Elizabeth Taylor

Elizabeth Taylor

A Private Life for Public Consumption

Ellis Cashmore

Bloomsbury Academic
An imprint of Bloomsbury Publishing Inc

B L O O M S B U R Y
NEW YORK · LONDON · OXFORD · NEW DELHI · SYDNEY

Bloomsbury Academic

An imprint of Bloomsbury Publishing Inc

1385 Broadway	50 Bedford Square
New York	London
NY 10018	WC1B 3DP
USA	UK

www.bloomsbury.com

BLOOMSBURY and the Diana logo are trademarks of Bloomsbury Publishing Plc

First published 2016
Reprinted 2016

Library of Congress Cataloging-in-Publication Data
Cashmore, Ellis.
Elizabeth Taylor : a private life for public consumption / Ellis Cashmore.
pages cm
Summary: "Uses the English-born Hollywood star as a lens through which to examine the
social changes that have yielded what we now call celebrity culture" — Provided by
publisher.
Includes bibliographical references and index.
ISBN 978-1-62892-070-3 (hardback) — ISBN 978-1-62892-069-7 (paperback)
1. Taylor, Elizabeth, 1932–2011. 2. Actors—United States—Biography.
3. Fame—Social aspects. 4. Celebrities. I. Title.

PN2287.T18C35 2016
791.4302'8092—dc23
[B]
2015034268

ISBN:	HB:	978-1-6289-2070-3
	PB:	978-1-6289-2069-7
	ePub:	978-1-6289-2068-0
	ePDF:	978-1-6289-2067-3

Typeset by RefineCatch Limited, Bungay, Suffolk
Printed and bound in the United States of America

—

"Everybody knows what she is."

Maxine Reynolds, mother of Debbie Reynolds, quoted in
Chicago Tribune, September 13, 1958.

CONTENTS

Life and times

Elizabeth Taylor, born London, England, February 27, 1932; died, Los Angeles, California, March 23, 2011

Legend
♥ Romantic relationship, actual or rumored
✚ Health-related condition
🅰 Aids, and Aids-related charitable work
MARRIAGE Taylor married eight times
NEAR-DEATH EXPERIENCE Taylor had two notable episodes on the brink of death

1932
FEBRUARY 27 Elizabeth Rosemond Taylor born in Hampstead, London, England, to Americans Francis Taylor, an art dealer, and Sara Viola Warmbrodt, stage name Sara Sothern, an actor.
She is born with a condition known as scoliosis, or curvature of the spine, which affects her for the rest of her life ✚

1934
Joseph Breen is appointed chief of Production Code Administration and enforces the Hays Code, drawn up in 1927 as guidelines for the film industry; code consists of eleven "don'ts" and twenty-six "be carefuls" (among subjects under scrutiny are blasphemy, nudity, illegal drugs, prostitution and miscegenation, this referring to relationships between actors considered to be of different racial types).

1936
Three-year-old Taylor gives recital for the Duchess of York, future Queen Elizabeth II of England, in London.

1938
Hedda Hopper begins writing her syndicated gossip column.
House Un-American Activities Committee (HUAC), a committee of the US House of Representatives, initially to uncover citizens with Nazi ties in the USA, and later to investigate allegations of Communist activity during the early years of the Cold War (1945–91), is established.

Robert K. Merton publishes his influential study "Social Structure and Anomie," which explains how American culture encourages aspirational consumption.

1939
Months before the outbreak of the Second World War (1939–45), the Taylor family moves to the USA, settling in Los Angeles, where Francis Taylor opens an art gallery patronized by the film colony.
Encouraged by mother Sara, Taylor auditions for Metro-Goldwyn-Mayer (MGM) and Universal studios; her parents sign her to Universal.
Sara introduces daughter Elizabeth to Hedda Hopper.

1942
Debut film: *There's One Born Every Minute.*
Ten-year-old Taylor signs contract with MGM after Universal cancels her contract, one of its casting directors declaring: "The kid has nothing . . . her eyes are too old."
Breaks foot during filming *Lassie Come Home* ✚

1943
Lassie Come Home, her first film with MGM, is released.
Sara takes Elizabeth to meet film producer Pandro S. Berman who is casting for the role of Velvet Brown of *National Velvet* and who initially suspects Elizabeth is too thin and fragile for the role a young girl who wins England's Grand National horse race disguised as a boy.

1944
Taylor suffers back injuries during filming of *National Velvet* ✚
Film is released in USA later in year; *New York Times* review hails Taylor: "Her voice has the softness of a sweet song and her whole manner in this picture is one of refreshing grace."

1945
National Velvet makes Taylor an international child star.

1946
Nibbles and Me, a book about Taylor, now fourteen, and her pet chipmunk is published.
While making *Life With Father*, mother, Sara, has affair with film's director Michael Curtiz.
James Stewart negotiates a percentage of profits deal with Universal for *Winchester '73*; it sets a precedent for actors wishing to remain independent of studios.

1947
Taylor, fifteen, meets football player Glenn Davis ♥
Appears on the cover of *Life* magazine (July 14); viewable here: http://bit.ly/18Oo5SP

1948
Davis accompanies Taylor to the 21st Academy Awards ceremony; her dates with Davis attract substantial press attention, prompting Taylor to reflect: "Maybe I should have fallen for a busboy, then the whole thing wouldn't cause so much attention."
Hedda Hopper writes of sixteen-year-old Taylor: "I will go far enough out on the limb to predict that she one day may likely be the Number 1 lady of the screen."
Taylor returns to London to make *Conspirator*.

The Kinsey Report, *Sexual Behavior in the Human Male*, is published.

Francis Taylor has gay relationship with married MGM designer Adrian Gaynor.

Rita Hayworth meets Prince Aly Khan in French Riviera and begins an affair that is generously covered by the media and creates a scandal.

1949

Taylor announces engagement to William Pawley, son of former US Ambassador to Brazil; engagement is canceled three months later amid rumors Taylor is seeing RKO boss Howard Hughes, who instructs his attorney to approach mother Sara to approve a marriage proposal; Taylor declines ♥

Taylor meets and befriends Montgomery Clift after MGM asks Taylor to accompany him to the premiere of *The Heiress*.

Ingrid Bergman is reported to be having an affair with director Roberto Rossellini, with whom she is filming *Stromboli* in Rome.

Hayworth marries Aly Khan; seven months later, she has a baby daughter.

Taylor, now seventeen, meets Conrad "Nicky" Hilton, 23-year-old son of the hotel magnate Conrad Hilton, in a Los Angeles nightclub ♥

1950

Bergman has Rossellini's child while still married to Peter Lindstrom.

FEBRUARY: Taylor announces engagement to Hilton.

Receives her high school diploma from University High School in Los Angeles after attending school on the MGM lot.

MAY: At eighteen, Taylor marries Hilton `MARRIAGE #1`

MGM capitalizes on Taylor's marriage by releasing *Father of the Bride*, in which Taylor plays a bride.

1951

FEBRUARY Divorces Nicky Hilton, who reflects: "I didn't marry a girl. I married an institution." *Marriage lasted eight months.*

Taylor plays her prototypical role as what the *New York Times* calls "a seemingly unattainable vision" in *A Place in the Sun,* a murder-romance-melodrama with Montgomery Clift.

Reports of relationship with director Stanley Donen ♥

MGM gives Taylor a role in *Ivanhoe* to be made in England as a way of breaking up her rumored affair with Donen.

While in England, Taylor meets actor Michael Wilding. ♥

I Love Lucy, featuring Lucille Ball, starts on CBS television.

1952

FEBRUARY Taylor marries forty-year-old Michael Wilding, the week before her twentieth birthday, at a London registry office `MARRIAGE #2`

Confidential magazine begins publication.

Taylor attends party at Stewart Granger's home; Richard Burton is also there, though they do not speak to each other.

1953

Gives birth by cesarean section to Michael Howard Wilding.

Surgery to remove shard of flint from Taylor's eye ✚
Collapses in Copenhagen with back problems ✚
The Girl Who Had Everything is released.
MGM announces that it will not authorize stories about its stars and their children: only "glamour" pieces.
20th Century Fox introduces CinemaScope in *The Robe*, a film that features Richard Burton.

1954
Four films (Taylor's busiest year), including *The Last Time I Saw Paris*.

1955
Gives birth by cesarean section to Christopher Edward Wilding.
Hospitalized with a pinched nerve and influenza ✚
MGM loans her to Warner Bros. to make *Giant* with Rock Hudson and James Dean.
Dean is killed, age twenty-four, in road accident in Cholame, California.

1956
After leaving a party at Taylor's house in Beverly Hills, Montgomery Clift crashes his car; Taylor saves him from choking by pulling two loose teeth from his throat and warns media against publishing pictures of injured Clift; there are no pictures.
Giant is released.
Taylor has close friendship with Kevin O'Donovan McClory, a producer ♥
Meets Michael Todd (real name: Avrom Goldbogen), who is five years older than Wilding, and twenty-three years older than Taylor ♥
Around the World in 80 Days opens and Taylor announces her engagement to Todd; she also files for divorce from Wilding citing "extreme mental cruelty."
Undergoes a five-hour back operation to repair a crushed spinal disk ✚

1957
JANUARY Divorces Michael Wilding. *Marriage lasted 4 years 11 months.*
FEBRUARY Marries Todd, whose Best Man is Eddie Fisher; Fisher's wife Debbie Reynolds is Matron of Honor MARRIAGE #3
Nominated for, but fails to win, Academy Award for *Raintree County*.
AUGUST Taylor gives birth by cesarean section to daughter Elizabeth Frances Todd (known as Liza, and later adopted by Richard Burton); baby almost dies and Taylor is advised not to have another baby.
Taylor has an appendectomy, i.e. surgical procedure to remove appendix ✚
Todd gives Taylor a suite of ruby and diamond jewelry by Cartier; he also presents her with an antique diamond tiara.

1958
Virus forces Taylor to say at home in Beverly Hills instead of flying to New York with Todd; ironically, Taylor's ill health saves her life ✚
MARCH Todd dies in a plane crash. *Marriage lasted 1 year 1 month.*
Todd's death interrupts filming of *Cat on a Hot Tin Roof*.
Taylor goes to New York; Eddie Fisher follows her; they are seen together, giving rise to rumors ♥

Fisher's wife, Debbie Reynolds, meets press on her front lawn; thirty-five years later, at a 1993 Aids benefit, Reynolds will precede Taylor on stage and joke, "Well, here I am, sharing something else with Elizabeth."

Debbie Reynold's mother Maxine tells *Chicago Tribune*: "Liz won't get hurt because nobody can hurt her."

"What do you expect me to do? Sleep alone?" quote is used by Hedda Hopper and heightens Taylor's notoriety.

Cat on a Hot Tin Roof, with Paul Newman, is box office success, in part because of the gossip surrounding Taylor and Fisher.

Taylor is nominated for an Academy Award for Best Actress for her role as Maggie in the film.

Michael Jackson is born in Gary, Indiana.

1959

Taylor converts to Judaism.

MAY Marries Eddie Fisher in a Las Vegas synagogue MARRIAGE #4

Minor surgery to remove tonsil nodes ✚

Taylor plays Katharine Hepburn's niece in *Suddenly, Last Summer*; she is nominated for an Academy Award for Best Actress for her role.

Hospitalized in New York with double pneumonia ✚

1960

Taylor plays a call girl in *BUtterfield 8*; "I hate the girl I play," she grumbles.

Demands $1 million to play the lead in 20th Century Fox's *Cleopatra* (she will eventually make an estimated $7m from the film).

Hospitalized in London with infection caused by abscessed teeth ✚

Federico Fellini's film *La Dolce Vita* introduces the term *paparazzi*.

Anita Ekberg, who is in *La Dolce Vita,* turns on a pursuant photographer with a bow and arrow in Rome, signaling the arrival of conflicts between real live paparazzi and their subjects.

1961

During filming in London, Taylor suffers a case of pneumonia complicated by anemia; emergency tracheotomy saves her life, but she remains on danger list for several days ✚ NEAR-DEATH EXPERIENCE #1

Media reports Taylor is dead; Joan Collins lined-up to replace her as Cleopatra.

"This brush with death seems, in some strange mythic way, to have divinized her," Camille Paglia writes later; Taylor regains public admiration.

Wins the Academy Award for Best Actress for her role in *BUtterfield 8*: "I knew it was a sympathy award, but I was still proud to get it."

Arrives in Rome for relocated production of *Cleopatra* with entourage consisting of five dogs, two cats, a retinue of aides, three children, and a husband (Fisher); stays in fourteen-roomed mansion off Via Appia.

Maria is born in Germany; she will be adopted by Taylor, and later become known as Maria Burton; Taylor begins the adoption application while married to Fisher.

1962

JANUARY Meets Richard Burton in Rome on set of *Cleopatra* ♥

Burton, who is married, frequents the mansion where Taylor and Fisher are staying.

FEBRUARY Fisher gives Taylor a $10,000 diamond ring for her 30th birthday.

Burton ends relationship with Taylor and leaves Rome.

Taylor taken ill with food poisoning in Rome; later reports suggest an overdose of sleeping pills may have been source of illness ✚

MARCH Fisher says to *Los Angeles Times* reports of an estrangement from Taylor are "preposterous, ridiculous and absolutely false."

Burton denies romantic involvement with Taylor.

SPRING/SUMMER Taylor is denounced by Italian media, American politicians, and the Vatican.

Burton and she are besieged by paparazzi at Porto Santo Stefano, a seaport town on the west coast of Italy.

Marcello Geppetti takes iconic photographs while unsuspecting Burton and Taylor tryst in Ischia, an island in the Tyrrhenian Sea.

Burton gives Taylor a suite of emerald-and-diamond jewelry from the Italian jewelry house Bvlgari; it is the first of a series of extravagant jewels he presents to her; later, Burton will reflect, "I introduced Elizabeth Taylor to beer and she introduced me to Bvlgari."

US tv show host Ed Sullivan pronounces: "You can only trust that youngsters will not be persuaded that the sanctity of marriage has been invalidated by the appalling example of Mrs. Taylor-Fisher and married man Burton."

AUGUST 5 Marilyn Monroe dies, age thirty-three.

Sex and the Single Girl by Helen Gurley Brown is published; it encourages women to seek physical gratification as well as an independent career.

1963

Cleopatra premieres at New York's Rivoli Theater: "Surely the most bizarre piece of entertainment ever to be perpetrated," according to Taylor.

The label "Liz & Dick" is introduced by the media.

Taylor has knee surgery while in London filming *The VIPs* with Burton ✚

Jacqueline Kennedy, described by Anthony Slide as "the first female megastar not created by the entertainment industry," ascends to public prominence after death of her husband President John F. Kennedy.

Sybil Williams divorces Burton on grounds of "abandonment and cruel and inhumane treatment," ending a fourteen-year marriage.

The Feminine Mystique by Betty Friedan is published; the author writes: "The only way for a woman, as for a man, to find herself, to know herself as a person, is by creative work of her own."

1964

Richard Burton plays in pre-Broadway run of *Hamlet* in Toronto, where crowds of 5,000 praise and assail him and Taylor.

MARCH 6 Taylor divorces Eddie Fisher. *Marriage lasted 4 years 10 months.*

MARCH 15 Marries Burton in Montreal; bride and groom give their respective religions as Jewish and Presbyterian; Burton gives Taylor an emerald-and-diamond pendant brooch, by Bvlgari MARRIAGE #5

Maria is adopted by Burton and becomes Maria Burton.

Taylor has knee surgery for dislocated cartilage ✚

Back and arm injuries after being mobbed by fans in Boston ✚

Beatles' first concert in USA; "Beatlemania" spreads.

Taylor makes up with Debbie Reynolds.

Two American destroyers are reported fired on in Vietnam where attempts to unify the country under a single communist regime have been in process since the defeat of the French colonial administration in 1954; the South Vietnamese resist the unification and align with the West.

1965

The Sandpiper, with Taylor and Burton, is released; the film is described by *Life* magazine as "$5.3 million sleeping pill."
US active combat units are introduced into Vietnam.

1966

Life magazine, on June 10, headlines, LIZ IN A SHOCKER, HER MOVIE SHATTERS THE RULES OF CENSORSHIP.
Taylor wins the Academy Award for her most acclaimed role in the film *Who's Afraid of Virginia Woolf?*
Taylor and Burton appear in Oxford University Dramatic Society's *Dr. Faustus;* Taylor plays the apparition of Helen of Troy.
Fractures big toe in Rome while making a film adaptation of Shakespeare's play *The Taming of the Shrew* ✚
Hedda Hopper dies.
Montgomery Clift dies.

1967

Taylor is hospitalized in Monte Carlo after fall on a rented yacht aggravates a knee inflammation ✚
The Taming of the Shrew features Taylor as the headstrong Katharina to Burton's wife-hunting Petruchio.
Lee Israel writes "The Rise and Fall and Rise of Elizabeth Taylor" in which she refers to the "para-fictive" character "Elizabeth Taylor" that is almost but not quite "completely independent of the real Taylor."
Taylor plays an adulterous Army major's wife in *Reflections in a Golden Eye*, with Marlon Brando.

1968

Tet Offensive launched by Vietcong and North Vietnamese Army is surprise attack on South Vietnamese cities, notably Saigon; shakes American confidence.
Taylor and Burton attend the high society wedding of Sharon Hornby and Peter Cazelet in England; other guests include the Queen Mother, Princess Margaret and Noël Coward.
Father, Francis Taylor, dies.
Taylor establishes a heart disease research foundation in memory of Clift and endows it with $1m.
Burton gives Taylor 33.19-carat Krupp diamond; later known as the Elizabeth Taylor Diamond, it costs Burton $300,000, and, after Taylor's death, sells at auction for $8.8 million.
Taylor undergoes a partial hysterectomy in London ✚
Burton gives Taylor an 8.24-carat ruby and diamond ring for Christmas.

1969

Burton gives Taylor La Peregrina, a pearl, ruby, and diamond necklace, discovered in the sixteenth century.

Taylor is hospitalized for back problems in Los Angeles ✚
Burton buys for Taylor the 69-carat Burton-Cartier Diamond, costing a rumored $1.5m; Taylor will sell this in 1979, following the couple's second divorce, for—again a rumored—$3m.
Over 500,000 US military personnel are stationed in Vietnam.

1970

Burton and Taylor appear in CBS tv's *Here's Lucy* with Lucille Ball.
The Mary Tyler Moore show starts on CBS; runs until 1977.
Fisher is declared bankrupt.
Jackson 5's first four singles, including *I Want You Back*, reach number one on pop music charts.

1971

Michael Jackson begins to record under his own name, while also continuing to perform and record with his brothers.
Cecil Beaton, the English photographer famous for his portraits of celebrities and the British Royal Family, takes photograph of Taylor and Burton at Chateau de Ferrières, near Paris; Beaton later records in his diary: "I have always loathed the Burtons for their vulgarity, commonness and crass bad taste, she combining the worst of US and English taste, he as butch and coarse as only a Welshman can be"; the photograph is here: http://bit.ly/1R5a5pS

1972

Taylor is forty; Burton gives her $1.5m Cartier diamond set in a necklace of smaller diamonds, and a heart-shaped diamond pendant, first given by the Mughal Emperor Shah Jehan (1592–1666, the builder of the Taj Mahal) to his young bride in 1621; Burton also gives Taylor a Bvlgari sapphire sautoir; in 2011, after Taylor's death, the Cartier Taj Mahal diamond, as it is known, sells for $8.8m, but the sale is canceled when the buyer balks, claiming the stone was not from the Mughal period as listed in the item's description—see below, 2015.

1973

America withdraws from Vietnam War.
Billie Jean King beats Bobby Riggs in televised tennis match purportedly symbolizing the "Battle of the Sexes."
Taylor is quarantined with measles in a hotel in Cortina, Italy ✚
Ovarian cyst, Los Angeles ✚
Amoebic dysentery, Soviet Union ✚
Meets Henry Wynberg; signs contract for product line of fragrances ♥
Announces separation from Burton via media statement.
Visits Lawrence Harvey who dies of cancer; within days of his death, Taylor is admitted to hospital with an ovarian cyst (which she suggests may have been carcinogenic; it is not) ✚
Following her recovery, Taylor spends time with Burton, prompting conjecture about reconciliation.

1974

JUNE Taylor and Burton are divorced; "There were too many differences. I have tried everything," Taylor tells the court. *Marriage lasted ten years three months.*

Patty Hearst is kidnapped; in 1976 she will be sentenced to thirty-five years' imprisonment, serving 22 months.

Conjectural news grows in currency.

Richard M. Nixon, the 37th President of the USA, announces resignation on television.

1975

Taylor travels to St. Petersburg accompanied by Wynberg to make *The Blue Bird*.

After completing filming, Taylor and Wynberg go to Geneva, where she meets with Burton; Wynberg leaves for London.

Burton, supported by Jeannie Bell, is drinking less.

An X-ray of Taylor's chest shows two spots on her lungs, though she does not have cancer.

OCTOBER Taylor re-marries Richard Burton in Botswana MARRIAGE #6

Richard Burton's fiftieth birthday party at London's Dorchester hotel; he drinks mineral water all night.

Burton meets Suzy Hunt; Taylor meets Peter Darmanin ♥

1976

Taylor calls off forty-fourth birthday celebration in New York and celebrates birthday with Wynberg in Beverly Hills.

Taylor attends Oscars accompanied by Halston, wearing one of his creations and helping establish him as one of the leading designers of the 1970s.

Taylor Meets Ardeshir Zahedi, Iranian ambassador to the USA; she later visits Iran with him ♥

Firooz Zahedi, cousin of Ardeshir, shoots what become an iconic series of images of Taylor; Firooz exhibits them here: http://bit.ly/1BGTLaA

Richard Burton travels to New York with Suzy Hunt to appear in *Equus* on Broadway.

AUGUST Taylor divorces Burton again, July 29. *Marriage lasted ten months*.

Suzy Hunt divorces James Hunt.

Burton marries Suzy Hunt.

DECEMBER Taylor marries Republican senator John Warner MARRIAGE #7 ♥

Falls off a horse on Warner's Virginia ranch and hospitalized for back injury ✚

1977

Taylor breaks finger while in Switzerland ✚

Taylor adapts to life as a politician's wife, campaigning to get her husband elected to the Senate by speaking at functions and attending charity benefits.

Hospitalized with bursitis and back problems in Washington DC ✚

Jimmy Carter gives interview to *Playboy* magazine, in which he confesses: "I've committed adultery in my heart." Carter will serve as President, 1977–81.

1978

Hospital doctor removes chicken wing bone lodged in Taylor's throat while campaigning with Warner in Big Stone Gap, Virginia ✚

Warner is elected to Senate.

1979

Taylor announces that she wishes to be known as Elizabeth Warner and declares: "I know my own identity, not as a movie star, but as a woman."

Michael Wilding dies; Taylor (or Warner, as she prefers) attends funeral in London.
Michael Jackson's *Off the Wall* album is released.

1980

Taylor/Warner opposes her husband's view that the military draft should be men-only.
Salivary gland infection ✚
Hospitalized with sinusitis ✚
Taylor attends Republican National Convention; Ronald Reagan is nominated as presidential candidate; he will go on to become US President, 1981–9.
Taylor sheds 40 lbs; she will later explain her weight gain as the result of her politician's wife lifestyle: "It was so boring. That's why I put on so much weight."
Burton discusses alcoholism, which he calls "a disease," on tv with Dick Cavett.
Lady Diana Spencer becomes a subject of media attention when it becomes known she is in a relationship with Prince Charles, eldest son of Queen Elizabeth II, heir to the throne; Diana first met Charles in 1977.

1981

Diana and Charles announce their engagement, initiating a zealous, worshipful and often prurient curiosity in Diana that is nourished by the media.
MAY 7 Taylor debuts on Broadway in revival of *The Little Foxes*; she is nominated for a Tony Award for her role; 123 sellout performances in New York.
MAY 16 Respiratory infection, torn and inflamed rib cartilage causes cancelation of *The Little Foxes* ✚
Skiing accident in Switzerland; arm in cast ✚
Taylor appears in daytime soap *General Hospital*, prompting rumors of a relationship with fellow actor Anthony Geary, over fifteen years her junior; the show is watched by 14 million tv viewers ♥
CNN launches as 24/7 news channel.
US Centers for Disease Control and Prevention (CDC) report five, young, previously healthy gay mean in LA, have become sick with unusual infections that indicate their immune systems are not functional; this is the first official reporting of what becomes the Aids pandemic; by the end of the year, there are 270 reported cases of severe immunity deficiency, of which there are 121 deaths ☀
Coty launches Sophia, a fragrance endorsed by Sophia Loren.
Taylor's spokeswoman, Chen Sam, announces Taylor is separating from Warner: "Each party accepts this change in their relationship with sadness but with no bitterness between them."

1982

FEBRUARY Burton is invited to Taylor's fiftieth birthday party in London; they see each other over the next several days and Taylor suggests they perform together in a stage production of Noël Coward's *Private Lives*, which she is considering.
Taylor is seen dining regularly with Mexican lawyer Victor Luna; he lives in Guadalajara, Mexico, and she 1,300 miles away in Beverly Hills ♥
NOVEMBER Taylor divorces John Warner. *Marriage lasted five years eleven months.*
ABC television is stymied by Taylor, who threatens legal action to stop a docudrama on her.

Michael Jackson's *Thriller* is released; it will sell over 50 million copies and help usher in the video age.
CDC uses term AIDS (later Aids) for first time ✗

1983

MAY *Private Lives* with Burton opens in New York.
JUNE Taylor's bronchitis and laryngitis forces show's suspension ✚
JULY Burton marries Sally Hay (during the play's run).
AUGUST Taylor announces engagement to Luna, who gives her a Cartier-designed 16.5 carat sapphire-and-diamond engagement ring; he will call off the engagement in September 1984.
Taylor injures neck and leg in car crash near Tel Aviv ✚
Taylor hospitalized ostensibly with bowel obstruction ✚
Taylor's first visit to Betty Ford Center; owns up to alcohol and pharmaceutical dependency ✚
While at the Center, Taylor records in her daily diary: "It's probably the first time since I was 9 that nobody's wanted to exploit me."
Madonna's first album is released.

1984

Burton, fifty-eight, dies of cerebral hemorrhage in Switzerland.
Taylor does not attend Burton's funeral but, later, visits his grave, where paparazzi wait.
Taylor returns engagement ring to Luna.
Taylor is seen with Carl Bernstein ❤
Taylor announces engagement to Dennis Stein ❤
Taylor attends a Jacksons' concert, but walks out of her VIP box midway through the performance; Michael Jackson apologizes personally.
Rock Hudson falls ill and is diagnosed as having Aids; this is not announced until a year later.
Jackson sustains burns during production of a Pepsi commercial; his use of painkillers will lead to dependency.

1985

Taylor announces "amicable split" from Stein.
Hospitalized in LA for back pain after injury incurred making tv movie *North and South* ✚
Rock Hudson has Aids, it is confirmed from Paris, where he is receiving treatment.
National AIDS Research Foundation, of which Taylor is a member, merges with New York-based AIDS Medical Foundation to form American Foundation for AIDS Research, or amfAR, to support Aids research, HIV prevention, treatment, education, and advocacy of Aids-related public policy ✗
Taylor meets Dr. Arnold Klein.
Taylor has food poisoning in Deauville, France ✚

1986

Taylor testifies before Congress to plead for funding for Aids care ✗
Wears surgical collar for neck injury ✚
Hospitalized in LA for complications after dental surgery ✚
President Ronald Reagan mentions Aids publicly for the first time, vowing in a letter to Congress to make Aids a priority ✗

Rock Hudson dies and leaves $250,000 to amfAR; at least one HIV case has been reported from every region of the world ☀

Taylor becomes friends with George Hamilton, with whom she acts in *Poker Alice*, a tv film ♥

1987

Elizabeth Taylor's Passion, her first fragrance for Parfums International Ltd., is launched; promotional tours follow; highest priced bottle is $200.

Taylor is seen in the company of Malcolm Forbes, chairman and editor in chief of *Forbes* magazine ♥

1988

Taylor goes on world tour to promote her book *Elizabeth Takes Off*.

Il giovane Toscanini (*Young Toscanini*) is released though not in USA.

Hospitalized with back pain caused by osteoporosis ✚

Betty Ford Center: second visit; pharmaceutical drug dependency ✚

Meets Larry Fortensky, a fellow patient at the center and twenty years Taylor's junior ♥

1989

Taylor speaks at Southeast Asia's first Aids benefit in Thailand ☀

The number of reported Aids cases in the United States reaches 100,000 ☀

Taylor presents Michael Jackson Soul Train Heritage Award; she is credited with describing him as the "King of Pop" at this award ceremony.

1990

Malcolm Forbes dies of a reported heart attack.

Taylor's friend Halston, the fashion designer, dies from Aids ☀

Taylor testifies before Congress to encourage passage of the Ryan White Comprehensive Aids Resources Emergency (CARE) Act, which prevented discrimination against people with HIV ☀

Taylor, now fifty-eight, is treated for three months in Santa Monica with viral pneumonia after undergoing a lung biopsy and being placed on a ventilator to assist breathing; it is her gravest illness since the near-fatal bout of pneumonia in 1961 ✚ NEAR-DEATH EXPERIENCE #2

Taylor scotches rumors that she has Aids ☀

Three of Taylor's doctors are accused of falsifying records to cover up the large amounts of addictive drugs they prescribe her; in 1994, they will receive reprimands.

Madonna debuts *Like a Prayer*, the title track of her fourth studio album.

Catholic leaders condemn Madonna's *Like a Prayer*, which features stigmata, burning crosses, statues crying blood and Madonna seducing a black Jesus; the Vatican had denounced Taylor in 1962.

MTV bans Madonna's *Justify My Love*.

1991

White Diamonds is launched by Elizabeth Arden; Taylor introduces Fortensky as her fiancé at the product launch in New York.

OCTOBER Marries Fortensky at Michael Jackson's Neverland Ranch MARRIAGE #8

Establishes Elizabeth Taylor Aids Foundation ☀

Freddie Mercury, lead singer/songwriter of the rock band Queen, dies of bronchial pneumonia resulting from Aids ⅄
The Jerry Springer Show launches.

1992

Taylor celebrates her 60th birthday at Disneyland, California; her first visit to the Magic Kingdom was in 1962 with Fisher and sons Michael and Christopher.
Receives the Jean Hersholt Humanitarian Award.
Elizabeth Taylor's White Diamonds wins Women's Fragrance of the Year – Broad Appeal (Popular Appeal) at FiFi Awards, a prestigious celebratory event of the fragrance industry.
Voices "Maggie Simpson" in *The Simpsons*.
AmfAR raises $20.6 million this year ⅄
MTV launches *The Real World*.

1993

Creates the Elizabeth Taylor Foundation for AIDs ⅄
Receives the American Film Institute's 21st Life Achievement Award.
Taylor describes Jackson as "the least weird man" she has ever known.
Jackson is accused of sexual molestation; Taylor stays with him in Singapore; later, Jackson will settle case out of court with Jordan Chandler.
Taylor flies with Fortensky to Mexico to be with Jackson; takes Jackson to London for treatment.
Jackson reveals his dependence on pharmaceutical drugs.

1994

Taylor undergoes left hip replacement surgery ✚
Tries to stop screening of planned NBC biopic.
Taylor plays in *The Flintstones* movie.
Sara, Taylor's mother, dies.
Jackson agrees to pay undisclosed sum to stop a sex abuse lawsuit.
Jackson marries Lisa Marie Presley; they will divorce in less than two years, in 1996.
Aids is leading cause of death for all Americans ages twenty-five to forty-four ⅄

1995

Taylor undergoes right hip replacement surgery ✚
Liz: The Elizabeth Taylor Story, with Sherilyn Fenn as Taylor airs on NBC.
Several new fragrances, including Black Pearls, are launched.

1996

Taylor features in four consecutive CBS sitcoms in storyline about missing black pearls.
Addresses General Assembly of United Nations on Aids ⅄
OCTOBER Divorces Larry Fortensky. *Marriage lasted five years*.
Jackson marries Debbie Rowe; divorces 1999.

1997

A benign golf ball-sized tumor is detected during a routine MRI (brain) scan; the tumor is successfully removed; nine days later, Taylor has a seizure (mini-stroke), is readmitted to the hospital and leaves a week later ✚

Taylor explains: "I get ill because I live too hard, I give too much — out of a lust for life. I never back away. I relish life and face it dead-on" (in *Life* magazine).
Diana, Princess of Wales, dies in Paris car accident.

1998

Taylor fractures vertebrae in a fall at her home on her sixty-sixth birthday ✚
Establishes "Elizabeth Taylor Trust," also known as "The Sothern Trust," this being a revocable living trust—a legal arrangement to hold assets, including property, and containing instructions about how assets will be distributed after death.

1999

Taylor has compression fracture of vertebrae in an accident at home ✚
Made a Dame Commander of the Order of the British Empire by Queen Elizabeth II.
While in London, Taylor is joined by her dentist Dr. Cary Schwartz, whom she will continue to see ❤

2000

Big Brother launches in USA and UK.
Mattel launches a range of Elizabeth Taylor Barbie dolls; the company will extend the range after her death, releasing commemorative dolls.

2001

Taylor appears uncharacteristically clumsy at Golden Globe award presentation.
These Old Broads with Debbie Reynolds.
Receives France's highest artistic award, the Commander of Arts and Letters.
Apocryphal story circulates of how September 11 attacks prompt Taylor and Jackson to flee New York, with Marlon Brando, following Jackson's concert at Madison Square Garden.

2002

My Love Affair with Jewelry is published.
Taylor is presented with John F. Kennedy Center Honors.
Receives radiation therapy for basal cell carcinoma, a curable form of skin cancer ✚

2003

Taylor falls and fractures several bones in her foot ✚
Voices for animated series *God, the Devil and Bob*.
Announces retirement from acting to concentrate on Aids work; she has steadily decreased acting work since 1980 ⅄
In a televised interview, Michael Jackson talks about sharing his bed with children.
Jackson is charged with various counts of child molestation and of administering an intoxicating agent for the purpose of a committing a felony; Taylor says: "I believe Michael is innocent and that he will be vindicated."
Taylor's former gardener, Willem Van Muyden, alleges that her butler, Jean-Luc Lacquement, provided sexual services to Taylor; he sues Taylor for breach of contract, sexual harassment, discrimination, and wrongful dismissal; Taylor's lawyer describes it as "pure fiction"; Taylor will settle the legal action in 2004.

2004

Taylor is sued under the Holocaust Victims Redress Act in an attempt to recover *View of the Asylum and Chapel at Saint-Rémy*, by Van Gogh, a painting that had been bought for her by her father in 1963; Andrew Orkin and three of his relatives claim their great-grandmother had been forced by the Nazis to sell the painting, but Taylor prevails in lawsuit; it is later sold at auction for $15.5 million—see below, 2012.

Surgery to correct seven compression fractures in Taylor's spine; discloses she has congestive heart failure, a disorder in which heart cannot pump enough oxygenated blood through the body; her health will progressively deteriorate beyond recovery ✚

"My body's a real mess," Taylor tells *W* magazine.

Taylor praises Dr. Arnold Klein: "He has helped save my life."

Michael Jackson, forty-five, pleads not guilty to seven felony counts of lewd or lascivious acts with a child under fourteen and two counts of giving the child an "intoxicating agent"; he is later indicted.

2005

Taylor expresses public support for Jackson during his trial in California on child molestation charges.

Jackson is acquitted on all ten felony counts brought against him, including four counts of lewd acts on a child under fourteen.

2006

Taylor appears on CNN's *The Larry King Show* and dispels rumors of about her health: "Oh come on, do I look like I'm dying? Do I look like or sound like I have Alzheimer's?"

Forms House of Taylor Jewelry, with Kathy Ireland.

2007

Taylor gives benefit performance of A.R. Gurney's epistolary play *Love Letters* in LA to raise $1 million for Aids; it is her final theatrical appearance; CDC reports over 565,000 people have died of Aids in the US since 1981 ☆

British newspaper reports that Taylor and Jason Winters, a Hollywood agent twent-eight years her junior, take a romantic vacation together at a Hawaiian resort ♥

2008

House of Taylor Jewelry announces insolvency $11 million in debt.

Reports that Jackson has newly revealed sickness requiring a lung transplant.

2009

Taylor opens twitter account with this tweet: "Spending time with my daughter Liza in my beautiful gardens. Hope the gardenias bloom soon."

Michael Jackson dies, age fifty; Taylor mourns his death on twitter: "We had so much in common and we had such loving fun together"; LA's coroner gives official cause of death as "acute propofol [an anesthetic] intoxication"; Jackson's physician Dr. Conrad Murray will be found guilty of involuntary manslaughter in 2011.

Taylor announces on twitter that she is to undergo heart surgery "so that my heart will function better"; later she tweets: it "was like having a brand new ticker."

2010

Taylor criticizes Dr. Arnold Klein for telling media Jackson was gay.

In the year following his death, Jackson earns $250m.

According to *USmagazine.com*, Taylor, seventy-eight, is engaged to Winters, forty-nine, now Janet Jackson's agent.

Taylor tweets: "The rumors regarding my engagement simply aren't true. Jason is my manager and dearest friend."

Violet Eyes fragrance is launched.

Taylor makes last visit to London, where she attends a royal gala at Buckingham Palace honoring Richard Burton; there is now a Richard Burton Theatre at the Royal Welsh College of Music and Drama, in Cardiff.

2011

Larry Fortensky faces eviction from his home.

FEBRUARY 11 News reports suggest that Taylor is taken to hospital "suffering intense abdominal pain and is now in a critical condition, surrounded by her family" ✚

FEBRUARY 12 More specific reports indicate that Taylor is admitted to Cedars-Sinai Hospital, Los Angeles, for treatment of "symptoms caused by congestive heart failure," a condition she has had since at least 2004, see above.

FEBRUARY 13 "She had a pretty good day Saturday (Feb. 12), and a good night, announces publicist Sally Morrison. "At this stage, with her [Taylor's] history, they're going to want to keep her in for a while just to make sure they've fixed what they needed to fix."

FEBRUARY 18 Reuters reports: "Elizabeth Taylor's health is improving following her hospitalization last week."

FEBRUARY 23 *The Hollywood Reporter* records that Taylor's publicist says, "She is in good spirits and continues to feel stronger every day."

FEBRUARY 27 Taylor spends her 79th birthday in the hospital.

MARCH 23 Taylor dies of congestive heart failure.

MARCH 24 Funeral at Forest Lawn memorial park.

Exhibition of Taylor's jewelry, costumes, art, and other personal effects tours world. Auction in New York; jewelry fetches $116 million; overall sale: $137 million.

2012

Auction of Taylor's artworks, haute couture, and scripts in London; a Van Gogh sells for £10.1 million ($15.5 million).

Taylor's earnings for year following her death: $210 million; makes her highest earning dead celebrity of year.

2013

Burton and Taylor a tv drama depicting the couple during the production of *Private Lives* in 1983, is shown by BBC and BBC America; it is the first dramatized account of Taylor after her death.

2014

A private letter, written in pencil by Taylor, left behind by Burton at a home he and Taylor rented in California while he filmed the 1974 movie *The Klansman,* is put up for sale.

A silkscreen print of Taylor by Andy Warhol from 1964 emerges when the artist's former bodyguard attempts to sell it at a Manhattan gallery, claiming Warhol gave him the artwork as a gift in the 1980s; lawyers for the Andy Warhol Foundation dispute this but arrive at a settlement.

Pictures taken at Taylor's wedding with Fortensky in 1991 and taken by Herb Ritts are released exclusively to *People* magazine.

2015

A dispute over Taylor's Cartier Taj Mahal diamond, sold at auction for $8.8m arises after buyer claims the stone is not from the Mughal period listed in the catalog and cancels sale; Christies contend Taylor's trust is obligated to pay back the proceeds of a rescinded sale but the trust refuses to return payment.

Five of Taylor's grandchildren continue her Aids work by presenting New York Democrat Congressman José Serrano with the Inaugural Elizabeth Taylor Legislative Leadership Award in recognition of his work supporting needle exchange programs ⋋

An oil painting by Richard Burton from 1963 is put up for sale on eBay; also placed on the online auction site is an unpublished manuscript by Sara Sothern, titled "Taylor-made memories".

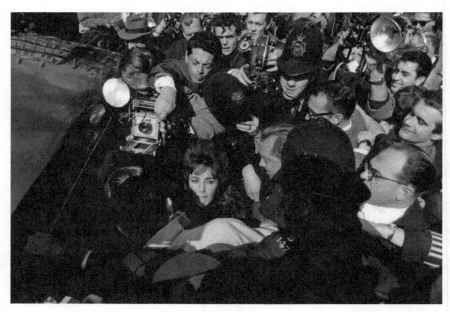

FIGURE 1 *Surrendering what once passed for a private life, Taylor learned to live in the ceaseless gaze of the media.*

Photo by Mondadori Portfolio via Getty Images.

1

The most public of private lives

"Elizabeth Taylor is the most important character she's ever played." Vincent Canby, of the *New York Times* was writing in 1986, when Taylor was fifty-four. "She's never had any real, sustained privacy, she's had to progress from childhood to middle age with what is, in effect, a bird on the top of her head." The bird was her reputation. "The public's identification with her highs and lows," as Canby called it, was incomparable; in the mid-1980s, there was no one who engaged the public in quite the same way as Taylor. She involved others in her life in a way that encouraged the kind of associations we find commonplace today.

It inclined some writers, including William Mann, to believe: "Everything about today's celebrity culture can be traced directly back to Elizabeth Taylor." In the early 1960s, when, for most people, paparazzi could have referred to a kind of pasta, she introduced new journalistic livestock to the world. With a combination of guile and grace, she "created a market for scandalous, often telephoto, pictures of the private lives of stars," Mann reasoned.

David Thomson agreed: "Liz was the first modern celebrity, playing herself at every moment and for every sly photographer." This established her as "among the first to reach that special category of celebrity—famous for being famous, for whom her work was inseparable from the gossip around it," as David Germain and Italie Hillel put it.

Are they right? After all, in the new world of celebrity, the kind of identification Canby had in mind has intensified into delirium; fans demand access to all quarters, leading to the frenzy of gossip, rumor, and tittle-tattle about private lives that Germain and Hillel suggest are vital to any celebrity's status. Surrendering what once passed as a private life is part of the deal offered in exchange for the fame, however fleeting, sought by aspiring celebrities.

Taylor "may not be the reason that celebrity love affairs now are part of the air we breathe," the *Chicago Tribune*'s Mark Caro concluded, "but she no doubt helped change and define our culture by serving as a template for modern-day stars whose real-life exploits are followed even more breathlessly than those on screen" (March 23, 2011).

Change and define? A template? Caro means Taylor created a model that others emulated. This must have been far from Taylor's own thoughts when she seemed to pursue scandal as if it were an accolade rather than a condemnation to hell. But Taylor held the philosopher's stone and could turn base ore into precious metal. Scandals had wrecked the careers, and in some cases lives, of other Hollywood stars. When Taylor behaved badly, the scandals were priceless. Even as late as the 1980s, entertainers had not fully understood the lessons Taylor had not so much taught as invented.

Madonna might have studied the template and decided to risk a promising showbusiness career by luring the media to her den, then shocking them with apparently reckless deeds that probably owed more to calculation than to impulse. She harnessed the public appetite for scandal to her own ends in much the same way as Taylor had twenty years before. Unlike Madonna, Taylor was not deliberately trying to create pandemonium. She was just being herself, but at a time when Hollywood stars were supposed to be living, breathing images of people created by the studio. Film stars had been managed practically since 1910 when Carl Laemmle, the pioneer mogul and later founder of Universal Pictures, discovered how a single actor, if well publicized, could sell a film.

"Taylor was a transitional figure," according to Lisa Kennedy, of the *Denver Post*, "a stunning product of the studio system and a rebellious force as its power waned." But the transition was not merely in the film industry: in the late 1950s and 1960s, when Taylor showed her desire to resist the technical authority of her studio bosses and the moral authority of the church, the media, and the public, there were all manner of other changes. Taylor withstood the abuse and opprobrium, resisting attempts to stifle her and never apologizing for what others considered her faults or errors. Disapproval, for her, became a reward more than a punishment.

So, when Kennedy concludes, "She benefited from gossip columnist Hedda Hopper's adoration and later survived the powerful writer's assaults," she might have added "and prospered from them." Adored or assaulted, Taylor proved people could not have too much of a good thing, or, in her case, a bad one. Audiences goggled at her as a restless ingénue, a rare beauty at the mercy of her mother's vicarious ambitions. They looked favorably on her first clean-cut suitors. But then recoiled as her first husband, rich and seemingly anodyne, turned out to be a boozy boor with a gambling habit and a tendency to lash out.

For much of the 1950s, no one could have thought Taylor was destined for anything but Hollywood stardom. It did not seem possible to look at her and think: "She will become one of the most notorious women in the world." But she became exactly that. Carefree and careless in her choice of romantic partners, she was impetuously extravagant in practically everything she did. As she matured, Taylor's English rose image wilted and in its place appeared a Venus flytrap.

Taylor the man-eater trapped and consumed any man she wanted and, to the horror of all, she wanted married fathers, like Eddie Fisher. But even before him, she snapped up two men old enough to be her father, the first married and, by her standards, bland. She left Michael Wilding for Michael Todd, a showman-cum-film producer with a gift for seducing the media and ticket buyers and who, many argue, introduced Taylor to conspicuous consumption. What made Taylor so peerless in this period was not so much what she did, but where she did it: in full view of the public. Unlike other actresses (the preferred term in pre-pc days), she repressed nothing, or so it seemed. Not for her furtive rendezvous and discreet affairs: her love life was blazingly visible. It was almost possible to see spirits of the damned following her about waiting for the Fall.

Taylor effectively turned her heresy inside out. In 1967, Lee Israel, reminded her *Esquire* magazine readers that other actresses had perished after sinning. (Israel's article was republished in 1970.) Taylor showed no remorse after her initial transgression, an affair with someone who had been best man at her wedding and who claimed to be one of her ex-husband's closest friends. Taylor's grief at the death of her husband appeared oddly affectless when she was in the company of Eddie Fisher. If anything she displayed *joie de vivre* and, for a grieving widow, an indecent amount of *joie d'amour*. Taylor was not the first female Hollywood star to have a dalliance, though she was the first to turn it to her advantage. How?

Refusing to explain herself or rationalize her behavior, she instead acquired an irresistible, coruscating power to captivate audiences. There were lessons for anyone who chose to look: love and hate were potent emotions, so anyone who could elicit them in others had a priceless resource. Audiences turned against Taylor, but they did not lose interest. Quite the opposite.

Then a transformation. Not yet thirty and stricken with pneumonia, Taylor drew near death and was given an emergency tracheotomy. For a while, it seemed she would die and, in haste, a replacement for her role in *Cleopatra* was sought. Taylor recovered, though, in a way, she was reborn, as Lee Israel wrote, "with dimensions of greatness."

Israel drew attention to the near-deific status conferred on Taylor after her initial indiscretion: "Instead of coming back from the valley of the shadow a repentant penitent washed in the blood of the lamb, Elizabeth Taylor went to Rome and did it again."

"Taylor," wrote Israel, "had been abused and misjudged prior to her illness" and, in a world where there was still a residual conviction that sinners suffer for their deeds, interest in her probably centered on how and when she would get her comeuppance. But the brush with mortality turned her into something other than a Hollywood star. "Other love goddesses, such as Rita Hayworth, Lana Turner and Ava Gardner, were not in her league in terms of public and press attention. Everything she did was news," recorded Britain's *Daily Telegraph* (March 23, 2011). This became indisputably clear when, soon after recovering, she became involved in what became the most shameful, ill-famed, spellbinding, and fabled romance of the twentieth century. Taylor did not just appear in the news: she *was* news.

In her 2014 study of how the media today turn girls into spectacles, the film and media scholar Sarah Projansky writes of a "rampant" theme in the way young women are represented and which she summarizes as "the simultaneous adoration and denigration of girls." While Taylor does not feature among her case studies, she might well have been the first. She was in many senses the prototype: people stood in awe, worshipfully admiring Taylor, while all the time maligning her promiscuity.

Projansky argues that modern media tends to divide female celebrities into high-achievers who attract adoration and others who are "at-risk" and tend to live on the cusp of, if not actually in trouble. Taylor was both. Resisting the typecasting tendencies of the media, even in the 1960s, she defied attempts to cast her out into the wilderness bearing stigmata and remained at the epicenter of the media's gaze—usually exhibiting the stigmata.

In 1999, when asked to reflect on her two spells in rehabilitation, Taylor told J.D. Reed, of *People* magazine: "One of the questions they first ask at the Betty Ford clinic, to find out if you're paranoid, is, 'When you walk down the street, do you feel a lot of eyes are looking at you out of windows?' I had to laugh at that."

Taylor never appeared uncomfortable in the public gaze; if anything she luxuriated in it, exposed but never vulnerable. Contrast her with her contemporaries who mostly sought to conceal what was conventionally thought to be their private lives as they lived them. Details of Marilyn Monroe's torment became known only after her death in 1962. David Lister of the British newspaper *i* believes: "We never really see a happy-go-lucky woman in the many happy-go-lucky parts that Marilyn Monroe played, because we know far too much about her real life pain."

We know *now*; but, during her lifetime (1926–62), audiences knew what they learned about Marilyn from movies and publications, making her private life seem rather colorless. By contrast, Taylor's private life was like van Gogh's palette.

At a time when celebrity couples are a staple and our demands and caprices make it impossible for celebrities to conduct relationships outside our range of experience or thought, Taylor's romance with Burton might seem *faute de mieux* normal. In the early 1960s, every aspect of it was extraordinary. Perhaps not quite every aspect: there had been relationships between married people, each with children, before—many of them in Roman Catholic countries—and probably several involving film actors or people prominent in other public spheres. It was the hysterical media reaction to the relationship that distinguished Taylor-Burton and effectively changed it from tryst into theater. As well as intimates, any number of observers were able to participate, vicariously perhaps, and at some distance. It was, in a sense, the first mediated love affair, conveyed to countless people through the agencies of newspapers, magazines, radio, and television.

Some writers, like the *Los Angeles Times*' Tim Rutten suspect the leviathan actor Burton cast a large shadow in which Taylor could develop her talent for straight-acting. "Taylor was a film star who discovered a powerful dramatic persona in the penumbra of Burton's influence," wrote Rutten in 2010. Perhaps, but if we look closer—as we will in the chapters to follow—what becomes clear is that the two were like subatomic particles in a see-through accelerator: once switched on, they collided with each other repeatedly at high speed, while others looked on, transfixed. Taylor may have polished up her technical acting skills, while Burton learned that being with Taylor meant giving up all proprietary rights to privacy. It is often said that Laurence Olivier once asked Burton, "Do you want to be an actor or a household name?" to which Burton replied, "Both." (Burton probably found the question insulting; on page 460 of his diaries, he describes Olivier as "a shallow little man with a very mediocre intelligence but a splendid salesman.")

Burton was an Oxford-trained thespian with a portfolio of Shakespearean roles and a few Hollywood film appearances before he met Taylor. She was apparently impressed by how he always seemed to have been given a script to learn, lost it amid a drunken binge, and, too embarrassed to ask for another, relied on intuition. And still managed to pull off a bravura performance.

His private life, like hers, became more interesting, immeasurably more interesting, than any of his films. And some of the films in which they appeared together, notably *Cleopatra*, and *Who's Afraid of Virginia Woolf?* were, in their own ways, richly compelling. Still, they were no match for what became known as Liz & Dick, a co-production as erotic, gripping, and fabulous as anything the Hollywood dream factory could produce. Mel Gussow, of the *New York Times*, uses the compression Dickenliz to underscore the similarities with more contemporary celebrity pairings, like Brangelina and Kimye. The media allowed audiences glimpses into what, at times, seemed a domestic cagefight, and, at other times, an affectionate soap opera. Indecorous, uncommon, and always engrossing, Taylor's life was a narrative in its own right.

In 2005, Reni Celeste argued that Hollywood stars were "most fascinating" when seen "simply eating at a café, entering an elevator, or using a lavatory. What happens off the screen will be as important as what occurs on it, and even undistinguishable." We take this almost for granted, even if we sometimes remind ourselves that the thrill of real lives is frequently not thrilling at all. The fact remains: audiences, or consumers, seem more interested in celebrities' selfies than their portraits.

Today's fans see in celebrities mirror images of themselves: they look and behave pretty much like everyone else. Taylor's life was not so earthbound: she loved passionately, raged savagely, spent profligately, ate and drank prodigiously, and self-destructed as if she wanted to relinquish every advantage conferred on her by birth. The media covered her in as much detail as she allowed; and, what she did not allow, they conjectured. Pleasantly fascinated, consumers became complicit in an epic exercise in mass voyeurism.

By the time the curtain eventually fell on Liz & Dick (Burton died in 1984), Taylor had assumed and abandoned the persona of a politician's wife, a part she played with her customary professionalism. It was a more patterned role that kept her and her husband John Warner in the limelight, though, in a sense a warm-up for the two new personae Taylor would assume in the late 1980s.

Today, it seems, there are as many celebrity perfumes and colognes on the market as there are celebrities. In 1987, the concept of linking a person with a product, though not completely original, was relatively untested. Elizabeth Taylor's Passion became one of the bestselling fragrances on the market and was the first of a range of perfumes from which Taylor made her late career fortune (she was estimated to be worth between $600 million (£374.6m) and $1bn at the time of her death).

Her life restructured by serious illness and dependencies, and the death of her friend Rock Hudson (in 1986), Taylor aligned herself with Aids charities and became the world's most prominent and influential campaigner. This is a book predicated on the view that Taylor reflected her times, but helped shape them too. While her Hollywood years are always the most fluorescently conspicuous, she was at her most persuasive in her mature life, when she embarrassed politicians into committing funds to Aids research, and cajoled shoppers into paying nearly $200 for signed *flacons* of her heady, floral scents (1987 prices too).

At a time, when the celebrity firmament seem to grow ever more congested as Hollywood actors were joined by rock stars, television presenters and, soon, reality tv contestants, interest in Taylor's private life might have declined. To an extent, it did, though a couple of spells in rehab, an eighth marriage and various dependencies were enough to keep audiences captivated. Taylor's friendships, romantic, platonic, real or made up, continued to fascinate.

As incongruous couplings go, Taylor's friendship with Michael Jackson was up there with the weirdest. Her bewildering and, in some ways, shocking friendship with the King of Pop, whom she met briefly in 1984 then developed a strengthening bond for the rest of his life, sucked her into new controversy—though not of her own making. At the start of their friendship Jackson was the world's leading male pop singer. Soon after, child abuse allegations surfaced, so that by the end of his life (in 2009) he was a somewhat tragic, haunted figure. Having been something of a social leper herself, Taylor probably figured out that a vengeful scandal-seeking media was out to get Jackson; so she stayed beside him during his crash, rise, downfall, recovery, and ultimate demise.

There are other points of comparison, discerned by Rafer Guzman, Gary Dymski, and Michele Ingrassia, in 2011: "Much like Michael Jackson, with whom she shared an unlikely friendship and oddly similar taste in clothes, Taylor became known more as an icon than an entertainer . . . Taylor lived nearly her entire life in the public eye." Taylor never failed to get a charge from this: being the object of others' voyeuristic fascination, far from fazing her, seemed her main source of energy. Jackson oscillated between exhilaration and fear.

"Just try telling the story of the second half of the 20th century without her," David Thomson dares writers. Of course, no one has tried telling the story of the second half of the twentieth century with her either. This, as the reader will now realize, is what I have chosen to do. Taylor's life is at the center of the book, but her times are equally important. I do not believe we can understand Taylor's life, or indeed anybody else's, without appreciating the context in which they lived. By context, I mean time and place, events preceding, following and surrounding people, and other background factors; all assist in fully understanding Taylor, both as an individual and a cultural figure.

Telling someone's life story in this nonlinear way implicates us in all manner of unexpected events and with people who seem to have no relationship to Taylor, at least not in a direct way. The reader will find out how Taylor's life intersects with the publication of the Kinsey Report on sexual behavior, in 1948, the assassination of President John F. Kennedy, in 1963, the Patty Hearst kidnapping of 1979, and the launch of Madonna's *Like a Prayer* in 1990. Taylor did not appear from a cultural void.

Jeff Simon, of *Buffalo News*, wrote shortly after Taylor's death in 2011: "Certainly her life, unsnobbish, hardly ethnocentric, filled with divorces and illness and material triumphs, with its political movements leftward and rightward, curiously mirrors the American decades from 1950 until now."

Simon likens Taylor to Elvis Presley in the sense that she is destined to stay an "inhabitant of the American imagination." I believe Simon is right, though he might have emphasized that she is in the world's imagination too and has been there for about six decades. So, when Saul Austerlitz, in 2010, wrote, "Taylor was far less than meets the eye," he was not being sarcastic nor even mildly critical. Taylor just supplied raw material: we put together the Taylor we knew, or wished we knew or just dreamed we knew. In this sense, as Austerlitz concludes: "Taylor's legacy lies off the screen. It lives on in the well-publicized travails of Britney and Paris and Jessica and Lindsay, the in slew of beautiful young actresses and singers upon whom the white-hot gaze of the media's eye briefly falls."

Like some of the other writers already mentioned, Austerlitz sees in Taylor, not just a person, but a kind of code for celebrity. Everything she did, she seemed to do in front of the media; it was sometimes as if she waited for photographers to arrive before she became herself. There was no core personality, as psychologists are wont to call it, there were fragments and experiences. It was "her iconic beauty, eight marriages (two of which were preceded by scandal), religious conversion, family, major illnesses, love of animals, political alliances and personal friendships, jewelry indulgences, that all produced 'Elizabeth Taylor' in the public domain," as Florence Jacobowitz expresses it. This was the "Elizabeth Taylor" everyone knew in some way. She led what Richard Corliss calls "the most public of Hollywood's 'private lives'," and Brenda Maddox, "the most public private life in the world."

Again, I am inclined to remind readers that, while today's celebrities are locked into a pact that obliges them to sacrifice their private lives in exchange for entrance to even the W-list, Taylor was not. She was just an ungovernable actor who opted to live differently. I am reminded of a headstrong child who, when presented with an unbreakable toy, instantly picks up a hammer and tries to break it. Taylor wielded a hammer and, in the process, changed culture. This is quite a claim, but one I intend to back up in the pages that follow. Whether Taylor takes credit or blame for the changes that followed her first indiscretions will depend on the reader's perspective.

Taylor is already a portal into imagined worlds. Her life, or episodes from it, has been disclosed to us in many different ways. There have been several feature films, two plays, paintings, in fact a whole portfolio of paintings, the first completed in 1982, by the American artist Kathe Burkhart. Andy Warhol used a still from Taylor's 1960 film *BUtterfield 8* for his 1964 silkscreen. She is in the background of Jess Walter's *Beautiful Ruins*, in which one of the central characters is a producer dispatched from Hollywood to Italy to sort out the chaos on the set of *Cleopatra* (the book's title is taken from a description of Richard Burton, when fifty-four, his once Adonic looks eroded by drinking liquor).

Taylor has also appeared spectrally in two J.G. Ballard novels. In *Crash*, she is an inhuman presence: the ultimate sexual thrill for the protagonist is to die in a head-on car collision with a car driven by Taylor. Her image appears on a 2008 edition of this title. In *The Atrocity Exhibition*, Taylor appears though in fragments, images, and projections, as if Ballard is, again, conceiving of Taylor, less of a person, more as an idea. As a living subject, Taylor was multifarious, though never elusive; in other words, she took many different shapes, and had many different aspects, but she was always available. She will be no less available in her death, if only because the Taylor everyone relates to is not the flesh-and-blood mortal, but the Taylor of the imagination. I will expand this argument in the chapters which follow.

Telling a story from beginning to end is the most straightforward but not always the most enlightening route. I have remapped Taylor's story, stalking celebrity culture to its lair. This is not a linear path. For this reason, I have provided a chronological timeline of Taylor's life (and times, of course) from the year of her birth, 1932, to 2015, four years after her death. This is on pages 1–17 immediately before this chapter. Like any other human, Taylor was surrounded by others, all of whom influenced her to some degree or another. After the main text of the book, I provide a who's who of the people who figured prominently in Taylor's life.

As the reader will have by now realized, I draw on many sources, often quoting or paraphrasing other writers, sometimes dipping into newspaper archives for reportage of events in and around Taylor's life. I have added a full list of sources in the bibliography at the end of the book, including, where available, shortened URLs (uniform resource locators) for readers who wish to return to the originals on the internet. Where it has been possible to include a page number in the text, I have done so immediately after the quotation. For example, (p. 45). So research-oriented readers can go back to sources if they wish. Where no page number is indicated, it will mean that the source document is unnumbered, or the document has now been uploaded onto the net with no numbering. Such are the challenges facing a didactic author: in common with other nonfiction writers, I strive to be informative and edifying, though without delivering a tutorial.

FIGURE 2 *Innocence gone, a new Elizabeth Taylor was unfolding. In addition to her many qualities, including beauty, glamour, money and a penchant for extravagance, there was now sexual voracity.*

Photo by Hulton Archive/Getty Images.

2

Animal delight

"The Elizabeth Taylor who's famous, the one on film, really has no depth or meaning to me. She's a totally superficial working thing, a commodity. I really don't know what the ingredients of the image are exactly—just that it makes money." In 1964, when Elizabeth Taylor offered these thoughts to *Life* magazine's Richard Meryman, she was married to Richard Burton.

Eight months before the publication of the interview, police had been obliged to block off West 46th Street in Manhattan when, as Ellis Amburn describes it, "thousands of the curious surged in from Times Square to catch a glimpse of the Burtons" (p. 216). Elizabeth arrived at the Lunt-Fontanne theater to see her husband appear in *Hamlet*. The "bedlam," as Amburn calls it was typical of the uproar occasioned by Elizabeth Taylor practically anywhere she went in the mid-1960s and beyond. She was then thirty-two and able to reflect on a decade of scandals of one kind or another. Taylor had been at the center of crises that would have terrified other actors or prominent figures from any sphere. She may have been terrified herself, but not for long. By 1964 she seemed to realize that scandal was not a chute but an elevator—it could take you up as well as down.

In disrupting every safe cliché with a mischievous, but usually effective intervention, she expressed her irritation with those who pored over her. "The public takes an animal delight in putting somebody on the top and then tearing into little bits. But I have never in my life believed in fighting back to 'cure' my public image . . . I'm not going to answer for an image created by hundreds of people who do not know what's true or false," she told Meryman (p. 81).

"Animal delight." What was she thinking of? A pleasure based on primitive sensibilities? Her mind must have been on her first experience of captivation red in tooth and claw. She might have been able to date it too: perhaps the night in September 1958 when she emerged with her escort Eddie Fisher from Musso and Frank's Grill in Hollywood. The flashes of light and pop of flashbulbs from waiting reporters were expected. But, the cry of "Whore!" and admonitions of "Shame on you" were probably not.

Taylor, at twenty-six, was a widow. Already twice divorced and a mother of three, she had been married to Michael Todd for only 414 days. Todd had died in a plane crash on March 22, 1958. His best friend and, in many ways, acolyte Eddie Fisher was overcome with grief. As such, he could empathize with Taylor. As J. Randy Taraborrelli put it in 2006: "[Fisher] was one of the few people in Elizabeth's life who truly grasped the deep impact his death had on her" (p. 139).

Fisher was devoted to Todd and, in the period immediately following his death, dutifully comforted his grieving widow, accompanying her to the funeral in Chicago while his wife Debbie Reynolds, also a close friend of Todd and, indeed, Taylor, stayed home in Los Angeles with their children. After that, Taylor and Fisher were constant companions—understandably so, given the circumstances. When they whispered, cried, held each other, they appeared to be engaged in acts of support and succor. There seemed nothing untoward or even unusual in two sorrowful souls easing each other's anguish.

In July 1958, *Modern Screen*, a popular film magazine, featured a picture of Taylor and Todd on its cover, with the promise of an article titled, "The most tender and tragic love story of our time." The title captured the collective sympathy for a woman, who with beauty, wealth, and the adulation of the world, was enduring unimaginable agony. In October, the same magazine again included Taylor in its cover photograph, this time with a composite shot of Fisher and his wife Debbie Reynolds. The strapline was an entreaty apparently from Reynolds: "Don't hurt Eddie . . . don't hurt my husband" (cited in Anthony Slide's *Inside the Hollywood Fan Magazine*, p. 174).

What happened to change the sentiment? Apart from returning to work—she was filming at the time of Todd's death—after an indecently hasty three weeks (she was back on set by April 14), she responded to murmurs about her togetherness with Fisher, in particular about whether it had become intimate. The grapevine was shaken on August 29, 1958, when *New York Times* columnist Earl Wilson reported: "Elizabeth Taylor and Eddie Fisher were dancing it up at the Harwyn [nightclub] this morning, Eddie having been Mike Todd's close friend and now sort of an escort service for Liz" (cited by William Mann, p. 223).

Wilson also revealed that Fisher had been with Taylor the night before, when they saw the William Gibson play *Two for the Seesaw* (later turned into a film). At a time when television was in its infancy, print media were the most trusted source of information. Wilson's delicacy in suggesting closeness between Taylor and Fisher contrasts with the blunter style more familiar to today's readers. But it was enough to arouse suspicions.

Taylor either opted or felt obliged to talk to Hedda Hopper, an aging but still influential figure in the Hollywood film industry at the time. We will discover more of Hopper later, but, for now, need only to remember her writing was syndicated in eighty-five American publications and her column had a daily readership of about 32 million (out of a national population of

160 million) in her heyday, the 1950s. She would die less than eight years after her fateful interview with Taylor in which she enquired about the solace she found in the company of Todd's best friend and whether this had developed into something less wholesome.

After Wilson's column, the rumors had been hissing like escaping gas, especially after Taylor spent four days at the same hotel as Fisher. When they showed up over the Labor Day weekend at Grossinger's, a resort in the Catskills, the media became interested. While press photographers were respectful and considerate compared to what we now recognize as paparazzi, pictures of the two filled spaces in newspapers. By September 8, the *Los Angeles Herald Express* was emboldened enough to run a story headlined "Eddie Fisher is dating Liz Taylor." Perfunctory dismissals from the principals followed, assisting the artfully ambiguous headline "Eddie Fisher Romance with Liz Taylor Denied" in the next day's *Los Angeles Examiner*. A denial amplifies whispers without the need for proof.

Hopper, a friend of Taylor's for nearly twenty years, had a reputation for separating half-truths from the real thing, and on September 11, called her friend directly for the definitive version. "Level with me," Hopper is said to have warned Taylor, "I shall find out anyhow." Hopper's pulse must have quickened as Taylor uttered an early contender for her own epitaph. "Mike's dead, and I'm alive," Taylor reminded Hopper. "What do you expect me to do, sleep alone?"

At the time Taylor was playing the role of Maggie "the Cat" Pollit in Richard Brooks's film adaptation of Tennessee Williams' *Cat on a Hot Tin Roof*. The script called for her to taunt her impotent husband who is pining for his dead best friend with, "Skipper is dead! And I'm alive! Maggie the cat is alive!" She could hardly be pastiching in such a solemn context. Could she? Whatever her intention, she had, in one sentence, contrived a transformation. Jeff Simon, of the *Buffalo News* unpicks the importance of the reply: "As an expression of total Hollywood entitlement from an actress whose beauty was legendary from the time she was only 9 years old, it's just about perfect." Simon goes on: "Its lusty frankness from an adulterous actress caught in flagrante delicto would be unusual even in the 21st century, but in 1958, it was almost unheard of" (2011).

"I'm not taking anything away from Debbie Reynolds," Taylor informed Hopper, "because she never really had it." Hopper might have inferred some truth from this callous-sounding attempt at establishing just cause. She chose instead to use it as evidence of a merciless, amoral homewrecker. According to David Bret, Taylor later contested both quotations (p. 116). But there were no legal challenges and Hopper was so experienced, it seems unlikely that she would risk publishing a fabrication. Hopper's account ran on the front page of the *Los Angeles Times* and was syndicated widely. "I only wrote down what you told me," Hopper is said to have told Taylor during a later interaction. "The words are your own." Taylor's response would have been more believable from an ingénue rather than someone who had been part of the Hollywood industry for eighteen years: "But I didn't think you'd print them."

Taylor's disclosure put a stop to the chatter, but started a scandal. She returned to Los Angeles from New York to find the press waiting. Nowadays we are used to celebrities trying to dodge chasing reporters at breakneck speed, Lindsay Lohan, Britney Spears and others seem unable to travel any other way. But it must have been unusual for a Hollywood star to escape a pursuant pack of reporters, as Taylor had to do, in the 1950s before the word paparazzi was even known. But, in a move worthy of Lohan herself, Taylor fled to a Beverly Hills hotel and, with her agent Kurt Frings, disappeared into the lobby. Frings remained to hold off the media personnel, while Taylor slipped out of a back door, into another car.

Taylor's affairs of the heart had been well documented since she was a teenager. This was different. Innocence gone, a new Elizabeth Taylor was unfolding. In addition to her many qualities, including beauty, glamour, money, and a penchant for extravagance, there was now sexual voracity. "Elizabeth Taylor's image changed from Grieving Widow to Scarlet Women," wrote Brenda Maddox, in her 1977 biography of Taylor (p. 139). One moment she drew the world's sympathies, the next its condemnation. She was notorious. Between them, she and Fisher received 5,000 letters of reprimand per week, according to Bret (p. 117).

The crucial words, Taylor's not Tennessee Williams', were, "enough to create the image of a woman with an insatiable sexual craving and a total indifference to public opinion," according to Maddox (p. 142). Given the currency a reputation like this would have today, we might suspect an element of calculation or at least forethought. "What do you expect me to do, sleep alone?" is a killer line, after all. In the late 1950s, it appeared to be a major clanger. Not because Taylor had a virginal persona: she already had three ex's, a vapor trail of discarded suitors, and a reputation that even Marilyn Monroe envied. Nor even because the man with whom she was associated was already married and had children. But because of his wife.

Debbie Reynolds was the same age as Taylor: signed to Warner Brothers at sixteen, she could act, dance, and sing. Blonde and well-scrubbed, she had a chaste princess quality that's almost impossible to find among today's A-listers. Katherine Heigl. Sandra Bullock, perhaps. Even this pair seems voluptuary by comparison. Reynolds embodied moral purity. She seemed sweet and innocuous. In reviewing the many articles on Reynolds prior to Taylor's intervention, Susan E. McLeland, in 1996, noted how they all tended to "present marriage as the quiet satisfaction of all her womanly desires" (p. 117). She and her husband were, as McLeland captures it, "The entertainment world's most romantic pair."

By the time she married Fisher in September 1955, the then 23-year-old daughter of a devoutly religious railroad worker was an established Hollywood star. Reynolds' most memorable film role was in *Singin' in the Rain* (1952). The year before the scandal broke, she had topped the singles best-seller charts with a sentimental ballad "Tammy" from the 1957 romcom *Tammy and the Bachelor* in which she played a sunny young woman who wins the affections of a recalcitrant bachelor.

Every move in her career, perhaps her life, seemed to be handled with near-balletic sublimity. When she agreed to stay behind and care for her children while her husband comforted the widow of one their friends, it seemed consistent with her over-generous character. "He went with my blessing," she reflected. But, as David Leafe asked in 2013: "How many women would be happy for their husbands to share a home with probably the most beautiful woman in the world, whether she was in mourning or not?" He answers his own question: "Perhaps only one like Reynolds who was aware, if only subconsciously, that her marriage was already approaching its end."

Reynolds herself recounted how, while Fisher was away, she frequently called Taylor at her hotel just for a chat. One time she called and, to her surprise, Fisher answered. "Suddenly, a lot of things clicked into place," she told David Wigg in 2010. "I could hear her [Taylor's] voice asking him who was calling." Reynolds told Fisher to "roll over" and let her talk to Taylor. He dropped the receiver and rushed back to California, where he told Reynolds: "Elizabeth and I are in love. I want a divorce." Reynolds replied: "If you marry her, she will throw you out within eighteen months." Reynolds' estimate was out by about two-and-half years.

When she appeared on the doorstep of her house to address a group of journalists who had gathered in anticipation of a reaction to the developing news of her husband's apparent faithlessness, Reynolds wore a veil of motherly serenity, even while she must have been crumbling inside. Diaper pins fastened to her shirt to remind everyone she was a dutiful parent, carrying a baby's plastic bottle to reinforce the point, her hair fashioned asexually into pigtails, Reynolds was word perfect: "I am still very much in love with my husband," she confirmed to the *Los Angeles Times*. And, with barely conceivable beneficence, she added: "Don't blame Eddie for this, though. It's not his fault. He's a wonderful guy" (September 11, 1958, pp. 1 and 26).

The media were Reynolds's helpful accomplices in projecting an emblem of taken-for-granted womanhood. She could have speaking for every woman when Reynolds announced to *Life* magazine: "It seems unbelievable to say you can live happily with a man and not know he doesn't love you" (cited by McLeland, p. 103).

And when the caption on the cover of the January 1959 edition of *Photoplay* read, "Can't daddy be with us all the time?" under a picture of Reynolds and her two fatherless children, everyone knew the answer.

According to M.G. Lord's 2012 book: "Reynold's antics made Taylor more defiant" (p. 66). The word antics suggests she thinks Reynold's behavior was contrived. Taylor presumably thought so too; her responses to media questions were unapologetic and she did nothing to counter the popular view that, like a capricious, destructive wind, she had just blown apart a functional, though not necessarily happy family. True to character, she refused to bolster Reynold's image of a motherly but fragile figure, pointing out that, showbusiness has a fortifying effect on its practitioners. She probably made jaws drop in disbelief when she suggested she might even be Reynolds' savior, rescuing her from a loveless marriage and releasing her to find someone she really loved. Even in the 1950s, it seems, the media knew how much consumers love to loathe people. Or maybe this was the point when they learned.

If Debbie Reynolds never seemed more than a pretty moppet under the benign control of studio executives, she broke free and asserted her individuality after her husband had abandoned her. She thrived in role of the wronged woman. In a 1958 readers' poll, *Motion Picture* magazine reported—predictably—that Taylor was the most interesting figure. Anthony Slide notes the runner-up was Reynolds, "whose career was suddenly of major import" (p. 174).

This was reflected in her earnings, which, according to Amburn, shot from $75,000 per year before 1958, to nearly $1 million thereafter (p. 159). Reynolds went on to make such classic films as *How the West Was Won*, and *The Unsinkable Molly Brown*, for which she won an Oscar nomination.

"The beauty ideal for adolescent girls as perpetuated by teen periodicals was the petite young woman as epitomized by Debbie Reynolds," wrote Georganne Scheiner in 2001 (p. 96). William J. Mann adds: "To the public, Debbie was the Good Mother. Elizabeth was anything but" (p. 252). In the philosophical vernacular, Taylor was Othered: positioned as someone, or something that was distinct from, or opposite to someone else who epitomized virtue. Dark and devastatingly beautiful, Taylor had éclat and vivacity in inverse proportion to Reynold's simple homeliness. She could probably have had any man she wanted. The shock was that she decided she wanted another woman's husband; the shock must have gone to every woman's core. The stinging rebuke she heard as she left the restaurant came from one disapproving customer but it probably echoed what a great many other women, especially married women, thought about Taylor.

Today's consumers may be more media savvy than their counterparts were in the 1950s and they rely less on a single source for their information. The print and, to a lesser extent—in the late 1950s—television reports offered a narrative, or, as McLeland calls it, "a plot": "Reporters' foregrounding of Taylor's and Reynolds's actions, while generally ignoring Fishers', creates a plot which plays the scandal out as a struggle between two women rather than the tale of an unfaithful husband" (p. 39).

Taylor did not demur from what was for her a new challenge, even when she must have known that she was about as popular as the evil witch Maleficent in Disney's *Snow White*, released around the same time (1959). Rather than deny, rationalize or plea for understanding, she issued an icy declaration: "You can't break up a happy marriage. Debbie's and Eddie's never has been." It was a self-conscious, almost threatening expression, a distillation of the sentiments of the coming decades. And she did not whisper it: the unapologetic comments were made in the context of an interview for *Life* magazine bearing the title, "Tale of Debbie, Eddie and the Widow Todd" (September 22, 1958). The heft of women who lived lives that were approximations of contentment were kidding themselves if they thought marriage was their guard. Taylor was demonstrating a new, subversive type of womanhood. Even the biological imperatives of children could not dissuade her that anything other than her own happiness was a priority. The only downside of being Elizabeth Taylor, it seemed, was having too many choices.

Several years later, Taylor and Reynolds made their peace. Reynolds even said she voted for Taylor when she was nominated for an Oscar. In 2001, they appeared in the tv movie *These Old Broads,* written and directed by Reynold's daughter Carrie Fisher.

"This will hurt you much more than it ever will Debbie Reynolds," Hedda Hopper cautioned Taylor. "People love her very much," Kitty Kelley recounted Hopper's counsel on page 153 of her biography of Taylor. The gossip maven knew how essential the happy-ever-after fantasy was to the American psyche. This was 1958, remember: the year to which director Gary Ross sent his time travelers in the movie *Pleasantville*, the title describing a fictional suburbia where there are *Leave It to Beaver* homes, manicured lawns, and uniformed milkmen delivering shiny bottles; and where the displaced characters wreak havoc by "introducing hipness, sensuality and '90s attitudes on sex," as *SFGate*'s Edward Guthmann put it (October 23, 1998). Yet Hopper had not read the runes accurately: Taylor would not get hurt at all. Quite the opposite.

What of Eddie Fisher, father of two, half of what once looked like a perfect marriage? A man with hitherto no track record of womanizing, nor the looks to be able to compile that track record, anyway. Not that he was repugnant, but, at just over 5 feet 4 inches tall and without the darkly imposing features of, say, Cary Grant or Clark Gable, he did not strike anybody as a match for someone widely described as the most beautiful woman in the world. In fact, he seemed slightly out of his depth.

They used to call singers like Fisher crooners—men who sang sentimental numbers in a soft voice. Bing Crosby, Dean Martin, and Frank Sinatra were among the most prominent crooners of the 1950s. Their quiet singing style was popularized by microphones and amplification. Fisher married fellow singer Reynolds in 1955 and featured with her in the musical comedy film *Bundle of Joy* in 1958. He met Taylor through his close friendship with Michael Todd. At the time, he was riding high with NBC television's *The Eddie Fisher Show* and a recording deal with RCA Victor. Before Todd's death, his marriage seemed hale and healthy, though, in the middle of the twentieth century it was not unknown for agents, managers, and studios to make matches almost independently of the principals involved. Daughter Carrie Fisher called her parents' entire marriage "a press release." Sam Kashner and Nancy Schoenberger, in 2010, pronounced: "The Fisher-Reynolds marriage was, for the most part, a studio-arranged mirage" (p. 154).

So Fisher's match may have been made in Hollywood rather than heaven. But, even if the Fisher family bliss was more apparent than real, there was no reason to believe his friendship with Taylor was anything but affectionate. In fact, Fisher was Todd's best man and sang at his and Taylor's wedding in 1957.

When he finally broke his silence Fisher declared his marriage was over and that, contrary to Reynolds' exculpation, it was, in fact, his fault. The public and industry reaction suggested most people believed him: after the full extent of his relationship with his friend's widow became known, Fisher was ostracized. His television show was dropped in 1959 and RCA Victor cancelled his recording contract the following year. Stores refused to stock his records. His record sales slowed and, once his RCA Victor contract had gone, he spent years performing on stage. It is possible that his career would have waned with or without his association with Taylor: after rock 'n' roll erupted in the mid-1950s, crooning became anachronistic. In fact, while most observers argue his relationship with Taylor started the rot in his musical career, it might actually have prolonged it. In a matter of months, he went from being a respectably successful, if unexciting, middle-of-the-road singer to the man who was sharing the same bed as the redoubtable Taylor.

Imagine every anodyne, tuneful, but bland and unadventurous singer you know pureed together and it was Eddie Fisher. He was a successful generic performer, his popularity based on *not* offering new or stimulating material. His biggest hit was the paean "Oh! My Pa-pa" (1954), which opened with the lines: "Oh my pa-pa, to me he was so wonderful. Oh! My pa-pa, to me you were so good." Had he not become involved with Taylor, his professional career would have probably unfolded gradually and predictably and, by the 1990s, if he had been very fortunate, he would probably have occupied the same kind of status as Jack Jones or Andy Williams. He must have realized that, after Taylor, his life and his audience would be different. Fans would no longer slump into their seats and let his music wash over them. They would grab him by the lapels and either say, "What on earth are you thinking of, leaving Debbie for that woman?" or "We didn't think you had it in you; well done!"

Fisher got some measure of what was to come in his first appearance in Las Vegas following his split with Reynolds. David Bret describes the first night as a "media-fest." Taylor had made it known in advance that she would be appearing in the audience at her new husband's performances. The reaction was mixed: "Liz Go Home" banners unfurled at the front entrance as she approached. *Newsweek* magazine asked a couple from Tennessee en route to the show which of the notorious couple they wanted to see. "Are you kidding?" they replied. "Liz." "At one time, the fans had clamored to see Fisher the crooner-par-excellence," writes Bret (p. 121). But, after the scandal, "audiences felt cheated unless Elizabeth was on full bejeweled display next to the stage."

Fisher, perhaps in an effort to bolster his self-confidence in the face of what must have been a humbling experience—performing to sellout crowds, most of whom were interested only in gawking at Taylor—introduced his new wife from the stage as "Mrs. Eddie Fisher."

The 1958 affair and its immediate aftermath left him relatively unimpaired. A steep decline in Fisher's professional career would come years later when Taylor emasculated him symbolically in full view of the world. Fisher could not have known that Taylor was not finished with scandals. The next one would ruin Fisher.

In February 1959, Debbie Reynolds was awarded full custody of her children with Fisher, who was ordered to pay her $10,000 alimony per year. Reynolds also took sole ownership of the family homes in Hollywood and Palm Springs, California. After his relationship with Taylor disintegrated, Fisher married three times again. He would die on September 22, 2010 at the age of eighty-two, survived by children Carrie, Todd, Joely, and Tricia Leigh, as well as six grandchildren. Perhaps the most piercing commentary on Fisher came from someone who did not know him and whose only acquaintance with him was through the media. Jackie Kennedy Onassis, former wife of the US President John F. Kennedy, imperiously pondered her own omnipotence: nothing she ever did or said, no matter how extraordinary or preposterous, would be questioned. "Anyone who is against me will look like a rat," she propounded. There was one qualification: "Unless I run off with Eddie Fisher" (cited by Burton Hersh, p. 468).

In 1949, when Ingrid Bergman was vilified for having an affair with Italian director Roberto Rossellini, condemnations were issued everywhere, even from the floor of the US Senate where Senator Edwin Johnson decried Bergman as "a horrible example of womanhood and a powerful influence for evil." When asked by Hedda Hopper whether she was pregnant by Rossellini, Bergman lied and denied it. She was declared *persona non grata*, fled the country and returned only after splitting up with Rossellini. Their affair began while they were making the movie *Stromboli*, which was banned in many places, boycotted in many more and bombed at the box office. All of her subsequent films were also flops. The 1956 film *Anastasia* to some extent restored her. "I've gone *from saint to whore* and back to saint again, all in one lifetime," Bergman reflected.

This was surely on the minds of MGM executives in the fall of 1958 when they contemplated the fallout from the Taylor-Fisher affair. The studio's concern was that the persistent news would affect—for want of a better term—public opinion on Taylor. Consumers might show their disapproval by deliberately avoiding her new film, *Cat on a Hot Tin Roof* in much the same way as they registered their disapproval for Bergman. For a film actor, the fate almost worse than death was losing box office appeal.

Taylor had been peerless for a decade but she was always vulnerable to public denunciation. In the twenty-first century, scandal is so valuable that showbusiness figures go prospecting for it. In the 1950s, stars and their handlers were much more circumspect. Affairs were hazardous. As were homosexuality and taking drugs. Some of the stories of how the Hollywood machine subdued or in some way massaged away minor transgressions are museum pieces now. Rita Hayworth became pregnant and fled to Europe after an abortion in the late 1940s, according to biographer Barbara Leaming. Robert Mitchum's drugs bust was hastily covered up by his studio so that it would not damage his promising movie career, revealed Lee Server. Movie actors and singers who broke codes and did not have a studio prepared and able to hush up their behavior were simply consigned to oblivion. Taylor could have followed them. Her second seven-year contract with Metro-Goldwyn-Mayer Studios was coming to an end, so the studio could have cut her loose and leave her to the hands of fate.

Taylor's agent was former boxer Kurt Frings. Whether he was prescient or just desperate when he said it, no one can be sure, but as the scandal gained momentum and the release date of her film *Cat on a Hot Tin Roof* drew nearer, he argued there was no such thing as bad publicity. It's the kind of aphorism usually credited to P.T. Barnum, the founder of the "Greatest Show on Earth" circus and originator of such gems as "Nobody ever lost a dollar by underestimating the taste of the American public" and "Advertising is to a genuine article what manure is to land: it largely increases the product." But Barnum, who died in 1891, would have been chastened by Taylor's provocations. Frings, on the other hand, had a vested interest and maybe a crystal ball.

His argument was a radical departure from the orthodox approach, but, as William J. Mann wrote in 2011: "It was a smart move because the picture that hit theaters just as the Fisher scandal struck, *Cat on a Hot Tin Roof*, featured Taylor as exactly the kind of seductress that she appeared to be in real life."

Mann had earlier written approvingly of Fring's risk-taking in his biography of Taylor, *How to be a Movie Star*. According to Mann, Frings actually encouraged Taylor in her "romantic exploits." "Old notions of how stars were 'supposed to' behave in public were being replaced by a radical new idea: that press coverage—*any* press coverage—was better than none at all" (p. 229).

While Hollywood imagined it had perfected a star system, what the scholar Joshua Gamson, in 1992, called "the assembly line of greatness," Frings, it seems, realized that consumer tastes made any kind of fame unstable, volatile, and demotic. Frings, in his own way helped sabotage the idea of stardom as something immutable and largely under the control of the powerful Hollywood studios. He probably realized that fans looked to stars in awe and admiration; they could also look in disgust and revulsion. Either way, they were engaged.

Frings was right. Ten years before, he would have been wrong, as Bergman's experience confirms. Frings, who died in 1991, would have been out of a job and regarded as certifiable had he advised clients to prompt outrage or provoke anger among audiences. But as the 1960s approached, he was tolerated, perhaps even humored; he had scarcely put a foot wrong so far in his career. So maybe he was worth listening to. There was little choice, anyway: *Cat on a Hot Tin Roof's* release was imminent and Taylor had no time to rehabilitate her image. In the 1950s, there was none of the repentance that habitually follows a celebrity transgression today. Taylor was utterly *un*repentant. "I'm not taking anything away from Debbie Reynolds because she never really had it."

The scandal was "the most explosive triangle of the past decade," contended Ezra Goodman in 1961. Mann concurred; in his 2009 publication, he wrote: "The Liz-Eddie-Debbie triangle was the first major scandal of the poststudio era" (p. 250). By *poststudio era*, he means from the mid-1950s when actors were no longer tied to studios under long-term contracts, but were still dependent on the major studios to provide the scale of production and distribution exposure necessary to make and maintain their fame. The studio era—a period from the 1920s usually refers to the period when a handful of Hollywood companies dominated the production, distribution, and exhibition of American films. Both writers, Goodman and Mann, are probably too guarded: the Taylor scandal had no precedents. No other celebrity event had horrified, outraged, repelled, disgusted, offended, unsettled, startled, and fascinated the media and their public. And it would not be eclipsed until Taylor again encouraged interest in her sexual proclivities four years later.

When Lord concludes, "Taylor's mistake, however, was not sleeping with Fisher. It was failing to grovel to Hedda Hopper," she misunderstands the context of the late 1950s. There was no mistake: Taylor was surefooted and confident. She would not have enjoyed being called a whore, nor being shouted at, as several later interviewers later confirmed. Yet the effect was undeniable: taking $11,285,000 at the boxoffice, *Cat on a Hot Tin Roof* was the highest grossing film of 1958, the tenth most commercially successful film in the history of MGM, yielding a profit of almost $2.5 million. The reviews were stunningly good; Taylor's notice, in particular, were the best of her career. "Taylor has a major credit with her portrayal of Maggie," reported *Variety*. "The frustrations and desires, both as a person and a woman, the warmth and understanding she molds, the loveliness that is more than a well-turned nose—all these are part of a well-accented, perceptive interpretation" (December 31, 1958). Taylor was nominated for an Academy Award (for the second consecutive year). Fans and critics alike purred at the film and Taylor's turn as the passionate, flirtatious Maggie. Even so, Maddox revealed, Taylor and Fisher, "dared not go out in public even for a drive; people would shout insults at them when the car stopped at traffic lights" (p. 143).

Maddox is probably underestimating Taylor's unblushing defiance in the face of disapproval. For example, in October 1958, shortly after Fisher's breakup with Reynolds (and before she filed for divorce), Taylor threw a party at her Bel Air home, in California. Fisher "got a warm welcome from the Widow Todd on his arrival," reported Seymour Korman for the *Chicago Tribune* (October 2, 1958). Korman described how reporters and photographers tried to force their way in and were "herded off the property by hired guards." Uninhibited by the presence of the media, Taylor emerged from the house barefooted with Fisher at 2:00 a.m., and dashed across her front lawn in full view of her audience.

Perhaps it was synchronicity, a near-simultaneous occurrence of two events that appeared related but had no discernible causal connection. Taylor couldn't have planned to start a relationship with Fisher so close to the release of her next picture. But, for all its artistic merits, the success of the film was bonded to the scandal—as what seemed to be damnation was ultimately bonded to Taylor's benediction. Far from destroying her, the Fisher scandal made Taylor anew. In that single episode, the value of scandal as a resource became clear. Recall her phrase: *animal delight*. This was surely the moment when Taylor, her staff, the studios and maybe everyone else realized that scandal could be, to use a word of today, monetized. Taylor's fee for *Cat on a Hot Tin Roof* was $125,000, a handsome amount in the 1950s. For her next film following the end of her MGM contract, Taylor negotiated $500,000. And that would double by 1961.

What changed? We did—obviously. Sensibilities, tastes, standards, our reactions to emotional, moral, and aesthetic influences; they all changed. We were still susceptible to shock and offence; but our responses were new—as if adaptations to a different environment. As the 1950s closed, the postwar consensus was drawing to an end and cultural upheaval would soon follow, releasing the paternalistic restraints and controls that had endured since the end of the Second World War. Amid the consumer affluence and the proliferation of values traditionally associated with the affluent, there emerged a cleavage to rival those of class, race, and sex. This concerned age; young people emerged as a self-conscious, independent group with their own particular and frequently outrageous values and lifestyles and a determination to stake out boundary markers between themselves and the rest of society.

"The children of the 1950s and 1960s, unlike the previous generation, were not interested in the same things as their parents," Robert J. Bresler observed in 1997, in his analysis of how the character of Hollywood was forced to change. Bresler explains; "The concept of a common culture that influenced the young and old alike was diminishing" (p. 64).

The cinema was given new purpose by the young: it "became a place where young people could be in a social setting of their own making," wrote the historian John Sedgwick in 2002. "By 1957 three-quarters of audiences were under 30 and half under 20 years of age" (p. 681).

There was an unfamiliar approach to life gaining currency among the young; this involved, among other things, reformulating moral standards. "Permissiveness" became a key concept of the 1960s. An active sex life was one of the prescriptions of the time. And, in this sense, Taylor became an unwitting and initially reluctant symbol. She would become a more potent figure in the years ahead. One epoch's immorality is the next's propriety. Several feminist writers, including eminent scholars, have rhapsodized on Taylor's influence in this period and beyond; I will consider their views in Chapter 19, when I assess Taylor's impact, politically and culturally.

At the time of the Taylor-Fisher-Reynolds scandal, American biologist Dr. Gregory Pincus was experimenting with a version of a pill that contained the hormones estrogen and progestin. Tested on Puerto Rican and Haitian women, the product suppressed ovulation and so served as an oral contraceptive. It did not become available on the market until 1961.The landmark *Roe vs. Wade* case that legalized abortion was not until 1973. Discrimination on the basis of sex was not addressed in federal law until the Equal Pay Act of 1963, and the amendment Title VII—that included sex as a protected class—was not added until a year later.

Imagine a world without these institutional features. If you can, you will sense not only that women occupied a different status in society, but a different status in the popular imagination. Not just in men's imaginations, but women's too. While there is no known evidence to support this, it seems reasonable to suppose that women in the 1950s felt more guilt than men: they had a history of being blamed for other people's behavior. If they were beaten, they probably annoyed someone; if they were raped, they must have aroused someone; if their children grew up to be delinquents (as young offenders were then called) they were poor mothers. The response to Taylor's moral trespasses has to be understood in the context of this cultural landscape.

What exactly was the response? We know Taylor was called a whore and Fisher was boycotted, while journalists clamored for stories and customers waited in line at the movies. Perhaps because the affair was thrilling: it evoked a sudden feeling of excitement and pleasure, a tremor of emotion that was both distasteful and agreeable. Who the hell does Elizabeth Taylor think she is? No sooner is her late husband buried than she's turned her wiles on a new man, who is married to one the nicest women imaginable and has two children by her. The answer, of course, was: Elizabeth Taylor.

Recall Jeff Simon's interpretation of Taylor's dismissal of Hopper in the fateful interview. He called it, "an expression of total Hollywood entitlement." He means that Taylor, in 1958, felt she had the right to do something—in this case, take another woman's husband—with impunity. The usual prohibitions or moral boundaries separating right from wrong didn't apply to her. She was a Hollywood star, not just any Hollywood star either. It is probably safe to assume Simons' reading of Taylor's reply is basically right: she was utterly unapologetic, never sought redemption and seemed almost puzzled by the alarm she had precipitated: "What do you *expect* me to do?" As if she had no reasonable alternative: she found herself drawn to a man, so she took him. Shamelessly. And in a way that would make her sexual history and future a matter of public record.

In doing so, Taylor invited consumers into her life, perhaps in a way no other Hollywood star or any famous person ever had. It was as if she had grown bored of the Hollywood moratorium that had held since the 1920s and which prevented the leak of information on private lives into the public sphere. It must have been like watching her life become a drama. But fans did not just watch the drama; they lived with it. Consumers became caught up in a star's life and at the star's own request. This meant that fans who had become accustomed to sitting back and appraising a decorous but distant spectacle could be part of that spectacle.

It is difficult to contemplate Taylor's praying for privacy to protect her guilty needs and desires; she seemed to adjust to the surveillance quite capably, like a child who plays with fire and gets singed, though not so badly that she is afraid to play again.

In 1961, Charles Winick, of the City University of New York, published the conclusions of a study of readers of *Confidential*, a fan magazine that had appeared on the newsstands in 1952 and which, according to Anthony Slide, "revealed [stars] in all their scandalous modes, without apology and without restraint" (p. 179). By the time of Winick's research (1954–7), the magazine was selling 4.1 million copies per issue, at 25 cents, and Winick, in his words, sought to "determine the reasons for the unprecedented success of the magazine" (p. 330).

Winick suspected that, while "the general public has always been interested in the private life of celebrities," the prosperity of the mid- and late 1950s had "in some way" helped "to unleash feelings of guilt which could express themselves by reading about celebrities who had sinned" (p. 332). Leaving aside Winick's account of the origins and functions of the curiosity (and his slightly pious language), his suspicions were well founded. *Confidential*'s success was based on its "frontal assault on the celebrity system," by which he meant the mechanism Hollywood used to suppress details of private lives. The magazine focused on itself "the sins and sex of the mighty" (p. 334).

"Realizing that the celebrity was an ordinary mortal with human failings," encouraged readers to think about themselves less guiltily. As Winick summarized the typical response: "We can't be so bad if they're doing the things they do" (p. 331). The portrayal of consumers exorcizing themselves vicariously may be a stretch, but there is plenty of value in Winick's findings. *Confidential* exploited a new curiosity, or perhaps—on Winick's view—a newly expressed old curiosity. It also fertilized it. (*Confidential* ceased publication in 1978 after the death of its founding proprietor.)

Fans knew what they wanted from Hollywood stars. They wanted characters that were symbols of glamour and opulence, models of conspicuous consumption. They wanted faces of hypnotic beauty, like those of Rita Hayworth or Ava Gardner and impossibly perfect bodies clothed in the most expensive gowns. They wanted to believe these celestial beings were halfway to the heavens, not condemned to the circular, eternal mundanity of virtue. They knew what they wanted: salacious details delivered with immediacy and without the protective sanitation of journalists, less still Hollywood publicists.

Confidential tried to provide the stories the Hollywood machine wanted slaughtered at birth. Its sales suggest it succeeded to an extent: it made Hollywood's untouchable characters living the Good Life seem like the magnificent idol of Nebuchadnezzar's dream, with feet "part of iron and part of clay." They too were flawed, just like everyone else. Taylor effected an important modification: here was at least one untouchable who, on her own admission, had very obvious human flaws. Her fate was to be of continuing interest to similarly flawed human beings, who no longer just admired, envied and were lovingly fascinated by her. Now they judged her.

There is something quite satisfying about judging others. "Disgraceful!" "Bravo!" "Shame on you!" "Good job!" We root for those we like and condemn those we dislike. We take pleasure from both types of pronouncement. Taylor virtually handed audiences temporary authority to make evaluations of her behavior. If she was taken aback by the "Go home Liz" directives and the surrounding mayhem every time she appeared with Fisher, that is probably because she had lived too insularly in her Hollywood cocoon. Or she may have anticipated the hue-and-cry and remained indifferent: perhaps she just reminded herself of her status and thought, "consequences be damned."

Whatever Taylor's thought processes, the results were to insinuate consumers into a moralizing discourse. Taylor handed fans what Winick called, "a kind of magical control over the famous and a vehicle for hostility against them, concealed behind expressions of morality and surprise" (p. 331). In other words, fans found new joy in being able to judge the very people they saw on screen. As long as magazines, tabloids, film quarterlies, and many other publications that proliferated in the middle of the twentieth century continued to chronicle the exploits of Taylor and the epigones who followed her, then there was source material. Fans could gaze at a distance, but feel they were pressing up close when they made their judgments.

Taylor probably troubled fans in the late 1950s. She gave them more raw material than they could have wished for. And what raw material: it was practically impossible not to judge her. She astonished the media and their consumers with her seemingly guileless honesty, excited them with the speed of her movements and dazzled them with her unexpected change of tastes. And all the time, the fans were building Elizabeth Taylor, an Elizabeth Taylor they imagined they knew.

In 1986, almost three decades after the Fisher affair, the *New York Times* critic Vincent Canby reflected on Taylor's status, comparing it with those of Bette Davis and Katherine Hepburn, both of whom were in the public consciousness for longer (Davis made her film début in 1931; Hepburn hers in 1932, the year in which Taylor was born) and featured in "more consistently entertaining and better films." The comparison is misleading, as Canby acknowledged: "Taylor occupies a slightly different spot in our history, being as much a figure of the audience's creation as of her own" (p. H1).

Canby's was a perceptive approach to Taylor: he realized that we, the audience, the consumers, the fans, were the true creators of Elizabeth Taylor. In a sense there have always been two Elizabeth Taylors: one the flesh-and-blood mortal, the other a creation independent of time and space, a product of countless imaginations, both changeless and ever changing. In 1977, Brenda Maddox had arrived at the same conclusion: "Virtually everybody carries a private Liz in his or her head" (p. 244).

Earlier in the book, I quoted Saul Austerlitz who called Taylor "an anomaly in American film history." "Taylor was far less than met the eye," he wrote, presumably implying that her complexity, profundity, and enigma were more to do with audiences' attempts to untangle her than with the woman herself. This is not a critique. In fact, Taylor realized this years before Canby, Maddox, and Austerlitz. I opened this chapter with her own reflection on the figure she had helped create: "The Elizabeth Taylor who's famous, the one on film, really has no depth or meaning to me. She's a totally superficial working thing, a commodity."

In 1964, when Taylor made this observation, she must surely have known how closely her persona and anima were fused. How could she not know that her public, screen roles were extensions of her private life? Think of three movies you most readily associate with Taylor. All of them will feature her playing the role of a sexually attractive, brazenly manipulative woman who wants her own way and uses any means she can of securing it. Her character is infused with wickedness but is no less entrancing for it. Think of a fourth role. It will probably work for that too. If Taylor made the commodity, she made it in her own image. But, of course, she did not: we did.

FIGURE 3 *"Her name is Mrs. Fisher," Eddie Fisher persisted. The 1958 scandal would change public perceptions of Taylor, though not in a way that would damage her long-term value.*

Photo by Silver Screen Collection/Getty Images.

3

Like a million dollars

Nothing succeeds like success. Taylor modified the maxim slightly: "There's no deodorant like success" (in the Meryman interview, p.82). She also provided proof: success creates the conditions under which it is possible to achieve even greater success—and remove foul odors. With *Cat on a Hot Tin Roof* pulling in crowds and stories of Taylor crowding practically every newspaper and magazine, the opportunities for bigger box office movies opened up. By November 1958, she had accepted offers to act in two films, *Two for the Seesaw*—recall that she went to see the Broadway play when in New York with Fisher—and *Suddenly, Last Summer,* which was also based on a play, this one by Tennessee Williams (author of the original play on which *Cat on a Hot Tin Roof* was based). The combination of Williams' plots and Taylor's screen presence made *Suddenly, Last Summer* the more bankable project and Taylor opted out of *Two for the Seesaw;* Shirley MacLaine took the role. It was commonplace for studios that held contracts with actors to allow them to work for rival studios and MGM permitted Taylor to make *Suddenly, Last Summer* for Columbia Pictures, which had offered a formidable bounty.

The rate Columbia offered Taylor was $500,000 against ten percent of the gross, meaning that she received a half-million upfront payment and, later, a backend income based on a percentage of the studio's share of box office receipts. The stipulation of *gross* meant she started earning from the first dollar the movie made; so even if the film eventually lost money for the studio, she would have still have earned her percentage (the importance of this arrangement will become clearer when we reach *Cleopatra*). Columbia also footed the bill for her European honeymoon with Fisher, of which more shortly.

The contract reflected Taylor's ascending value and meant she approached the earnings capacity of the highest-earning men. Columbia paid William Holden the then highest single film fee of $1 million for 1957's *The Bridge on the River Kwai*, directed by David Lean. It barely needs stating that film studios were industries, not charitable foundations, and, as such, prioritized money over morality. Taylor's complicated predicament made her a deeply divisive presence in all but one—the most significant—respect: she turned a penny.

"She *was* the target of scorn and rumors," states William J. Mann in his book on Taylor. "What Elizabeth faced as 1958 turned into 1959 was not a crisis of career, but of public relations." Mann's point is supported by the amount of coverage Taylor got from magazines. Anthony Slide documents how Taylor dominated cover stories, not just for these years, but for two decades from 1953 (p. 172).

But was this a *crisis* of public relations? Mann's statement suggests she faced a time of intense difficulty or danger. Or could he mean she reached a turning point? The aura of glamour and mystery once attached to the Hollywood stars of the 1940s and early 1950s was, on Slide's account, disappearing and, while studios persisted in promoting wholesome, righteous, and honorable stars who they hoped would be accepted as respectable, magazines like *Confidential* and its compeers and their readers were turning to more provocative figures, like Marilyn Monroe, Ava Gardner, and Rita Hayworth. So Taylor's combustible public image chimed with the times. From one perspective, "Elizabeth Taylor had reemerged in the course of the fracas as a spoiled, materialistic, callous woman—a callous home wrecker whose selfish needs and hedonistic sex drive knew few limitations." C. David Heymann offers a dramatic interpretation of the popular image that had disseminated around the world—not as quickly as it would in the post-internet age, of course—but quickly enough to guarantee the name Elizabeth Taylor was internationally known. Austin Pendleton offers a different perspective. "Elizabeth Taylor, more than any woman in America, symbolizes not greed to people but healthy appetite," wrote Pendleton in 1986 (p. 29).

Whether her seduction of married men reflected the avaricious inclinations of an indulgent woman who wanted everything within her grasp, whether jewelry, clothes, or human beings, or was just what every other woman would like to do remains a matter of perspective. But the heady mixture of outrage and fascination it elicited was, in a genuine sense, the making of Elizabeth Taylor. Whatever people thought about her, they *thought*—and that was what counted. If they had just forgotten about her, her status might have shrunk. In the event, the scandal excited the kind of interest that translated into box office receipts.

Fisher dissolved his existing marriage on May 12, 1959, and married Taylor at a Las Vegas marriage-licensing bureau on the same day. The license cost $10. After the wedding, Taylor and Fisher headed to the Mediterranean for their honeymoon. Some reports put the couple on a yacht moored off the coast of Barcelona, while others suggested they removed themselves to Lookout Mountain, a mountaintop resort in Georgia. Unassisted by a camera-ready public, as they are now, journalists in the 1950s were at the mercy of traditional methods of reporting.

Shortly before the wedding ceremony, held at the Temple Beth Shalom, Taylor had converted to Judaism. Mann suspects this was "an act of defiance," an act of "flouting the sacred canon," and, in short, "'fuck you' ... to her critics" (p. 264). Taylor's erstwhile husband Michael Todd, like Fisher, was Jewish and Taylor maintained that he rather than Fisher was the main influence in her decision, though there is no evidence that Todd had ever asked his wife to convert. Raised a Christian Scientist, Taylor apparently grew dissatisfied with her faith and studied the reform philosophy of Judaism before making her decision. Debbie Reynolds, incidentally, was also a devout Christian and, in 1962, with Bob Thomas, wrote an advice book for young women, *If I Knew Then* (still available) in which she encourages her readers to stay in daily contact with God by saying grace.

"In 1959, Reynolds was the wronged wife, and all the stories were in her support," writes Anthony Slide about American coverage (p. 174). But in the UK, Reynolds was not such a popular figure and Taylor was British, after all. She was born in Hampstead, London, and retained her British passport as well as a trace of accent. She was followed as avidly in Britain as she was in the US. So, in May 1959, when she and Fisher, newly married, arrived in London to start filming *Suddenly, Last Summer* at Shepperton Studios, in West London, she might have expected a warmer reception than she had experienced in the US. She was due to film for eight weeks.

Scandals did not disseminate so quickly in the 1950s as they do today, but the mixture of outrage and fascination was familiar. Surprised and possibly disappointed that the British press's interest in her was no more sympathetic than America's, Taylor banned reporters from the film set and refused to give interviews. As a result: "The Fishers found themselves ostracized in conservative Englefield Green, near Windsor [southern England]," according to Ellis Amburn (p. 160).

Fisher was given a paid role as her guardian. His own career had stalled and his professional commitments were few. His name was now twinned with his wife's and, while he repeatedly corrected journalists who called her Miss Taylor—"her name is Mrs. Fisher," he persisted—he was and perhaps still is "the guy who married Elizabeth Taylor." For a while he assumed custody of the Elizabeth Taylor brand, even though in the 1960s, people did not think of people as brands, as we do today. He started the Fisher Corporation with a remit to produce films featuring his wife, though none of his projects materialized. His main duty seemed to be as Taylor's factotum and tribute bringer. Taylor's well-documented enthusiasm for exotic jewelry had usually been met by generous suitors. Fisher continued the tradition, though, in his case, the baubles were paid for out of a joint bank account. Taylor was not always gracious in receipt. On one occasion, he presented her with a diamond-encrusted necklace to be asked, "how much?" Several accounts agree that Fisher proudly answered, "$50,000," only for Taylor to dismiss the trinket, "there's not a decent stone in here."

Remarking on a wantonness in Taylor that became apparent to many around this time, Marjorie Rosen, of *Biography Magazine*, wrote in 2003: "Taylor married Fisher in 1959 . . . he would soon become expendable" (p. 72).

Taylor's role in *Suddenly, Last Summer* was more than faintly familiar: the gorgeous and provocative cousin of a gay man who uses her to draw men. She dressed in an opalescent white swimsuit, skimpy by 1960s standards. As in *Cat on a Hot Tin Roof,* she was cast as a woman capable of tempting practically anyone with XY chromosomes: a sexual *force majeure.* The congruence between her on screen persona and popular conceptions of her was unmistakable. So, when Taylor, in the 1964 *Life* interview, meditated on the depthless, meaningless, superficial moneymaking commodity called Elizabeth Taylor, she presumably had the *Suddenly, Last Summer* archetype in mind. This was the film from which she started, on her own account, to earn "big money." So we can infer some calculation: could she really have not seen the symmetry of popular images of her and the bewitchingly, ravishingly, shamelessly immodest characters she essayed in her films?

"I have I supposed behaved immorally," she told Richard Meryman in 1964 (p. 82). Sam Kashner and Nancy Schoenberger, in 2010, contended: "Notoriety had continued to fuel the unstoppable engine of Elizabeth's white hot career" p. 38). It is difficult to see how Taylor herself could not have arrived at a similar conclusion when she plotted her film career and her life.

Sex was not invented in the late 1950s, but, in a sense, it was created. The word itself was probably popularized in America. Sigmund Freud (1856–1939), who theorized on the sexual origins of neuroses, aroused great controversies in the early twentieth century. And the two Kinsey Reports on sexual behavior were published in 1948 and 1953, encouraging open discussion about a subject that had previously been strictly taboo. Only from the 1960s, did sex become a commodity: it realized value as a product in a consumer marketplace. This was not a lightbulb idea that suddenly dawned on a mid-century Steve Jobs or Mark Zuckerberg-type visionary. But through the relaxation of censorship rules, a progressively influential women's movement, ever-more convenient forms of contraception, and the disappearance of all manner of cultural prohibition, sex emerged as an exploitable resource. Whether or not Taylor intended to exploit her own sexuality is not important: others certainly did, and she shared their spoils.

Hollywood's more traditional approach to sex was probably exemplified in Universal Picture's *Pillow Talk*, which was released in 1959, around the same time as *Suddenly, Last Summer*, but which dealt with the subject in a familiar and comfortably reassuring way. The eternally virginal Doris Day played opposite Rock Hudson, then an exemplar of apollonian masculinity.

Tall (6 foot 5 inches) and muscular, Hudson, at thirty-four, always looked as if he had arrived straight from a cosmetic makeover session: his skin was flawless, he had a full head of black hair, succulent lips, and eyes as white as wolves' teeth. Day bore comparisons with Debbie Reynolds in her primness; crisp, neat, and seemingly unstained, she was—in the proper sense of the word—immaculate. Their relationship in the film was implicitly sexual, but its character was romantic.

There was irony in Hudson's casting as an unambiguously heterosexual woman-chasing man: only years later did it become widely known that he was gay, though he never voluntarily disclosed this. Taylor was one of a circle of confidantes and Hollywood insiders who knew what was, in the 1950s and 1960s, a closely guarded secret. I will move onto this in Chapter 14. Taylor's close friend Montgomery Clift was also gay and, as was the Hollywood custom of the time, also disguised this fact in the interest of, among other things, his career. Taylor secured him a lead role in *Suddenly, Last Summer*, which was a daring attempt to integrate a gay theme into a mainstream movie. The script of *Cat on a Hot Tin Roof* was rewritten in a way that made one of its central character's homosexuality indeterminate. But in *Suddenly, Last Summer*, the plot trigger was a gay man's death at the hands of a homophobic gang. The gay character is not seen on screen. Among the other themes of the gothic tale were cannibalism and prefrontal lobotomy.

The Legion of Decency, which was one of the principal agencies responsible for the regulation of film content decided *Suddenly, Last Summer* was "morally legitimate but with some elements 'beyond the capacity of some adults'," as Richard A. Brisbin Jr. put it in 2002 (p. 13). The censorial Production Code Administration (PCA) required the director Joseph L. Mankiewicz to make cuts in order to portray the victim's lifestyle in a way that was not considered offensive. "Since the film illustrates the horrors of such a lifestyle, it can be considered moral in theme even though it deals with sexual perversion," wrote Boze Hadleigh in 2001 (p. 23). Tennessee Williams objected to this slant on his play and distanced himself from the film, at the same time criticizing Taylor for becoming involved with the project. It was originally unrated in the USA and given an X certificate in the UK, meaning it was considered suitable for adults only—like Taylor herself, in fact.

Another film of the era, J. Lee Thompson's 1961 original film *Cape Fear*, later remade by Martin Scorsese, refers to an "attack," on a woman; censors in the 1960s regarding even a mention of the word rape as unacceptable. *Suddenly, Last Summer* was, like *Cat on a Hot Tin Roof,* an adventurous attempt to deal with sexuality in a framework that had begun adjusting to the liberalization that would eventually characterize the 1960s, but could not accommodate the kind of openness we are used to today. Much of the language that featured in the original Broadway play of *Cat on a Hot Tin*

Roof was expurgated for the film. "During the latter of half of the 50s,
Taylor was a star whose persona challenged the stringent production code,"
reflected Florence Jacobowitz and Richard Lippe in 2012 (p. 44)

As an aside: Katherine Hepburn, who also played in the film, reportedly
felt threatened by the attention lavished on Taylor by Mankiewicz, who, for
his part, allegedly hated Clift, at that stage a heavy drinker who could work
no more than half a day at a time. (I will return to Mankiewicz in Chapter 7.)

Taylor received Academy Award nominations for both *Cat on a Hot Tin
Roof* and *Suddenly, Last Summer* for her performances as what James
Verniere called "the sexually incendiary female leads." Camille Paglia thought:
"She [Taylor] represented a kind of womanliness that . . . was rooted in
hormonal reality" (cited by *Salon* in 2011, p. 2). She means that Taylor
expressed her sexuality robustly, as well as "naturally and beautifully." I will
discuss Paglia's overall assessment of Taylor's influence in Chapter 19.

Collectively the two roles "catapulted her [Taylor] from mere Hollywood
fame to international superstar," argued Verniere in 2011. But he exaggerated
the importance of the film roles as entities in their own right: they were
injected with relevance because they seemed to reveal the woman playing
them. Taylor did not just play sexual beings; she appeared to inhabit them;
and everything people heard or read about the "real" Taylor complemented
this impression.

The Golden Age of Hollywood refers to the period beginning in the late
1920s when five powerful American studios dominated the film industry and
the cinema was the paradigm for popular entertainment. In 1948, a landmark
legal case known as *United States v. Paramount Pictures, Inc.* reduced
the major studios' power and started a process that would end the epoch.
The studios not only made films but owned the theaters where the films were
shown, meaning they controlled both production and distribution, an
arrangement the Supreme Court concluded was not consistent with antitrust
principles and effectively perpetuated a monopoly or at least an oligopoly—a
state of limited competition in which the market was shared by a small
number of sellers, in this case 20th Century Fox Film Corporation, RKO
Radio Pictures, Columbia Pictures Corporation, Universal-International,
Warner Brothers, and Loew's, which owned MGM—to which Taylor was
contracted. Actors were employees tied to particular studios, but could ask
for temporary release to work on projects for rival studios. One immediate
implication of the 1948 ruling was that the studios would have to sell off
their movie theaters and the new owners would have more freedom to pick
and choose films. Studios suffered a drop in revenue and cut back on the
number of films they could make.

An arguably more damaging development to Hollywood came with the
arrival of television. At the time of the ruling, less that 9 percent of the US

population had a television set. By 1960, 87.1 percent had at least one tv set. And by 1965, this was up to 92.6 percent. This reflected an astonishing rise in popularity for an innovation about which the film industry may have initially been dismissive, but soon realized was a potent competitor. While tv grew in the 1950s, film lost about 40 percent of its audience.

Like the other major studios, 20th Century Fox was vulnerable to the changes affecting the entertainment industry. And yet it was fearless. Its roster of contracted actors included Marilyn Monroe and John Wayne. It had also loaned Elvis Presley from Paramount to make his first movie, *Love Me Tender* in 1956 (Presley was under contract to Paramount, but had not made a film at this point). 20th Century Fox had introduced the widescreen format CinemaScope in 1953 in *The Robe*, a film set at the start of the Christian era that featured Richard Burton as a Roman tribune who angers Caligula and is sent to Jerusalem where he supervises the crucifixion of Jesus; the film made over seven times its budget. On the other side of the balance sheet, the same studio was responsible for expensive turkeys, such as John Huston's *The Barbarian and the Geisha* in 1958, and, for all its accomplishments, the studio was struggling. 20th Century Fox's President of the time Spyros Skouras was a Greek who had emerged from a poor migrant background to own a chain of movie theaters and become a major stockholder in the company, merged in 1935 from Twentieth Century Pictures and the 20th Century Fox West Coast Theater chain. Skouras became president of 20th Century Fox in 1942 (until 1962). Forced to adapt to a declining market in the late 1950s, he charged his executives with the task of combing through the company's backcatalog in search of films that seemed ripe for a remake.

Buried in the backcatalog was a 1917 film made by the early film theater chain owner and founder of the original 20th Century Fox Film Corporation, William Fox. *Cleopatra* was a silent film directed by J. Gordon Edwards, featuring Theda Bara as the eponymous queen of Egypt 47–30 BC. Obviously, as a silent film there was no screenplay, but the story arc seemed promising: after her liaison with the older Julius Caesar, Cleopatra formed a political and romantic alliance with Mark Antony, a Roman general and triumvir (a triumvir is one of three officers jointly responsible for administrative affairs), who initially supported Caesar. Cleopatra and Mark Antony's ambitions brought them into conflict with Rome and she and Antony were defeated at the Battle of Actium in 31 BC. Both Antony and Cleopatra committed suicide, she by plunging her hand into a basket containing an asp, allowing the venomous snake to bite her.

Skouras must have been reminded of 20th Century Fox's success with *The Robe*. But more probably saw comparisons with MGM's *Ben-Hur*, which was due for US release in November 1959. William Wyler's "epic," as it was billed, cost under $16 million and would eventually gross over $70 million. It became the model for a number of other films with biblical or pre-Christian themes that were known as "swords-and-sandals" movies. At this stage, Skouras could not have known how spectacularly successful *Ben-Hur* would become and was understandably cautious: he appointed Walter Wanger as producer of a *Cleopatra* remake, gave him a modest budget of $2 million and allowed him only sixty-four days shooting. Joan Collins was under contract to 20th Century Fox; she had shown her slithery glamour as Princess Nellifer in the Howard Hawks film *Land of the Pharaohs,* in 1955, and was a natural for another regal role in ancient Egypt. Collins screen-tested for the part. But Wanger had different ideas. Excited by the prospect of a new *Cleopatra*, he commissioned his own treatment independently of 20th Century Fox, producing new storyboards and models of scenery to present to Skouras. By mid-1959, the arm twisting had resulted in a $5 million budget. Wanger and Skouras started to contemplate bigger box office draws than Collins.

Several names were mentioned, including Dorothy Dandridge, an African American who would have presented an adventurous and risky proposition at a time when America was still legally segregated. Wanger had produced *I Want to Live* in 1958 and favored the star of that film: Susan Hayward had played a prostitute who specialized in luring her johns into fixed card games. Audrey Hepburn also surfaced as a possible: she seemed gifted with the Midas touch and followed *Breakfast at Tiffany's* in 1961 with a sequence of boxoffice successes. Sophia Loren, who had played with Cary Grant and Frank Sinatra in *The Pride and the Passion,* in 1957, was a strong contender. But the figure Wanger and Skouras kept hearing and reading about and who was, for all practical purposes, inescapable in 1959 was Elizabeth Taylor.

One can imagine the scene. "Where is she?" asks Wanger in a room crowded with studio executives. "In Europe, I think," someone answers. "Doing what?" "Another Tennessee Williams job, I think." The room goes silent for a while before Wanger brings up a practical question: "Is she still with MGM?" No one knows for sure, though someone offers a thought: "Coming to the end of her contract, I'm sure. She owes them one more film, but they'd probably let us have her if we negotiated with them." "Good," says Wanger. "Get her on the phone."

"One day Walter Wanger called and Eddie Fisher answered the phone. Walter said he wanted me to play Cleopatra." Taylor recollects the call: "I thought the idea was ridiculous and said to Eddie, 'Tell him I'll do it for a million dollars. You know—ha ha. Walter said OK'" (in Meryman, p. 74).

Like all good stories this one has been embedded in the popular imagination for decades. One million dollars! For a woman? This was unheard of, beyond any actress' wildest dreams. And both Taylor and 20th Century Fox were only too happy to subscribe to what, on closer inspection, seems to have owed more to myth than reality. But of course, where Elizabeth

Taylor was concerned, myth frequently overpowered reality: our fascination with her has led to a preparedness to accept almost anything. Actors do not typically negotiate film deals with studios, or anyone for that matter. But, as the axiom dictates: don't let the facts spoil a good story.

Another version of the million-dollar-deal story states that a dumbstruck Wanger put down the phone, called Skouras, returned to Taylor (or Fisher) after an hour and agreed to her demands. More realistically, Taylor's agent Kurt Frings would have received the initial approach or been involved at an early stage and he would take responsibility for early negotiations.

The actual deal Taylor and Frings closed with 20th Century Fox guaranteed her an upfront payment estimated (by Bret, p. 133) as improbably low as $125,000, but as high as £1 million by Kashner and Schonenberger (p. 11), but with the crucial ten percent of the gross clause, which gave her a revenue source once the eventual film opened. Given 20th Century Fox's weakening financial position, this made more sense: the headline figure for Taylor's fee was raw material for publicity and, as Brenda Maddox points out: "Taylor's 'million' was, of course a kind of symbolic reference to what she actually was to be paid" (p. 158).

20th Century Fox, an ailing studio, was publicly seen to be awarding a contract that made history. As I noted previously, only William Holden had commanded a million for his role in *The Bridge on the River Kwai*, in 1957. As today, male actors were usually the highest earners. So there was cultural capital for 20th Century Fox in signing the first million-dollar woman. The studio arranged a signing ceremony to which the media were invited—just to witness Taylor inking the contract.

It proved a brilliant deal for Taylor, more brilliant than she could have imagined in 1959 when she put pen to paper. Frings included other clauses that made the contract one of Taylor's most valuable. These included a provision for time: the upfront payment covered Taylor's fee for sixteen weeks only. After this, her rate spiked to $50,000 per week. Wanger or Skouras, or perhaps both of them, must have anticipated a silk-smooth schedule. This proved to be either fearfully naïve or extraordinarily hopeful; whatever, Maddox likens it to a *folie à deux*, a delusion shared by two people.

There were other features of the contract that were weighted in Taylor's favor too. She was given director approval, meaning she was contractually entitled to pick and choose the director. And fatefully she insisted that the film would not be shot in the United States. This may have been advantageous to her tax situation though it seems likely that she wanted to escape the United States where the stigma she earned with her adulterous affair remained.

Taylor also demanded that *Cleopatra* would be filmed in Todd-AO, this being her late husband Michael Todd's high resolution, widescreen technology, rather than the by then tried-and-tested Cinemascope. After

Todd's death, Taylor assumed an interest in the company that developed the system. So this gave her another source of income from the project.

While her other contractual demands seem modest compared to those of the likes of Mariah Carey or Lady Gaga, Taylor insisted on $3,000 for expenses, first class travel for her and her retinue, and a chauffeured Rolls-Royce Silver Cloud for her personal use. She also stipulated that her clothes would be designed by Helen Rose (who was responsible for her wardrobe for *Cat on a Hot Tin Roof*) and that MGM hairdresser Sydney Guilaroff should travel with her. The last would prove to be quite a troublesome clause.

Once satisfied this was a contract fit for a Queen, Taylor agreed. Her long-term contract with MGM was coming to an end and she apparently presumed the studio would release her to make *Cleopatra* for 20th Century Fox. MGM was not quite as obliging as she thought. Legally, she was obliged to make another film for MGM and, while she had no appetite to make it, the studio intended to compel her, or impose on her a two-year suspension. This would have forced 20th Century Fox to look elsewhere and, of course, Taylor would have lost out.

"I resented that so much. It inhibited my freedom. I called it my penal servitude," Taylor told Ray Richmond of the *Hollywood Reporter* in 2005. She made an unconvincing serf.

The head of MGM production, Sol Siegel, received personal visits from Frings then Taylor herself. He was unmoved by her request for a release and clairvoyantly maintained that his project would earn her an Oscar. It was the lead in the film adaptation of a 1935 John O'Hara novel, *BUtterfield 8* (the title refers to an abbreviation for telephone exchanges used at the time. BUtterfield 8 was an exchange that provided service to ritzy precincts of Manhattan's Upper East Side). The central character was a femme fatale who might have migrated from a film noir, but was actually based on the life of Starr Faithfull, a promiscuous "society girl," whose body was found on Long Island beach in 1931.

Faithfull's diaries, found after her death, recorded graphic accounts of her many sexual exploits. O'Hara's barely disguised character was Gloria Wandrous, who makes a habit of picking up men, having sex with them—sometimes for money—and then discarding them. Siegel must have thought he was gifting Taylor a perfect role: an alluring, selfish woman, ambitious, strong, clever, daring, ironic—after sleeping with a man, she awakes to find he has left her money, which she leaves, daubing in lipstick on the mirror, "No sale." It might have been the most brazenly erotic female role since 1946, when Rita Hayworth's *Gilda*, who, when asked by a prospective male partner, "Doesn't it bother you at all that you're married?" answers, "What I want to know is, does it bother *you*?"

If Taylor did not see the potential, or perhaps the correspondence between the role and her popular image as the uninhibited seductress, MGM saw both. The fee was $125,000, a trifle compared to the riches on offer for *Cleopatra*. But legally she had little choice but to accede or face suspension, which would have meant giftwrapping the role for Joan Collins, or one of the others. Perhaps in retaliation, Taylor insisted she wanted Eddie Fisher, by no means an accomplished actor, in the proposed film, *BUtterfield 8*. And she wanted filming to take place in New York, rather than in California, where public hostility to her had still not abated.

For all her grumbling, Taylor played Gloria Wandrous but in a way that reminded critics and, presumably, fans that the person she was unmistakably playing was Elizabeth Taylor. Writing for the *New York Times*, Bosley Crowther notes how, in the film, Gloria's/Taylor's admission, "I was the slut of all times," sounded agreeably implausible. "At no point does she look like one of those things. She looks like a million dollars, in mink or in negligée" (November 17, 1960). When *Variety*, concluded, "The picture's major asset is Taylor," it corroborated MGM's expectations (December 31, 1959).

Despite her avowed loathing of the film, its script, her role, and the contract that obliged her to appear in it, Taylor's performance earned her a first Oscar success. It also disclosed how well she could navigate through a script and remain recognizably Elizabeth Taylor, the commodity, as she described herself. She was probably realizing how valuable that commodity had become. A small but revealing episode offered evidence of this. Taylor had a history of ill health. Some suspect she used sickness to her advantage on occasion. On February 29, 1960, two days after her twenty-eighth birthday, with filming of *BUtterfield 8* underway, she complained of feeling feverish and, while her temperature was normal, this was the first of a series of sicknesses that afflicted her during the schedule.

Over the period of filming Taylor was smitten by a variety of ailments, including commonplace colds and flu, plus migraine and a sprained ankle. "Sections of the media found it hard to distinguish when Elizabeth was genuinely sick or attention seeking," writes David Bret (p. 126). No doubt the production crew were similarly confused. Perhaps even Fisher, who was in close attendance for every illness.

Taylor's consummate grasp of her own power—not just as an actor, but as an all-round public figure—inclined her to use illness, not just to irritate MGM producer Pandro Berman and her director Daniel Mann, or sabotage a film she said she despised, or even, as Bret suggests, to draw attention to herself. But to capitalize on her growing reputation as an overindulged creature who needed pampering and close ministration in all aspects of her life. Even allowing for a psychosomatic component in her illnesses, the episode to which I refer seemed to reveal her purposes. Stricken with breathing difficulties, she was rumored to have contracted pneumonia and rushed to the hospital with Fisher, as always, in close attendance. As the ambulance approached the hospital, Taylor, mindful that her every indisposition offered the media a story, paused to ask Fisher to recover her lip-gloss from her purse. Only after applying the cosmetic and preparing herself for the waiting press, did she emerge from the vehicle. Even in sickness, she remained in "look-at-me" mode.

Having reconnoitered Italy and Turkey, Skouras decided on 1960s England as his double for Rome and Egypt circa 48 BC. Filming *Cleopatra* in London had several advantages. First it satisfied Taylor's demand for a location outside the USA. But it also offered tax advantages. Under the UK's Eady Levy (as it was known), filmmakers received incentives as long as they employed Brits on the production. So Skouras told his producer Wanger to start converting twenty acres of farmland at Pinewood. Majestic papier mâché temples, statues redolent of ancient civilization and palm trees began emerging incongruously about eight miles away from Heathrow airport. The cost of recreating the past was $600,000. English actor Peter Finch, then forty-four, was cast as Julius Caesar; Irish actor Stephen Boyd, twenty-nine, who had been in *Ben-Hur*, was to play Mark Antony. The director was to be Rouben Mamoulian, whose directing credits included *The Mark of Zorro* (1940) and *Silk Stockings* (1957). The script was sourced from a variety of distinguished writers, including Shakespeare, George Bernard Shaw, and C. M. Franzero (author of *The Life and Times of Cleopatra*, 1969). Its story arc started with Caesar's first encounter with Cleopatra and ended with her death. In between there were historic episodes such as Cleopatra's entry to Rome, the assassination of Caesar, and the Battle of Actium. Dale Wasserman was given the job of shaping the historical material into a narrative. Taylor would outlast the two main actors, the original director and the scriptwriter, all of whom were replaced. Filming was scheduled to begin on September 28, 1960.

There was an ill-omened first day of shooting: the British hairdressers' trade association (i.e. labor union) was upset that Taylor had brought Sydney Guilaroff from the USA to England and issued a protest, delaying the production. A settlement was reached: Guilaroff was allowed to style Taylor's hair, but at her hotel rather than the set. Remember, Taylor, while not the pariah she was in California, was not especially well liked in England, where the media had been unforgiving. So her diva-like insistence on having her own stylist—an American at that—did not endear her to the predominantly British production staff. The inauspicious start was compounded by the weather: summer had passed and a damp fall played havoc with the scenery. Bad enough; but worse was to come.

Taylor fell sick with a sore throat and was unable to work for two weeks. Mamoulian was then tasked with filming without the film's central character. Scenes involving Finch and Boyd were shot, as were those in which the thousand extras featured. The costs grew to about $100,000 per day and still Taylor ailed. By mid-November, there were few signs of recovery and Taylor's tribulations, if anything, worsened; indeterminate ailments continued to lay her low.

Meanwhile the British winter approached and Roman peplos (shawls) were puny shields against the elements; extras stood around valiantly pretending to be in a toasty Mediterranean climate while shivering in about 35 degrees (about 1.6 °C). Even after rewriting the script to accommodate Taylor's enforced absence, Mamoulian had exhausted all scenes that did not involve Cleopatra and the production effectively came to a standstill. It was decided to shut down production for a month. Taylor herself had long since fled London for the gentler climes of southern California, where she relaxed amid the restorative mineral springs of Palm Beach.

By the time filming resumed in January 1961, there were only seven minutes of usable footage in the can and the cost had reached $7 million. MGM's ultimately successful *Ben-Hur*, which cost less than $16 million, was considered profligate—especially as a quarter of its budget was absorbed by the eleven-minute chariot race scene. Mamoulian was left to shoulder much of the blame for what was already looking like a folly. He offered his resignation to Skouras, perhaps in the expectation that the 20th Century Fox boss would reject it. He did not: instead he consulted Taylor, who recommended Joseph L. Mankiewicz as Mamoulian's replacement. She knew Mankiewicz from another film in which they worked together, *Suddenly, Last Summer*. Her contract stated that she had the right to approve or reject *Cleopatra*'s director. Mamoulian left and Mankiewicz arrived.

Mankiewicz had a somewhat different vision of the entire project: two separate films, the first focusing on Cleopatra's relationship with Caesar, the second—to be released simultaneously—covering her romance with Mark Antony. Several two-part films have been released simultaneously since; for example, Sergey Bondarchuk's *War and Peace* (1966), Steven Soderbergh's *Che, Part 1* and *Che, Part 2 (2008)*; other two-parters have been released sequentially, Quentin Tarantino's *Kill Bill, Volume 1* (2003) and *Kill Bill, Volume 2* (2004), David Yates' *Harry Potter and the Deathly Hallows: Part 1* (2010) and *Harry Potter and the Deathly Hallows: Part 2* (2011). Two-parters are now quite commonplace. In 1961, Mankiewicz's concept must have sounded an innovative way of maximizing boxoffice receipts.

Conceptually, Mankiewicz's approach seemed more in line with Taylor's recent output. "The writer-director saw her [Cleopatra] as the first woman to rule in a man's world and in a man's way," writes Donald Spoto in his 1995 book. "With such ideas, Mankiewicz fired Elizabeth's imagination" (p. 177). The only trouble was: Mankiewicz wanted to rewrite the entire script and this necessitated a further delay. He arrived in London in February 1961 and started work on his project, working through the night on a new screenplay.

Cleopatra seemed set for a literary re-boot: Mankiewicz cited as inspirations Shaw, Shakespeare, and Plutarch (the Greek biographer, c. AD

46–120). He also enlisted two writers to help him, the novelist Lawrence Durrell (whose *Alexandria Quartet* was the basis for Mankiewicz's *Justine* script) and the screenwriter Sidney Buchman (*Mr. Smith Goes to Washington*). Wanger was encouraged to think his money was being well spent.

The terms Mankiewicz were offered made him a rich man, but the film took its toll on his personal wellbeing. He later joked that *Cleopatra* was, "The toughest three pictures I ever made. It was shot in a state of emergency, shot in confusion, and wound up in blind panic" (quoted by David Shipman, in the *Independent*, February 8, 1993).

Despite the rest, Taylor's health showed little sign of improvement and she returned to London in only marginally better condition than when she had left. Paradoxically, her renown was in rude health: every new development in what had become a kind of medical saga was chronicled by the media, then largely dominated by the print media but with television replacing the newsreels—which were short (about ten-minute) compendiums of news items shown at cinemas before the main feature. But, being Elizabeth Taylor, she thrived on paradox—and inconsistency.

In another era, her prolonged sickness might have been hailed by some as restitution for her moral turpitude. Perhaps it was then too; but that method of interpreting illness was popularized only after the Aids pandemic of the early 1980s, as we will see later in the book. In the 1960s, her sickness was a healing process of sorts. A cultural healing process. Reading of her colitis, anemia, meningitis, broken ankle, and her many other infirmities or watching her ambulated by wheelchair, sick but radiant in her lip-gloss, might have been boring compared to her familial destruction enterprises. But it kept her in the headlines and, in a sense, validated her world fame. Here was a singular woman: she made news even from her sickbed.

On screen, Taylor was burning it up in *BUtterfield 8*, making men feel anxious about female independence and women envious about exactly the same thing. Given its subject matter, it was surprising the film was nominated for an Oscar. But, in February, while Taylor was preparing to return to her role as the Queen of the Nile, that is what happened. It was her fourth nomination and perhaps it indicated the film industry's acknowledgment that, as William Mann reasoned in 2009, "the tide of public opinion seemed to be turning in Elizabeth's favour" (p. 289).

Then a scalpel played its crucial part in rescuing Taylor from a doomed life of infamy, albeit a retreating infamy. Confined to in her hotel bed at the Dorchester, London, initially complaining of head and back pains, Taylor had developed influenza when the nurse called in on March 4, 1960. Worried that Taylor's breathing was labored and irregular, the nurse sought further medical advice. One of the hotel guests was a qualified anesthetist, Dr. J. Middleton Price, who made his way to Taylor's room where she was unconscious and gasping for breath. The doctor later said she was fifteen minutes from death.

This was Taylor in her most dramatic non-dramatic role. The press was waiting outside her hotel, taking photographs of her in a kind of discordant presage of the paparazzi's fateful pursuit of Princess Diana in 1997. Fisher was at her side screaming, "Let her alone! Let her alone!" as photographers leaned in to get pictures of the unconscious but unfailingly photogenic Taylor. At the hospital, Taylor was diagnosed with staphylococcus pneumonia. Staphylococcus is a bacterium that causes pus formation in the skin and membranes; Taylor's lungs were dangerously congested. Taylor was twenty-nine. Some sections of press were a little premature, revealed David Kamp in 1988: "The diligence of the Fleet Street press ensured that within hours an international deathwatch was in place, some papers already reporting that Taylor was dead."

Remember: Taylor was upset with the British press for not defending her during the American media's vilification. After the Fisher scandal broke in 1958, Taylor declined requests for interviews. She maintained her silence for the next few years. Brenda Maddox called it her "Garboization," an allusion to the ultra-reclusive Swedish actor of the 1930s, Greta Garbo. The paradox of such policies is that they do not so much allow media license to conjecture but impose it on them. One famously false news report that Taylor was dead reached as far as Skouras and beyond (Marilyn Monroe is said to have called her publicist to tell him, "Elizabeth is dead"). Technically, the report could have been accurate: Taylor herself later confirmed that she stopped breathing on four occasions while in the hospital. On one such occasion a surgeon named Terence Cawthorne made an emergency incision in Taylor's windpipe and inserted a tube connected to a respirator to induce breathing: the emergency incision in the windpipe to permit breathing proved a lifesaver. For the next five days, Taylor remained critical.

It is possible to loathe, detest, and abhor someone, yet value them all the same. They are valuable, if only as reminders of the way we should not think or behave, or as symbols of all that is wrong. Taylor may not have been one such representative, but, in the early 1960s, it must have been impossible not to know of her and difficult not to have an opinion. This made her valuable. So, in the days following the emergency procedure when her condition remained critical, people who had tut-tutted about her indiscretions were reminded how much they appreciated her. "The crowds that had railed against her . . . suddenly rallied in support," wrote Lord in her 2012 book *The Accidental Feminist* (pp.93–4). Fisher, who stayed at her bedside, reported all-night vigils outside the hospital. Flowers were laid in gratitude rather than memory: people were validating their relationship with someone who had almost demanded not just their attention but their emotions. Six days after being admitted, Taylor was taken off the critical list but remained in the hospital until the end of March.

"The perilous melodrama of dying and coming back to life became one of her most prized roles," propounded Kitty Kelley in 1981 (p. 191). Myths about people always grow bigger, often much bigger, than the actual person. Single incidents are capable of creating such myths. The African American heavyweight boxer Jack Johnson was believed to have been refused passage on the maiden voyage of the *Titanic*, which struck an iceberg and sank with the loss of an estimated 1,490 lives in 1912. Johnson was thought to have the grace of God. There is no conclusive evidence that he even tried to buy a ticket, but the story gave rise to an enduring myth. Maybe Taylor did not have comparable benefaction; maybe she did.

Some figures *invite* myth. Taylor must fall into that slim category. Obviously, she did not encourage what became known as her near-death experience, but, like every good pro actor, she was able to dramatize, embellish, and mythicize it to maximum effect. "I went to that tunnel, saw the white light, and Mike [Todd]. I said, Oh Mike, you're where I want to be. And he said, 'No, Baby. You have to turn around and go back because there is something very important for you to do. You cannot give up now.' It was Mike's strength and love that brought me back," she told Dann Dulin in 2003, reiterating her recollections of a spiritual assignation with her late husband.

Two months after the tracheotomy, she gave a scene-stealing master class at the Academy Awards ceremony, appearing with Fisher, before ascending unsteadily to the stage to collect her Oscar. She eschewed wearing a necklace, so that traces of a scar on her neck were still visible. Her acceptance speech was a breathy and actorly: "I don't really know how to express my gratitude for this *after everything*. I guess all I can do is say thank you. Thank you with all my heart." Later she passed out in a restroom.

Taylor won for her performance in a film she detested and which she agreed to make only to fulfill her contractual obligation to MGM. Shirley MacLaine was nominated in the same category as Taylor for *The Apartment* and was favored to win. Filming in Japan at the time, MacLaine explained: "When Elizabeth Taylor got a hole in her throat, I canceled my plane," meaning she expected a swing in sympathy toward Taylor. MacLaine later joked, or possibly half-joked: "I lost to a tracheotomy" (quoted in Kilday, 2012).

Marjorie Rosen, in 2003, wrote of Taylor: "Her near-death experience restored her to Hollywood's good graces and helped her win an Oscar" (p. 73). But Taylor did not need to redeem herself to the film industry: her box office credentials were known. Taylor would return to the podium six years later.

The story of Taylor's medical condition was not exactly new: as we will see, she had experienced poor health since childhood and had undergone a reputed thirty procedures up until this point—the narrative would continue for the rest of life. Up until the near-death experience, she had a variety of intestinal and gynecological disorders, she had three spinal discs removed and replaced with parts of a hipbone, plus a broken leg, among other injuries, according to Lester David and Jhan Robbins, writing in the *Miami News* (p. I2A). The latest development was an extension, but with a new after-effect. It seemed to absolve her of past sins, as if the brush with mortality was penance. At least that is how many saw it.

A less sentimental interpretation is that the cultural and moral background had changed. It was two-and-a-half years since Taylor's injudicious interview with Hedda Hopper and one byproduct of the cultural alchemy that turned her from tragic widow to scarlet woman was that she commanded the interest of, well, practically everyone. In the intervening period, she had, at the first practical opportunity, married Fisher, which seemed to suggest their liaison had more depth and strength than initially suspected. In any case, Debbie Reynolds's ostensibly tender displays of sorrow and forgiveness were, over time, beginning to look more like posturing—intended to convey an impression rather than reflect her genuine feelings. She seemed well rid of Fisher.

In 1959, the year after Fisher's departure from her life, Reynolds placed fifth in the Quigley Exhibitor's Poll of Box-Office Champions (though it did not reflect actual box office receipts, the Quigley survey of movie theaters was regarded as a reliable indicator of a star's box office draw; see Elizabeth, 2003). She retained that position in 1960. Also in 1960, Reynolds signed a three-year, $1 million agreement with ABC to produce a series of television specials called "A Date with Debbie," and headlined at the Riviera Hotel in Las Vegas. Barely a year after her split with Fisher, she married Harry Karl, a wealthy shoe store magnate. The pain occasioned by the rift with Fisher was palliated by these other developments, suggesting that Taylor's seemingly caustic remark, "I'm not taking anything away from Debbie Reynolds because she never really had it," may have been truer than at first thought. Within twenty-four months, Reynolds had reconstituted her life and, to use contemporary vernacular, moved on—and, in her case, up.

The wholesome decade of the 1950s and the suburban life Reynolds seemed to represent were coming to an end. Decent, shiny, upwardly aspirant families were giving way to rebellious men and dissident women in search of energizing freedoms. However improbably and unwittingly, Taylor's roles as hellions, sirens, and vamps, all striving for a kind of self-reliance, gave voice and presence to this. The methods she chose to seize the deeds to her own destiny in her personal life were not to the taste of many. But her exploits suited the pulse and brio of the 1960s much better than they did the 1950s.

⊂⊛⊃

"I have never wanted to be a queen! Cleopatra was a role, and I am an actor, so it was fun to play one, but it's not real. The real Cleopatra had an incredibly complicated life, and she had to be very, very canny to survive as long as she did." Elizabeth Taylor was talking to Kim Kardashian, who, understandably, conflated Taylor and her portrayal. Their conversation was recorded by Laura Brown in 2012 (p. 412).

The allure of Cleopatra for Hollywood lay in the legendary queen's reputation as a creator of fabulousness. As Lucy Hughes-Hallet wrote in 1990: "When Cleopatra becomes a movie, then frequently the movie becomes a kind of Cleopatra, deplorably but thrillingly spendthrift" (p. 284). The queen of Egypt and descendant of Ptolemy, one of Alexander the Great's generals who created a dynasty that ruled Egypt for 300 years, Cleopatra VII was known for her excessive and fantastic wealth, her exotic opulence and what we would now probably call conspicuous hyperconsumption (that is, the extravagant consumption of commodities for display rather than functional utility). She was the personification of *tryphé*, this being of an ancient Eastern concept meaning abundance, indulgence, and the enjoyment of life—and the softening of morality it entailed. To imperial Romans, the *luxuria* of the East represented moral and cultural decay. So, the assignment of the role of Cleopatra to Taylor was not so much typecasting as superimposition—both figures would still be evident. As Sally Riad put it in 2014: "The [Egyptian queen's] decadence was embodied by Taylor, with burgeoning accounts of her grotesquely excessive tastes and indulgent habits" (p. 8).

So, when the insurers of 20th Century Fox's *Cleopatra* suggested to Skouras that the filmmakers should consider replacing Taylor, they met with short shrift. Lloyd's of London had paid $2 million, a hefty sum at the time, to cover the cost of Taylor's unavailability, and their adjusters had evidently decided Taylor was a bad risk. Names such as Ava Gardner, Sophia Loren, and, perhaps Marilyn Monroe, all of whom had been considered before, were suggested again. But Skouras was adamant: Taylor's flirtation with death and her ultimate triumph with that adversary had given her an aura of invulnerability to complement her other Cleopatra-esque attributes.

Skouras subscribed to the "in for a penny . . ." doctrine: his intuition was to see the undertaking through, however much time, effort, or money this entailed. Cost to date (mid-1961): $12 million—and counting at about $500,000 per week. There was no room for sentimentality in Skouras's plans: he had under contract the biggest star in the world, her box office value now even greater than when she signed. Taylor's name would sell the movie, he reckoned. Chastened by the London experience and realizing the monstrous sets had been rendered unusable by the British winter weather, Skouras announced *Cleopatra* would resume production in summer, 1961, but at a new site: Hollywood. Of course, Taylor was contractually entitled to scotch this. So Skouras looked further afield and decided on Rome, meaning another expensive relocation. To fund this, he sold 260 acres of the 20th Century Fox studio's property to Alcoa (the Aluminum Company of

America) for $43 million. The property included 20th Century Fox's backlot, this being the outdoor area in a film studio where large exterior sets are made and some outside scenes are filmed. So Skouras was staking the company on a single film that had been in production for almost a year and had yielded nothing apart from publicity—no bad thing, of course; but not an adequate substitute for tangible film. He had to appeal to 20th Century Fox shareholders for support, though, in a way, they had no choice other than to back him; the alternative would have probably been bankruptcy. Skouras announced September 21 as the date production would re-commence.

Mankiewicz had worked on an entirely new screenplay and, though not finished, he was effectively starting a new film. He took with him to Italy a new director of photography, Leon Shamroy. There were other changes in personnel. Peter Finch and Stephen Boyd (Caesar and Mark Antony, respectively) had filmed several scenes, but both had prior commitments that prevented them continuing. Finch was paid $150,000 for his unusable work. Boyd received a lesser amount. Skouras would not have been troubled by these departures: there was only one name above the credits that mattered.

Laurence Olivier and Trevor Howard turned down the role of Caesar. Another English actor, Rex Harrison, took the job even though he knew he was effectively fourth choice. Marlon Brando looked right for Mark Antony: he had already played Antony in Mankiewicz's 1953 film *Julius Caesar* and his sleepy handsomeness made him a good match for Taylor. In the event, Brando was either not offered or did not take the part and the search continued. Taylor herself had an idea: she had seen the musical *Camelot* during its Broadway run and was impressed by the actor who played King Arthur. The same actor had appeared in Henry Koster's *The Robe* in 1953, which was, of course, a 20th Century Fox film set at the time of Christ's crucifixion. The studio offered him $250,000 and bought him out of his *Camelot* contract for a further $50,000. He took the deal. He was Richard Burton.

FIGURE 4 *Alfred Kinsey's influential research Sexual Behavior in the Human Male, better known as "The Kinsey Report," was published in 1948, when Taylor was 16.*

Photo by Silver Screen Collection/Getty Images.

4

With human failings

La vendetta è un piatto che va mangiato freddo. Elizabeth Taylor had probably never heard this phrase when she was dropped by Universal Pictures in 1941. At age nine, she was old beyond her years: confident, clever, quick thinking and, abetted by a forceful mother, ambitious. She had just completed a film directed by Harold Young, *There's One Born Every Minute*, which was released the following year. Executives at Universal apparently considered Taylor adequate but not exceptional enough to qualify as a new Shirley Temple, who had been the top box office star four years in a row, from 1935 to 1938. But, at thirteen, Temple could no longer entrance audiences as she did as a child. When in 1940, 20th Century Fox terminated Temple's contract, the studio underlined how merciless the film industry could be. Taylor must have got the message. In a now famous memo, Universal's casting director Dan Kelly dismissed Taylor's potential: "The kid has nothing ... Her eyes are too old. She doesn't have the face of a kid" (quoted *inter alia* in Taraborrelli's 2006 biography, p. 41). Every studio was searching for a replacement for the complete singing, dancing, acting prodigy, but Temple remains arguably the most popular child star in Hollywood history.

Metro-Goldwyn-Mayer did not dismiss Taylor so lightly and gave her a role in a 1944 production, *National Velvet*. It may be an apocryphal but a story that still circulates is that Temple had earlier turned down the role. If so, it was a fateful decision: the film made Taylor a major movie star. Every studio would covet her, but, by the time they realized Taylor's developing prowess, she had committed to MGM. At twelve, Taylor was what she would later describe as a commodity—as I have noted. From that point, she had an unbroken skein of successful movies and her value increased progressively until she became Hollywood's first million-dollar woman. It was revenge of sorts and, even if Taylor could not translate the Italian axiom, she would have intuitively grasped its meaning: revenge is sweeter when delivered after it has had time to cool down.

She was born Elizabeth Rosemond Taylor on February 27, 1932 in Hampstead, London. Her mother had acted before her marriage under the stage name Sara Sothern, while her father Francis Taylor, who had been born in Kansas, had relocated to England as a buyer for his uncle, an art dealer in St. Louis, Missouri. Later, Taylor started his own gallery in Old Bond Street, a major shopping street in London's West End. The family—Elizabeth had one brother, Howard—lived in London and Elizabeth attended a private school where she took ballet lessons from Betty Vacani, who was better known as Madame Vacani and whose clients included members of the royal family. While there are some doubters over the authenticity of this, Taylor claims to have danced at the London Hippodrome when aged three; the future Queen Elizabeth II and her sister Princess Margaret (both students of Mme. Vacani) were in the audience, she recalled in the 2001 tv documentary *Elizabeth Taylor—Britain's Other Elizabeth*.

Victor Cazelet was a Conservative Party politician who represented Chippenham, Wiltshire, from 1924 until his death in 1943. A friend of Francis Taylor, he became Elizabeth's godfather. He owned an estate in Kent, where the young Elizabeth learned to ride horses—a skill that equipped her well when she featured in *National Velvet* (the plot revolves around a twelve-year-old girl who masquerades as a male jockey and rides to victory in England's Grand National horse race). Cazelet's sister Thelma Cazelet-Keir was so well connected, she was able to take Sara to the coronation of King George VI in 1936. (The 2010 film *The King's Speech* tells the story of George's radio broadcast announcement of war in 1939.) The Cazelets were influential friends (see the "Players" section at the end of this book for more on Victor Cazelet and the rumors that surrounded him and the Taylors.)

Shortly before the start of the Second World War, the family, like many Americans, returned to the US. The Taylors settled in Los Angeles by way of Pasadena in 1939. Francis opened an art gallery in Beverly Hills, while Sara concentrated on the children. Older brother Howard arrived in the USA just two months before the war broke out. The priority of most parents might have been to secure their children a good education and place them in an environment where they could enjoy a happy childhood. Indeed, Sara did place both her children in a private school in Pasadena. But there was something else: Elizabeth, it seems, became the repository of her mother's displaced ambitions: Sara's aim was to get her daughter the show business breaks that had eluded her. To this end, she enrolled Elizabeth in dance classes, riding lessons, and instilled in her the importance of physical appearance. "She [Elizabeth] consented, as many girls will not, to being elaborately dressed and beribboned," wrote Brenda Maddox in 1977 (p. 32). Her thick black hair needed particular attention. Surprisingly, perhaps, there is no record of a single instance when Elizabeth resisted what for many children would be an overbearing mother's unreasonable demands. She seems to have been happy to participate in her mother's grand project (and the word project is not inappropriate: Sara's enterprise was planned to achieve a particular aim).

By all accounts, Sara was what we now call a pushy mother: self-assertive and ambitious, sometimes unpleasantly so, Sara hawked her daughter to auditions and interviews with key figures in Hollywood. Fortuitously (perhaps), Francis's art store attracted a clientele that included several Hollywood actors, producers, journalists, and other personnel connected with the industry. One such client was journalist Hedda Hopper, a friend of Victor Cazelet and Thelma Cazelet-Keir, and one of the first customers at the new gallery. Thelma had asked her a favor: write an approving review of the new gallery in her newspaper column. Hopper obliged with a small item about the gallery's proprietors, Sara's unfulfilled promise on the stage, and the couple's "beautiful eight-year-old daughter." This was Hopper's first mention of a woman on whose life she would make an indelible imprint.

Hopper later made a claim to have "discovered" Elizabeth Taylor and, in a sense, she did; though, in another sense, she did not need discovering. It was her mother's industrious lobbying of casting directors rather than a namecheck in gossip columns that brought results. Shirley Temple was fading rapidly, remember; other former child stars like Deanna Durbin, were, to be cruel, past it. Metro-Goldwyn-Mayer had Mickey Rooney under contract. The same studio would also benefit from Margaret O'Brien, who became valuable after her appearance in 1942's *Journey for Margaret*. So studios hunted for children who could attract audiences.

Universal was the first studio to offer Taylor a chance. Her audition proved satisfactory and they extended her what were then usual terms: $100 week over seven years. To any ordinary nine-year-old, this would have been a dream come true: an end to normal schooling, a fledgling career in Hollywood, and an income that equated to about a hundred or more times the pocket money of any other kid—apart from those contracted to the studios. Not good enough for Elizabeth Taylor. Even at that age, she had a conception of the Hollywood hierarchy and knew that Universal, while a big player in the industry, was not the biggest. That would be MGM.

Sara persuaded her that, when Universal improved the terms of the deal, it was worth taking. But it turned out to be disappointing. The contract effectively just prevented her from finding suitable outlets elsewhere. After a year, all Elizabeth Taylor had to show was three days' work on *There's One Born Every Minute* and a scalding review from Universal's production chief Edward Muhl, who concurred with his casting director's verdict and added, "her mother has to be one of the most unbearable women it has been my displeasure to meet" (quoted in Heymann, pages 38–9). Universal had a clause in the contract that allowed the studio the option to sever after a year.

Understandably downcast, Sara and Elizabeth were forced to reflect and reconsider the future. Perhaps a more conventional career beckoned. No: "Sara Taylor dragged her daughter to Hedda Hopper's Beverly Hills home and told Hedda of the fiasco," records C. David Heymann, writing in 1996 (p. 37). This was 1942, when Elizabeth was ten. At her mother's request, Elizabeth sang "Blue Danube" to prove to Hopper how Universal had failed to notice what a genuine talent she was. Hopper's verdict: "One of the most painful ordeals I've ever witnessed" (in Heymann, p. 37).

In the 1940s, Hedda Hopper was often described as "an actress trying to be a columnist." Writing in Los Angeles' *Saturday Evening Post* in 1947, Collie Small reported how she turned to writing after falling out of favor with casting directors, but, within a few years, circumstances combined, "to establish Hedda Hopper as an autocrat of the Hollywood gossip exchange whose power is at times literally frightening" (p. 15). Anthony Slide describes her as "untouchable by the studios."

From 1916, when she was thirty-one, Hopper found work as a bit-part actor in Hollywood films, though without ever approaching the level of, for example, Lillian Gish or Claudette Colman. Hollywood was awash with aspirant actors, male and female, and the film industry was an oligopoly: a small number of employers and a surfeit of potential employees. In the Martin Scorsese film *The Aviator*, Howard Hughes (played by Leonardo DiCaprio), for a while a film producer sneers: "Actresses are cheap in this town."

Not that Hopper's time scrabbling for work as an actor was valueless: in 1936 during one of her longer periods of unemployment, she floated the idea of a newsletter in *Movie Classics*, a weekly magazine. She earned $50 for each article, but that was soon dropped to $35 and Hopper lost enthusiasm. The scraps of tittle-tattle she picked up while trying to find work as an actor were the raw material for the column, which went largely unnoticed until 1938 when she was approached by the *Los Angeles Times* and syndicated. Her snippets of information on the personal lives of Hollywood actors provided a contrast to the official versions pushed out by the studio's publicity departments.

By 1947, Hopper's column was syndicated in 110 newspapers (under the sponsorship of the *Chicago Tribune-New York News* Syndicate) and commanded a readership of between 23 million and 32 million at a time when the total US population was 160 million. This is the equivalent of a twitter following of about 40–50 million—somewhere between Katy Perry and Taylor Swift. Many of her readers were regular letter-writers and she would publish extracts, so there was a twitter-like exchange of information. Validation of her arrival as a major national figure came when she was shown on the cover of *Time* in 1947 (July 28).

By her own admission, her spelling and punctuation were poor, but, with the aid of a literate assistant, she put together bulletins that, combined with her radio broadcasts, brought her about $200,000 per year; way more than the actors she wrote about. Hopper's advantage over other writers on film was that she maintained an interest in professional acting. Even when she was making money from her columns, she took on acting roles, often credited (e.g., *Queen of the Mob*, 1940) but sometimes uncredited (e.g., *That's Right—You're Wrong*, 1939). So she had insider knowledge.

"But Hopper also saw herself as a political figure and activist," writes historian Jennifer Frost, who has studied Hopper (in her 2011 article "Hollywood Gossip as Public Sphere," p. 86). Hopper believed communist sympathizers had infiltrated the film industry and were using cinema for propaganda. So, when the House Un-American Activities Committee (HUAC) was created in 1938 to investigate the beliefs and activities of individuals and organizations suspected of having communist ties, she found a natural ally. (The committee was initially interested in Nazism in the USA but broadened its scope to include ideologies considered contrary to the interests of the USA.) She targeted specific figures and films, even films she considered "un-American" in the sense that they advanced stark, realistic and, sometimes, scathing images of American life. Richard Brooks's praised-by-many *Blackboard Jungle* (1955), with Glenn Ford and Sydney Poitier, and a rock 'n' roll soundtrack, was one such film. There was irony in her opposition to movies that strove to be realistic: her columns were based on exposing the reality behind the supposed Hollywood façade.

Her gossipy writing reflected her political contributions: as Frost reveals: "Hopper's gossip column was never just empty or directionless opinion" (p. 99). There was judgment and a mandate for action, whether letter-writing or boycotts. Recall how Hopper denounced Taylor for her liaison with Eddie Fisher: this functioned not just as a public declaration of Taylor's wrongness, but as authorization for others to judge her similarly.

Collie Small, whom I quoted earlier, called Hopper *an* autocrat rather than *the* autocrat of the Hollywood gossip exchange. Mention of her name usually evoked another: Louella Parsons. The rivalry between Hopper and Parsons was mutually productive: in their efforts to outdo each other, each enhanced their own and the other's reputations as gossip mavens. Parsons was the first to disclose that Ingrid Bergman was pregnant in 1950 and so gave rise to an international scandal. Hopper, whom Bergman earlier told she was not pregnant, had to wait nine years before she scooped Taylor's "sleep alone" interview, and effectively started a more uproarious scandal.

Hopper and Parsons surfaced as forces in the film industry and, in a sense, American life at a time when the nation was emerging from the Great Depression (1929–39). The economic measures introduced by President Franklin D. Roosevelt in 1933 and known as the New Deal took effect slowly, but by the late 1930s were taking effect; the war effort effectively kick-started the economy and ended the depression. In 1938, the sociologist Robert K. Merton published the results of his influential study of "a society, which places a high premium on economic affluence and ascent for all its members" i.e. America. Merton was at pains to expose the workings of a "system of cultural values extols, above all else, certain common symbols of success ... while its social structure rigorously restricts or completely eliminates access to approved modes of acquiring these symbols" (p. 680).

Movie stars personified success and embodied a version of the good life to which all Americans, in some measure, aspired. Merton was interested in how Americans strove to achieve success, often using "amoral intelligence" to short-circuit institutional barriers (he meant they stole). While he did not concern himself with the effects of Hollywood, he provided a grammar that makes it possible for us to understand why the lines of communication established and enlivened by Hopper were not just conduits carrying information but means of maintaining contact—lifelines.

It was not a mere fluke that Hopper's articles grabbed an enthusiastic readership in the late 1930s into the 1940s. Changes in American culture providentially turned her gossip into hard currency: she appealed to a readership that was both aspirational and voyeuristic, eager to bring their own lives into harmony with those of the stars. By offering information on the putative secrets of figures that were popularly admired, emulated, and envied, and making pronouncements on their conduct, Hopper et al. were brokering relationships.

Julie A. Wilson believes the relationships had their genesis in what she calls identification. "That identification was central to relationships between stars and audiences is born out in the popular fan magazine *Modern Screen*, which was established in 1930," wrote Wilson in 2010 (p. 27). She means audiences associated their own position or experience with those of successful actors. *Modern Screen* and other publications of the time depended on what Wilson calls a "cozy relationship with the Hollywood film studios for their content."

Hopper, Parsons, and the other gossip writers, the most notable of whom were Walter Winchell—who was dominant in the 1920s—and Mike Connelly, were subversive. While the studios controlled both official and unofficial discourses on the stars, writers like Hopper specialized in the stories the studios preferred to stay under lock-and-key.

At least that was the orthodox view. Anne Helen Petersen suspects that Hopper et al. would purport to break unsanctioned scoops, "but in reality they were heavily involved with studio politics, protecting or damaging a particular star as a favor or a matter of loyalty" (p. 65). This suggests that the studios controlled both formal and informal discourses and, while Hopper et al. were ostensibly independent, they had limits. They specialized in content the studios would rather have kept protected rather than released, but they rarely, if ever, undermined the studios.

Whether or not Hopper and other "star makers, fabricators and gossip mongers," to use Slide's florid description, intended to be antagonists or associates of the Hollywood studios is actually irrelevant: they were accomplices, whether they liked it or not. They were instrumental in revealing to fans what they considered to be intimate details of the lives of film actors and so establishing a familiarity or identification that was crucial to the success of cinema and, by implication, the entertainment industry.

Together, "Parsons and Hopper helped alter the parameters of the public disclosure of private lives," argued Kathleen A. Feeley in 2004. In other words, the studios, since the 1920s, had set the conditions of the films industry's operations, establishing limits that defined the proper scope of practically every process, including publicity. Feeley emphasizes the role of Hopper and Parson in changing those limits. There were other factors.

"It is a scandal sheet. It is the gossip columnist with dementia praecox." Anthony Slide quotes an article from *Fortnight* magazine, dated July 1955 (p. 179) and headlined, "*Confidential*: Between you and me and the bedpost." (Dementia praecox is an old-fashioned term for schizophrenia.)

In December 1952, Robert Harrison, the son of Russian migrants, raised in the Bronx, launched *Confidential* magazine. The publication was a departure from the fan magazines that had been on sale since 1911. *Confidential* broke with the "cozy relationship," to use Wilson's term again, and opted for an approach that "devastated the private lives of hundreds of celebrities," as Victor Davis put it in 2002. Its importance lay in its wider effects. Davis again: "Other publications, magazines and tabloids, were emboldened to venture further than they'd ever gone before in printing scabrous material" (p. 77). The adjective scabrous suggests that content became salacious, indecent—at least by 1950s standards—and, unlike the tidy and polished stories sanctioned by the studios, rough. Other similarly unrestrained magazines followed, though *Confidential* led the field with a circulation of four million and outlets all over the USA and England.

Proprietor Harrison's inspiration for the magazine was, bizarrely, the US government investigation into organized crime headed by politician Estes Kefauver in 1950–1. According to Charles Winick, this alerted Harrison to "the fact that there was excitement and interest in the lives of people in the headlines and getting behind the story" (1961, p. 22). A typical issue of *Confidential* contained five or six articles about prominent figures, especially actors, who had secrets they preferred not to disclose. Those secrets might include visiting prostitutes, committing felonies in early life, or having lesbian relationships. These seem tame nowadays and celebrities can thrive on disclosures of this kind. In the 1950s though, they were hushed-up whenever possible. The cautionary case of Roscoe "Fatty" Arbuckle functioned as a reminder of the costs of scandal.

Arbuckle died in 1933, but his specter roamed the backlots of Hollywood for decades: he was a silent screen actor, writer, and director, who, in 1921, when aged thirty-four, became involved in the century's first major Hollywood scandal. He was falsely accused of rape and manslaughter. It took three well-publicized trials to clear him and by the time he was acquitted and granted an apology, his showbusiness career was over. His films were banned and employment opportunities vanished, leaving him destitute. He died a penniless smackhead in 1933, aged forty-six. Forewarned, actors after Arbuckle, dared not risk any kind of scandal for fear of the potentially ruinous consequences. And, if they did, studios were vigilant in cover-ups. Ideally, the studios would have liked to move their contracted actors around like life-size chess pieces on a board. In actuality, the actors were often more like characters in World of Warcraft, theoretically controllable but liable to behave unpredictably.

Against this background, *Confidential* was an interesting experiment: even three decades after the Arbuckle case, Hollywood stars and their employers avoided controversy. So a publication with scandal as its raison d'être would have been like the polecat at a picnic: the picnickers would not welcome the malodorous interloper, but imagine the amusement it would give onlookers. "There appeared to be a special gratification to the reader in being able to know about the errancy of his presumed betters," reasons Winick, on page 331 of his 1961 study (which I quoted in Chapter 2; *errancy* is term from the past—it means straying from accepted standards). "He" (though the typical reader was more likely to be a 'She') "enjoyed realizing that the celebrity was an ordinary mortal with human failings," Winick delivered his conclusion. It was like a Delphic soothsaying at the time; now it is a truism.

Hopper and her fellow gossip columnists gave human characteristics to the once remote and untouchable stars, accessorizing magnificent idols with feet of clay. Fans identified with stars, as Wilson suggested (and I assume she means fans regarded themselves as having links with stars), but they also experienced *intimacy at a distance*. This was a term introduced by psychologists Donald Horton and R. Richard Wohl in a 1956 article, "Mass communication and para-social interaction: observations on intimacy at a distance."

A para-social interaction describes the relationship fans have with figures they have never met, nor probably ever will meet but whose persona has appeared on the screen or on paper. The persona is that aspect of a person that is presented to or perceived by others; in other words, the outwardly recognizable being seen in the media (and this was 1956, when tv was growing like weed). Horton and Wohl qualified this: "But the persona's image, while partial, contrived, and penetrated by illusion, is no fantasy or dream; his performance is an objectively perceptible action in which the viewer is implicated imaginatively" (p. 216).

So, the interaction is oneway interaction, but this does not lessen its impact on the fan who might experience the relationship as genuine and just as valid as other kinds of social interaction. This may be a technical way of approaching what is, after all, a seemingly obvious feature of contemporary culture. But in the 1950s, it was a novel and perplexing development: why did people feel so intimately attached to other people who did not know them, made no material impact on their lives and who, in all probability, were not remotely interested in them? Without an answer, the spell Elizabeth Taylor cast remains a mystery. Why were audiences *implicated imaginatively* with her?

"Celebrity gossip not only tells stories about contemporary culture but also constitutes it and shapes its formation," argued David Beer and Ruth Penfold-Mounce in 2009 (paragraph 5.2). Taylor's life was lived by countless people: alongside her own lived experience, there was another narrative composed of what others imagined was going on in her life. Gossip constituted and shaped the way the world thought about and understood her.

When she endured listening to the uncommonly ambitious ten-year-old wailing "Blue Danube," Hedda Hopper probably had no conception of the influence she would wield over the next decade or two. Don Romesburg, in 2000, wrote of Louella Parsons: "She and Hedda really could 'make or break.' They could instill the fear of God in movie star and mogul. They had real power" (p. 20). There may be an element of overstatement in this, but the influence of Hopper and Parsons is undeniable. Sara Taylor was clearly aware of Hopper's potential either as friend or foe. The former was preferable, she concluded. Her daughter was less apprehensive.

Hopper's influence eventually waned. *Confidential*'s arrival in 1952 stole some of the gossip maven's thunder. Hopper had spent the best part of the previous two decades promoting the idea that truth had to be sought: it did not just arrive, tied with a bow, courtesy of the big studios. She was probably mindful that stardom itself was launched on a hoax. That was in 1910, when Carl Laemmle, the pioneer entrepreneur and later founder of Universal Pictures hatched a plan to stage a bogus auto accident involving Florence Lawrence – up till then known as just "The Biograph Girl." Lawrence's unexplained disappearance after the wreck was turned into a mystery by the newspapers and, when she returned unscathed, her memorable name went up in lights. The era of the star was launched on a studio machination. Hopper probably saw her ventures as part of a more comprehensive unmasking of Hollywood undertaken by HUAC. Her political allies included Joseph McCarthy, who instigated the widespread investigations into alleged communist infiltration in public life, J. Edgar Hoover, the director of the FBI, Howard Hughes, the industrialist, aviator, and film producer who wanted to marry Taylor, Ronald Reagan, who was a Hollywood actor before entering politics, and William Randolph Hearst, the media tycoon who was the model for the central character of Orson Welles' *Citizen Kane* (1941). Hopper actually aided McCarthy in outing "liberal" actors and helped Reagan into politics.

She spent the early years of the 1960s appearing in cameos, sometimes as herself, in television shows, and she kept writing gossip. But her approach was too preachy for the 1960s, when the kind of behavior she reprimanded became the de facto norm for a generation. Hopper died in 1966; so she lived long enough to see Taylor endure the precipitation from the Fisher scandal, then become involved in another that made it pale.

Taylor's voice: Hopper hated the sound of it; MGM studio bosses loved it. Actually, they did not so much love it, but appreciated how it would sound when put to use with a good script. In fairness to Hopper's appraisal, Taylor was not asked to sing in *National Velvet*. Taylor still had an unforced English accent, which was still posh enough to pass as upperclass. Fellow Brit Angela Lansbury was also in the cast, as was Mickey Rooney, both of whom were to go on to distinguished acting careers. But, as a 1945 *Chicago Tribune* reviewer put it, "no one outshines little Elizabeth Taylor as Velvet. The child is completely natural and unaffected, with a very sweet expressive face and the most beautiful soft blue eyes I've seen on the screen in a long time" (quoted in Haggerty, 2011).

Taylor remained contracted to MGM for the next eighteen years, all but the final two of which were harmonious. Her performance as the belle Velvet presaged several more portraits of innocence and several more of decadence. During the filming of *National Velvet* Taylor fell from her horse. The ensuing back injury was to recur in later years; it was but one of a succession of ailments that contributed to a prodigious history of illness and which obliged her repeatedly to take medication throughout her life.

National Velvet was Taylor's fifth film. She played a supporting role in *Lassie Come Home*, before MGM offered her the seven-year contract, starting at $100 per week. Once in the employ of a studio, actors in the 1940s had little say in their films: MGM dictated that Taylor play in *Jane Eyre* (1943) for Fox. This was Robert Stevenson's film of Charlotte Brontë's 1847 novel, which has been the source of many films and television plays. Taylor played Jane's schoolfriend Helen Burns. Orson Welles played Rochester with Joan Fontaine as the adult Jane. The other film in her early portfolio was *The White Cliffs of Dover*, a wartime romance released in 1944 and directed by Clarence Brown, who was also scheduled to make *National Velvet* (Brown was known for his many films with Greta Garbo and Joan Crawford). Initially told she was too short for the part, Taylor resolved to grow in height, invoking the power of mind as decreed in Christian Science teachings. Her parents were adherents of the beliefs and practices of the Church of Christ Science and, as such, held that only God and the mind are the ultimate reality, and that prayer and faith can overcome everything—including being too short presumably.

Louis B. Mayer, then studio boss at MGM, improved Taylor's salary to $300 per week. There are several conflicting reports of how much Taylor earned at this time, but, even on the most conservative accounts, she was a very well paid teenager; and, at thirteen, she was a major Hollywood presence. Taylor's father resisted Mayer's attempts to change his daughter's name and the color of her hair; he also stopped an attempt to remove a mole from her face. But Francis Taylor grew progressively detached from his family and left the business of his daughter—and she had become something of a business—to his wife, who, in her mid-forties, dedicated herself fulltime to her project. After the disappointment of the experience with Universal, she had fashioned an auspicious cluster of appearances for her daughter.

Mindful that Elizabeth Taylor, child star, was a product that would self-obsolesce, MGM quickly featured Taylor in *Courage of Lassie*, in which she again shared billing with an animal and again played a smart, pure-as-driven-snow girl, as opposed to young woman. It was released in 1946 and was her final performance as a child actor. Years later, Taylor would complain about the Hollywood system and how it used her. She would also say: "I wouldn't wish being a child actress on anyone. It takes your childhood away" (quoted in Richmond, p. 22).

Yet there is little evidence of her discomfort at the time she was a film prodigy. Quite the opposite: she actually seems to have been born to the life of a star. Most celebrities, at some stage—usually very soon after they rise to some level of fame—write (or have someone write for them) a book. Taylor's first foray into publishing came when she was thirteen: the book was *Nibbles and Me*, an account of her pet chipmunk; it was published in 1946 and was most recently republished by Simon and Schuster in 2011. At an age when most pubescent people are so driven by hormonally induced imperatives that they can barely spare enough time to do their homework, Taylor appears to have joyfully committed to diarize an account of her experiences with a striped ground squirrel—or at least recounted them to a publisher-appointed ghost writer. Brenda Maddox, in 1977, discerned in this, "the beginning of a compulsion to explain herself to the public—to make her life a myth" (p. 53).

Compulsion: the noun suggests an irresistible urge to behave in a certain way, as if Taylor was coerced into sharing details of her life. Whether Maddox thought there was an outer-compulsion from her pressuring mother, or some sort of internal drive to externalize is not certain. But, from that point, Taylor lived, according to Maddox, "the most public private life in the world."

Other child stars of the period slipped almost unnoticed out of the limelight. Shirley Temple, of course, simply failed to make the transition into adult star, largely because the studios ignored her. Judy Garland—ten years older than Taylor and also signed to MGM—found comfort of sorts in alcohol and prescription drugs as she navigated uncertainly from child star to adulthood. She died from a barbiturate overdose in 1969, aged forty-seven.

Countless other child actors were consigned to oblivion. Even actors who were mature when they achieved commercial success in Hollywood sought escape routes. By far the most mythic retreat was that of Marilyn Monroe who was found dead in 1962, aged thirty-six, in circumstances that were never satisfactorily explained and continue to fascinate us. Grace Kelly absconded from Hollywood at the peak of her film career, age twenty-six, opting to live as Princess Grace of Monaco after marrying Prince Rainier III. She played in the western classic *High Noon* in 1952, then three notable Alfred Hitchcock films. She died in a car accident on a dangerous coastal road in 1982, suffering a stroke and losing control of the vehicle. By stark contrast, Taylor seemed to luxuriate in stardom and, later, in scandal.

We can only speculate, but even at thirteen, Taylor seems to have an intuitive grasp of what, many years later, Gwen Stefani was to call "the game." In 2005, Stefani, when complaining, "You never quite get used to being public property" to the *Independent Magazine*'s Nick Duerden, shrugged, "I understand how the game works" (quoted in Duerden, p. 12). She meant that, in the twenty-first century, fame is a less a state, more an activity in which one party engages and sometimes competes with another: individuals surrender some portion of their private lives to a media that liberates it through their channels and fabricates fame. While there are no explicit regulations or principles, there are unwritten codes in operation and, on Stefani's account, these are just *understood* to govern practice.

In the 1950s, the rules of the game were framed by the Hollywood studios. Hopper, as we have seen, worked as a kind of pariah interlocutor—someone ostensibly cast outside the system, but who was, in reality, part of the dialog between Hollywood and consumers. Hopper was like family to the Taylors. As a friend of Thelma Cazelet-Keir, she assumed the role of a good-natured, favorite aunt-cum-fairy godmother when Taylor moved to the USA. Hopper apparently liked Taylor much more than her mother, Sara, whom she (in common with several others) regarded as overbearing. Taylor almost certainly did not wish to offend Hopper.

Taylor's life was circumscribed by both MGM and Sara Taylor; both had an interest in conveying a public image of her as enjoying an ordinary teenage life while ensuring she did anything but. Even at fifteen, she was not seeing young men, at least not men she met in what might pass as ordinary circumstances. Her "dates" were all stage-managed affairs, with no room for the spontaneity, choice or randomness characteristic of life as a teenager. Among her eligible suitors were Arthur Loew Jr., the son of the film producer and MGM president, and Tommy Breen, whose father was the chief Hollywood film censor. Yet there is no evidence that Taylor was ever discomfited, cramped or unsettled: she appears to have been a willing party to a life organized around by prerequisites of Hollywood.

Mindful that Taylor was unlikely to rebel, lose control, or behave in a manner that was unacceptable to her employers or mother, Hopper, through her syndicated column in 1948, reflected on how Taylor had changed in the four-and-a-half years since she had last been to her home. "What a metamorphosis," wrote Hopper. "It is breathtaking ... Her delicate expressiveness, together with the beauty that has matured her into a thoroughly ravishing young lady make her—in my mind—a potential young [Ingrid] Bergman" (*Toledo Blade,* August 29, p. 4).

Within two years, Bergman was all-but crushed by the weight of the scandal of 1950 when she became pregnant by Roberto Rossellini. Even after resuming her Hollywood career, she never recaptured her glittering status. Hopper, as we know, would be instrumental in plunging Taylor into a scandal that eclipsed Bergman's, but, as we will discover, helped *make*

Taylor. Hopper could not have imagined how prescient she was. The story, incidentally, was headlined "Moppet matures to whistle bait: despite slim film diet Elizabeth Taylor is a potential star." "Whistle bait" is a 1940s expression for a sexy young woman who attracts wolf whistles; the "slim film diet" referred to the meager roles MGM had chosen for her.

"I will go far enough out on the limb to predict that she [Taylor] one day may likely be the Number 1 lady of the screen," wrote Hopper in the same story. At the time of publication, Taylor was making *Little Women* (1949), Louisa May Alcott's classic story set in the 1860s. After its completion, MGM sent Taylor to London to film *Conspirator* (1949), in which she played a woman who falls in love with a communist spy. By then, her own love life was part of the public record.

Not many Hollywood employees would ever have deliberately made an enemy of someone as imperiously, frighteningly powerful as Hopper was thought to be. So Taylor probably did not want to risk offending her. But eventually one of them trespassed. For Hopper, it was her young protégé— remember, she believed she had "made" Taylor—who had wondered into an unchartered moral zone without her guiding hand when she became the spiteful woman that destroyed Debbie Reynold's seemingly happy marriage with Eddie Fisher.

When Taylor later asked Hopper to explain what seemed to her an astonishing betrayal of a trust they had built over the years, Hopper is reported to have dismissed her with, "You didn't say it was off the record" (quoted in Mann's 2009 book, p. 235).

Taylor matured in full view of the world, changing from an eye-catchingly attractive youngster into an ineffably beautiful woman acclaimed by Hopper. She was the standard or point of reference against which other women would compare themselves. Arriving in London in 1948 to play her first lead role as an adult, sixteen-year-old Taylor (back in Britain for the first time since 1939) discovered public interest in her was more widespread than she might have expected. In Britain the high school leaving age was fifteen, so, in a sense, she was as much a schoolgirl as a sex goddess. California law required that Taylor spend three hours per day studying and to this end the Los Angeles Board of Education sent a supply teacher to London with Taylor. MGM paid for everything else, including a side trip to Paris, luxurious accommodation and, naturally, a chauffeured car on standby.

Taylor's first boyfriend of record was a well-known All-American football player from West Point Academy. Like Taylor, Glenn Davis was wholesome and respectable and, perhaps unlike her, conventional. While Taylor did not manifest any leanings toward the then incipient beat generation, she was hardly conventional: no formal education, no adolescence in the way her peers experienced theirs, no meaningful life outside the parameters drawn

by her studio and mother and, of course, more money than she could hope
to spend. Davis served in the Korean War of 1950–3. While in London, she
suggested they were engaged to be married. But by March 1949 she had
split with Davis and met William Pawley Jr. He was the son of a friend
of Taylor's wealthy uncle, Howard Young. Again, an engagement was
announced and called off (Pawley's archly conservative family did not want
him involved with a Hollywood "actress"). Both relationships were media-
friendly affairs, choreographed by others, presumably with the rubberstamp of MGM. High-flown blind dates with alpha-males.

Another match made by others was with Ralph Kiner, a baseball player
for Pittsburgh Pirates. Bing Crosby was a part owner of the Pirates. "One
day, I paid a visit to Crosby in his office on the Paramount lot," recalled
Kiner. "He asked me if I'd be interested in having a date with Elizabeth
Taylor. He explained that she needed someone to accompany her to the
premiere of the Gregory Peck war film *Twelve O'Clock High* at Grauman's
Chinese Theater on Hollywood Boulevard" (quoted in Peary, 2014).

Taylor's movements were so restricted that it is probable that all her male
friends were screened and subject to approval by third parties. Amazingly,
Taylor never demurred: like a painting from one of her father's galleries, she
was passed from dealer to patron, packaged and exhibited—always for the
delectation of others. Perhaps it is not so amazing though: Taylor had never
glimpsed the alternatives. She was always surrounded by advisors, some
technical, others moral. Every facet of her life was organized for her; so, she
probably thought the only way to meet men was via other, older men.
Protocol superseded infatuation in Taylor's life. Excitingly unpredictable
relationships were not part of the procedure.

The courtship that never was involved Montgomery Clift who was
devilishly handsome and, as such, promoted as what was then known as a
heartthrob—a star whose good looks excite amorous feelings in women.
Taylor was cast opposite him in *A Place in the Sun,* directed by George
Stevens. The six Oscar-winning adaptation of Theodore Dreiser's novel *An
American Tragedy*, it featured Clift as a poor but ambitious fortune hunter
who lands a job in his uncle's factory, dates (and impregnates) a fellow
worker but soon falls for Taylor's character, a rich, beautiful young woman
above his station. Clift and Taylor huddled together for long hours on set,
discussing their roles, and Stevens shot their romance—notably an iconic
lakeside scene—in intimate close-ups that conveyed their doomed desire.
And, as today, publicists were inclined to tease the media with life-follows-
art stories about their intimate involvement. Although it was never
adequately explained at the time, the best-laid plans came to nothing. It
would have been believable too: at seventeen, Taylor had acquired womanly
qualities that most young men with a fully functioning complement of
hormones would have found irresistible. As Kitty Kelley put it: "In 1949,
Elizabeth Taylor personified the outer reaches of male fantasy" (p. 51). But

Hollywood would not dare let gay men declare their sexual preferences for fear it would destroy their box office appeal. Clift followed the fate of Hollywood's other gay male actors and remained in the closet.

Hopper was no doubt aware of Clift's secret and was curious enough to tiptoe into the studio to the apparent annoyance of Clift, who, as a method actor, aspired to complete emotional identification with his part (Clift spent a night in a real jail to assimilate what his character in the movie would experience). Taylor had never had any formal dramatic training; she was a product of an environment that promoted entertainment rather than theatrical performance. To her, it was natural to give interviews, pose for photographs and cooperate fully with the media. She was perplexed by Clift's indifference to Hollywood's ministrations to the media. Hopper added 2+2 and offered one of her less-than-clairvoyant divinations: "Those magnificent lovebirds are very soon going to be married" (quoted in Bret, 2011, p. 43).

Taylor's familiarity and affection for gay men was to become a feature of her life. Her own father had affairs with men, one well-known with MGM's chief costume designer, who was in what was called a "lavender marriage," in which one or both partners were gay, but remained married to maintain the impression they were straight. Such connubial arrangements were common in Hollywood. Rock Hudson was lavender-married to Phyllis Gates (I will return to this later in the book), Judy Garland was married for a while to gay director Vincente Minnelli (father of Liza). (Gay actors were not the only ones pressured by studios into marriage: Sammy Davis Jr. was forced to marry singer and fellow African American Loray White, in 1958, after having an affair with Columbia's biggest box office draw Kim Novak, who was white; the marriage was intended to end speculation about a liaison between a black man and a white woman that endangered the careers of both.)

While some gay men made a practical accommodation to both the cultural and legal prohibitions on homosexuality (the USA did not begin repealing its sodomy laws until 1971), others, like Clift, endured the torment of the damned before his early death. He did have romantic relationships with women—famously, with singer-actor Libby Holman, sixteen years his senior, a state of affairs that would have been considered scandalous—though Taylor, it seems was not among them. They were paired up again years later in *Raintree County* (1957), a Civil War romance in the style of *Gone with the Wind*. It was a film that tragically changed Clift's fortunes. During filming in 1956, he went a dinner party in Los Angeles at the canyon-side home of Taylor, who was, by then married (to her second husband Michael Wilding). Clift excused himself early, drove down the hill and crashed his car into a telegraph pole. He suffered a broken jaw and nose, and lost four teeth. His upper lip was split in half. Taylor helped rescue him and, sensing the gathering crowd of ghoulish reporters at the scene, ordered them not to take photographs of the hideously disfigured Clift. If anyone defied her, Taylor warned: "I'll make sure every damn one of you is banned."

The Clash's 1979 track *The Right Profile* is about Clift and includes references to the accident: "Monty's face is broken on a wheel/Is he alive?"

Clift was patched up as well as anyone could be, but the most handsome male face in 1950s Hollywood was gone forever. He completed *Raintree County* but then he started to drink heavily and became dependent on painkillers. This, combined perhaps with a thyroid condition only diagnosed posthumously, made him appear slurred and disorientated in public. He died aged forty-six in 1966, the same year as Hopper's death.

Unlikely at it sounds today, Clift was probably more intimate with Taylor than any of her more romantic partners. By intimate, I mean very closely involved rather than sexually familiar. She was presented with a string of suitable consorts, though her friendship with Clift endured. Some forbidden fruit theories suggest that she desired him more because he was unattainable. Vaunted as one of the most desirable women in the world, someone who could have whoever she desired, she was excited by someone she could *not* get.

What could possibly be so interesting about Alfred C. Kinsey? The professor of entomology (an insect-scientist), born in Hoboken, New Jersey, married one of his university students only to discover there was something not quite right about their relationship. After seeing a consultant about their problem, Kinsey had a *Eureka!* moment and realized it was to do with sex. In the 1940s, the subject was strictly for disciples of an Austrian neurologist-turned-psychoanalyst who thought it was the secret key to explaining mental development. More puritanical Americans thought this was a typical European crackpot theory, like those of Karl Marx and Charles Darwin. Yet Kinsey championed someone who was suspected to be a pervert and risked becoming known as a pervert himself.

Kinsey carried out his pioneering studies into sexual behavior by interviewing 5,000 subjects. He concluded among other things that almost all men masturbate, that women peak sexually in their mid-thirties and that homosexuality is not some one-in-a-million anomaly. He published his first set of findings in 1948. *Sexual Behavior in the Human Male*, better known as the Kinsey Report, led to his being reviled as a fraud whose bogus science legitimized the gay movement, Roe *vs.* Wade, sex education, the glamorization of pornography and the relaxation of sex-offender laws, among other instances of moral degeneracy. The book sold 200,000 copies within three months, a staggering quantity for what was primarily an academic text. A second volume focusing on female sexuality followed in 1952. This was a long time before gender or women's studies entered the college curriculum (Cornell and a handful of other universities introduced women's studies in the 1969–70 academic year). Women were still locked into "the domestic sphere to raise children and attend household needs," as Liberty Walther Barnes put it in 2014 (p. 12). The case notes of women, married and unmarried, defying traditional roles and ignoring the moral codes that were thought to underpin them must have made uneasy reading. Masturbation, petting, sex dreams, premarital coitus, and animal contacts were all recorded. The report made no distinction between love and lust.

The British were as unnerved by the reports as Americans. *The People*, a Sunday newspaper, commissioned its own research that unearthed the finding: "British women are much more moral, more conventional, and more faithful to the marriage bond than the American women of the Kinsey Report" (in Kinsey Institute). Taylor, of course, was British, but lived in the USA.

Eventually, the public attacks gave way to more analytical appraisals and Kinsey is now considered one of the most influential thinkers of the twentieth century, who helped usher in the so-called "sexual revolution" of the 1960s. But the point is: the initial response to the Kinsey Report in 1948 reflected, in many ways, the way Americans thought about sex and about other people's private lives. Did they really want to know whether such-and-such was a maelstrom in bed or you-know-who indulged in sexual perversions (as many of the practices recounted by Kinsey would have been regarded)? Even if the answer was "yes," no one was likely to admit to such prurience. Curiosity may be part of the human condition; exercising it is subject to cultural mores. Today, there are practically no limits to our desire to learn more about other people; inquisitiveness is normal; in fact, indifference is unusual. But at the time of Kinsey's iconoclastic research, an interest in others' lives was unhealthy, perhaps unnatural. Following Kinsey were beat poets, anarchic novelists, and rebellious housewives looking for what the psychologist Abraham Maslow, in 1954, called self-actualization. All were, in their own ways, challenging the moral order of the day.

Taylor in her teens might have been what Hopper had described as a "thoroughly ravishing young lady," but her premarital escorts were not expected to ravish her. Delightful and entrancing as she may have been, she was ornamental: decorative and not functional, at least not sexually functional. Of course, the public was not privy—nor indeed are we—to the nature of the relationships Taylor had with her early male partners. But it was probably widely assumed that she would remain a virgin until she married. Bizarre as this may seem today, in the mid-twentieth century, it would have been a common expectation. Taylor was exceptional. But her beauty did not give her license to breach essential moral conventions. *Confidential* did not begin publishing until 1952, so the grapevine was in the grasp of the studios and the gossip mavens, who were the main sources of information on private lives, were probably far less seditious than imagined.

Taylor did not singlehandedly convert everyone into voyeurs; nor did her dalliances turn them into neurotics with a faith in their own right to know others' secrets. Yet the fact remains: reports of her trysts arrived at a time when ordinary people were discovering—or perhaps rediscovering—an interest in the habits, including sexual habits, of others.

FIGURE 5 *Practically anyone who even escorted, let alone married, Taylor was guaranteed attention. But media attention has not always been as beneficial as it is today—as Eddie Fisher discovered.*

Photo by Archive Photos/Getty Images.

5

Inseparable from the gossip

Howard Hughes, aviator, film producer, industrialist, and obsessive-compulsive, was a known admirer of Elizabeth Taylor. In this respect, he was not alone. He was over sixteen years her senior. In 1946, Hughes, already a stupendously successful aircraft company owner and breaker of many world aviation records, narrowly escaped death in a plane crash; thereafter he became a recluse and experienced anxiety disorders. Even after buying a part of RKO Pictures in 1948, he never visited the studio and largely confined himself to a room on the top floor of the Desert Inn, Las Vegas. In 1949, on one of his few sojourns to California, Hughes stopped by Francis Taylor's art gallery in Beverly Hills. There, he made several purchases and ordered more paintings from Europe. He also expressed a desire to meet the celebrated daughter of the owner. Hughes invited the Taylor family to stay with him at one of the hotels he owned in Reno, Nevada. Elizabeth was not keen. But Hughes, as head of RKO and a customer of the gallery, was a potentially valuable friend.

Dismayed at her daughter's lack of enthusiasm, Sara salvaged the situation by flying with husband Francis and some other friends to Reno, where Hughes entertained them and made an astonishing, if indecent proposal. Hughes, nearing forty-three, offered to buy Elizabeth, then seventeen, her own film studio or give her a million dollars (versions differ) on the condition she married him. Sara did not doubt he had the wherewithal. Some mothers might have laughed off the preposterous offer; others might have taken offense; still others might have replied, "Let me talk to her." Sara did just that, summoning Elizabeth to Reno. Never one to defy her mother's authority, Elizabeth obeyed, arriving the next day to meet someone described in 2013 by *Forbes'* Zillow as (in the 1940s), "the richest man in the world, with vast holdings and control over real estate, aviation and Hollywood."

Ten years before, Hughes had rescued Katherine Hepburn, whose acting career had gone into a tailspin. A combination of Hughes's benevolence and the media's interest in celebrity couples was sufficient to send Hepburn back to the top with films such as *The Philadelphia Story* (1940) and *Woman of the Year* (1942). Perhaps Sara Taylor was mindful of his catalytic effect.

Elizabeth Taylor rebuffed the request. She was notionally still involved with Glenn Davis, then serving in Korea, though she may have started seeing William Pawley at that stage; there was some overlap in the relationships. It could hardly escape Taylor's attention that other people were pushing the fast-forward button on her life. Even deeply personal and fundamental decisions were deliberated at levels almost beyond her control. When she did marry for the first time, her motivation could have been simple—love. Or it could have been to shrug off the competing interest groups vying for her favors. Maybe to escape a manipulative mother whose ice-cold rationality superseded matters of the heart. Or even to appease her studio, which was featuring her in a family crowd-pleaser called *Father of the Bride*, in which Spencer Tracy played the titular dad, and Taylor a blushing virgin bride. The director was Vincente Minnelli. The marketing possibilities of a tie-in with a real-life wedding would be obvious today. Perhaps less so in the early 1950s, when the film was made. But when, after a couple of false starts, Taylor did get married in May 1950, MGM picked up the tab for everything, including the bride's wedding gown (designed by Helen Rose, who also created Grace Kelly's wedding dress). And the studio released *Father of the Bride* within weeks, inviting comparisons between her character in the film and Taylor herself. The juxtaposition was perfect.

Her husband was Conrad Nicholson Hilton Jr., usually known as Nicky Hilton. He was not as wealthy as Hughes, but, as heir to the Hilton Hotel Corporation, he was hardly strapped. He held stock in Hughes's airline TWA. Today, the name Hilton is joined as if by word association to Paris. Nicky was the great-grandfather of the omnifarious celeb. Taylor first met him at a bridal shower for fellow MGM player Jane Powell, in October 1949, five months after the announcement of her engagement to Pawley. The go-between was Peter Lawford, onetime brother-in-law to the Kennedys, member of Frank Sinatra's Rat Pack and avid consumer of alcohol and cocaine. Hilton shared his enthusiasm for intoxicants; he was also an enthusiastic gambler. And unbeknown to his father, he slept with Conrad Sr.'s second wife and his own stepmother Zsa Zsa Gabor. But, on the surface, he must have seemed marriageable material: Taylor was eighteen, Hilton 23.

Many years later, the British newspaper, the *Daily Telegraph* reflected on Taylor: "Everything she did was news" (March 23, 2011, p. 33). Perhaps not everything; but everything after May 6, 1950, the day of the wedding. "The wedding attracted the kind of crowds that Hollywood had not seen since Jean Harlow's funeral [in 1937 when thousands crowded outside a private, guarded mortuary in Glendale, California]," writes Brenda Maddox (1977, p. 88).

To maximize the marketing possibilities, MGM decorated the church so that it resembled the one in the *Father of the Bride*, then only weeks away from release. This was 1950, before paparazzi were heard of and when the pop of flashbulbs was music to the ears, especially of MGM executives.

There was no sense in which the media interfered with or pursued the newly-weds overzealously. At eighteen, Taylor savored the attention; in the years that followed, she would bask in it.

The couple were divorced January 29, 1951. It was the shortest of all of Taylor's marriages. But the movie was a success. So much so that MGM made a sequel *Father's Little Dividend* and asked Taylor, Tracy, and Joan Bennett, who had also been in *Father*, to reprise their roles. The film was released in April 1951. When, years later in 2011, David Germain and Hillel Italie wrote of Taylor, "her work was inseparable from the gossip around it," we understand why: even at eighteen, the film industry used her in a way that tempted audiences to see in her film roles a reflection of her precocious off-screen life.

Most accounts of the marriage stress Hilton's proclivities for drugs and gambling as the source of conflict. He was also thought to have struck his wife. But, when Hilton in trying to summon a kind of a defense for his behavior, claimed, "I didn't marry a girl. I married an institution," he unwittingly (perhaps) and inadvertently (maybe) offered counsel (Hilton is quoted in Bergan, 2011, p. 17). Taylor had become a nascent phenomenon, an alliance of personality and media. From the get-go, Hilton must have been mystified: Taylor was accompanied on her honeymoon by an entourage of a dozen or so, fourteen trunks filled with clothes and accessories and a poodle (his great-granddaughter might have got the idea from Taylor). And, of course, the media corps was never far from her. There was also the unseen presence of MGM, which wielded an intrusive if benign influence in practically everything Taylor did.

Officially, the grounds for divorce were indifference and mental cruelty. Taylor told the court her income from motion pictures was sufficient for her support and would waive alimony, though she asked for the return of her maiden name. Following the divorce, which was finalized in January 1951, Hedda Hopper noticed how "the parade of suitors began."

Hilton died in 1969, aged forty-two, after marrying twice more.

Shortly after her divorce, Taylor became involved with the director Stanley Donen and news circled the world. The *Courier-Mail*, in Brisbane, Australia, for example, on February 14, 1951, reported that Taylor had become "linked with Stanley Donen who is directing her new picture ... but when the rumours of romance were referred to her, Elizabeth replied 'Rubbish'" (p. 6). Twelve years in the US and she still used the British vernacular. Donen was only eight years Taylor's senior, but married. This set a precedent of sorts: Taylor's attraction to married men became part of a pattern. Donen co-directed (with Gene Kelly) the 1952 film *Singin' in the Rain*. Donen's wife, Jeanne Coyne, filed for divorce and threatened to name Taylor, then nineteen, as co-respondent, according to David Bret. This did not materialize, though one wonders how it might have impacted on Taylor's career. MGM clearly had this possibility in mind when it intervened. After an emergency meeting, the studio decided to cast Taylor in *Ivanhoe* so she would be well away from Donen. "We agreed that the best way to separate them was to send her abroad to make a picture . . . and she left for London," an MGM executive reflected to John B. Allan in the 2011 edition of his biography of Taylor.

Donen directed Taylor in a 1952 potboiler *Love Is Better Than Ever*, in which she played opposite Larry Parks, who was a hot-ticket actor at the time. The House Un-American Activities Committee (HUAC) put an end to his career, when it summoned him. He could have followed the same course as a great many other film industry personnel and, when asked about communist affiliations, taken the Fifth (i.e. stated: "I respectfully decline to answer the question on the grounds that this is privileged information under the Fifth Amendment of the Unites States Constitution.)" Hedda Hopper, remember, was a stalwart supporter of HUAC.

While filming *Ivanhoe* in London, Taylor met Michael Wilding, who was acting in another movie, *Trent's Last Case*, in the same studio complex. Wilding would eventually became an unwitting factor in the demise of Hopper, whose influence waned in the late 1950s and who perhaps imagined she was still untouchable in the early 1960s. In 1963, she wrote a memoir, *The Whole Truth and Nothing But*. "In it she wrote that she had summoned Elizabeth Taylor to her house and tried to dissuade her from marrying Michael Wilding," wrote actor David Niven in his 1975 memoir, because Wilding was not only "too old for her but had also long indulged in homosexual relations with Stewart Granger" (p. 86).

Hopper must have thought she was still omnipotent. But, on this occasion, was forced to settle. The offending passages were deleted from subsequent editions of the book. "Hopper's loss meant financial damages and public humiliation," writes Jennifer Frost, in *Hedda Hopper's Hollywood* (p. 197). Hopper's credibility was damaged.

According to David Bret, Wilding's gay "relationship would continue well into his association with Elizabeth" (p. 63). Paradoxically, MGM, in an effort to pair Taylor up with a more suitable man, fixed her up with the handsome New York actor Tab Hunter, just a year older than Taylor and filming in London. Hunter eventually came out of the closet in 2006.

Taylor became engaged to Wilding in the fall of 1951, even while he was still married and her own decree absolute was still pending. In the same year, her contract with MGM was approaching an end. She had to consider renewing her deal and remaining in secure employment with the studio or gambling. James Stewart gambled when, in 1950, he played in the movie *Winchester '73* for 50 percent of the net profits rather than his usual fee of about $200,000. John W. Cones explains net profits were "defined in the contract as the point at which the film earned in gross receipts twice its negative cost . . . breakeven point" (p. 20). The film was a success and Stewart earned a reputed $600,000 spread over the next few years. The deal is conventionally regarded as the beginning of the end for the longterm studio contracts that tied actors to particular studios. Taylor was earning about $2,000 per week.

Taylor married Wilding in February 1952, days before her twentieth birthday. The marriage took place at Caxton Hall, a register office in Westminster, London (it closed in 1979, though the building still stands). The wedding was a huge media event with "a crowd that would have done credit to the [Football Association] Cup Final," as the Gaumont British News put it. In those days the Cup Final attendance was 100,000, but, even allowing for hyperbole, the crowds were substantial. The footage is still viewable at: http://bit.ly/TlWOQG (accessed September 2015).

MGM offered her a new seven-year contract at $5,000 per week (for 40 weeks per year) with a three-year deal for her new husband and a job for her mother. It looked an unmissable opportunity, but, of course, it tormented her in the years that followed. Wilding followed Taylor to California, leaving behind a tax bill of £35,000, then about $115,000.

By the time of *Love Is Better Than Ever*'s release in March 1952, Taylor was Mrs. Michael Wilding and was referred to as such by journalists such as Bosley Crowther, of the *New York Times,* who, in reviewing the film on March 4, delineated: "Mrs. Wilding is a very shapely lady, in case you didn't know, and her dark, round madonna beauty is almost too luscious to be true." Bear in mind: it was 1952.

Taylor's marriage to Wilding lasted five years; *it was to be her longest.* She had two children, the first, Michael, born in January 1953. She was a month shy of her twenty-first birthday. The following year, Taylor again became pregnant. Her second son, Christopher, was born in February 1955. After this, rumors of Taylor's interest in other men multiplied. Among the reputed inamoratos were Victor Mature, beefcake in the Sylvester Stallone mold, and Frank Sinatra.

During her marriage to Wilding, Taylor began to suffer from ailments typically associated with older people. For example, in 1953, she suffered from what was reported to be a heart attack. Two years later, she had sciatica and had to walk with the aid of crutches. She was hospitalized after being hit in the eye by a splinter of steel. These were parts of a sequence of illnesses that were to become a kind of parallel narrative to her life. There was rarely a period of good health when she was not either ailing or taking medication of some sort. In fact, it is probable that, from the time of her first child, she was continually medicated.

The union of glamorous young, covetable starlet with an apparently glittering future and a middle-aged, workaday Brit actor apparently blessed by good fortune looked doomed. But Taylor and Wilding were rightly partnered, at least for five years. Wilding was, by all accounts, a pragmatist, sensing a career move of breathtaking beneficence. A common claim is that several of Taylor's partners *used* her. That seems an unduly cynical assertion, particularly when Taylor's many other attractants are taken into consideration. Still, there were advantages to being associated with Taylor.

Practically anyone who even escorted, let alone married, Elizabeth Taylor was guaranteed attention, not just from the film industry, but from media. But media attention has not always been as propitious as it is today. Eddie Fisher discovered this. Wilding's career did not change trajectory, at least not in a way that significantly advantaged him. Wilding picked up prominent roles in Michael Curtiz's *The Egyptian* (1954) and *The Glass Slipper* (1955), among others. But his Hollywood career was shortlived and he specialized in television parts in his later life. He died in 1979, age sixty-six.

It is also easy to mischaracterize Taylor's status in the early 1950s. Scandal-free and apparently virtuous, she was a popular and promising Hollywood star. But, not in the same class as Grace Kelly, whose part in *High Noon*, in 1952, began a sequence of successful film and tv roles, culminating in *High Society* in 1956. Kelly had been earmarked for what became Taylor's most celebrated role in this period: *Giant*, the 1956 film based on the Edna Ferber novel of a Texan ranching family. MGM loaned out Taylor to Warner Brothers for this production in Marfa, Texas. The production pitched Taylor in with two of the most seemingly eligible actors of the period, both possessed of good looks and without wives or children.

Giant would be James Dean's last film: he died, aged twenty-four, in an accident in 1955, shortly after completing the film. A maverick figure, Dean is still remembered as a symbol of rebellious youth in the mid-1950s. He was actually a year older than Taylor, though in many ways a complete contrast. She was twice married, a mother and a paragon of righteousness (divorce was hardly a sin). He was Hollywood's answer to rock 'n' roll.

By 1955, the music condemned by some as primitive "jungle music," had been appropriated from African American artists by whites and rendered a marketable product. "Rock around the clock," was a blues number that was picked up by Decca re-recorded by Bill Haley and the Comets, a white band, and turned into a number one hit record in the USA and Britain. Other white musicians followed. The frantic rhythms of the genre were carried largely but not exclusively by white artists (Little Richard and Chuck Berry were notable black rockers) and, as we know, changed music. The influence was not confined to music: rock 'n' roll was a cultural centrifuge: everything was affected in some form. Dean, with Adonis looks, swept-back hair, blue jeans, and arrogance in every step, looked the complete package. In films like *East of Eden* and, especially, *Rebel Without a Cause* (both 1955), he captured a kind of alienated, dissolute youthful desire to resist conformity and oppose practically everything though without actually knowing why. He would not have looked out-of-place in the Killers or the Foo Fighters.

Even the manner of his death—in a Porsche Spyder—seemed ghoulishly appropriate. He remains a posthumous icon of the era. After his death,

Hedda Hopper claimed intimate familiarity with the grief of Dean fans: she reported that she had received thousands of letters every week from mournful devotees. Not that the notoriously conservative Hopper burnished his rebellious credentials. Justin Owen Rawlins argued in 2013 that, in Hopper's writing, Dean "came to symbolize not an agent of antiestablishment change but rather a conscientious objector to the perceived erosions of preexisting racial and gender hierarchies" (p. 29).

It seems like practically every man mentioned in the book so far has some sort of gay inflexion, and Dean is no exception. This was explored in the 2012 film *Joshua Tree, 1951: A Portrait of James Dean.*

While making *Giant*, Taylor met Rock Hudson, with whom she formed a close friendship that endured until his death in 1985. Like Dean, strikingly handsome, Hudson heaved into view as likely raw material for a Taylor affair. There were no doubts that Hudson was anything other than an emphatically heterosexual hunk. The indeterminate friendship between Taylor and Hudson never became an affair, but grew into a strong, lasting union that played an important role in Taylor's later life, as we will discover later in the book.

Wilding visited his wife in Marfa while she was filming *Giant*. He left abruptly after a series of public arguments. There was talk of a kind of love triangle with both she and Hudson vying for the affections of Dean. Taylor's apparent admiration for Sinatra was also a source of tension, and it seemed the marriage was dissolving in the Texan heat. *Giant* was released in November 1956, six weeks after Dean's death and the circumstances no doubt contributed to its success (in the same way that Heath Ledger's death in 2008 boosted boxoffice for *The Imaginarium of Doctor Parnassus*, his final film; and River Phoenix's death in 1993 increased interest in his last complete film *The Thing Called Love*, released in the same year—he partially completed another project which was put on hold after his death). *Giant* grossed $7 million in its first year of release and gave Taylor leverage to argue for parts in big budget films.

In an effort to capitalize on Taylor's profile, MGM cast her in *Raintree County*, based on a bestselling novel of the American Civil War by Ross Lockridge Jr. The intention was probably to fashion a sort of *Gone With the Wind II*, almost two decades after the original. Taylor played a headstrong southern belle not unlike Scarlett O'Hara. A budget of $5 million made it the most expensive film ever made in the United States. During shooting, Montgomery Clift, who also had a part in the film, suffered the road accident that left him disfigured. Taylor arrived at the scene and helped rescue him, as we learned earlier. *Raintree County* was released in October 1957 but did not replicate *Giant*'s success at the boxoffice.

Taylor was still married to Wilding, but her appearances with him were perfunctory. She was seen frequently with Kevin O'Donovan McClory. A County Dublin-born producer McClory had an interesting background.

Born in 1939, educated in Ireland, New York, and London, he joined the merchant navy (marine) at fifteen. After the Second World War, he worked in the building trade in England and, after a brief period as an actor and a tin prospector in the Belgian Congo (the former name for the Democratic Republic of Congo), found work in the film industry. McClory served as assistant director for John Huston on *The African Queen* (1951), *Moulin Rouge* (1952) and *Moby Dick (1956)* before being hired as an associate producer on a huge film project based on Jules Verne's 1873 novel *Around the World in 80 Days*. Although he is rarely mentioned, McClory was to become a pivotal character in Taylor's life.

In July 1956, MGM announced that she and Wilding were separating; this meant Taylor, at twenty-four, was facing her second divorce. Taylor would file for divorce four months later and ask for custody of the two boys, then aged three-and-a-half, and one-and-a-half. Presumably, mindful of the announcement, Taylor had become emboldened to be seen in public with McClory, who, in 1959, suggested to author Ian Fleming a James Bond film set in the Bahamas. McClory and Fleming collaborated on *Thunderball* (1965, the third in the longrunning series) and a subsequent legal dispute resulted in McClory, who died in 2006, becoming owner of significant elements of the 007 mythos. Several sources suggest that Taylor and he had discussed getting married. But the director of *Around the World in 80 Days* and thus McCrory's paymaster at the time, Michael Todd, urged caution. There was method in his madness: within months, Todd had insinuated his way into Taylor's affections and become her prospective third husband.

"MGM announced in May 1953 that it would no longer authorize stories about its stars and their children," reveals Anthony Slide, who continues: "It would be okay to publish 'glamour' pieces on Esther Williams, Jane Powell, or Elizabeth Taylor, but there could be no acknowledgement that they had a family life" (p. 171). A glamour piece is a magazine or newspaper story that showcases a particular figure, featuring a picture that accentuates her (or, less often, his) appealing or attractive qualities, but with no background, context, or detail; the story may be sexually suggestive in some cases, though this was not MGM's intention.

Television was beginning to loom as a threat to the Hollywood's dominance of the entertainment industry. Lucille Ball's career gained a new lease on life when she appeared in *I Love Lucy* on CBS in the 1951. After years in the film industry, she ventured into what was, for some, the faddish new medium and became a spectacular success. Like many other Hollywood figures, she was interviewed by HUAC and submitted sealed testimony about her alleged political affiliations.

One of the film industry's responses was to offer audiences what television could not: size and color. Widescreen film and television is the norm today, but, prior to 1953 when 20th Century Fox introduced CinemaScope, images on both were square. CinemaScope was initially breathtaking: an image of about twice the usual width was squeezed into a 35mm frame and then screened by a projector having complementary lenses, giving the viewer a panoramic vista. *The Robe* (1953) featuring the aforementioned Victor Mature, and Richard Burton (of whom much more later) was the first film in CinemaScope. Full color cinematography had been available since the silent film era, Technicolor being the process. Significant improvements in quality in the 1930s encouraged more filmmakers to use color, though the competition from television, which used black and white, made it imperative. Film, in other words, sought to make cinema a visually more enriching experience in any way it could.

The film industry also wanted to reverse what Lucille Ball and many other actors were doing: far from appearing familiar and ordinary, it wanted film actors to be remote and extraordinary. The aim was to restore what Slide calls "the aura of mystery" to movie stars. Television characters were like frequent visitors into viewers' homes; they became familiar, making possible the "intimacy at a distance" discussed in the previous chapter. By contrast, Taylor and other Hollywood actors were exotic, remarkable, and anything but ordinary. So seepage of gossip on her *affaires du coeur* entailed no great cost, at least not to her image or MGM—her marriage, maybe.

In his own way, Michael Todd assisted both responses. "A five-foot-nine, 152-pound bundle of energy and wonder: gifted, grandiose and resourceful, a bold man fighting middle-age as if he is going to beat it," is how Art Cohn eulogized his friend Todd in 1956 (p. 9). Born Avrom Hirsch Goldbogen in Minneapolis, son of a Polish rabbi, he adapted his name from his nickname "Toad." He got married at twenty. A self-styled producer—though he preferred the designation showman—he launched his first Broadway show in 1939, aged thirty-two, went into bankruptcy with liabilities over $1 million eight years later and, in 1950, formed a company to experiment with a wide, curved cinema screen process. He later refined this into what he trademarked as Todd-AO (the AO stood for American Optical). The first film to employ this technique was Fred Zinnemann's version of the Rodgers and Hammerstein musical *Oklahoma!* in 1955. Todd had been widowed in 1947, then married again, divorcing after two years.

Todd himself had never made a film but had something of an *idée fixe* about the Verne classic *Around the World in 80 Days*. He had started to produce a Broadway musical version with a Cole Porter score and featuring Orson Welles, in 1946, but withdrew from the project. When he resurrected it, his vision was for a lavish movie version in Todd-AO filmed at thirteen locations all over the world, with four principal characters and fifty cameo roles played by well-known actors (Cohn reckons this meaning of the word cameo originated in the film), and over 68,000 extras. It was an enormously ambitious, extravagant, and perilous undertaking, especially for a first-time producer. Even the director Michael Anderson was a risk: he had made the

British film *The Dam Busters* (1955) and a 1956 screen version of George Orwell's *1984,* but had no experience with the kind of budget associated with this film; the best estimate put it at $6 million, but Todd's book keeping was so labyrinthine that no one knew for certain. The film was also independent of the major studios; Todd had raised the money from several different sources. In fact, Todd claimed one of the studios offered him $10 million to take control of the project and he refused.

Cohn maintained that Todd's mission was to make a spectacle that would overshadow television's most popular show. "He [Todd] knew he had at last found something Ed Sullivan couldn't do" (p. 11). Sullivan's Saturday night variety show on CBS ran from 1948 to 1971 and featured extracts from the top Broadway shows as well as every worldclass act. "He [Todd] has brought the vintage Jules Verne novel to the wide screen with a roll and a flourish, embellishing the story with big and colorful visual values and a healthy sense of humor that shapes it into perhaps the most entertaining global story travelog ever made," concluded *Variety* (October 24, 1956).

It was typical of the reception. In the 1950s and 1960s, before digital recorders, DVDs, or film channels, it was not unusual for films to play in theaters for years. *Around the World in 80 Days* played in New York for over a year and comparable lengths of time elsewhere, making it the second highest grossing film of 1957 behind *The Ten Commandments.*

Todd, stocky with a square jaw, could have passed as a junior-middleweight boxer; he was living with Evelyn Keyes, who had played a Parisian tart (the cast description) in his film, at the time he met Taylor, which was June 1956 (about six weeks after Montgomery Clift's accident). Taylor was invited by Todd to a short cruise on the Pacific. Todd was forty-six. Taylor was still married to Wilding, but estranged and involved with McClory. Hedda Hopper discerned Todd's motives in approaching Taylor. "After Mike had made *Around the World in 80 Days,* he wanted someone to help sell it. Who else but the queen of movies?" she wrote with James Brough in a 1963 story provocatively (for the 1960s) headlined "Todd taught Liz everything about sex—good and bad" (p. 24). Clift shared this view (if not the headline). Todd might not have been able to give his queen a state to rule over, but he gave her an antique diamond tiara fit for a queen, with an estimated value of $60,000 to $80,000.

McClory and Keyes melted away once Todd had made his decisive move: he proposed marriage and bombarded Taylor with extravagant baubles, including a $43,000 black pearl ring, and a $92,000 diamond ring (previously given to Keyes). "It was actually Mike who started Elizabeth down the road of collecting expensive jewels," contends Randy Taraborrelli (p. 126). If so, Todd should take credit for initiating a collection accreted over five decades that was eventually valued at a record-breaking $116 million (£75 million) when auctioned in 2011. I will return to this history-making auction in Chapter 18.

Even if Todd was not so mercenary as Hopper and Brough suspected, there is no doubting Taylor's utility as a marketing instrument for the film. She did not feature in *Around the World in 80 Days* (Shirley MacLaine, in her third film role, played the female lead), but Taylor made it known she would be in Todd's next project, *Don Quixote*, sourced from the Cervantes classic. The courtship was relatively short—Todd was notoriously direct—and the official engagement was announced in October to coincide with the official release of Todd's masterwork.

"Conspicuous consumption" does not do justice to Todd's ostentatious devouring of every conceivable commodity. Flushed by the success of his film and the companionship of his bride-to-be, Todd splashed out on a Rolls-Royce Silver Cloud and installed two phones (long before the days of cell phones, of course) and a bar. He commissioned his own custom-rolled cigars. He bought two cinemas in Chicago, leased a mansion in Beverly Hills, a resort in Palm Springs, Florida, and an estate in Westport, Connecticut. Every Saturday he gifted Taylor profusely with clothes, accessories, and works of art (mink stoles, sapphires, Renoirs!) In a sense, Taylor became *his* accessory. She accompanied him and showed no obvious embarrassment, even at Todd's coarsely objectifying language. On one famous occasion, Todd informed a journalist, "Any time this little dame spends out of bed is wasted" (in *The Scotsman*, March 23, 2011).

Taylor consented to what, at times, seemed her own infantilization: Todd treated her not so much as an infant but in a way that denied her maturity in age or experience. "I get my hands on a few dollars occasionally," he said to journalists, "and I think there is no better way in the world of spending it than trying to spoil Elizabeth." Spoil? This is a verb typically used to describe being too indulgent or excessively kind with a child to an extent where it harms them. Todd was not embarrassed about this, giving the impression that he was exhibiting Taylor, as a proud father shows off his daughter.

Perhaps it was the showman in him that impelled Todd to turn his private life inside out. Kitty Kelley recounts how, at a dinner party, he picked up a chicken leg and motioned across the room to Taylor, "I'm going to eat this and you, too." Far from flinching at his crudities, Taylor joined in: she felt no compunction about discussing their sex life to others, on one occasion separating Todd from the company of a journalist with the simple explanation: "I want to fuck you this minute." Perhaps it was for show; but, if so, it suggested Taylor had developed the tendency to attract and keep attention: after a few well-placed allusions to her sexual proclivities, every journalist was *en garde*. (The uninhibited quote appeared on page 106 of the 1981 edition of Kitty Kelley's biography and was reproduced in subsequent editions.)

Love was a consciously public affair for Taylor; it was as if she had suddenly become fascinated with her own private life and been incited to share it. Taylor's newfound propensity combined perfectly with Todd's well-established extraversion. While Kelley thinks Taylor's plasticity allowed Todd to shape her, this does little justice to Taylor's own willingness to play a role more flamboyant and cheerfully reckless than any of her films, husbands, parents or MGM had ever allowed.

"When we were making *Giant*," said Rock Hudson, "Elizabeth was a big star, but she was not news" (in Maddox, 1977, p. 121). Since her marriage to Wilding four years before 1952 there had been no football crowd-like gatherings; only respectful applause and appreciation from media and public alike. Professionally, she had advanced to the upper echelons of Hollywood, but she managed to maintain a warrantable private life with Wilding, who was more thespian than celebrity and had no interest in repackaging himself for Hollywood.

Were someone to script Taylor's life to this point, it would be a tale of a youngster afforded every material gift she wanted but deprived socially and emotionally, awaiting one of those miracles that always seem pending but never materialize. Her first husband offered only an illusion. The second brought her only what Kelley called "a lifeless marriage." Then came an experience of good grace that transfigured her life on at least three levels. "The transformation wrought by Todd was total," declared Maddox in 1977. "He woke Taylor up sexually, professionally and financially" (p. 121).

This was the late 1950s: studios were, as I have noted, providing different fare to the blander output of earlier generations; responding, no doubt, to the salacious palate cultivated by *Confidential* and other gossip magazines. Consumers were changing: they demanded more than fabulous images of fabulous people with fabulous lives: they wanted narratives—real accounts of people they could recognize and perhaps identify with as human beings with the same kinds of strengths and weaknesses as themselves. Better still: events, stories, histories or chronicles that carried with them a moral or lesson in what is right or prudent, bad or foolish. In other words, they wanted to interpret, judge, and evaluate rather than just absorb: they wanted to engage. Taylor had brought audiences to the box office before, she had even drawn them to her wedding ceremonies, but, after meeting Todd, she captured them, engrossed, absorbed, and occupied their attention like no other Hollywood star in history.

"She appeared in the newspapers and magazines, every day, every issue. Every facet of their lives was exploited for the benefit of love-starved fans. Gold poured into the box office for her pictures and his *Around the World* [sic]," wrote Hedda Hopper (with James Brough) in 1963 (p. 24).

Even a medical condition was no longer just an illness: it was new material for the unfolding narrative. So when she tripped on a staircase and hurt her back, it presented an occasion for a new dramatic turn. Rushed to hospital in New York, tests revealed damaged vertebrae. A four-hour surgical procedure to fuse parts of her spine was a success. Todd briefed the media on her medical condition; but not comprehensively: he neglected to include the detail that she was pregnant.

The prospect of a birth motivated Taylor, or, perhaps more likely, Todd to push for a quick divorce. Wilding was not opposed to this, of course and, after an initial denial, a second petition was granted in Acapulco, Mexico. Wilding returned to California immediately after the divorce, and then to England. Taylor and Todd remained in Mexico to marry on February 2, 1957. Taylor was single for less than a week. Todd was forty-seven and Taylor was twenty-four.

Theatrically, Todd brought in the mayor of Acapulco to officiate at the civil service, which was followed by a typically animated reception. The maid of honor was Debbie Reynolds and the best man was her husband and close friend of Todd, Eddie Fisher. The couple had married two years before in 1955 on Reynolds's twenty-fourth birthday. They had a four-month-old daughter, Carrie.

There is a consensus among Taylor biographers and commentators that Todd changed Taylor. He certainly projected her in a way that, as Hudson had alluded to, made her news. Taylor graduated from Hollywood stardom to what an MGM employee, speaking to Maddox, called "the royalty of America" (p. 135). Actually Maddox, in 1977, dissented from this view: "Royalty would not dare to court such a bad press." In the 1970s maybe. In the Princess Diana era, British royals accepted the dare; for example when Diana herself confronted Camilla Parker Bowles over her affair with the Prince of Wales, demanding she end the relationship, and later revealed details of the conversation (see Matt Born and John Steele's 2004 article).

"They seemed to thrive on a public display of their relationship, in all its passion or violence," wrote Kelley in 1981 (p. 133). Probably because, as M. G. Lord pointed out in 2012: "Each aspired to the same goal: overriding a viewer's logical left brain by engaging his or her intuitive right" (p. 60). The implication is that audience's emotions dominated over analytical or critical reasoning. Lord believed Todd and Taylor became grasping and greedy, using their own life, or rather reportage of their life, as a way of maintaining a grip on public attention.

Todd's purpose in this was obvious: he wanted to promote his film and establish himself as a major Hollywood player. Taylor's is less transparent: perhaps it was liberation of sorts after what might have been a stifling marriage to the urbane and undemonstrative Wilding; or perhaps she just took pleasure from the admiration, adoration, and celebrity-affirming attention she received as Todd's wife. Hers was a dazzlingly imagined real life drama: all she had to do was live her life, while media-assisted audiences did the rest—with their imaginations. Todd filed press updates almost daily, feeding the media a constant flow of information on his and his wife's comings-and-goings.

There may have been sound logic in this: Todd wanted to stay at the forefront of the public consciousness, but, at a time when scandal magazines were gathering pace, he probably sought to head off any unwelcome stories. Todd was a known associate of Robert Harrison, *Confidential*'s proprietor. It is interesting to note that, for all her prominence, Taylor escaped scandal until after Todd's death. Todd supplied so much copy, that had the press pursued infelicitous stories, they would have risked biting the hand that fed them. This had literal as well as metaphorical meanings. For instance, Todd celebrated the one-year anniversary of the release of his film by hosting a party at New York's Madison Square Garden for 18,000 people. A cake fourteen-foot tall, thirty-foot diameter with a single giant candle was sliced up. There is still decent video footage of the event at: http://bit.ly/1goPUny (accessed September 2015). The monster-size cake could have been metaphor for Todd's ego.

The celebration was Taylor's first public appearance after giving birth to her third and last biological child. Elizabeth Frances Todd, known as Liza, was born on August 6, 1957. As with the other births, this was again by caesarian section, but it was troublesome and Taylor, on medical advice, had a tubal ligation, better known as having her fallopian tubes tied, a minor surgical procedure that prevented her becoming pregnant ever again. Another pregnancy could have been fatal. Inevitably mother-and-baby pictures covered newspapers and magazines and almost as inevitably, Taylor rejoined her husband as soon as her health permitted.

Unusual as it may seem today, it was important for celebrity couples to be seen to adhere to moral codes in the 1950s. Those who did not, risked ruin, as Ingrid Bergman discovered. Rita Hayworth only narrowly escaped being stigmatized after her baby was born seven months after her marriage to Aly Khan in 1949; the couple claimed it was a premature birth. Simple arithmetic would have alerted most to the probability that baby Liza was conceived in November 1956, when Taylor was still married to Wilding. Todd was media savvy enough to spin out a premature birth story and, aided by Hedda Hopper et al., somehow managed to navigate away from the more awkward questions that would have hurt Taylor *then*. Of course, in the years that followed, her sexual activities became a prominent feature of the Taylor narrative.

Straight after the Madison Square Garden extravaganza, Taylor and Todd resumed their touring. The tour was interrupted in Tokyo when Taylor insisted on flying back to US to have appendicitis treated. It was a sidebar to the main narrative, but one well documented by the media. The diversion was temporary and Taylor soon returned to touring. It seemed she had settled into the role of an ambulant news item and neglected her vocation. There were even hints that Taylor might follow the example of Grace Kelly who retired from acting in 1956, aged twenty-six, when she married Prince Rainier of Monaco. Todd had claimed she would be in his next film and even the one after that (Tolstoy's *War and Peace* and *Anna Karenina* were mooted), but Taylor was under contract and her value to MGM was peaking after *Giant* and the new synergy from her relationship with Todd.

MGM had optioned Tennessee Williams' Pulitzer Prize-winning play *Cat on a Hot Tin Roof*, which ran on Broadway for eighteen months from March 1955 with Barbara Bel Geddes and Ben Gazzara playing the central roles of Maggie and Brick respectively. Burl Ives played Big Daddy. MGM kept Ives, but wanted to replace Gazzara with Paul Newman, then in his early thirties. Taylor seemed a natural for the Maggie role. Todd, having already cast her in his next production, was probably preparing himself for a fight with MGM, and was almost certainly anticipating this would be her final project with the studio. We might note here that, like Montgomery Clift, Newman was an acolyte of Stanislavsky and practiced method acting, which involved immersing himself into a character so deeply that he could empathize. Taylor, who had never had a formal acting lesson, spurned preparation of this sort. In fact, she often skipped read-throughs and just turned up ready to film her part, then disappeared immediately after it was completed. The director chosen to pull together the disparate parts was Richard Brooks. Filming began in March 1958.

As Taylor recommenced her acting, Todd became consumed with a different project. Maybe it was a feeling of being unconquerable or a Midas-type delusion that made him invest in another cinematic innovation that he thought would match Todd-AO, which had been well-received by film critics and audiences alike. Smell-O-Vision was not such a success. This was a piece of technology that released odors during the screening of a film in such a way that the audience could smell particular fragrances as they appeared in the plot. For example, someone smoking a cigarette might enter a room and the audience would smell the tobacco. In theory, it looked a good idea and Todd, encouraged by the reception of his widescreen effects, pushed ahead. Who knows? It might well have become a success eventually. But Todd did not live long enough to see it through to its fruition.

It must have been an unbearable journey. What on earth did they say to each other? If anything. In the car was Rex Kennamer, Taylor's personal physician and the doctor who had supervised Clift's rehabilitation after his crash. With him was Dick Hanley, Todd's executive secretary. They were heading for Schuyler Road in Beverly Hills, where Taylor and Todd were renting a home. It was early Saturday morning. Taylor would be in bed. She had been there since Wednesday when she came down with a fever and a temperature of 102 degrees. Kennamer and Hanley were the bearers of unspeakably bad news.

They got to the house as quickly as they could in case someone else picked up the news from the radio and told Taylor. When they arrived one of the domestic staff opened the door. Kennamer took the liberty of walking into Taylor's bedroom. Hanley stood back and braced himself. Kennamer later remembered: "The minute we walked in that bedroom door, Liz knew why we were there" (quoted in Bacon, p. 5). The scream was loud enough to be heard by the neighbors. Taylor ran from her bedroom still in her nightdress shrieking uncontrollably. She tried to run outside but Kennamer subdued her and together he and Hanley took her back to bed where she submitted to sedatives. Even so, the sedatives took several hours to take effect before she fell into a sleep. Todd was dead.

On March 23, 1958, the *Los Angeles Times* reported on page one: "Showman Mike Todd, fifty, died in the flaming crash of his private plane in high mountains southwest of Grants, N.M., early yesterday morning. With him were his friend and biographer Art Cohn, and two pilots." Todd, who was actually forty-eight, had been on his way to New York City, where he was to be honored as Showman of the Year by the Friars' Club, a prestigious private club. The wings of the plane iced up while in flight and, while the de-icing equipment had been checked, the plane ran into difficulties while passing over Arizona into New Mexico and went down in a mountainous region, exploding on impact. The wreckage was scattered over half an acre. The newspaper report noted how, in previous months, Todd had traveled thousands of miles by air, promoting his film. Days before the crash, he had addressed 2,500 students at UCLA on a proposed exchange program with Russia. The newsreel is still available at: http://bit.ly/1r8mYVJ (accessed September 2015).

As with all his recent public appearances, he would have been expected to have been accompanied by his wife. On this occasion, Taylor had been laid low by a virus and decided to stay in California. She was in the middle of filming *Cat on a Hot Tin Roof* and had interrupted the schedule. It was only the third time since their marriage thirteen months before that he had traveled anywhere without her. In fact, the couple had capitalized on their publicized travels by endorsing TWA, the now-defunct airline, in an advertising campaign.

The visitors to the Beverly Hills house in the aftermath of the news were Michael Wilding, Debbie Reynolds, Kurt Frings, and his wife Ketti Frings (the acclaimed writer). Taylor had recently signed up with Kurt Frings, who was personally recommended by Todd as a press agent. Also invited to visit was James Bacon, an Associated Press writer who specialized in Hollywood stories. Bacon reported that Todd's plan was to arrive in New York on Saturday, spend the rest of the day doing promotional work, then attend the Friars' Club function on Sunday before flying to Chicago to see the middleweight world title fight between Sugar Ray Robinson and Carmen Basilio on March 25. He called her from Burbank Airport just before takeoff and promised to call again from Tulsa, where the twin-engine plane would refuel. Todd's body was recovered and taken to Chicago by train for burial.

Taylor flew to Chicago, where she was met and comforted by Todd's friend, husband of Debbie Reynolds and, of course, best man at the Acapulco wedding, Eddie Fisher.

Todd was a friend of Robert Harrison. His frequent lunches with the owner of *Confidential* were, it seems, part of his strategy for ensuring he and his wife were not prey for the scandal-hunting hacks on whom Harrison drew for sordid details and unsavory facts. The brief marriage was often like a mixture of combustible elements: the couple argued publicly and, on more than one occasion, Todd handled Taylor roughly, pulling her hair, shoving her and even slapping her across the face. Today, behavior like this would be evidence of domestic abuse, but, in the 1950s it just made an ostensibly happy marriage seem more ordinary than the made-in-heaven Hollywood matches.

At the time *Confidential* "terrorized Hollywood," as Anne Helen Petersen put it in 2013 (p. 56). Harrison was effectively Todd's get-out-of-jail card before he even got arrested. As William J. Mann wrote in 2009: "The 'official version' of his love story with Elizabeth Taylor became virtually the only version" (p. 180).

With Todd, so went the card: Taylor instantly and inevitably became rich, raw material for the predatory and sensationalistic prosecutors of what was then called "yellow journalism." She was no longer just a movie star: Todd's exhibitionism, his commerce with the media and his insistence on making as many aspects of his life visible had turned Taylor into news. The difference was: she was now unprotected. So, when she went to Chicago for her late husband's funeral, the media were ready for her. (Later, in 1977, Todd's remains were desecrated by robbers, who broke into his casket looking for a $100,000 diamond ring, which, according to rumor, Taylor had placed on her husband's finger prior to his burial.)

Mann believes Todd was a visionary in many respects; one aspect of his vision was television. Unlike the orthodox perception, he saw no necessary opposition between the film industry and what many regarded as its upstart rival. Todd, according to Mann, realized that tv was humanizing previously untouchable figures. "No longer distant deities on the silver screen, stars now appeared right there in Americans' living rooms," wrote Mann in 2009 (p.195). In other words, he grasped intuitively what some psychologists were calling para-social interaction (which I explained in the previous chapter).

Today, no one asks why we, the consumers, the fans, the audience, are so fascinated by the private lives of people who make no material impact on our own lives. Why do we wish to engage via the media, including social media, with people who never promise to bring peace on earth, or save the planet from its own ecological destruction, or help find a cure for many of the diseases that bedevil the human population? Why are we prepared to spend so much of our time, energy and money on products and services associated with people who are, in most respects, just like us? Questions like these seem to deserve answers only in the same way as, Oprah Winfrey's question to Lance Armstrong, about whether cyclists take dope. "We have to have air in our tires or we have to have water in our bottles," answered Armstrong (quoted in Goldman's 2013 article).

The answers are so obvious that they barely warrant a sensible answer. And yet for the first half of the twentieth century, we were content to look at actors on the screen or on stage, or read about them without necessarily wanting to probe. Their lives were spent playing roles, entertaining us with their art, performing for our delectation. The satisfaction we took from stars or other less celestial performers lay in the consumption of their official work, not their private lives. Of course, there was gossip. But that was supplementary: like *divertissement*, a minor diversion from the main entertainment.

Had Taylor married Todd in 1947, ten years before she actually did, she and her husband would not have captivated audiences as they so manifestly did in 1957–8. Their exploits would have been covered by newspapers, fan magazine, and traditional gossip columnists. Perhaps. Or the couple might have been consciously ignored, dismissed as flashy, vulgar, offensively pretentious, self-publicists, whose personal lives held no interest for the common people on whom they relied. "Elizabeth Taylor is an actress," someone might have responded. "We enjoy watching her play roles. Why should we want to pry into her private life? None of our business."

Yet she became our business, and in the years that followed, everyone who aspired to fame became our business. In the 1950s, audiences gazed at Taylor in cinematic chiaroscuro, or in the flickering monochrome of television. Yet, with Taylor, paradoxes flourished: audiences learned how to combine feelings of wonder and reverential respect with an ability to identify emotionally, and experience strong personal associations with the stars. They took the chance to inspect and empathize close up, as well as the invitation to applaud from the back seats of the balcony. All of which prompts the question: what would have happened if Todd had survived the plane crash?

Taylor insisted that, had her husband lived she would have remained Mrs. Michael Todd until her death. Then again, she habitually committed herself to men for life, only to divorce them. Macabrely Todd was the only one of seven husbands she did not divorce. After Todd's death, Taylor would marry five more times, eight in total. Her average marriage lasted about four years, eight months. This seems a crass statistic, but the point is: Taylor would, in all probability—in spite of her claim—not have stayed married to Todd much beyond mid-1961.

She would have played in Todd's projected *Don Quixote* if the film had ever been made. Given the parlous stage of Todd's financial affairs on his death, it is not certain whether such a movie would have reached the light of day. Todd lived high on the hog and *Around the World in 80 Days* grossed an impressive $42 million (it cost only an estimated $6 million, remember). But his finances were never transparent: the Cervantes project would have necessitated extensive borrowing and, without the institutional security of a major studio, Todd was always at risk. Were *Don Quixote* not to replicate the success of *Around the World in 80 Days*, Todd would have been seen as a one-trick pony and Taylor's credibility would have suffered.

The extravagant world tours, the ostentatious parties and the unrestrained consumption might have become tiresome. Fan fatigue is a familiar condition nowadays; in the 1950s, who knows? It is at least possible that audiences would lose interest in the couple that had everything and made sure everyone knew it. So the Liz and Mike show could have carried on spinning around the world; but, audiences were likely to stop following it.

Of all the unanswerable questions, the most tantalizing is: would she have made *Cleopatra*? Presuming she was still in-demand and married to Todd in 1961, would he—and she seemed comfortable allowing him to make her career decisions—have agreed to 20th Century Fox's proposal? Probably: $1 million was a staggering fee, even if the contract was loaded with clauses that made that amount contingent on many other factors. Todd would have warmed to the prospect of enriching the couple's finances and their egos in the process. Taylor would not have traveled to England and, later, to Rome as a once vilified, now redeemed jezebel. But, even without the fascinating mix of vice and virtue, her charisma would be intact. And she would still have become involved in a relationship that held the world spellbound for the next fifteen years.

FIGURE 6 *The love affair that destroyed two marriages, turned a film production into a confusion of art and life, and heralded the arrival of a new kind of celebrity culture.*

Photo by Express/Hulton Archive/Getty Images.

6

Dismantling the fantasy

You are Richard Burton. You used to be Richard Jenkins. You are the twelfth of thirteen children born to Dic and Edith Jenkins, who were married in 1900 and lived their whole lives in Pontrhydyfen, a small coalmining village in South Wales. Edith died young, aged forty-four, when you were only two, so the childrearing duties fell to sister Cecilia, or Cis, as she was known, and her husband Elfed. Most people in this part of the world follow their father; so you will probably become a coalminer. It's a dirty, dangerous job that damages your lungs, your legs, and your head, and you see evidence of this in your dad who constantly looks worn-out: you don't understand why he drinks so much but it is probably something to do with trying to compensate for his dreary life.

Your favorite brother Ifor followed Dic and worked in the mines. He is nineteen years older than you and you look up to him; in fact, you regard him as a surrogate father. He is a lover of poetry and you learn the beauty of words from him. And an outstanding rugby player: you would like to be as good a player as he is. When you start earning decent money, you will give Ifor a job as your personal assistant.

The Welsh mining community will always have its hand on your shoulder: wherever you go and whatever you do, you will feel its warm, protective comfort. But restlessness and a yearning to reach beyond the valleys will take you away from Wales. The journey starts as soon as you start reading. In years to come you will build your own private library filled with the works of John Donne, William Shakespeare, and your beloved Dylan Thomas, who becomes, in many ways, a kindred spirit. Men of letters fascinate you and, for most of your life, you will strive to become one. But your destiny is different: you will speak words with a clarity and power that will leave others in awe; your sole contribution to literature will be a miscellaneous assembly of personal reflections that will be edited, deposited, and curated at the University of Swansea.

One thing becomes clear as you grow up: you will not follow your father and work in the mines. You will, however, follow him in some other respects: like him, you will become a prodigious drinker and smoker; you will also lead something of a nomadic life. Dic often left home for days on end, leaving others to worry about his whereabouts. He would always return and, without explanation, resume his daily work. You too will find settling an uncomfortably sedentary experience. In a sense your life will be a story of resistance: resistance, that is, against the life offered by the Welsh mining community. And yet it will never leave you.

As mining gives way to the steel industry as the main source of employment, the big factory at nearby Port Talbot becomes the local magnet for young men. Not you though: you gain a scholarship when aged eleven and this means you can carry on your education, even as far as university if you wish. Your teachers think you have ability. Of course, rugby is still high on your priorities and, while you will never become a good player, you will play hard and remain loyal to the Welsh international rugby team for your life. In later years, you will travel abroad, but will always try to stay in touch with the rugby results. Carrying a Welsh flag in your suitcase will help maintain your association with the land of your fathers.

Delivering newspapers; collecting old newspapers for wrapping fish-and-chips; shoveling horse dung for reselling as fertilizer: these are some of the activities you do to scrape together a few pennies. It is only pocket money, but you use it to go to the local cinema and to buy books or clothes. For a while you leave education and take a job at the local Co-operative, a sort of early version of what we now call a supermarket. The Co-operative organization is still going. It surprises many that you leave your academic studies for a job that pays, but is hardly gratifying. The job provides you with no satisfaction. Not like sports: as well as playing rugby, you also play table tennis, or ping-pong, and even try your hand at boxing. Yet it is only when a youth center opens that you begin to glimpse your true vocation. The youth center is a small-scale club based at your school, Port Talbot Secondary School. The leader of the center's drama is Leo Lloyd, an enthusiastic follower of the stage who gives up his free time to promote drama. You will later write of him: "He persuaded me that acting was infinitely fascinating . . . [he] made me want to be an actor."

With the Second World War still raging, most people suspend their ambitions, wondering whether there will ever be an end to what seems an interminably long conflict. Like many boys or young men anticipating they will be needed in the Allied war effort, you are a member of the Air Training Corps, or ATC as it is known. It is two years since hostilities started and there is still no end in sight. After eighteen months away from the academic world, you return to school disenchanted with life working in a store and more resolved to study harder.

The ATC was a voluntary organization, started in 1941 with the purpose of giving young men some experience in the military (the organization is still operational). You enjoy the outdoor activities, such as rock climbing and rifle shooting so the taste of military life is not quite as sour as you anticipated.

And the people you meet at the Port Talbot ATC, 499 Squadron are often educated, cultured men. Your commanding officer, for example: he is also one of your teachers at school and has a love of poetry and literature, which he shares with you. He becomes the most inspirational figure you know. At first, he is a bit scary: too organized, neat, and precise for your tastes; he does not have the spontaneity you find so thrilling. He is an ordered man and, from him you learn, that you need order in your life; the alternative is to dissipate your creative energies.

Philip Burton was born in 1904 in Mountain Ash, South Wales. He lost his father in a mining pit tragedy when he was fourteen. A graduate of the University of Wales, he moved to Port Talbot to teach mathematics and history as well as drama, though he strove to be in the theater. To this end he wrote plays, produced, and occasionally acted on BBC Radio in Cardiff. Naturally, he took charge of school plays. Later, he moved to the USA to take up a position as director of the American Music and Dramatic Academy in New York; he continued to write and produce. He died in 1995.

Philip Burton is old enough to be your father and, in many ways, he instructs you as a father would his son. He craves a protégé to replace Owen Jones, who won a scholarship to RADA, the Royal Academy for the Dramatic Arts, in London. He joined the Royal Air Force as a fighter pilot and died in the Battle of Britain in 1940. So your arrival is more than a slice of good fortune: it is an answer to his prayers.

If anything, you, young Jenkins, have even more potential than Jones. Under Philip Burton's tutelage, you learn to use your voice in a tympanic way, broadening your range and developing a style of delivery that is somewhere between Tom Jones and Vincent Price. It becomes a voice that can bring gravitas to the most flippant dialog. At times, you will recite Shakespeare while standing on the hills above Port Talbot. This is brilliant tuition for theatrical roles. In the process, Burton will help you refine your accent. You spoke only Welsh until you were ten. Those who know the effect Philip Burton is having on you, smile when they see you playing Professor Higgins in your school's production of Shaw's *Pygmalion*. Your schoolmaster is something of a real life Professor Higgins to your Eliza Doolittle.

You are invited to play in one of Philip Burton's own plays called *Youth at the Helm*, which is broadcast on BBC Radio. You and Burton grow closer and he develops a strong affection for you. So strong that he wants to adopt you as his son. There is also an expedient reason for this. Philip Burton supports you in every way he can, helping you gain an offer to study at Oxford; he believes you stand a better chance of acceptance if you are his adoptive son. Bureaucracy prevents you doing this but you agree to change your family name to his, at first just for stage purposes, then legally by deed poll. For all intents and purposes, at the age of eighteen, you are Richard Burton.

There are myths about Richard Burton: philandering, hard-drinking, self-destructive Celtic artist in the mold of Dylan Thomas but with the looks of a Trojan king. He escaped the clutches of his ancestry but never quite shrugged the curse of his forebear: he drank heroically for all but short, temporary periods in a life that was always disorderly, often magisterial, but frequently pathetic. Yet even damaged, frail, and aging, he had a voice that would dignify the poorest of scripts—and there were many of these in his career, particularly over the final few years of his life.

After his discharge from the military in 1947 (28 months after the end of the war), Burton, as he was then officially known, restarted his acting career, picking up a few parts in plays, then making his film debut as a shepherd in *The Last Days of Dolwyn*, a tiny budget revenge drama released in 1949, its title changed to *Women of Dolwyn* for the American market. Also in the cast was an extra, Sybil Williams, a girl from the Welsh valleys, also hoping to pursue a professional career in acting. She and Burton called each other "boot" in the way couples today might address each other as "babe": boot is a Welsh-accented abbreviation of beautiful. They had a short courtship and married in 1949.

Sybil continued her acting for only a short while. She appeared in a West End drama and even in a 1951 Stratford-upon-Avon season: she played Lady Mortimer in *Henry IV, Part 1*, speaking her lines in Welsh. Her husband played Prince Hal. She can still be heard in the classic BBC Radio production of Dylan Thomas's *Under Milk Wood* in 1954, in which she played the dressmaker Myfanwy Price. The production can be heard at: http://bit.ly/1hitftX (accessed September 2015). But when her husband's career started to take off, she abandoned her own acting aspirations to follow Burton's star and to raise their two daughters. In the early 1950s, the couple moved to Hampstead, London, not far from where Elizabeth Taylor was born.

Sybil Burton, as she became, was a model of discretion and, for the fourteen years she was married, resigned herself to being the wife of a prolific womanizer: according to one biographer, Tom Rubython, Burton averaged three bouts of extramarital sex per week. On Rubython's 2011 account, the faithlessness started the day after Burtons' wedding when the then seventeen-year-old Claire Bloom became part of a kind of *ménage à trois*. Richard Burton's affair with Bloom, with whom he acted in the 1953 production of *Hamlet* at London's Royal Victoria Theatre (better known as the Old Vic) and the 1959 film *Look Back in Anger*, endured for several years, establishing an arrangement to which his wife seems to have been resigned. Sybil never threatened, less still filed for divorce, and was eventually prompted to do so by Burton himself. Burton, it seems, was a charmer; winningly funny when drunk, forcefully magnetic when reciting; he frequently beguiled audiences with his impromptu orations in pubs and at parties. Burton radiated what might pass as charisma touched by a boyish irresponsibility; he became a virtual absentee parent to his two children.

During his season at Stratford, Burton distinguished himself as a possible heir to Laurence Olivier, then regarded as the finest living Shakespearean actor (though not by Burton: in his diaries, he writes, "Dear Larry, my dear, a Lord yet. I mean it's absurd. He's practically a dwarf. He has the most contrived voice, all affectations. And that vulgar streak in him is shaming", p. 512 in *The Richard Burton Diaries*, edited by Chris Williams in 2012). Olivier was in his mid-forties, when the 26-year-old Burton impressed as Prince Hal and attracted interest from Hollywood. Twentieth Century Fox offered him a part opposite Olivia de Havilland in a film version of Daphne du Maurier's novel *My Cousin Rachel* (1952). During filming in Hollywood, Burton found himself at a party, as usual slightly the worse for wear after drinking, and doing his familiar shtick; Thomas recitals, Shakespeare declamations, and so on. The party was at the home of Stewart Granger. Also at the party was Elizabeth Taylor, then aged twenty and married to Michael Wilding. She did not apparently register on his radar. Perhaps he was too preoccupied: he was seeing Jean Simmons, wife of the party's host. The relationship with Bloom was still live too. And he had various other women on retainers. Once a callow provincial from the Welsh valleys, Burton seems to have adapted well to the voluptuary environment of Hollywood.

The arrival of his wife and eldest daughter in Hollywood made no difference to his carousing. For the most part, Sybil seems to have been indifferent. Only on one occasion did Sybil make a scene: when her husband kissed Simmons long and passionately in public while she was in the same room. Sybil erupted, whacking Burton across the face and storming out. Her humiliation was not so much because her husband was having affairs, nor even that his infidelities were well-known; but because he tried to demonstrate that he could simply disregard his wife's feelings in public. His relationship with Bloom came to an end in 1957 (at least temporarily) when she discovered he was sleeping with American actor Susan Strasberg, nine years her junior, and, perhaps creepily, with a resemblance to a younger Bloom.

Burton's initial foray in Hollywood was productive professionally too. He was nominated for an Academy Award for his performance and quickly rewarded with another film part in *The Desert Rats* (1953), a wartime drama featuring James Mason as Field Marshal Rommel (Burton crossed paths with the Desert Fox once more in 1971's *Raid on Rommel*, when his adversary was played by Wolfgang Preiss). His third Hollywood film was in the sword and sandals genre: *The Robe* (1953) was a box office success, grossing $17 million on a budget of $5 million and was, as we have noted, instrumental in securing Burton the role of Mark Antony in *Cleopatra*.

Flushed with success, Burton and his family returned to London to make what remains his most lasting dramatic impact. In 1953 and 1954, he appeared at the Old Vic to play *Hamlet* and *Coriolanus*. The critics rhapsodized over Burton, then approaching his thirtieth birthday and perhaps his artistic peak. For a while, it seemed like Burton had scratched an itch by going to Hollywood, making a couple of movies and then returning to his natural role as an actor in the tradition of Ralph Richardson, or John Gielgud who played Hamlet more than 500 times. But idealism did not figure high on Burton's motivational hierarchy: money did.

Like many successful figures who have bootstrapped their way out of humble origins, material wealth was a consuming motivation. Burton made no secret of his priority: he wanted to make as much money as he could. Some suspected a Mephistophelean offer when Hollywood beckoned a second time. Burton would sacrifice his dramatic soul if he succumbed to money. But succumb he did. Burton was no Van Gogh, Hemingway or Brian Wilson, all tormented by their own creativity and continually striving for some sort of artistic perfection: he was happy to do whatever it took to earn and become one of the highest paid actors in the world. When he eventually succeeded in this venture, it was due in no small part to his association with Taylor rather than an honest recognition of his talent.

Burton had heard the traducers before: after his stunning debut at Stratford, he welcomed the advances of Hollywood and had no hesitation in heading west. Artistic purity was all very fine, but the son of a Welsh miner, who has experienced rather than just read about social deprivation, has material prerequisites. Burton bought houses for all of his siblings and put brother Ifor on his personal payroll.

Burton strapped on the sandals once more when he played *Alexander the Great* (1956), no doubt intended as an extension of his great Shakespearean roles. Like Hamlet and Coriolanus, the enigmatic King of Macedon, conqueror of Persia, Egypt, Syria, and founder of the city of Alexandria, had a life that was the stuff of legend. The film itself was not, like the stories surrounding the Shakespeare figures, a tragedy, though it was not a box office success either, leaving Burton with a doubtful reputation, as Michael Munn reflected in 2008: "The word in Hollywood was that Richard Burton was box office poison."

Claire Bloom played Barsine, Alexander's mistress. While not a proponent of method acting, Burton seems to have favored the technique in this particular aspect of his preparations. Many commentators have noted his penchant for rehearsing his onscreen sexual encounters with what were then called "leading ladies." He played opposite Bloom again in the British film of John Osborne's play *Look Back in Anger* (1959). Her relationship with Burton was a sporadic affair and, at the start of filming they were in an "off" phase, which soon switched to "on." It was during the making of this film, she discovered him with Strasberg. Six years later, they would appear together for the final time in the film *The Spy Who Came In From The Cold*. By that time, Burton was married to Elizabeth Taylor.

Some marveled at his wife's abundant tolerance; or was it weakness? Burton's indelicate promiscuity was an open secret; not only did everyone know about it, everyone knew his wife knew too. It provoked no ire from Sybil. So why did she accept or endure it? Burton was good-natured, and not just in his sexual favors; he provided for his wife and his daughters amply. Perhaps Burton himself was not the only one to trade with Mephistopheles. Sybil lived a well-upholstered life, her every material comfort provided. She kept a low profile and attracted little interest while all the media were trained on Burton. The situation, unbearable as it may strike outsiders, was, it seems, sufficiently rewarding for her to remain in it. Nor did her husband ever agitate for a divorce.

Practically every writer on Burton buys into the precept "Men want sex, women want relationships" and depicts him as a roué, debauchee and serial seducer of women, usually neglecting the roles of his various seducees in the liaisons. Often, they were married women, like Bloom (who first married in 1959), Simmons (first married 1950) and, later of course, Taylor. So it is misleading to imagine the skirt-chasing Lothario as unassisted: his partners seem to have submitted enthusiastically to the dalliances, perhaps themselves representatives of a kind of liberation that was, in the late 1960s, to take shape as a political and social movement.

Burton's fervent pursuit of sex with married women was more than matched by his pursuit of being inebriated: he prosecuted both pursuits with equal zeal, often amazing his colleagues with his spry early morning appearances on set after a night of serious alcohol abuse. Even more amazing was his capacity to remember his lines word perfect. Nor did age seem to wither this: right into his forties and even fifties, he could get roaring drunk but still hit his mark and nail his lines.

Periodically, he went on the wagon, but, unlike Taylor, he never checked into rehab, though he did spend six weeks in a hospital recovering from an alcohol-related condition. Unlike today, when the whiff of scotch on somebody's breath at the wrong time of day is enough to designate them as having a dependency and in need of help, drinking functioned in Burton's heyday as a method of validating masculinity. "Drink was ... proof of machismo in a world where it mattered to be a man," wrote Burton biographer Melvyn Bragg in 1989 (p. 571). It sounds facile, but in the 1950s, drinking was a constituent part of a man's social identity and, in Burton's case, something of a motif, as distinct as his womanizing and his association with Taylor. But there were times when Burton had the self-discipline to stay sober, even if for only limited periods.

In 1957, Burton and his wife moved to the small Swiss village of Céligny, near Geneva. He bought a family villa, which remained his property and, officially, his home until his death. "Officially," that is, for tax purposes. Britain's Inland Revenue (the tax collecting authority; now Her Majesty's Revenue & Customs) rules dictated that someone could spend a maximum of 90 days on UK soil in any given year without paying tax in Britain. Switzerland's tax system was less punitive than either the UK's or the USA's. Mephistopheles might again have brought his influence to bear: the relocation effectively put paid to his stage career in London or Stratford. Shortly before his death he was planning to reemerge in an English production of *Hamlet*, though this never materialized. When his natural father, Dic, died in 1957, aged eighty-one, Burton did not return to Wales for the funeral.

At this stage, Burton was thirty-two and drinking incontinently. He had started seeing Strasberg, making it seem that his marriage vows with Sybil had now become little more than a tax-efficient covenant. Not quite so: within months of moving to Switzerland, Sybil gave birth to a second daughter. It was Burton's. Professionally, he focused on Hollywood, featuring in mainly forgettable films, but interspersing his roles with the occasional project that kept his thespian credentials intact. For example, *Look Back in Anger* and a lead part in BBC Television's production of *A Subject of Scandal and Concern* (1960). Then came an offer that would change the direction of his career.

After the success of the musical *My Fair Lady*, based on George Bernard Shaw's *Pygmalion*, the writers Alan Jay Lerner and Frederick Loewe turned their hand to creating a stage musical of T.H. Whites' tetralogy *The Once and Future King* (1958), which is about the legendary King Arthur and his exploits with the likes of Guinevere, Merlin, Sir Lancelot, and knights of the round table. The show's title was taken from the place where Arthur held his court *Camelot*. The term's associations with glittering romance and lofty ideals lent it a special resonance at a time when John F. Kennedy stood ready to become the youngest man ever to be elected US President (at forty-three). A staunch supporter of civil rights, the handsome Democrat seemed to herald a new age in American politics. His wife Jacqueline Kennedy (as she then was) actually used the term after seeing the musical and the word Camelot became forever linked with the Kennedy era. While Jacqueline meant the comparison to be positive, highlighting the hope and potential ushered in with the inauguration, it is actually rooted in the tale of a weak and cuckolded leader. One aspect of the plot is the adulterous romance between Arthur's queen, Guinevere, and Sir Lancelot. (Kennedy, as became clear years later, was in the same class as Burton when it came to philandering.)

While Burton had no history in musicals, the idea of his playing an English king (Camelot is thought to have been built in Chester, in northwest England, in the fifth or sixth century AD), not unlike Shakespeare's Lear except with a few good tunes, was not so ridiculous. Certainly Burton had the pomp and solemnity of a king; but did he have the voice? The *Boston Globe* thought so. "The timbre of his baritone made the lyrics of Alan Jay Lerner sound more like Tennyson or Mallory [sic]," the paper recalled its original review in 1984 (p. 1). Judge for yourself at http://bit.ly/1pLKxiE

(accessed September 2015). "How to handle a woman" was Burton's *pièce de résistance*. "Simply love her," is the song's prescription, by the way.

Burton stayed off the alcohol, at least during rehearsals. Once the run had started, he resumed his more familiar habits. Julie Andrews, who also played in the show, was apparently oblivious to the change: even after drinking up to a bottle of vodka, Burton was on-point. The show opened to mixed reviews, but had a commercially successful Broadway run after opening in Toronto and Boston. Sybil and the two children followed him to the USA. It was a bounteous appointment for Burton: he was paid $4,000 per week plus a percentage of box office receipts. It was bounteous in another sense too. Burton rendezvouzed with M'el Dowd, who was also in *Camelot*. But, soon after settling into Manhattan, he discovered Jim Downey's Steak House. "The place was full of young actresses and chorus girls and Burton had the pick of them," wrote Gene Lees in 2005. Burton's head was turned. "M'el Dowd evidently had been replaced. Burton was frequently seen in Downey's with Pat Tunder a blond [sic] and beautiful dancer from the Copacabana" (p. 201).

Camelot gave Burton "a level of public exposure in the USA (including an appearance on the *Ed Sullivan Show*) that he had not enjoyed since 1953," reflects Chris Williams, editor of *The Richard Burton Diaries* (p.9), alluding to the year when *The Robe* and *The Desert Rats* were released. Remember how, after *Alexander the Great*, Burton was regarded as toxic by Hollywood. On Broadway, it was a different matter. In 1961, Burton won a prestigious Tony (New York Drama Critics' Circle award). Unlikely as it would have seemed when he was playing at Stratford-upon-Avon or the Old Vic, Burton reached the apogee of his career to date in a Broadway musical.

Christine Norden also featured in Burton's life. She was an actor, born in Sunderland in England's northeast, and had been in several British movies before transferring in 1960 to Broadway where she played in the musical *Tenderloin*, the show named after a red-light district in Manhattan. She achieved notoriety in 1967 when she became the first person to go topless in the comedy *Scuba Duba*. While writers on Burton often refer to his "conquests," in Norden's case it appears Burton was the conquered party. Her own dance card bore the names of several illustrious stars, including Ava Gardner.

Burton's seemingly invulnerable marriage had endured since 1949 and Sybil had never, it appears, felt threatened by Burton's sexual partners. She seemed to think the marriage was like an elastic band that would resume a normal shape despite being stretched. When the elastic band eventually snapped in 1963, it was an unpleasant surprise for her. But, rude awakenings often have favorable consequences. Sybil would remain in the USA with her daughters and, in an astonishing career volte-face in 1965, open a nightclub called Arthur in New York City. (The name of the club is thought to have been inspired by a line from the Beatles' 1964 film *A Hard Day's Night*:

asked by a reporter, "What would you call that hairstyle you're wearing?" George Harrison replies, "Arthur.") The club would quickly become a haunt of celebrities and fashionistas. The resident band was known as the Wild Ones and, in 1966, Sybil would marry the band's lead singer Jordan Christopher, in the process discarding the name that had, by the mid-1960s become indivisible from "Taylor." Sybil Christopher, as she would be known, had a child with her new husband and revisited her theatrical beginnings, founding the Bay Street Theater, at Long Island's Sag Harbor. For a while she also worked as a literary agent. She would die in 1996.

In 1960 Federico Fellini's film *La Dolce Vita* disclosed what was for Americans and British a different kind of world: Rome. In particular Via Vittorio Veneto (often abbreviated to Via Veneto), a famously elegant, expensive, and fashionable street where those who can afford it congregate to drink, eat, and fraternize. One of the film's central characters is an enthusiastic freelance photojournalist named Paparazzo. Fellini took the name from a character named Coriolano Paparazzo who appeared in the English nineteenth-century writer George Gissing's travel book *By the Ionian Sea: Notes of a Ramble in Southern Italy*. The character was a restaurateur rather than a journalist, but the name had resonance for Fellini who believed it evoked thoughts of annoying sandflies that make an annoying buzzing noise. The Italian for sandflies is *pappataci*. The journalist was intended to be like a small insect, an unwelcome bloodsucker that irritates and transmits diseases and never sits still long enough to be swatted. The plural of paparazzo is paparazzi, a term that is familiar to every reader.

In the Fellini film, Paparazzo earns a living from his pictures and scours the streets of Rome in search of newsworthy stories of celebrities and socialites. Where they do not exist, he creates them. He goads his subjects into reacting, threatening, often striking at him. At the critical moment, he snaps and gets his story. While he was Fellini's construction, he represented a new generation of Italian journalists, who were more aggressive and invasive than their predecessors: they prowled surreptitiously before leaping into view in places they were least welcome. They showed scant regard for others' privacy and accessed all areas for their own purposes. They did not wait for stories to arrive: they operated more like search parties in the westerns, hunting down their prey.

Italy was relatively inexpensive at the time, so many films were made at Rome's Cinecittà studios where production costs were lower than in Hollywood or London. The arrival of movie stars from the USA, Britain, and elsewhere in Europe provided Italian journalists with a perfect environment. Some actors, like Audrey Hepburn ignored them completely. Franco Nero famously struck an uninvited journalist. The Swedish actor Anita Ekberg should have won a prize for originality with one of her responses: in a move worthy of Robin Hood, she pointed a bow and arrow at a journalist's crotch. Actually, the image of a fuming Ekberg emerging, bow in hand, in stocking feet from her chauffeur-driven Fiat Seicento is still viewable at http://bit.ly/1h3N5ZC (accessed September 2015).

The historian Stephen Gundle argued that La Dolce Vita was, in many ways, liminal. "The movie marked a transition in the way stars were perceived" he propounded in 2002. "In the United States studio publicity departments were accustomed to exercising complete control over the flow of news about stars, presenting flawless images that stressed their admirable qualities" (p. 115). Pictures and stories emerging from Rome appeared decidedly real compared to the airbrushed visions of Hollywood.

Gundle went on: "In Rome, where there could be no such control, the stars seemed real and were often shown to be flawed" (p. 115). They also seemed to chime with the kinds of tales leaked into the public domain by Confidential and lesser scandal sheets. The stars behaved a lot like the audiences who followed them: they drank, often quite a lot, they lost their tempers, frequently and viciously, and they were fully capable of making complete fools of themselves, as when the previously-mentioned Ekberg—a favorite target of photojournalists—took a dip in the largest and most famous Baroque fountain in Rome, Fontana di Trevi—as I will recount shortly.

While paparazzi were thought to be the bane of socialites and actors, Gundle suspects that some of the purportedly candid shots "were not spontaneous" at all and owed something to Hollywood-style staging. "Still, the genuine conflicts that arose between celebrities and press photographers around the Via Veneto lent an air of authenticity," wrote Gundle (p. 113).

Actors in the late 1950s/early 1960s were used to intrusive journalists, and journalists had no respect for American protocols. In contrast to their deferential counterparts in the US and elsewhere, the Roman journos did not depend on studios, publicists, agents or anyone else; they were truly independent operators.

So who was the first paparazzo? Even before the word came into common currency, there must have been photojournalists who carried cameras with them as part of their daily luggage and snapped opportunely when their subjects least expected and mostly resisted being photographed. Erich Salomon is a likely candidate: born in Berlin in 1886, Salomon received a doctorate in law from the University of Munich but practiced only briefly. His career as a freelance photographer began in 1928, when he bought an Ermanox, one of the first miniature cameras equipped with a high-speed lens, which enabled him to photograph in dim light. He cunningly concealed the camera in an attaché case and, on one occasion, under his hat, and secretly took photographs of a sensational murder trial. The resulting pictures sold so well to news periodicals that he became a fulltime photojournalist. Salomon died in Auschwitz in 1944.

Salomon effectively changed the relationship between the photographer and the subject: no longer a voluntary engagement, the interaction was one-sided, dictated in large part only by the person taking the picture. Salomon's slyly covert methods meant subjects often did not even realize they were in focus. The power swung further toward the photographer after the development of the telephoto lens. The innovation dated back to the 1920s, but was used by the Germans for surveillance during the Second World War. Only its prohibitively high price prevented its widespread use after the war, but by the late 1950s, the telephoto lens for use on 35mm cameras was in regular production and became affordable. So, in a way, the lens connected modern paparazzi to war photographers.

The inspiration for Fellini's character was the shot of Anita Ekberg in Fontana di Trevi, taken by photographer, Pierluigi Praturlon, and published in the magazine *Tempo Illustrato* in 1958. This was not, strictly speaking, a paparazzi venture: Ekberg had spent the evening with Praturlon and decided to cool off by climbing into the fountain. Fellini recreated the scene in *La Dolce Vita* (In 1995, German supermodel Claudia Schiffer also waded into the fountain for an ad campaign for designer Valentino). According to John Hooper, writing in 2006, the scene was truly iconic, marking "a turning point in postwar Europe . . . while Ekberg's low-cut, dark evening dress may look back to the formal 50s, her insouciant transgression points unmistakably ahead, into the subversive 60s."

Yet the transgression was not so much Ekberg's or indeed that of any other subject who came into zoom lens range; the act that went against established codes of conduct was not even confined to the photojournalists who defied the tacit agreements between the media and stars. The transgressors were readers, viewers, audiences, the people who consumed the output of paparazzi. These were the real violators. Reason? They were not outraged, insulted, or embarrassed by the representations that proliferated in popular magazines and newspapers. Their illusions may have been shattered by narratives that disclosed celebrities as hapless fools, mindless drunks, obnoxious assailants, and indiscreet lovers. But what replaced them became more satisfying. And the tendency for stars to rebel against the intrusion of the lens made the new images even more satisfying.

The French called them *images volées* or "stolen images" and they became the paparazzo's stock-in-trade: stars staggering from bars, politicians dancing gauchely, models reclining on the deck of a yacht—practically any image in which the subject was unaware was valuable. And there was additional value if the subject objected, as was the case when Tazio Secchiaroli earned his reputation as an "assault photographer" on the night of August 14, 1958, during the *Ferragosto*, or Feast of the Assumption, holiday in Rome. Secchiaroli took a picture of King Farouk of Egypt, who had been deposed a few years earlier, sitting in a café with two women, neither of them his wife. Farouk, a redoubtable playboy tried to break

Secchiaroli's camera, while another photographer, Umberto Guidotti, caught the moment. Secchiaroli also snared notable prey when he captured the afore-mentioned Ava Gardner and Anthony Franciosa kissing at Bricktop's, an American nightclub. Franciosa was married to Shelly Winters. There was another physical confrontation.

Secchiaroli's masterwork featured Anita Ekberg and her husband, Anthony Steel, a British actor, who was visibly inebriated as they left Vecchia Roma, another nightclub. When Steel saw the baiting photographer, he lunged at him drunkenly, providing Secchiaroli with perfect raw material. The beauty of this sequence of images is that they required no captions: every picture told a story. The paparazzi of the time strove for stolen images, but images that conveyed more than a moment: they provided a gripping account of connected events; the photojournalists were storytellers. The difference between them and earlier photographers was that their stories were rarely the ones their subjects wished to be told.

There was also an antagonistic element to a relationship that appeared on the surface to be symbiotic: both journalist and subject benefited, even though the subjects may not have realized it in the immediate aftermath of a picture's publication. The antagonism was summed up by Secchiaroli: "We photographers were all poor starving devils and they had it all—money, fame, posh hotels" (quoted in Boxer, 1998).

They were not starving for long. "Two things happened after Tazio Secchiaroli and his friends started to make real money from their photographs of the rich and famous," wrote George Porkari in 2013. First, celebrities realized they were now the "the subject of constant surveillance for profit" and, second "a bond was made between publicity departments and paparazzi to stage events." This was an attempt to co-opt renegade journalists into the system. An early example of this came in 1968 when Italian actor Sophia Loren felt harassed by photographers trying to get pictures of her newly born son. Loren secretly arranged a meeting with Secchiaroli at a park where he took supposedly spontaneous pictures of the two of them playing. Loren profited from the exposure and Secchiaroli got the most valuable pictures of the time.

Compared to the anarchically edgy pictures from Europe, the homegrown products of America must have seemed as dull as the neighbors' holiday photographs. Some mavericks, like the man formerly known as Ascher Fellig, or Weegee (played by Joe Pesci in the 1992 film *The Public Eye*) built a reputation following police cars and ambulances on emergency calls in the 1940s. But the journalist who most closely resembled the Europeans was Ron Galella, whose significant innovation was stealth. Rather than confront subjects, Galella pursued them invisibly, sometimes staking out their homes, or tracking them from distance. He specialized in celebrities of the 1960s and 1970s, his most famous and most reluctant subject being Jacqueline Onassis, formerly Kennedy, the widow of the deceased President. Onassis took him to court twice for harassment; the first case ended in a restraining order of 150 feet being placed on Galella and the second with him having to give up photographing her for life. Later subjects of paparazzi attention were to do likewise. Amy Winehouse, Halle Berry, and Pippa Middleton were among several people who secured legal protection against invasive paps. In 2009, then Governor of California Arnold Schwarzenegger signed an anti-paparazzi bill that made it easier to sue media outlets that published photos that invaded celebrities' privacy.

There was more than a hint of delusion in Galella's obsessive pursuit of Onassis. Even sixteen years after Onassis's death (she died in 1994), Galella claimed: "She liked being pursued" (quoted in Babb, 2010). Porkari detects "envious complicity" in Galella's practice, "like a teenager who wants to join the party but can only watch the adults drinking and flirting from a distance." That may have been true when journalists were ancillary. Or when popular culture was less pictorial. But the value of photojournalists grew markedly in the 1960s. Some paparazzi's earnings rivaled that of their subjects. They may have skulked like teenagers, but there was no envy; they could earn enough to drink and flirt with the same gusto as the adults they were watching.

Earlier in the book, I quoted from Charles Winick's 1961 American study, a study that was minor in tone but major in its relevance. "These respondents enjoyed realizing that the celebrity was an ordinary mortal with human failings," reported Winick (p. 331). Winick's focus was *Confidential*, which he maintains, "made a frontal assault on the celebrity system." That "system" dispensed idealized images of the stars and, according to some, the America they represented. In Europe another prong to the media-instigated assault was in operation. Both, to quote Winick again, "represented the recognition of the public's interest in learning about celebrities and in learning about their less admirable as well as their more visible facets" (p. 334).

There has been no escape from the paparazzi. Today, they continue "generating evidence of celebrities in newsworthy (and publicity rich) contexts, whether in terms of scandal, romance or action settings," wrote Kim McNamara in 2011, noting that, the days of freelancers like Secchiaroli were numbered when international news agencies began to specialize in entertainment-based news (p. 515).

The impact of the paparazzi can scarcely be exaggerated: it is difficult to think of a single aspect of contemporary culture that has not in some way been touched by their devilish divination. Magazines that "used to peddle a fantasy of loveliness," as Virginia Hefferman put it in 2007, "now traffic in dismantling the same fantasy" (p. 20). Hefferman discerned their effect on her own relationship with celebrities: "The magazines taught me to care, and mistake the new unkempt images for intimacy" (p. 20). Intimacy at distance, as I have called it earlier in the book.

The paparazzi instigated what eventually became a cultural shift; but their coruscating arrival secreted menace: after seventeen years of trailing Princess Diana and, in the process, changing her status from a nursery nurse into arguably the most captivating being on the planet, paparazzi were instrumental in her death. The speeding Mercedes in which she died on August 31 in 1997 was being pursued by paparazzi. "She may have incited the paparazzi by teasing them earlier in August with news of a 'big surprise,'" surmised Ronald Bishop in 1999 (p.103).

Diana was perhaps the most precious paparazzi subject of all. She was preceded by Princess Grace of Monaco, Jacqueline Onassis—the first figure outside the Hollywood orbit to transfix paparazzi—and, of course, Elizabeth Taylor. When captured by paparazzi, these women were like lava lamps, producing a constantly changing pattern or sequence of elements. This, I believe, is what Porkari has in mind when he submits: "They [paparazzi] had intuitively discovered . . . something that artists, poets and philosophers were dealing with." He explains: "an Abyss that is as much a part of the internal psyche as it is a part of 'reality.'"

This is puzzlingly expressed, but suggests, I think, that paparazzi gave consumers the license to interpret images in multiple ways: in a single shot there were many possible meanings. Anthony J. Ferri offered a similar idea when he wrote of a "'Pseudo environment' made up of the images in our heads of the world outside. These external images are the product of others' interpretations, or 'opinions' of events. The media help produce these images," submitted Ferri in 2010 (p. 407). We, the audience, became part of the performance; and I use performance in a similar way to Scott Duchesne, to describe "the interaction of fan and celebrity" (p. 27). While Duchesne, writing in 2010, does not expand, I presume he means that all parties are necessary players in the same part-improvised drama. Paparazzi did not so much close the space between fans and stars, but brought them together in the same performance. We became players. And stars no longer had control over their own reputations.

In September 1961, Burton arrived in Rome, the city that had 2,000 years before played host to Cleopatra. He was to play the role of Mark Antony in a film that had been in production for over a year but had only a few minutes of usable material. Stephen Boyd had already shot some sequences as the legendary Roman general, but the production delays and change of location clashed with his schedule and he, like his fellow player Peter Finch (playing Caesar) were forced to pull out. Burton was effectively a substitute. Rex Harrison stepped in as Caesar after Laurence Olivier had declined the role.

Twentieth Century Fox identified Burton as a likely Mark Antony, but had to buy him out of his successful Broadway run in *Camelot*. It cost 20th Century Fox $50,000. Burton was lured by $250,000, plus $1,000 per week expenses and transportation for him, his wife and two daughters. Sybil and the girls shared a villa and household staff with Roddy McDowall, who had also transferred from *Camelot*. McDowall, like Taylor, had been a child star;

in fact, he had appeared with her in *Lassie* in 1943. Their home would be on the Appian Way, the principal road southward from Rome in classical times (named after Appius Claudius Caecus, the magistrate, actually). Pat Tunder, the dancer who had been Burton's main romantic interest during *Camelot* was the third person associated with the Broadway production to relocate to Rome, though her arrival was understandably played down.

Burton's biographer Melvyn Bragg believes that, at this point in his life: "He was on top of the world. After this he thought he would go back on to the English stage. The *Cleopatra* money would finally secure his future" (p. 191).

The paparazzi treated Burton as a hunter on safari might treat a wild boar: why bother when there was seriously big game in the territory? Otherwise there would surely have been headlines like ESCLUSIVO: BURTON FA SESSO CON LA BALLERINA. Instead, he was allowed to maintain what must have been, for him, a satisfying arrangement initially established in New York: "What's that moving in the bushes over there?" "Oh, just a boar. Don't waste your ammo; let him go. We're after a big cat."

All the same, it would have been interesting to see how Burton would have reacted had the paparazzi got on his case: "I'm an artist, a Shakespearean actor, better than Olivier," he might have declaimed indignantly. To which a paparazzo might have replied: "But all the world's a stage, and all the men and women merely players. So just keep playing and we'll keep watching." In the event, all paparazzi eyes were trained on Taylor, her popularity imperiled by her liaison with Fisher, but now in the throes of a restoration after a brush with death. She was the only game in town, so to speak.

Burton had three personae. One: the poor Welsh kid who clawed his way out of poverty to become one of the world's best-known purveyors of the Bard of Avon's work. Two: the womanizing sot with more conquests than Genghis Khan. Three: part of a love affair that destroyed two marriages, turned a film production into a conflation of art and life and heralded the arrival of new kind of celebrity culture.

So you have arrived in Italy. I hope you know what you are doing: this film *Cleopatra* is already a car crash. The budget changes every month; it was supposed to be made in London; it has already burned off Finch and Boyd, whom you are replacing. Why would you want to do another Roman epic, anyway? Remember what you said about *Alexander the Great*? No? Let me remind you: "I knew all epics are crap, but I felt this one could be different. How could I have been so wrong?" I suppose the quarter of a million you are getting paid helped you make your decision.

So far, you have managed to keep your personal life out of the glare of the media. People in the business know you like a drink. And you make no secret of your amorous ways. I think showbusiness types turn a blind eye to this kind of thing. The media do not regard it as any of their business either. But you should be on guard: the Italians are different: they seem to have an appetite for this kind of stuff, anything that could lead to a scandal. You may be hard-pressed to keep a lid on your relationship with Pat Tunder, especially as she is moving to Rome for the duration of the film. They still call it adultery over here. As a matter of fact: it *is* adultery.

Paparazzi, as the photojournalists in Rome are called, are tenacious: do not expect them to treat you with the respect you have become accustomed to in Britain and the USA. You might also be a tad more cautious when you discuss Elizabeth Taylor. This is the biggest movie star in the world, remember. I know you met her briefly several years ago, but that was before she became Hollywood royalty. She has been married four times, has three children and she is not yet thirty. She has many gay male friends too, by the way. Make of this what you may. One of them, Roddy McDowall, is scheduled to play in *Cleopatra*. Montgomery Clift too is a good friend of hers and he is gay. Rock Hudson? Well, it is known in the film industry though he has not declared he is gay. Maybe she likes gay men because she knows where she stands with them: they are friends without ulterior sexual motives. Straight men are understandably attracted to her: she has been called "the most beautiful woman in world" many, many times.

Unlike you, she has no private life to speak of. Her every move is sedulously chronicled by the media. Her late husband Michael Todd capitalized on this by teaching her how to be comfortable with her own public image. Other movie stars find this unmanageable, but Taylor seems to have aligned personal and public spheres: there seems nothing in her life that is not potentially consumable. That includes her husbands. She once radiated displeasure with the media, especially after her notorious interview with Hedda Hopper. That was shortly after Todd's funeral when she was habitually seen with Eddie Fisher. Now she seems as relaxed with the flashbulbs as you are with the Klieg lights. There is a whisper that she sits in front of the mirror rehearsing facial expressions, or "looks." Is this sickening narcissism or professional scrupulousness, or one and the same thing?

She is unlike other women you have known. Her confidence is as overwhelming as a hurricane: when asked to play in this film, she did not even bother walking to the phone, but instructed Fisher to demand a million. Imagine: a million dollars—for a woman! Even top male actors do not command that much. The best part is: she got it. This is a woman used to getting her own way. The habit must have started when she was an eleven-year-old making *National Velvet*, in which she rode a horse. After the movie was completed, she asked the producer if she could keep the horse. The request went all the way up the food chain to Louis B. Mayer, then the boss of MGM. She got the horse and later complained that it cost too much to keep. I wonder if she thinks of Fisher in the same way she thought about that horse.

Her publicity says she sleeps only with the men she marries. This provides a canopy of respectability and she is resolute about keeping this intact. She was vilified after her relationship with Fisher became known. "Once bitten, twice shy," is probably ringing in her ears.

It seems worth mentioning all this because there is a hint that you have been boasting Taylor will be another notch on your bedpost. She is a married woman with children and, by all accounts, will not take kindly to this *braggadocio*. And remember the part about her sleeping with only with the men she marries. You are already married and have children of your own. So this seems to rule you completely out. She also seems a little bit—how can I put this? -- *dangerous*. But given your record, you will probably need to discover this for yourself. After all, you are Richard Burton.

FIGURE 7 *Unaware of the presence of a paparazzo, Taylor rendezvouzed with Burton off the coast of Italy.*

Photo by Keystone/Hulton Archive/Getty Images.

7

Believing and wanting to believe

On January 13, 1962, Associated Press carried a report headlined CEIL CHAPMAN'S FASHIONS TURN TO DAYS OF CLEOPATRA. Chapman, a high-end fashion designer, who had made dresses for Grace Kelly, Marilyn Monroe, and Elizabeth Taylor was calling her fall collection "Daughters of the Nile," its inspiration being the upcoming *Cleopatra* (*Reading Eagle*, January 13, 1962, p. 9). Even today, when marketing for a film can start ten months before its theatrical release, the launch of a themed line of clothing while the film was still in production, would seem premature. Or prescient.

Six days before Chapman's fashion statement, Elizabeth Taylor came face to face with Richard Burton on the set of *Cleopatra*. It was the first time they had met since their chance encounter in 1952 at a party at Stewart Granger's house back when she was a contract player at MGM and married to Michael Wilding. While with Michael Todd, Taylor had actually been in the same room as Burton, though without speaking, on two occasions, at a London restaurant and a party in New York.

At the point of resumption of production Taylor had not appeared in any of the usable footage, which amounted only to about seven minutes anyway. Joseph Mankiewicz was now at the director's helm. He had seen earlier versions of the script and watched rough cuts of the early footage before deciding the entire project needed to be re-thought. Mankiewicz, it should be pointed out, was not an obvious choice for replacement director. His strengths lay in films driven by dialog and structured like plays, such as his *All About Eve*. Perhaps producer Walter Wanger was mindful of Mankiewicz's people management skills: he had finessed the egos of Taylor and Katharine Hepburn on *Suddenly Last Summer*, and Bette Davis on *All About Eve*. All the same, Mankiewicz's decision to accept what seemed a hopeless cause must have been motivated by money. At fifty-one, Mankiewicz was tempted by Wanger's offer: not only a salary but a $3 million fee for Figaro, a production company Mankiewicz co-owned. In other words, Fox offered him a chance to become seriously rich with one film.

Calamitous as Taylor's near-death experience and its aftermath had been for the production, it did have the benefit of affording Mankiewicz six months, which he spent rewriting the script. Its benefits for Taylor were more abundant: her reputation as a homewrecking nymphet had been replaced by a cross between an ailing princess and a plucky survivor. As Mankiewicz had not got any footage featuring Taylor, it made sense for him to dispose of the existing material and start the whole film from scratch. Thus began what was effectively a new production of *Cleopatra*.

The revised *Cleopatra* script was still a work-in-progress in January 1962. Once more, production was started with haste rather than speed. President Spyros Skouras wished to present his 20th Century Fox board of directors with a film that would save the studio, a studio with limited revenue streams and few other films in production. In fact, other films were canceled in order to divert funds to *Cleopatra*, by then effectively Taylor's show. Taylor requested to Skouras that Rex Kennamer, her personal physician, be added to the payroll. Skouras agreed and flew in Kennamer at a cost of $25,000. His sole duty was to take care of any ailment Taylor might have. Husband Eddie Fisher was also on a $150,000 salary essentially for making sure his wife got to work on time. Privately, Skouras, Wanger, and Peter Levathes, a legal advisor at 20th Century Fox, who was appointed by Skouras to the production team, entertained doubts about her physical ability to stand up to another period of filming. But Taylor, approaching her thirtieth birthday, was intimidating, and, as David Kamp points out in his 1998 *Vanity Fair* article, "in her presence they lost their resolve and genuflected."

Taylor's every request was accommodated. Wanger booked her a fourteen-room mansion in Rome called Villa Papa and had food flown in from New York especially for her. It was rumored that shooting schedules were timed so that her appearances did not clash with her period. Her justification was that, if she was playing the most beautiful woman in the world, she had to look her best.

There was a more pragmatic reason to bend over backward. Taylor, at this point, was not insurable. The film's insurer Lloyd's was so alarmed at her fragility, especially after the near-death encounter, that the firm instructed Wanger to replace her with Shirley MacLaine (who had been in *Around the World in 80 Days*) or even Marilyn Monroe (who would die in 1962). Wanger refused and persisted with Taylor, presumably mindful that the entire existence of 20th Century Fox rested on the film *Cleopatra* and the film rested on Elizabeth Taylor. It is no exaggeration to say Taylor became costlier by the day. Under the terms of her contract, she was, from November 17, 1961 on overtime, meaning that she was paid a weekly wage of $50,000 per week (some writers suggest the overtime rate began even earlier on August 1, but the point is that she had become an even bigger gamble than at first envisaged).

In his efforts to minimize the shooting schedule Mankiewicz directed by day and wrote the still-unfinished script by night, an exhausting routine that wrecked his health and rendered him dependent on medication, at least during the shooting and probably beyond. There was near-pandemonium when new actors arrived to find half-finished sets, incomplete wardrobes and a script that was being written only hours before filming. Burton, having arrived September 19, found himself idle and left to amuse himself by drinking.

Elementary oversights in the reconnaissance resulted in further delays and expenses. For example, live explosive mines from the Second World War were discovered at a beach at Torre Astura, where a gigantic replica of the ancient city of Alexandria was under construction. It took $22,000 to render the beach safe. Cinecittà had no facilities for processing Todd-AO (which had to be used, according to Taylor's stipulation), so rushes had to be sent to New York and returned before they could be viewed. The extravagant scale was sometimes manic: the Roman Forum was actually bigger than the real thing and, at $1.5 million wildly more expensive. At one point, the film needed so much steel tubing that there was a nationwide shortage that affected the Italian building industry. The expenses side of the balance sheet was loaded further by Fox's creative bookkeeping: with few other films in production, the Rome project was made to absorb out-payments from a miscellany of sources. And, of course, the petty larceny that afflicts any film production was expanded in *Cleopatra*.

So, as the cast re-assembled, augmented by some new actors and depleted by some others, the new production looked just as desultory, chaotic, and inefficient as its London-based predecessor. Only the weather was in its favor and even that threatened to join the mischief: an unseasonably wet fall in Italy meant several lost days of outdoor filming, leaving contracted actors such as Roddy McDowell, Hume Cronyn, and Martin Landau to languish while Fox paid them, respectively, $2,500, $5,000 and $850 per week.

Mr. and Mrs. Eddie Fisher were not a healthy couple when production of *Cleopatra* re-started. Fisher had, for all practical purposes, surrendered his singing career when he started a relationship with Taylor. The backlash against both of them had been severe, but she had weathered it and emerged as box office gold. He was still popularly regarded as her fulltime minder. This was not very far from the truth. Fisher had also incurred a dependency on methamphetamine, having been given shots by Max Jacobson, aka "Dr. Feelgood," who provided a similar service for, among others, John F. Kennedy, Tennessee Williams, and songwriter Alan Jay Lerner. Taylor herself was inured to meds, particularly painkillers and sedatives; she was also drinking. (Jacobson enjoyed a burst of popular currency in 2013, when the 1960s-set tv series *Mad Men* featured a character, "Dr. Shelly Hecht," apparently based on him.)

Burton arrived burdened with high expectation: he had been Mankiewicz's choice to replace Stephen Boyd as Mark Antony. Producer Spyros Skouras wanted someone more immediately recognizable. Burton had flickered briefly in Hollywood, but the stage was his natural environment and, as Wanger said, he "doesn't mean a thing at the box office" (quoted in Kamp, 1998). But, having yielded to Mankiewicz, Skouras and fellow skeptic Wanger agreed that he was a thorough professional, turned up on time, remembered his lines and was admired by his co-workers for his literary knowledge, barroom raconteur skills, and all-round charm.

Taylor ran into Burton before they started filming. She remembered the occasion: "The first day I saw Richard on the *Cleopatra* set . . . he sort of sidled over to me and said, 'Has anybody ever told you that you're a very pretty girl?'" It was trite, perhaps deliberately so. But it amused Taylor, mainly because it jarred with his reputation: "Here's the great lover, the great intellectual of Wales, and he comes out with a line like that," she laughed to Richard Meryman in 1964 (p. 80)

Burton was fresh and sober enough to comport himself decently on that occasion. By the time it came to shooting their scenes, he had lapsed somewhat. "The first day we worked together he had a hangover and was looking so vulnerable," Taylor recalls January 5, 1962. "He was trying to drink a cup of coffee and his hand was shaking, so I held the cup to his lips."

Burton had been wasted the night before; as indeed he was on most nights. But he was ready for his call and, fortified by a coffee, strode in front of the cameras to deliver his usual reliable performance. It is possible that Taylor had bumped into Burton earlier, although she had a well-documented habit of showing up only when absolutely necessary and Mankiewicz would not dare waste her time. The first time Taylor and Burton shared the camera, there were no lines: they just looked at each other. Retrospectively, members of the cast and crew have claimed "electricity" was in the air when the two appeared together. Taylor herself has admitted she was smitten at the outset. But Burton, six-and-a-half years her senior, never offered clues and, despite many accounts, Chris Williams' seems most plausible: "Quite what Burton's state of mind was at any given point in what was eventually a fifteen-month period when he hovered between his wife, his children and his lover is probably impossible to judge" (p. 10).

Initially, there was no melodrama. Yet a few things were known: (a) gossip circulated inside and outside the production; (b) Burton denied he was having an affair; (c) Burton was lying. In fact, he probably lied about Taylor: he was a braggart of the first order and, given his stalwart guardianship of his masculinity, may have fabricated stories to satisfy the prurient curiosity of his audience. The tales of his first encounters with Taylor are legion: in cars, behind scenery on sets, and so on. But neither party ever disclosed the moment they became lovers. Their companionship was clear to all: after acting their scenes, they would relax over lunch, often with several glasses of wine and liquor. They also spent many evenings evidently appreciating each other's company and the fulfillments of alcohol. But of course, Burton was living with Sybil and their two daughters in Rome *and* had Pat Tunder secreted not too far away. Sybil, given her insider knowledge of her husband, may have known about Tunder—and vice versa. But neither would have been privy to his incipient friendship with Taylor.

Apart from the two principals, the closest person to the machinations was Tunder herself. As the "other woman," she was strategically placed: Burton could not have deceived her into thinking he was anything but a married man with two children; so, when he installed her in Rome, she would have been fully aware of her status. Still, she must have been shaken when Burton truncated her Roman holiday and dispatched her back to the USA, where reporters waited. As the crescendo built, newspapers persisted and offered inducements for her firsthand account of events. Her refusal to disclose anything earned her the admiration of many, including syndicated columnist Dorothy Kilgallen, who, in 1963, wrote: "One of Richard Burton's past amours, showgirl Pat Tunder, is showing considerable taste by turning down big money offers to write the 'lowdown' on her romance with him" (*Toledo Blade*, June 24, 1963, p. 24).

Kilgallen went on: "Dickie [Burton] is displaying abominable manners with his statements for publication, which are his way of having sport with the press while insuring daily bulletins on his affair with Elizabeth Taylor." Her implication was that, far from shying away from the media, Burton actually wanted to orchestrate the coverage. This was mid-1963.

Six months later when Taylor announced plans to marry Burton, Tunder broke her silence, very briefly, and Kilgallen (in a separate article in 1964) conveyed her reaction through her newspaper column: "I wish him [Burton] all the happiness in the world—but not with her!" (p. 12). She was not referring to Sybil. Tunder sought near-zero visibility and refused to dish dirt on Burton, but she was evidently aggrieved at her hasty dispatch back to the US shortly after Burton had become ensorcelled by Taylor in early 1962.

Taylor's marital bond was much more brittle than Burton's. Remember: Fisher was Taylor's fourth husband and she had married him at a time when she must have been heartbroken by the loss of Michael Todd. Even those who challenge Taylor's overall sincerity must surely acknowledge the inexpressible sorrow, anguish, and perhaps desolation she must have experienced in the immediate aftermath of her husband's death. Todd died March 22, 1958. Taylor married Fisher May 12, 1959. The available evidence available suggests by January 1962, she had drifted away from Fisher to the point where she was receptive to Burton's advances.

Martin Landau recounts how he was in makeup at about 7:30 a.m., chatting to Taylor when Burton walked in and brazenly kissed her in a way that suggested their friendship had entered an intimate phase (in the documentary *Cleopatra: The Film That Changed Hollywood*, 2001). "I said to myself, 'Oh, my God.' They had not gone to their respective homes that night," recalled Landau, who played Rufio, one of Caesar's commanders. (The *Los Angeles Times'* Susan King recorded the incident in 2013)

Fisher arrived on set at about 11:00 a.m. and Sybil a half-hour later." This indicates that the affair was never more than perfunctorily secret. Even if Landau were a confidante of Burton's—which he was not—the makeup artists were present and would have witnessed the kiss. Landau did not specify the date of the gesture, but, the probability is that it was between January 22, when Taylor and Burton filmed their first scene and January 26, when Mankiewicz met with Wanger to share confidential information: "I have been sitting on a volcano all alone for too long, and I want to give you some facts you ought to know." He must have then paused for an intake of breath: "Liz and Burton are not just *playing* Antony and Cleopatra" (quoted in Kamp, 1998).

Today, a film producer, on hearing news such as this might cast eyes upward and whispered, "there *is* a god." In 1962, Wanger was probably apprehensive. There were several variables to consider. The first was: how secure is the studio? Hollywood was well versed at suppressing and releasing news to suit its own imperatives. Even gossip specialists like Hopper et al. relied on contacts. So news of an unsuitable relationship would not necessarily reach the light of day. But in Italy in the early 1960s, it might be more difficult to contain.

And what of the consequences? Taylor had rehabilitated her image and, at the same, was magic at the boxoffice. But would yet another misalliance, again with a married man with children, incite hatred all over again? And, if so, would that hurt or—improbable as it sounded—help boxoffice? Anyway, the whole affair could have fizzled out by the time the production wrapped. Burton already had two women in tow. He would probably claim bragging rights about ravishing another leading lady and then file under "T." Or he might not. There were too many incalculable elements that could and almost certainly would affect the fortunes of a film that was already looking hoodooed. But the meeting between director and producer was of only academic importance: neither could actually do anything that would stabilize what was set to become an unruly force. Having withstood inclement weather, a life-threatening illness, labor disputes, and too many other tribulations to list, the film now had a rogue relationship. And by rogue, I mean it was an aberrant and unpredictable presence, and possibly dangerous.

Whatever the content of the Mankiewicz-Wanger conversation, there was nothing of consequence they or their employers could do. As Anne Helen Petersen reflected in 2013: "Twentieth Century Fox couldn't force Taylor not to cheat. She was a freelance star. They couldn't force Burton not to seduce her. He too was freelance" (p. 56). It would not be long before they could not suppress the evidence either. "Because," as Petersen points out, "they were gallivanting in full view of dozens of Italian paparazzi."

In fact, they were not gallivanting: Taylor and Burton were, if anything, circumspect. Well, relatively; as circumspect as one can be, when kissing in full view of colleagues. But, Burton flirted coltishly with practically every good-looking woman he met. It was his way of endearing himself. Nothing wrong with that, the producers could have assured workers who had sensed a growing affection. That was just Burton being Burton. To an extent, they would have been right: Burton's penchant was well known and he was in the company of one of the most extravagantly beautiful women in the world. It would have been surprising, perhaps shocking, if he had *not* made a move on her. This, broadly speaking, was Mankiewicz's reaction: according to his son, the director "didn't try to stop it [the affair]" (quoted in Taraborrelli's 2006 biography, p. 186). Both Burton and Rex Harrison were "theater people," which meant they were reliable professionals who would turn up on time and never muff their lines. Mankiewicz's priority was getting the film finished rather than the gossip circulating around it.

It is impossible to determine for sure, but Taylor probably enjoyed, endured, tolerated or just experienced her unique status: that of being admired, loved, and revered and of being best known for deeds regarded as mostly bad but occasionally good. A particularly tempestuous mashup of idolatry and infamy. Even after three years of relative calm with Fisher, she still had the potential to be, as far as the media was concerned, a perfect storm. As such, tabloid and mainstream journalists the world over were alive to any murmur.

Presumably, Taylor knew that the studio would contain her open secret; and, as both she and Burton were married (and in Burton's case also enamored of *demimondaine*), it made little sense to gallivant, if by this Petersen means going around from one place to another in pursuit of entertainment. There was also a cordon of paparazzi around Cinecittà, hoping and, in a Roman Catholic country, probably praying for any kind of indiscretion from Taylor. A mobile unit accompanied Taylor. "Elizabeth had her own paparazzi that shadowed her everywhere she went," wrote Vicky Tiel in 2011. "There were never fewer than 4 photographers or more than 20 every day" (Tiel was a member of Taylor's entourage).

As January passed, the ever-hypnotic Taylor's behavior began to mimic Burton's: she drank with him, giggled at his jokes and seemed captivated by his familiar Shakespeare recitations. The conviviality gave rise to fanciful suspicions and the whispers grew louder. Yet the studio somehow contained the gossip immaculately. But the self-inflicted damage limitation exercise was shortlived.

In February, the whispers became loud enough to be heard in the USA. Specifically by Louella Parsons, whose gossip antenna rivaled that of Hedda Hopper. Parsons was guarded in her reports, but wrote that Taylor's marriage was in trouble and that the star's interests had wandered. She did not name Burton. Fisher picked up the story while on a break in New York. He immediately called his wife and asked her to nip the rumors in the bud. His suggestion was a press conference and a flat-out denial. Taylor declined, citing timing: she was in the middle of filming, of course; so a press conference to issue a denial of what was only tittle-tattle seemed an unnecessary distraction. Her decision must have done little to assuage any doubts Fisher entertained.

When he returned to Rome, Fisher was barely over his jetlag when his phone rang in the middle of the night. It was his friend and ex-army colleague Bob Abrams, who also happened to be in Rome. "There is something you need to know," said Abrams. Fisher finished the call and turned to Taylor who lay in bed. "Is it true?" She confirmed that she was sleeping with Burton.

Men react differently to the news that their wife or partner is seeing someone else. Fisher was not prone to histrionics. But nor did he make a dignified exit. After a night away from the Villa Papa, where he and Taylor were staying, he returned and resumed his role as her aide, taciturn and apparently chastened, but presumably prepared to tolerate his wife's infidelity in the hope that it would run its course. In the meantime, Fisher had to stand back and watch while his wife captivated her curious audience; and practically everyone was part of that audience.

Fisher did not drink much, a feature of his makeup Taylor found tiresome. Burton, of course, drank to excess every night; Taylor joined him enthusiastically. During days, when filming permitted, they had assignations at the rented apartment of Taylor's secretary Dick Hanley. C. David Heymann, among others, relates in his 1995 book a chilling story in which Fisher was forcibly made to witness the vindictive demolition of his honor in public. He and Taylor, in what seems a papery attempt to project an image of normalcy, threw a dinner party at their temporary home. During the evening, Burton appeared, uninvited and decidedly unwelcome (at least, by Fisher). Roaring drunk, Burton barged in and demanded to see Taylor. Fisher had been resting upstairs, but descended in carpet slippers and monogrammed robe. "I'm in love with that girl over there," slurred Burton, pointing at Taylor.

Fisher told him to leave, though Taylor, in full view of twelve guests, stayed impassive. "You are my girl, aren't you?" asked Burton, walking toward Taylor. This was, of course, the time for Taylor to support her husband's plea and ask the conspicuously intoxicated Burton to leave. "I think it would be a good idea for you to go now, Richard. I'll see you on set tomorrow, eh? Thanks for stopping by. Goodnight." This was *not* Taylor's reply. She just answered: "Yes." Burton then issued an instruction that must have made the guests squirm and Fisher grimace: "Stick your tongue down my throat." Taylor obliged, walking to him and engaged him in a passionate French kiss. Fisher slunk back to his room, leaving his guests to consider the main event of that, or, for that matter, any other evening's activities.

Perhaps it was Taylor's near-instinctive sense of drama, her unerring capacity to make theater out of anything no matter how mundane. Actors act. In submitting to Burton, she was performing for her dinner guests: it was a spectacular, dramaturgical emasculation of Eddie Fisher. Next day, Burton appeared on set hung-over but with his usual nonchalance. Fisher started preparing to leave. But not without tossing one tiny pebble in the pool.

Understandably aggrieved at his open humiliation, Fisher contemplated his riposte. He must have known Taylor was impervious. Burton could be riled; he knew this because, in mid-February, he made a mischievous call to Sybil Burton. It probably had not occurred to him that, for Sybil, another Burton affair was like having to put gas in your car. No one likes to do it, but it is not onerous and it makes the car run. Burton had been married to Sybil for thirteen years and had strayed on countless occasions. Sybil had no reason to suppose that the latest affair would be any different: it would occupy him agreeably for a while and, when it was over, he would still be married. So the ripples Fisher expected did not materialize: the pebbled just plopped in the water. At least, that is how it appeared at first. Sybil left Rome days after the conversation.

Taylor, like Fisher, misunderstood the Burtons' flexible yet sturdy marital arrangement: the other men in her life, after meeting her, typically experienced an emotional epiphany and suddenly lost interest in other women. At least that was her perception. She knew of Sybil, of course; but probably not of Pat Tunder, who departed discreetly around this time, almost certainly at Richard Burton's behest.

The Burtons' arrangement, successful as it was—at least for them—was predicated on covertness. Richard's various affairs were handled with tact, and never discussed. It was just understood. Fisher had disrupted Burton's personal tranquility a little more than he initially realized. So when Fisher called Taylor, he got an unexpected ear bending from Burton who answered the phone and threatened him for having the temerity to snitch on him to his wife. But Fisher's intervention clearly took Burton by surprise and, on February 16, he told Taylor their brief encounter was over then promptly took off for Paris, where he was due to film a small part in another Fox film, *The Longest Day*, about the Normandy landings of 1944 (D-day). This film eventually became an unexpectedly big box office success for the studio.

Unaccustomed to being dumped, as opposing to dumping other people, Taylor went into shock, failed to turn up for work the next day and was taken to the Salvator Mundi Hospital with suspected food poisoning. At least that was the official version. She had taken Secanol, a prescription sedative. "It was not a suicide attempt," Taylor later insisted. But her hospitalization and subsequent denial (often a telltale sign of the truth of whatever is being denied) augmented the gossip.

The narrative was, by then, unfolding by the day: on February 19, Burton issued a press statement that was as bold in its insincerity as it was timid in its inventiveness. He referred to "uncontrolled rumors . . . about Elizabeth and myself." (Question: whenever are rumors not uncontrolled?) There were transparently false explanations of why Sybil and Fisher had fled town. Burton made this statement under his own steam, without 20th Century Fox's approval. The studio's publicity team had decades of expertise in managing crises and would have certainly created an artifice more plausible than Burton's sham. Its manifest falseness was compounded by Burton's clump-footed avoidance of straight repudiation. Years later in 1998, US President Bill Clinton issued his famous "I did not have sex with that woman" pronouncement on his relationship with Monica Lewinsky. This proved equally as untrue as Burton's ordinance, but, at least, it bought him some time. No one believed Burton was not having an affair with Taylor. By mentioning it in a public discourse, Burton inadvertently and clumsily validated the affair as a topic for public discussion. So when he announced to the press that he would never leave his wife, the obvious question in the media's collective mind was: who said you were?

Ten years hence, Taylor would celebrate her fortieth birthday at a riotous party in Budapest where Burton would be filming; he would present her with a $500,000 heart-shaped diamond, inscribed with the name Nur Jahan, the wife of the Mughal Emperor Shah Jahan who built the mausoleum known as the Taj Mahal. But on February 27, 1962, Fisher moved back to the villa and hosted a thirtieth birthday party for his wife. He gave her a $10,000 diamond ring and an emerald Bvlgari mirror in what seemed an attempt to persuade everyone that what they thought was smoke was not a visible suspension of carbon in the air at all. So there was no fire either. The film was barely half-finished, meaning it was impossible for Taylor and Burton to stay out of each other's way even if they wanted to, which does not appear to have been the case. Fisher's pretense proved to be as feeble as he seemed to be, though, in a sense, he had little alternative.

About a month after her initial warning shot, Louella Parsons wrote in her syndicated column: "It's true—Elizabeth Taylor has fallen madly in love with Richard Burton. It's the end of the road for Liz and Eddie Fisher." Fisher immediately retorted that the report was, to use his word, ridiculous. "Fisher admitted that his wife refused to issue a statement denying reports of their estrangements," an Associated Press report appearing on the front-page of the *Los Angeles Times* on March 31, 1962, confirmed. "He [Fisher] said rumors of a breakup with Miss Taylor were 'preposterous, ridiculous and absolutely false,' adding . . . 'you can ask a woman to do something and she doesn't always do it.'"

His announcement was like a man being sucked into a black hole shouting, "I'm still here!" Three weeks later, he disappeared for good. Shortly before his departure, Taylor had become conspicuously bossy. On one occasion, she ordered him out of a bar after his impromptu singing interrupted a drunken conversation with Burton. The relationship was laced with enough passion and brio to be combustible even without alcohol; but the drinking binges—of which there were many during spring 1962, and beyond—made the relationship explosive. There was even a scene within a scene during which Burton warned Taylor, "Don't get my Welsh temper up," as he pushed her aside during a volatile exchange. Shakespearean scholar that he was, Burton would have recognized his own love was like that of *Romeo and Juliet*, "Being vex'd, a sea nourish'd with lovers' tears."

With their respective spouses and, in Burton's case, lover, gone, Taylor and Burton were free to spend as much time together as they wished; and free to lay bare their feelings. Stephen Gundle, suggested in 2012: "The abundant leisure that the drawn-out production afforded gave them an opportunity to take short vacations on Ischia, an idyllic island where passion took over." Ischia, which is an island in the Bay of Naples, about 170 miles southeast of Rome, would be the base for the filming of the battles of Pharsalia, Philippi, Moongate, and Actium, which are germane to the Cleopatra story.

"The paparazzi wouldn't exist in the same form if she hadn't gone to Rome in 1962 to make *Cleopatra* and fallen in love with Richard Burton, thereby creating a market for scandalous, often telephoto, pictures of the private lives of stars," maintained William Mann in 2011, (p. 8).

Marcello Geppetti was in the then adolescent paparazzi business: he worked at Meldolesi-Canestrelli-Bozzer, one of the biggest news agencies in Rome, which had connections the world over. He prowled Via Veneto and had captured Anita Ekberg's famous assault of the paparazzi with bow and arrow in 1960. At twenty-nine (his age in 1962), he must have heard press statements like Fisher's many times over and regarded them all in the same way. Press releases claiming fidelity usually carried with them an implicit directive: do not believe this. Even if they were true, it was his task to find an image that conveyed some hitherto undisclosed aspect of a narrative. His signature was the stolen aesthetic: images that had the quality of being misappropriated property. It was as if he shoplifted moments of other peoples' lives then made them available for everyone.

Like other paparazzi, Geppetti had kept a vigilant eye on the Cinecittà studios. Unlike other paparazzi, he was willing to stalk his subjects predaciously, stealthily following them, armed with his telephoto lens, ever ready to exploit an opportunity and purloin a secret. So Geppetti must have felt like a genie had sprung from an old lamp and asked him for a ride on his Vespa (the scooter of choice for paparazzi) to Aladdin's cave. "I'll give you directions, and when we get there you can take your pick." The genie—well, actually it was Taylor—took him to the coast. Taylor had arranged carefully and prudently a rendezvous on a yacht moored to the coast. Isolated, discreet, and intentionally unobtrusive as it was, it had not escaped Geppetti.

Today, we associate paparazzi with threatening, aggressive, and abusive behavior, perhaps unfairly. In this instance, Geppetti's approach had more in common with military reconnaissance, locating his subjects then ascertaining a strategy, in this case a long-range shot as the couple relaxed in the Mediterranean sun. Taylor never sought public affection nor begged approval, though she had both in spades. Would there be enough to serve as a bulwark against what was to come?

Into focus came two people who may have been the most perfectly partnered couple in history, or two hapless beings doomed by whatever force guides impassioned lovers toward disaster. Burton appeared in swimming trunks, Taylor in a polka dot one-piece swimsuit that rode up as she reclined on a beach towel she threw down on the yacht's lounge deck. A pack of cigarettes was within reach. Burton lay to her right so that he could incline his head above hers. He craned slightly forward so that faces aligned and lowered his head. Their lips met. Geppetti gently depressed his camera's shutter release. He might have thought he had captured what later generations of paparazzi were to call the money shot; but he had also conjured an image that was to change not just the media or the film industry, but almost every aspect of popular culture.

His photograph was not just of union, an illicit kiss of two star-crossed people. It was not just one of his trademark stolen moments. It was a message: the private life is over. If the biggest star in the world, supported by the mighty apparatus the film industry affords its treasured possessions cannot protect her privacy, who can? On his way back to Rome to deliver his film to the agency, Geppetti might have felt the genie riding pillion, and heard him say: "I was only out of the lamp on bail when I met you earlier today. But now I'm out for good."

The rumors (they are lovers), the gossip (they are leaving their spouses), the hearsay (they argue), and the lies (she is actually sleeping with Mankiewicz and the Burton story is just a smokescreen) were all fuel to the media, but, until the Geppetti shot, they lacked one important feature: evidence. Now, there was an image that proved unequivocally that Taylor and Burton were lovers. Geppetti had captured a kiss that was not that of a brother and sister or the kind exchanged by people who like each other: it was a prelude to sex. He had caught the couple *in flagrante delicto*, during the very act of wrongdoing. This was proof and it was circulated around the world. Newspapers everywhere eagerly published the definitive news: despite all the public disavowals and protestations of innocence, Taylor and Burton were indeed lovers.

Ironically, the Fox studio had grumbled that, considering its enormous cost, the production had not attracted much media attention during its formative months of production. In spring and summer 1962 it was the most publicized film production in history, squeezing important geo-political news into smaller columns of the front pages. Coverage of the Mercury-

Atlas space missions and the US–Soviet tension that built toward the Cuban missile crisis were eclipsed by the phenomenon that Burton, with customary pretentiousness, called *Le Scandale*. Perhaps he confused French with Italian: *Lo Scandalo* would have been more appropriate.

As some measure of the reverb, consider the response. Quite apart from the mainstream coverage, the Roman Catholic Church got involved. Italy is a Catholic country, of course. The weekly Vatican City publication, *L'Osservatore della Domenica,* devoted 500 words to an "Open Letter" that began formally "Dear Madam" and included this passage: "Even considering the [husband] that was finished by a natural solution, there remain three husbands buried with no other motive than a greater love that killed the one before. But if we start using these standards and this sort of competition between the first, second, third, and the hundredth love, where are we all going to end up? Right where you will finish—in an erotic vagrancy . . . without end or without a safe port." It was signed "X.Y." The phrase *erotic vagrancy* seemed loaded with purpose: it suggested Taylor was someone who wanders from man to man in pursuit of sexual excitement. Today, someone like Kristen Stewart or Mila Kunis would laugh off such a charge; Miley Cyrus or Rihanna might rejoice in it. But in 1962 it was a damning evaluation and one that probably occasioned a degree of unease even in someone who had withstood arguably the biggest showbusiness scandal in history four years before.

If Taylor imagined the media had forgotten and forgiven her earlier trespasses, she was wrong. Lester David and Jhan Robbins, in 1976, translated a juicy passage from a 1962 edition of Roman newspaper *Il Tempo* in which Taylor is described as: "This vamp [who] destroys families and shucks husbands like a praying mantis."

On May 30, American newspapers reported that: "Iris Faircloth Blitch, has put into The Congressional Record what has been on the minds of many of her fellow Americans. She objects to the over-publicized carryings on of English-born actress Elizabeth Taylor in Rome." Faircloth Blitch was a member of the US House of Representatives from Georgia, a Democrat who supported racial segregation. She found good reason to oppose Taylor's reentry to the US. The report continued: "She thinks it might be well to bar both the actress and actor Richard Burton, a British citizen, from entering the United States, on the ground they are undesirable persons" (*Daily Times*, May 30, 1962, p. 6). According to Faircloth Blitch, the scandal had damaged the USA's foreign aid program and foreign policy. Not even Cleopatra herself could have drawn rebuke from both church and state so exquisitely.

The paparazzi had been giving voltage to the supercharged saga of Taylor and Burton, but they cranked up the electromotive force at Porto Santo

Stefano. The couple had fled Rome for what was ostensibly a quiet coastal town about a hundred miles north of Rome. Were they naïve, or cunning? If they genuinely believed they could shrug the attentions of the paparazzi even for an Easter weekend, they were naïve to the point of stupidity. So perhaps they suspected they would have a tail wherever they went and issued a kind of passive invitation to the media. By Easter, 1962 (Good Friday fell on April 20), the scandal was truly international and reporters from outside Italy had been flown in.

Taylor called it "hell." Journalists had either followed them or just heard about the break and invaded what was ordinarily a quiet little retreat. "When we were driving somewhere, they ran us into a ditch by jumping in front of the car," Taylor remembered. Paparazzi staked out the cottage where she and Burton were staying. Several managed to get inside either by stealth—one journalist disguised himself as a priest in order to gain entry—or adeptness. Some scaled walls. In the 1990s, pap invasions such as this became commonplace whenever Diana tried to find seclusion. In 1962, it was a new phenomenon: Italian paparazzi were known for their intrusive habits, but this was guerrilla journalism. Their output was published internationally. The normally sober *Times* of London, for example, carried the story.

Burton's wife, by then back in England, learned of the tryst through the media. Again, the idea of learning of a partner's indiscretions via the popular media is nothing unusual today; but at the time it must have been staggering to learn of a husband's dalliance from the *Times*. Sybil knew about Burton's latest relationship; after all, it was this that hastened her retreat to England. But Burton's previous experiences had been occluded, allowing Sybil to preserve a veneer of self-respect. Only showbusiness insiders and select journalists knew of Burton's extracurricular activities. In any case, he was not a big enough star to warrant scandal sheet coverage. So what gossip there was remained confined to an inner circle. Now, she was degraded; her shame was public. She flew back to Rome to await Burton's return, presumably with Taylor.

But Taylor returned first, alone. News of a heated argument at the Porto Santo Stefano suggested a serious falling-out, perhaps even a violent clash between Taylor and Burton. Taylor even went to the hospital. Dark glasses might have concealed a black eye or bruising. Whatever the state of Taylor's face, filming was delayed for over three weeks. Taylor later maintained she was hurt when the car in which she was riding turned into a curve and she bumped her nose.

She was not the only member of the production crew to suffer sickness: the strain of directing during the day and writing or rewriting the script and reviewing rushes at night took effect on Mankiewicz, who needed a cocktail of medications to keep him going. The pressure on him intensified as it became clear that the destiny of 20th Century Fox rested on his film.

The only other film then in production was *Something's Got to Give* featuring Marilyn Monroe and, in June, Monroe was fired. She was later rehired, but died in August 1962, and the film was never completed (a 37-minute version remains). In Hollywood, Wanger was ousted and Darryl Zanuck took over as producer of *Cleopatra*. Wanger heard the news while in Rome, but stayed on to oversee production, even though his salary had been stopped. Fox's saving grace was *The Longest Day*, which was rushed to theatrical release and proved a box office success, taking over $18 million in its first year.

It was almost as if some divine architect was crafting a special project, configuring the elements with such delicacy that they coincided with the filming of *Cleopatra*'s most magnificent set-piece, the Egyptian queen's entrance into Rome. A quick ancient history tutorial will provide a little context: in 51 BC, Cleopatra ascended to the throne of Egypt at the age of eighteen on the death of her father Ptolemy XII. Her eight-year-old brother Ptolemy XIII was co-regent and, as ancient Egyptian custom dictated, they were married. The two were in perpetual conflict, much due to Ptolemy's opposition to Rome, then the center of the world's most formidable empire. Unlike her brother, Cleopatra saw Rome as a strategic ally. In 48 BC Julius Caesar, then fifty-two, arrived in Egypt where he met Cleopatra, thirty years his junior. She apparently smuggled her way into his room rolled in a carpet. They began an affair and Cleopatra, who had been exiled by her brother, was reinstalled as queen with Roman military support. In 47 BC Cleopatra had Caesar's child, Caesarion—though Caesar never publicly acknowledged him as his son. Cleopatra followed Caesar back to Rome. Her grand entrance was perfect raw material for the filmmakers. They wanted to realize an event that was as spectacular as anything ever seen in motion pictures: a vivid cinematic *trompe l'oeil*, which, when screened in Todd-AO became panoramic.

Ptolemy XIV died mysteriously at around this time, and Cleopatra made her son Caesarion co-regent. After Caesar's assassination, Cleopatra returned to Egypt. As originally conceived, this event would conclude the first film. The second feature was designed to focus on Cleopatra's relationship with Mark Antony, a Roman general who was in dispute with Caesar's adopted son Octavian over the succession to the Roman leadership. Antony was married to Octavian's sister. He began a relationship with Cleopatra which was both romantic and political. The couple had three children. In 31 BC, Mark Antony and Cleopatra combined armies to take on Octavian's forces in a great sea battle at Actium, on the west coast of Greece. This battle, filmed near Ischia, was the film's climactic conflict. Octavian was victorious and Cleopatra and Mark Antony fled to Egypt. Octavian pursued them and captured Alexandria in 30 BC. With his soldiers deserting him, Antony took his own life and Cleopatra chose the same course, committing suicide in 30 BC after which Egypt became a province of the Roman Empire.

The historical digression does have contemporary relevance. Consider: Cleopatra was twenty-two when she met Caesar, fifty-two and one of the most powerful men in the world. Taylor had been attracted and married to two much older men, Wilding and Todd, the latter of whom had Caesar-like qualities, including the ability to manipulate people to his own ends, and an appetite for power. Cleopatra's great love with Mark Antony had all manner of ramifications, many of them political and economic. Romans considered Mark Antony's marriage a betrayal: the marriage effectively ceded Egypt, once under Roman patronage. Octavian declared war on Cleopatra and Antony. In the middle of 1962, it must have seemed like several parties had declared a war of sorts on Taylor and Burton, her Antony. Such was the confusion of art and life during the production of *Cleopatra*.

The real entry of Cleopatra into Rome in 45 BC or 46 BC was probably nothing like the breathtaking extravaganza conceived by Mankiewicz. But he was a film director, not a professor of classical studies; he had audiences, not students, to think about. The spectacle lasted over nine minutes and invited yet another comparison: in the film, the reception awaiting Cleopatra could determine her future. If the crowd awaiting her or perhaps Caesar himself gave Cleopatra and her son a muted greeting, it augured poorly; whereas a warmer response would indicate acceptance. Mankiewicz's set designers had conjured a pageant that included snake dancers, elephants, warrior-dancers, and dwarfs preceding a gigantic replica of a sphinx drawn by 300 Nubian slaves. At the top of the 30-foot high sphinx sat Cleopatra and her son Caesarion, who would be carried down and presented before Caesar, flanked by an incredulous Antony. Taylor's outfit for this scene alone cost $6,500 (about $126,000 at today's prices). The scene is viewable at: http://bit.ly/1ijJA1J (accessed September 2015).

Six thousand extras were recruited to play Roman plebeians awaiting the arrival of Cleopatra; their job was simply to cheer excitedly as the queen makes her entrance. Given the Vatican's condemnation of Taylor, it was by no means certain that the extras would comply. No one knew whether Taylor's notoriety had turned her into a marked woman. In the event, the extras screamed their approval, at one point hailing *Leez! Leez!* and *Baci!* meaning kisses.

The acceptance was by no means universal. Two years after the Rome scandal, Taylor recalled the revilement when she and Burton went out in public: "We were spit at . . . What used to kill us was when people would say, 'We don't care what they do in private life, but do they have to air their dirty linen in public?" She was talking to Richard Meryman (p. 82). "God we were doing everything we could not to make it public."

It is difficult to know whether Taylor was being serious, in which case she was hopelessly naïve (unlikely) or dishonest (more likely). If she and Burton wanted to conduct a secret affair, they would have still been found out by the most resourceful and inquisitive journalists the world had ever seen. Even so, the lovers could have given them a run for their money. "Burton and Taylor flaunted their togetherness on the Via Veneto," writes Dani Garavelli. And, the Tre Scalini restaurant in the Piazza Navona. Then later at Taylor's Chalet Ariel in Gstaad, Switzerland. And many other places where they were easy targets for photographers. The only part of the relationship that was not made available for chronicling was the sex—and even that came close to being documented by Geppetti.

We often talk of divisive figures; those characters who cause disagreement or even hostility between people. Taylor, in 1962, was something of an archetype: castigated, loathed, denounced by some; venerated, treasured, idolized by others. She excited greatly differing passions as well as thoughts in people. It was impossible not to care. Today, it is a priceless commodity: if people care about someone enough to like, dislike or excite some kind of emotion, that someone has traction. From a celebrity's perspective, the thing to avoid at all costs is the opposite: neglect. It matters little whether audiences are repulsed by or attracted to someone; indifference is the problem.

By the middle of 1962, when Taylor finally left the set of *Cleopatra* and returned to the USA, it is hard to imagine anyone in the world (not just the Western world) did not know of her. Just as importantly, she behaved in a way that invited that most satisfying endeavor, evaluation. People judged Taylor. So far in this book, I have used crude typifications to represent the ways people thought about Taylor, like homewrecking nymphet, sexual *force majeure*, and ailing princess. These are just convenient but inadequate generalizations: actually, Taylor was what linguists call *polysémique*; in other words there were countless, coexisting meanings for her. It was as if there was one Elizabeth Taylor, a flesh-and-blood mortal. Then there were other Elizabeth Taylors, free of time and space, creations of everyone's imaginations. Everyone imagined they knew something, perhaps a little, or maybe a lot about her.

By 1964, when Taylor had managed to make sense retrospectively of the events of two years before, she sounded self-righteous. "I'm not going to answer for an image created by hundreds of people who do not know what's true or false," she told Richard Meryman. "Who reads that made-up stuff and believes it *wants* to believe it and is going to think it regardless of what she reads" (p. 81). It was a slightly confusing conclusion, but it possessed insight. Audiences were marching in time with the media and both had changed direction. Perhaps the media whetted the consumers' appetites by exposing them to the seamier side of Hollywood life through *Confidential* and, later—and more significantly—the Italian paparazzi. Charles Winick concluded his study in 1961 perceptively: "[*Confidential*] magazine represented the recognition of the public's interest in learning about celebrities and in learning about their less admirable as well as their more visible facets" (p. 334).

Neither gossip magazines nor paparazzi could not have thrived as they obviously did had there not been hungriness in the first instance. It is hard to conceive now, but, in a slightly different cultural climate, the kind of material dispensed by scandal sheets and paparazzi could have appalled readers. "These scurrilous people have no right to call themselves journalists: they are hell-bent of dishing dirt on anyone in the public eye and when they can't find evidence, they just fabricate it. It is nauseating." It sounds absurd, but earlier in the twentieth century, the reaction may not have been so different. An audience reared on Hollywood, newly-habituated to television and beginning to understand how the beings they saw on their screens were much closer to them than they had once thought welcomed the development. Even more, they gave their consent to evermore-invasive coverage. Where rumor remained unsubstantiated, "the made-up stuff," as Taylor called it, filled in. She was right when she said the people who believed it *wanted* to believe it. Yet she did not make the next logical connection: the globalization of what became known as the Liz & Dick scandal suggested everyone wanted to.

FIGURE 8 *Andy Warhol's silkscreen images of Taylor, Marilyn Monroe and Jackie Onassis—three women who were, in different ways, iconized as symbols of the twentieth century.*

Photo by Rudolf Dietrich/ullstein bild via Getty Images.

8

Beyond condemnation

Marilyn Monroe was in torment: she was getting $100,000 for her next film *Something's Got to Give* (1962). So it seemed like sour grapes when she whined: "Fox should start paying as much attention to me as they are paying to Elizabeth Taylor." Taylor's affair with Eddie Fisher in 1958 had awakened audiences to the guilty pleasures of scandal: all the yammering about the indiscretion meant that, like or hate her, everyone knew her. The studio might have trembled when it heard how much Taylor was demanding for her services, but her dalliance had brought an unexpected if highly ambiguous bounty: global notoriety. "Larry," Marilyn addressed photographer Lawrence Schiller when they were discussing a photoshoot, "If I do come out of the pool with nothing on, I want your guarantee that when your pictures appear on the covers of magazines, Elizabeth Taylor is not anywhere in the same issue."

Schiller relates the story in his 2012 memoir *Marilyn & Me*. Exasperated by the global attention—and money—Taylor was attracting even before the Burton affair broke, Marilyn, then thirty-three (she was six years older than Taylor), was prepared to fight scandal with scandal. She duly stripped, plunged into the pool and emerged naked before sliding into a blue terry towel bathrobe. Schiller recalls how he took the shots, and instantly and excitedly called the picture editor of *Paris Match*, assuring him he had "the first nudes of Marilyn in over ten years. The pictures are going to blow your mind!"

The *San Francisco Chronicle* secured an American exclusive for the pictures and, on June 18, 1962, alerted its readers with the front page headline: MARILYN'S NUDE WAR: AMERICA'S FRIGHTENED LOVE-GODDESS BATTLES FOR HER THRONE. The collection may not have become as iconic as Geppetti's stolen images, but it confirmed Marilyn's position as the most shamelessly intemperate Hollywood star of the time. Yet Marilyn's torment continued when she was fired by 20th Century Fox, in part because of the enormous budget overrun of Taylor's film. Marilyn's poor health caused several delays to *Something's Got to Give*'s production and, even though 20th Century Fox relented, and rehired her, the movie was never completed. Marilyn died on August 5, 1962. She had been married and divorced three times and was childless. The following year, Marilyn's close friend President John F. Kennedy was assassinated. In both cases, the loss of life was immediately followed by a cultural reincarnation; both figures remain alive in our imaginations.

"You're already famous, now you're going to make me famous," Schiller recalls advising Marilyn as they prepared for the photoshoot. "Don't be so cocky," Marilyn laughed, "photographers can be easily replaced." But lovers were not so interchangeable. After his first sexual interlude with Taylor, Burton is rumored to have announced: "I am worth four million dollars more than I was yesterday." There is no evidence that he actually uttered that sentence. Its import was probably accurate though. What we might call the Elizabeth Taylor Factor was the sum added to an ordinary price simply because the commodity was associated with Taylor. Cologne, films, jewelry, men: they were all subject to the premium.

Burton had no problem in accepting that he had become a commodity; his only struggle was in pricing himself at the top end of the market and, in this sense, he shared a career orientation with Marilyn. The Liz & Dick scandal had much the same effect on him that a ✶✶✶✶✶ rating from *Car* magazine has on a car's sales. Its effect on Taylor's market value was less certain. Schiller was twenty-six at the time he photographed Marilyn and went on to become an Emmy award-winning film producer and director as well as a respected photographer. Imagine what would have happened to Marilyn's marketability had it become known that she was having an affair with a married man, who happened to hold the highest political office in the USA.

In the early 1960s, there were no reliable guides, apart from Taylor herself, who had emerged from one major scandal, her market appeal enhanced. But what would have happened to the President? His clandestine relationship started in Palm Springs, California, in March 1962, making it roughly synchronous with Taylor's second scandalous affair in Rome. JFK's intentions were, according to some, similar to Burton's, "another notch— albeit an impressive one—on his bedstead," to use J. Randy Taraborrelli's phrase (2010). We can safely surmise the impact of disclosure on Kennedy's career would have been a lot less providential than it was on Burton's.

In any scandal, there are winners and losers. Apart from Burton, who seemed flushed with success after the attention he had suddenly commanded, the paparazzi were earning several times their usual fees. Naturally, Fisher numbered himself among the losers and insisted on recompense for the damage done to his singing career. He eventually received a figure thought to be about $500,000, a hefty settlement in the 1960s (the equivalent of about $8.8 million today). By the time of the official announcement in March that Taylor and Fisher were to separate, the fragile pretense had disintegrated: everyone knew; this was just an *ex post facto* confirmation of the obvious.

What of *Cleopatra*? Was she, or rather it, a winner or loser? Twentieth Century Fox was confused to the point where it could not decide whether Taylor's vagrant eroticism had cost the film or not. A denunciation from the Vatican did not augur well. Did it? Absurd as it sounds today, 20th Century Fox was undecided; to be safe, Peter Levathes, who had worked as a legal assistant to Spyros Skouras before rising to executive vice president, dictated a letter intended for Taylor in which he suggested she "desist involvement with Richard Burton" or risk being sued by Fox for violating a moral clause in her contract. The incident is recounted by C. David Heymann (p. 286). The contents of the letter reached Kurt Frings before the letter was mailed. He transmitted them to Taylor, who had finished the majority of her work on the film and had probably estimated her own value: priceless. Her response was the equivalent of a middle finger salute: "Nobody tells me who to love or not to love." Twentieth Century Fox actually did press ahead with its legal case and, a year later, sued Taylor.

And Sybil? After finishing his part in the film, Burton went to his home in Céligny in Geneva, Switzerland, about 85 miles away from where Taylor was relaxing in Gstaad. Sybil and their two daughters (Kate and Jessica) were with him. For a while, it seemed as if his relationship with Taylor had lived its course. Burton had a boomerang quality and, no matter how great the distraction, he always returned to Sybil. Yet Taylor offered more than any other *inamoratas*. "She represented the promise of global superstardom and million-dollar film assignments," Ellis Amburn pointed out in 2011 (p. 203).

Burton knew when he was onto a promise. Clearly, this was not one to be missed. The interlude in Céligny with his wife and children was not a return but a departure, or at least the beginning of a protracted departure that was to extend over the next several months. Burton spent a couple of weeks with his family before reuniting with Taylor and the now-familiar retinue of photojournalists, all competing for scraps like animals at feeding time. The scraps were nutritious. Burton made no dramatic announcement of a divorce; Taylor said next to nothing, but remained mindful that she had a global audience. "When Elizabeth went out to make an appearance, it was always in a major gown and Richard in a tux. She went the whole nine yards—diamond tiara, necklace, three bracelets, five diamond rings with major stones, sables, couture gowns, and killer makeup. Going out was a performance and would be recorded in every paper," writes Vicky Tiel who was, for a while, a member of Taylor's staff.

At some point during the second half of 1962, Burton must have realized his situation would force him to rethink his modus operandi. Taylor, like some other women in his past, had beauty, but she also had power. She must have been a revelation to him: reckless, domineering, fearing no one, she mesmerized pretty much everyone within her purview. This included media, studio executives, fellow actors, everyone. When it came to earnings capacity, she was untouchable. Sex, power, money: what more could there be for an actor? Burton could no more walk away from all this than he could a glass of Rémy Martin XO.

In 1962, on hearing that her husband John Glenn had been selected as one of the astronauts to orbit earth in the spacecraft Mercury-Atlas-6, Annie Glenn went straight to church to ask her pastor if a man was allowed to leave God's planet, even temporarily, and if it was true that the "the heavens weren't actually heaven." After lengthy consultation with the Bible, the pastor could find no reason for John not to go; so he did, while his wife sat at home on the living room rug and prayed. It is not known whether Spyros Skouras, the head of 20th Century Fox consulted the same pastor before he resigned in June 1962. If he did, he might have asked if a man was allowed to leave a studio after gambling the entire studio's future on a single picture, which was still unfinished. The pastor would probably have told him: "Hell, no. You started this whole débâcle and now you want to quit with the studio on the verge of bankruptcy? Wasn't it you who signed off on Liz Taylor's million bucks? You stick around till it's finished."

Skouras, on whose vision the film was based, suffered with deteriorating health and sensed his time as head of 20th Century Fox was nearing an end. From his point of view, a speedy turnaround and theatrical release would at least validate his original concept, fanciful as it seemed. But there were Machiavellian stratagems at work and Darryl Zanuck, whose family was still the single largest shareholder of Fox stock, maneuvered himself into a powerful position so that he could take control of the stumbling company he had co-founded in 1933. Skouras announced his resignation on June 26, and assumed the largely ceremonial chairman-of-the-board role. Zanuck closed down practically all 20th Century Fox productions apart from *Cleopatra*, which was in its final phases. Taylor was no longer required and had finished three days earlier, her total remuneration eventually reaching about $7 million. Recall her initial demand for a million dollars was considered outrageous. Shooting transferred to Egypt for some final battle scenes, but Taylor was now free to pursue other projects. (Zanuck himself was forced out of 20th Century Fox in 1971, and died in 1979.)

Hollywood is like a pyre that consumes all things, but occasionally, Phoenix-like, renews them in curious new forms. Perhaps Zanuck saw in *Cleopatra* an allegory of 20th Century Fox: a once-great empire riven with conflict over one enthrallingly, perilously enticing woman. Or maybe he recognized that love and power are fantastic box office twins and that the story of Cleopatra and Mark Antony was barely distinguishable from Liz & Dick, especially if the mists of time and the blizzards of publicity rendered audiences unable to see the difference between the struggles of the great queen and, well, the struggles of the great queen.

Cleopatra for Skouras might have been a majestic tragedy, a story for all time; for Zanuck it was an instrument for making money and saving the studio.

A film is by no means over once filming is finished: postproduction involves editing, overdubs and other processes. As far as Mankiewicz was concerned the original concept of two separate films, released concurrently, with audiences having to pay twice, was his brief. Zanuck, however, had been following events in Italy and realized three material facts. First, there was a perception of symmetry: Elizabeth Taylor was not just playing Cleopatra, she was facing her; there was an uncanny correspondence between her own life and that of her subject. He also realized that, while scandals had sunk many other stars, Taylor had an unsinkable quality and would probably surface in style. His third finding was that, given the burgeoning interest in Taylor and her affair with Burton, everyone would want to see her live that out on screen. So a film that focused on her relationship with Caesar, played by the less interesting Rex Harrison, would have no pulling power. In short, *Cleopatra and Caesar* and *Cleopatra and Antony* were burned and, from their ashes rose *Cleopatra*, a single motion picture focusing on Cleopatra/Taylor and Antony/Burton.

Mankiewicz worked with his editor, Dorothy Spencer, hewing his material into a luminous fable of love, power and death. He presented his new boss Zanuck with his masterpiece, a film that ran five hours and twenty minutes. Zanuck was not impressed. In fact, he hated it. In particular, he considered the battle sequences amateurish and unconvincing. His response was to fire Mankiewicz. It was a rash response. In time, Zanuck appreciated that Mankiewicz's ability to shoot plausible battle scenes was incurably constrained by his budget. Still: they would make the film laughable and had to be reshot. Zanuck found an additional $2 million and asked Mankiewicz to film two key sequences again, this time with Zanuck himself at his shoulder. They went to Almería, Spain, to film the battle scenes again.

The compression into a more tolerable length was necessary simply because movie theaters would be able to show only two performances per day and would balk at exhibiting such an obviously noncommercial item. Again, Zanuck stuck close to Mankiewicz when he pared the film down to four-hours and three-minutes, its original premiere length. Mankiewicz was aggrieved that such a gigantic, ambitious and, in more ways than one, historical drama had been miniaturized. Although he did not know it at the time, the film would be reduced further to a mere three hours twelve-minutes, only 60 percent of the director's initial cut; this is the form in which it was popularly distributed (though the 4 hour+ version was restored for DVD release in 2013). Taylor herself was dismayed at this. "The only things I was proud of in *Cleopatra* Fox cut out with unerring accuracy," she said to Meryman in 1964 (p. 76).

The total cost of the film was $44 million (£29 million) which, when indexed to inflation, makes it one of the most expensive films ever made. (Adjusted for inflation, it ranks it as second, behind 2007's *Pirates of the Caribbean: At World's End,* according to Kirsten Acuna, of *Business Insider UK,* 2014.) Fox then had to find extra money to fund a marketing campaign that absorbed the best part of $10 million. One element of the campaign was an exclusive premiere at New York's Rivoli Theater, the owners of which paid 20th Century Fox a record high $1.25 million to screen the movie exclusively. "Program Publishing Company of New York paid Fox $350,000 for the right to print and sell the souvenir program for one dollar each," reported Kim R. Holston in *Movie Roadshows* (p. 167).

Even the huge signs to advertise the film caused a commotion. Top priced tickets for the opening night were $100 (then about £45). Mindful that consumers' curiosities had been piqued by Taylor's illicit liaison, the original posters featured her reclining languidly with Burton close by. Rex Harrison was furious and reminded 20th Century Fox's advertising agency that a clause in his contract stipulated that his image should appear in all marketing. His head-and-torso was superimposed, slightly incongruously, in later editions of the poster.

Time magazine set the scene of the premiere: "Cleopatra. In scarlet letters volted with excitement the notorious name hung throbbing and enormous in the night sky over Broadway. Beneath it 10,000 rubberneckers milled on the macadam and roared at the famous faces in the glare. One by one, smiles popping like flashbulbs, they disappeared in the direction of the screen. What did it hold for them? Surely no Shavian conversation piece could conceivably have cost all that money" (June 21, 1963) ("Shavian" means relating to the work of George Bernard Shaw, one of the sources of the film's screenplay.) The absence of Taylor and Burton was not so much conspicuous as flagrant. The New York premiere is preserved on Pathé news: http://bit.ly/1stvqiY (accessed September 2015). A jostling assembly of thousands of fans screaming and clamoring worshipfully was a precursor for the gatherings that were to become commonplace.

The *New York Times'* film critic, Bosley Crowther called *Cleopatra* a "brilliant, moving and satisfying film" in which "Elizabeth Taylor's Cleopatra is a woman of force and dignity, fired by a fierce ambition to conquer and rule the world—at least, the world of the Mediterranean basin—through the union of Egypt and Rome. In her is impressively compacted the arrogance and pride of an ancient queen" (1963). This was about the most positive of reviews: others were mostly middling and some were wholly negative. Judith Crist, of the *New York Herald Tribune,* added to her own reputation for put-downs, when she described the film as "a monumental mouse" (quoted in Martin, 2012).

Early signs were promising: the picture was sold out in advance for the first four months. Of course, there was no DVD version available and without the internet, no other way to see the film apart from traveling to New York. It became the top grossing film of 1963, taking $15.7 million in the USA alone; nowhere near enough to break even; the film actually moved into profit in 1966 when ABC television paid Fox $5 million to show the film on television; by then Taylor and Burton were married. *Cleopatra* tropes filtered into popular culture. Apart from the themed fashion lines introduced by Ceil Chapman and others, the effects of the film were felt in hairstyles that mimicked the symmetrical cut favored by Taylor in the film. Taylor's kohl-eyed queen influenced ranges of cosmetics. There was a distinct Cleopatra look and, for a while in 1963 it seemed the film might yet become the all-conquering mother-of-all-epics its creators had hoped for. It was nominated for nine Academy Awards, though none for Best Actress, and won four, all in technical categories.

In the aftermath there was a flurry of legal actions and threatened legal actions, and two books in the "making of . . ." genre: Walter Wanger and Joe Hyams' *My Life with Cleopatra* (2013), which upset Skouras; *The Cleopatra Papers* (1963) by the film's publicists Jack Brodsky and Nathan Weiss (which also upset Skouras). So *Cleopatra* was, in its own way, the mother-of-all-epics. The film was only part of it.

Sam Kashner and Nancy Schoenberger offer a theory to account for how Taylor consciously made herself into a living narrative. They argued in 2010: "She drew on her theatrical roles to provide direction and add luster to her life" (p. 58). This "reverse method acting" implicated her in a kind of role playing. While they do not cite her infamous 1958 interview with Hedda Hopper ("sleep alone?"), they might have. Her acting had bravado, however preposterous and unbelievable the character (a pre-Christian Egyptian queen who speaks English with an American accent?) And so did her life: everything she did was intended to impress or (perhaps and) intimidate. At the risk of distorting Kashner and Schoenberger, I venture that they would agree that Taylor assimilated ideas and knowledge she took from her films and made them part of her own identity. The writers go further in claiming Mankiewicz became complicit in this process, writing the *Cleopatra* script in a way that assisted this assimilation, but also invited audiences to blur the person and the role; he wrote ambiguities into the script in a way that made audiences wonder: is this Cleopatra speaking or Taylor? Kashner and Schoenberger submit: "He [Mankiewicz] could not have known how closely Cleopatra would anticipate the arc of Elizabeth and Richard's thirteen-year love affair," write (p. 58).

If 20th Century Fox was undecided about the marketability of Taylor and Burton (remember, the studio sued the couple, though later dropped the action), MGM had no doubt about how the real life drama when transposed onto screen could bring benefits. No other couple in history had commanded the media's attention and bewitched consumers in same way as Taylor and Burton. A film would have to be execrably tenth-rate not to succeed when its two main players were locked in an international scandal. Actually, the 2003 romcom, *Gigli,* managed to flop even while the romance between its stars Jennifer Lopez and Ben Affleck dominated headlines. Bennifer, as the rocky relationship was known, broke up in 2004; it was a tabloid staple. But, while the film failed, neither Lopez nor Affleck suffered in career terms.

MGM had lined up Burton and the Italian actor Sophia Loren to play in *The VIPs,* produced by Anatole de Grunwald, who knew Burton from his 1949 production *The Last Days of Dolwyn,* Burton's first film. In terms of allurement, voluptuousness, and glamour, Loren, then twenty-nine, was as weaponized as Taylor. It would have been surprising if Burton had not tried to maintain his track record. Joan Collins, with whom Burton played in a 1957 film, *Sea Wife,* recalled of Burton: "He admitted to me that he would 'f***' a snake if it was wearing a skirt!' He also told me that if I did not succumb to his charms, I would ruin his record of sleeping with all his leading ladies" (2010).

This helps explain what would, in other circumstances, be an incomprehensible decision: Taylor, by far the most famous and most bankable actor of the time, without reading a script or negotiating a fee (and she was in the process of earning $7 million for *Cleopatra,* remember) made it known to MGM that she wished to be in *The VIPs* in the role assigned to Loren. It was a British production with a modest budget of $3 million. Even so, Taylor took a sizable $500,000 upfront fee plus 10 percent of the gross. The film was no *Gigli* and did healthy business, bringing Taylor an additional $4 million.

Taylor attended the British premiere of *Cleopatra* in August 1962, though only under pressure. In the same month, Marilyn Monroe died. Taylor returned to London to make *The VIPs.* She and Burton stayed at Taylor's usual hotel, the Dorchester on Park Lane. They checked into separate but adjacent suites. Burton was in what he called a state of "suspended animation." His attachment to Sybil had not been threatened by his serial affairs, probably because his paramours had never required more than a share of his affections. Several were married themselves. So Burton had never contemplated divorce. This must have been irritating to a woman already on her fourth husband and preparing to move to a fifth. Burton worked on the film during the week and spent weekends with his wife, while Taylor remained at the hotel. Questioned about whether he intended to leave Sybil, Burton told journalists he did not. If this was to be believed, it left Taylor without a love interest in her life for the first time since she was sixteen and met Glenn Davis. I repeat: if this was to be believed.

With *Cleopatra* playing to full houses and the Liz & Dick chronicles progressing beyond their first chapter, it seems extraordinary that Burton would even talk about the subject to the media, let alone continue to deny what everyone else presumed was inevitable. As if to perpetuate the façade, Sybil regularly attended the set of *The VIPs* and behaved as if there were no marital discord or any other kind of discord for that matter. Perhaps she had experienced Burton's centrifugal tendencies so many times that she expected him to return to his natural center in due course.

Once more, audiences were induced to become guiltless peeping toms: the publicity for the film blared, THE MOST TALKED-ABOUT, THE MOST READ-ABOUT, THE MOST FAMOUS COUPLE IN THE ENTIRE WORLD . . . TOGETHER FOR THE FIRST TIME IN A MODERN LOVE STORY. Taylor played a woman planning to leave her husband (Burton) for a handsome, playboyish Louis Jordan. Taylor's character tells her husband she is leaving him in a note at home. A flight delay means he has time to read it and follow her to the airport (this was in the days before the multiple security checks at airports). By the time of the film's release, just three months after *Cleopatra*, audiences were familiar with Burton's own equivocations about leaving his wife. Taylor's character was Burton; Burton was Sybil. The critical reception was lukewarm, but audiences voted with their feet and the film grossed $15 million (five times its budget).

"Jacqueline Kennedy was the first female megastar not created by the entertainment industry," Anthony Slide points out (p. 202). By the time her husband President John F. Kennedy was assassinated on November 22, 1963, she was already a paradigm of elegance: beautiful, refined, polished, she was the most decorous First Lady in history. Surviving the hugely popular JFK, she was, in many senses, the most exquisite grief-stricken widow imaginable. She appeared to have a new 1960s-style outfit for every appearance; her jet-black hair was perfectly coiffed on all but one occasion when her nemesis paparazzo Ron Galella caught her in a 1971 photograph. The image is at: http://ti.me/1qtOpFZ (accessed September 2015).

Before she married Kennedy, Jacqueline Bouvier was unknown. She became famous by association. As Schiller did after photographing Marilyn, and Burton did by having a relationship with Taylor. Both these men had reputations independently before their associations, but their fame came only after. "Fame has nothing to do with merit," contends Slide, noting a change in the mood of time. "There really is little meritorious about Jackie Kennedy." There did not need to be: in the early 1960s, consumers' interests derived more from voyeurism more than admiration. Followers of Jackie Kennedy were not concerned by what she had achieved, her tangible accomplishments, her corpus of work. They were fascinated by how she lived, who she loved, what she wore, *her*.

Jacqueline freighted the haunting memory of her husband with her for a while, but her load lightened as she became delectable in her own right. Journalists, who had handled her with care, were emboldened to chase, even confront her and Galella became involved in a no-holds barred pursuit, which eventually required legal intervention. By the time Jacqueline Kennedy remarried in 1968, this time to Aristotle Onassis, the media treated her with the scant respect they afforded figures from the entertainment industry. Like Taylor, she accrued a following of paparazzi wherever she went. C. David Heymann reckons, the Kennedy-Onassis wedding was the only event that could "create the same degree of public excitement" as Taylor and Burton (p. 293).

We—and I mean all of us—duly respond to what we consider genuine achievements. Traditionally, we applauded, even genuflected to the great explorers, prominent military leaders, leading lights of religion, and inventors of technology or medicines that introduced tangible changes in the way we live. At the start of the twentieth century, entertainers were trivial characters who did nothing of substance. They were agreeable diversions, hardly deserving admiration and certainly not respect.

The man responsible for what was effectively a cultural revolution was Carl Laemmle, pioneer mogul and later founder of Universal Pictures. Let me remind you of his great discovery. In 1910, he staged a fake car accident in which actor Florence Lawrence—until then known simply as "The Biograph Girl," after her studio—vanished without trace. The norm was for screen performers to appear relatively anonymously; they did not sell a film. But the media furor occasioned by Lawrence convinced Laemmle and other Hollywood bosses that they could foreground actors' names to draw audiences. Hollywood's next task was to persuade audiences that actors, or stars as they were called, were human beings who were just like anyone else save for one thing: their abundant talent in playing make-believe roles. That talent made them special. The lifestyle they enjoyed was a just dessert. There was no way of knowing for sure whether consumers would buy this: after all, these stars might just be lucky enough to snag a job in a fledgling film industry. They were not responsible for an act, a deed, an exploit or any kind of attainment that actually bettered life. They just performed in a way that was enjoyable and amusing. That was not the response, however: consumers accepted the messages handed down on the tablets of Tinseltown.

Despite the myth that stars were born, they were really promoted by studios; there was no foolproof method of elevating workaday actors to the level of stars, but the Hollywood studios came up with a system that held sway until about 1950. And we—again, all of us—wittingly or not, became parts of that system. We accepted that fame was not just a byproduct of great achievements: it was something that could be created by steadfast promotion. The screen glitterati supplanted traditional leaders, possessors of charisma and adventuring pioneers as the most famous people on the planet. Fame was decoupled from achievement.

Jacqueline Kennedy was not a star, of course; at least not a Hollywood-produced star. She was just as photogenic and immeasurably more enigmatic—and I use the word in its proper sense: impenetrable, unfathomable, and secretive. She married an ambitious, thrusting young politician with good connections. After his death, she married a Greek billionaire. She refused to discuss her marriages, her private life, banned friends who talked to the media, and died in 1994 as recondite and inscrutable as Greta Garbo. Not until twenty years after her death, when a stash of letters she had written to an Irish priest was discovered, did anyone gain what passes as insight into her thoughts.

Jackie O, as she became known after marrying Onassis, is a pivotal, perhaps epochal figure, not because of anything she did or said, although marrying a future President is in itself something of a deed. She just delivered a quality: she obeyed no laws or protocols, played no games with the media, confessed to nothing, and dared not to do anything of consequence. Yet she was mesmerizing.

Vicky Tiel thinks: "It was Elizabeth and Jackie Kennedy who aroused the public's interest in off-screen celebrity lifestyles. Fashion trends would be launched from the way they tied their Hermès scarves" (2011). She may be right. But she could also ask: why was there any interest to be aroused in the first place? Provoking or exciting interest, or, for that matter, emotions is not a straightforward case of stimulus-response. At another time, in another place, a star-crossed actor and a taciturn First Lady might prompt attention, but in their accomplishments. Kennedy, like Taylor, fired peoples' imaginations with her sheer presence. By *being* Jacqueline Kennedy Onassis, *being* Elizabeth Taylor.

It is not surprising that we take for granted our interest in other people. After all, we live though blurrily fast cultural shifts of unplanned obsolescence and celebrity evaporation. Consumers can be absorbed in someone's life then oblivious to it, sometimes within a one-month span. Yet it is a relatively recent development. It could be argued that both Kennedy and Taylor had fascinating and glamorous auras of mystery, a distinct atmosphere that surrounded them both. But the air of secrecy surrounding Kennedy would not have been of any consequence if no one were interested; and the nimbus of glamour, romance, and passion that seemed to surround Taylor could well have gone unnoticed if that collection of changeable folk we call the public was peering elsewhere.

Jacqueline represented a change in public orientation as dramatic as the earlier shift in which entertainers ascended to the level previously commandeered by people who had made palpable contributions. Hollywood stars could claim to have worked for their status: their films represented a body of creative work and, in this sense, their art could be compared to that of writers and other artists. But Jacqueline was just a kind of cipher in whom people invested importance; they also sympathized, empathized, and somehow thought they understood and shared her feelings; what we called earlier an intimacy at distance.

Taylor elicited comparable responses. True, she could legitimately claim a portfolio of creative work that would stand up to scrutiny for years. But, in a sense, this was secondary: her primary attraction was herself. There is no contradiction here: Taylor was the source of fascination: the films offered a way of seeing her act out her own life in dramatic form. Jacqueline curated her own mystique, while Taylor dramatized her own life. In Richard Corliss's phrase: "Taylor made film only as a visiting dignitary, vacationing from her good works, her incorrigible celebrity" (from his 2011 article).

Twentieth Century Fox accused Taylor of "suffering herself to be held up to scorn, ridicule, and unfavorable publicity as a result of her conduct and deportment." This was part of its legal case against her and Burton and, while the case was eventually dropped, the phrase includes an archaic use of the verb to suffer. "Suffering herself," means to tolerate or allow someone or something to do something, in this case the media, which generated publicity. Taylor did allow the media to turn her life into theater, but, for the most part, showed little resistance and expressed no discomfort. Nor made any apology for either of these.

Dave Kehr, of *Entertainment Weekly*, notes in 2011 that Taylor's had "few memorable films [and] left behind no signature role (unless you count *Cleopatra*)." I actually do count *Cleopatra*, but accept Kehr's overall point. He goes on: "Taylor did create something: a new category of celebrity, one whose life was vastly more dramatic off screen than on." Consumers did not just look at Taylor's life: they were parts of it; she was "a woman who lived every moment in public," as Corliss said. After *Cleopatra*, the complex narratives of Taylor's life piqued and provoked, prompting audiences to ask more questions. She duly responded, though not always with direct answers.

One of the questions that was raised in the aftermath of *Cleopatra* was: will Burton ever leave Sybil? He had publicly declared on more than one occasion that he would not and, yet, he must have realized as soon as the first receipts from *The VIPs* arrived that Taylor's impact was undeniably immense. To take another phrase from Corliss, "she made him a star." Sybil Burton did not file for divorce until December 1963.

Burton was, of course, a successful actor in his own right, rich enough to have become a tax exile in Switzerland. But he was unabashed about his pursuit of money and never concealed his avarice. Taylor's colossal fees compared to his own merely big earnings probably irked someone with his traditional male-oriented background, but he could probably envisage equal billings for as long as the Liz & Dick phenomenon had life. The scandal did not die quietly after the release of *Cleopatra* in June 1963, or even after *The VIPs*, which was rush-released three months later in September to capitalize—successfully—on the surging interest in Taylor and the married father-of-two, who would not be leaving his wife even for one of the most desirable women in the world.

When, in September 1963, Burton went to Puerto Vallarta, Mexico, to make *The Night of the Iguana*, Taylor went with him; as did a posse of paparazzi. The couple hired a gun-carrying bodyguard, Emilio Fernández to protect them from the media. Never one to disappoint her media, Taylor arrived in what the *Los Angeles Times* (October 13) described as "a specially-outfitted VIP plane," accompanied by seventy-four pieces of luggage (even Lady Gaga would be in awe). Mexico, like Italy, is a Catholic country and a convent near the production site broke its vow of silence to protest against Taylor's and Burton's apparent co-habitation. Taylor and Burton rented a nine-bedroomed villa, which they eventually bought and to which they frequently returned. Kashner and Schoenberger describe the "Beatlemania-like frenzy" in the ordinarily sleepy tourist resort. The reference is to the collective fan hysteria that accompanied the Beatles, who first played live in America five months later in February 1964.

The opprobrium might well have affected other movie stars, perhaps even ruined them. But Taylor had lived through one almighty scandal and was probably tutoring Burton on the fly. "Burton and Taylor were beyond condemnation," Stephen Gundle wrote in 2012. "Neither allowed their conduct to be determined by what others thought of them." In a way, they reversed the process, helping determine how others should think about them; they were able to do this because of the enormous power they had both to attract the media and influence its reportage, and because widespread attitudes to sex, love, and marriage were not lingering.

Meanwhile, Eddie Fisher, who had been issued with divorce papers, was watching from afar, trying to revive a showbusiness career he had put on hold when he became Taylor's husband, personal assistant, and, for another while, cuckold. Unsurprisingly, there was little sympathy for him; he had ditched the perennially popular Debbie Reynolds when Taylor beckoned, left his children and become a factotum. Yet he still had fight in him and was holding out for a favorable settlement. During their time together, he and Taylor had adopted a German girl, Maria. After the birth of her third child, Taylor had consented to a tubectomy for her own wellbeing. She still wanted children, so adoption seemed sensible. Fisher's name appeared on the adoption papers though he agreed to relinquish this and cede custody to Taylor. This was part of a complicated series of exchanges over the division of their property and wealth that reached an end but not until March 5, 1964, when Fisher refused to contest Taylor's petition for a Mexican divorce.

Burton must have felt like Dorothy, the orphaned Kansas girl swept by a tornado into a fantastical world called Oz, yet striving to return to her aunt and uncle. One moment Burton was a respected Shakespearean actor with all the dignity that attends such a role. The next, he was one half of Liz & Dick. Perhaps a return to the Bard would help restore some solemnity to his public image. To this end, Burton announced he would play Hamlet in a

Broadway production directed by fellow thespian and Shakespeare luvvie
(as Brits call effusive or affected actors) Sir John Gielgud. There would be a
pre-Broadway run in Toronto. In normal circumstances, Burton would have
expected a warm welcome from the media, perhaps a few promotional
interviews, followed by a rapturous reception from full houses at Toronto's
O'Keefe Centre. These were not normal circumstances.

As Burton and Taylor approached their hotel, the King Edward Sheraton,
where they planned to stay, they were obliged to cross through a line of
protesters carrying placards that read: "Daughter of the flesh" and "Drink
not the wine of adultery." Gielgud dismissed them as "Ghastly crowds of
morons," but they were little different from the demonstrators Burton had
become used to over the previous few months. The protests were only part
of an overwhelming response. "The city couldn't contain itself," Dave Bidini,
of the *National Post* remembered in 2013. Gielgud noticed how "Every
drink and conversation is photographed and reported."

Taylor and Burton had to be escorted everywhere, police sometimes
cordoning off streets to allow them safe passage. Although they stopped
short of disguising themselves, Taylor and Burton swaddled themselves in
scarves and turned-up their collars as they entered and exited via service
elevators and back doors, always accompanying by a cortège that included
security staff. The familiar mixture of moral panic, antic adulation and what
we would now call celebrity worship forced Taylor and Burton to contrive
a cocoon-like protection, never venturing into public unaccompanied. For
Taylor, this was nothing unusual. Burton's adaptation was predictable: to
drink more alcohol.

This was the first episode in which Liz & Dick was made to address
crowds in a major international city. In Rome, they were two individuals
having a suspected affair; by the time they reached Toronto, they were a
media phenomenon. Recall Rock Hudson's observation that, when making
Giant, Taylor was an actor, but not news. By January 1964, Brenda Maddox
points out: "Miss Taylor moved into the news and off the entertainment
pages" (p. 180). In her 1977 book, Maddox quotes from the *Los Angeles
Times*: "Public appearance is her [Taylor's] trade." It was not Burton's: he
still cleaved to his actorly credentials; though he must have sensed that they
were being invalidated, especially after the hammering his *Hamlet* took
from the Canadian critics. "Elizabeth would have to teach Burton how to be
private in public now that she had brought him into her world," wrote
Kashner and Schoenberger in 2010 (p.92).

It got worse for Burton. Writing two years on in 1966, syndicated
journalist Drew Pearson summarized the position: "Burton, then in Canada,
was scheduled to do a benefit performance at the Lincoln Center in New
York, and the Democratic Congressman from Cleveland [Michael Feighan]
proposed that the Immigration Service stop him at the border" (p. 8).
Feighan's attempt failed and Burton entered the USA with Taylor, who was

a US citizen. The incident illustrates the levels at which Taylor and Burton were debated.

Sometimes "raising the stakes" becomes laughable: the very idea of obstructing an individual's path into a country—not any country, but the land of the free—because of that person's indiscretions with a married woman sounds ludicrous. But remember to consider: time, place, people, preceding events, surrounding circumstances; in other words, *context*. The mid-1960s were a time of transition in the Western world. The US army was only months away from sending its army into Vietnam, where it would wage war for the next several years, eventually withdrawing in 1973. This in turn would precipitate a counter culture of young people opposed to war and, indeed, all manner of violence. But the pulses of liberalism and permissiveness sent out by what became known as hippies were only just being felt at the time of Burton's entry in the US. Prevailing moral standards dictated that his domestic arrangement with Taylor was sinful; they were living "over the brush." Out of wedlock, in other words. Humorous as this seems today, a politician's attempt to deny entry on these grounds was in 1964 considered, even if not considered too deeply and eventually rejected. I include the episode as a way of conveying how Taylor and Burton's presence, let alone behavior, was seen by even affluent Western societies as transgressive.

The couple was in Toronto when Taylor's divorce came though. She and Burton escaped what had become something close to confinement and headed northeast, marrying in Montreal on March 15. It was an expedient wedding, a quick functional affair with no time for a honeymoon. Burton was due on stage the next night. After taking his usual curtain call, he made a special point of introducing his new wife to the audience and, in typical Burtonian style, repeated lines he had spoken earlier in the evening from Act III, Scene I of *Hamlet*: "Go to, I'll no more on't. It hath made me mad. I say, we will have no more marriages." We will have no more marriages? Burton would marry three times again, including once more to Taylor and Taylor would marry three more times.

Burton experienced what we might call cultural osmosis: a process by which the qualities and character of Taylor's life passed through an invisible membrane into his. He had forcibly become accustomed to the idea of not having what used to be a private life: even if he had negotiated a precarious entente with some paparazzi in Rome, the mayhem at Porto Santo Stefano in Easter 1962, had served as a harbinger. The benefits though were palpable. *The VIPs* had drawn audiences quite out of proportion to the scale of the film. Gielgud's *Hamlet* made more money than any Shakespeare play in history and offers of films indicated that he was in-demand. No one called it the A-List back then, but, if they had, Burton had joined. Twice in a year, he appeared on the front cover of *Life* magazine.

In Chapter 6, I reasoned that some people suspected Burton had accepted a Mephistophelean offer when Hollywood beckoned. This time, it seemed Lucifer had not just sent his evil messenger: he came himself, offering Burton everything he had ever craved: money, primo film roles, and a wife with the face that launch'd a thousand ships. In return, Burton would surrender any remaining vestige of his private life.

Taylor's circus of secretaries, chauffeurs, pilots, hairdressers, lawyers, and hangers-on was "a far cry from 1925 and the helpless poverty of the valleys," as Chris Williams puts it. But it was also a far cry from the prestige, affluence, and prominence of recent memory. Barely two years before, when playing *Camelot* on Broadway, Burton would slip out after a show to Jim Downey's Steak House, on 44th and 8th, have a few drinks and check out available women (or reptiles, according to Joan Collins).

Now, after every performance, a Rolls-Royce would be waiting at the front entrance of the Lunt-Fontanne Theater. As a police-fortified barrier held back the crowd, Elizabeth Taylor Burton, as she now was, would alight regally and acknowledge her acolytes before disappearing into the theater. When she returned, she would be accompanied by her husband. Downey's was only a block from the theater and the Copacabana, where Pat Tunder used to work, was also within walking distance. But Burton would have needed a false beard, a backup security team and maybe a rescue plan to snatch a Jack Daniel's in either.

The parts Burton was offered were, like Taylor's, tailored to fit him, often too snugly. For example, the couple played in their third film together as anomalous lovers, he a married Episcopalian priest, she an unmarried, free-spirited nonbeliever, determined to break every social norm she can. Taylor's character describes herself as "an amusement" and expresses doubt over whether it was possible for a man to love her. *Time* reported that, when Burton first read the script of *The Sandpiper*, he remarked, "it hits pretty close to home" (July 16, 1965). Despite poor reviews (*Variety* called it "trite and often ponderous"), its worldwide gross was an incredible $14 million; even with Taylor and Burton's inflated fees, the film cost only $5.3 million.

Eleanor Perry, in her 1965 review of the film for *Life* magazine, relates how, during filming, Burton and director Vincente Minnelli became involved in a heated exchange about the staging of an indoor scene. Finally Burton conceded and snapped at Minnelli: "For the money we will dance." The "we" suggested he and Taylor came as a package. "The money," wrote Perry, "was enough to get both the Burtons to act in what is possibly one of the most tedious, inane and ludicrous films ever made" (p. 22).

Burton's earnings started to match his new status: his percentage take from *The VIPs* came to $2.8 million, far more than he had ever earned from any other film. This gave him a lever for bargaining similar fees for *The Night of the Iguana*, and *Becket*, both released in 1964. With the confidence that he now had legitimate drawing power at the box office, whether in theater or film, Burton had agreed to a percentage of the receipts for *Hamlet* and ended up with about $900,000. Burton must have realized that the source of his newfound allure was curiosity not so much about him but of his relationship with Taylor. She was fascinating without him; irresistible with him. He was rumbustiously interesting without her; wickedly charismatic with her. Liz & Dick had discovered a human version of synergy, the interaction of elements that, when combined, produce an effect greater than the sum of its part.

Theirs was an America, or a world, where following celebrities was once foolishness; now it was amusement, and soon it would become business. When Stephen Gundle writes, "The Taylor-Burton scandal marked the beginning of epoch," he alludes to the period in history when voyeurism became respectable.

FIGURE 9 *Taylor displayed "The Elizabeth Taylor Diamond," as it became known, at every opportunity. Her exhibitionism helped shape her public image. After Taylor's death, the ring was sold for $8.8m.*

Photo by Express Newspapers/*Hulton Archive*/*Getty Images.*

9

The devil's work

Celebrity culture has democratized the world. Anyone and everyone have thoughts, opinions, anxieties, expectations, and dreams. We all make evaluations of others, if for no other reason than we are human and humans are curious: we examine, criticize, appraise, evaluate, and judge. By the 1960s, no other actor, male or female, had made him or herself available to scrutiny and judgment like Taylor. She was thirty-two at the time of her marriage to Burton. It is difficult to imagine any other film actor who had attracted nearly as much newsprint, much of it scathing, some of it laudatory. She had fulfilled every gossip columnists' fantasy wishes and then some. No one had ever offered herself up in quite the same way: adore or loathe her, it was impossible not to form some sort of judgment of Elizabeth Taylor. When she was not basking in the glory of her films, she was luxuriating in scandal: her life was less a journey, more an odyssey from one crisis to the next, making a richer, more evocative drama than any of her films.

In 1964, newly married to Burton, her notoriety at a peak, her status as the world's premier actor assured, Taylor gave one of her most thoughtful interviews to Richard Meryman. I opened this book with a quotation from this interview; it was the one in which she stood back from herself and revealed that "Elizabeth Taylor" was an artifice without "depth or meaning" and useful merely because "it makes money." "I love not being me Elizabeth Taylor, but being Richard Burton's wife," she disclosed. "I adore fighting with him" (1964).

Much of her effort was to distance herself from popular conceptions, though she appeared to contradict herself with the striking admission, "I have I suppose behaved immorally because I broke the conventions," at the same time stressing that, from her perspective, she did not "feel immoral or dirty." She seemed a woman imprisoned by an image of her own making, a chatelaine of her own artifice. The "working thing," as she called it, broke the conventions? Or did *she*?

Later in the interview, Taylor seemed to suggest they are one and the same thing. "We were doing everything we could not to make it public," she says of her and Burton's apparent attempts to conceal their infamous liaison. By kissing on set? By humiliating Fisher in public? By frequenting Hostaria dell'Orso, one of Rome's most fashionable restaurants and a human aquarium where the paparazzi watched different species of celebrities feed? Her strenuous attempts to escape the media rarely took her out of zoom lens range.

And the complexities multiply when Taylor said of her creation: "I'm not going to answer for an image created by hundreds of people who do not know what's true or false." This was 1964, remember; a time when consumers' enthusiasm for probing into others' lives was a new, perplexing and, for some, unwholesome development. "The public takes an animal delight in putting somebody on a pedestal and them tearing them into little bits," Taylor bristles, almost certainly with herself in mind. A persecution complex—an irrational feeling that one is the object of collective hostility or ill treatment—can be a comfort (though it is rarely a serviceable guide for future conduct). Incidentally, Taylor herself was not averse to theriomorphic excitement: on March 15, 1974, she wrote to Burton, "I wish I could tell you of my pure animal pleasure of you" (quoted in Lauren Effron's 2013 story for *ABC News*).

In many ways, Taylor gave an unmannered account; in other ways, she affirmed what many had suspected: that, while she proffered a kind of Jekyll and Hyde split, the two facets of her personality, character or self were indistinguishable, perhaps indivisible. She did not metamorphose into another person, a Mr. Hyde, when she was in public. She remained in role. Forty-seven years after the interview in 2011, when reflecting on her life, Dave Kehr wrote: "Elizabeth Taylor's most memorable role—and greatest accomplishment—was Elizabeth Taylor."

"For about five years after *Cleopatra* [i.e. 1968] the public's curiosity about the sexual combination of Taylor and Burton remained insatiable," wrote Brenda Maddox in 1977 (p. 190). It is untenable to believe Taylor was not just fully aware of this, but ready to exploit it. Abetted by a film industry willing to pour her into custom-fitted roles, like that in *The Sandpiper*, she embarked on what might qualify as a project. The project was a collaborative enterprise, carefully planned to achieve the aim of making Taylor and Burton, or Liz & Dick, the most glorified, most lauded, even most idolized couple in the world. Far from trying to shy away from the gaze of their public, as Taylor contended they had in Rome, the couple seemed to stride into range of every camera lens, talked into every mic and posed for every journalist who ever shouted: "Liz! Just one smile please!" These were just the distractions, the minor entertainments that broke up the main drama: the main plot was played out on the big screen. It was in the 1964 Meryman interview that Taylor first uttered a line that could have served as her motto: "I have learned however that there's no deodorant like success." Exactly what she meant by success became clearer over the next several years.

In contrast to Taylor, Burton made no attempt to conceal his accommodation of the media or their often invasive methods. "Why shouldn't the press and the photo corps have a go at us?" he asked writer Budd Schulberg, while filming *The Night of the Iguana*. "We make an absolutely enormous amount of money for an absurd bit of work," Burton was quoted by Heymann (p. 306).

A percentage of that "enormous amount" was blown on an extravagant lifestyle that, following the deaths of super-sybarites Aly Khan in 1960, King Farouk in 1965, and Porfirio Rubirosa in 1965, set the gold standard for self-indulgence. Today, celebrities appease their fans with a reckless wastefulness; no one wants a celebrity who shows restraint and moderation. Fits of profligacy are of no interest to audiences: fans expect a continuous flow of free spending. Movie stars in the 1960s were typically not narcissistic, at least not overtly. Audiences had to be coaxed into believing stars were wealthy, enjoyed a luxurious lifestyle, and had earned these perks on merit. No one wanted to risk the potentially ruinous consequences of rubbing consumers' faces in it. Until Taylor and Burton.

When, in 1899, the American economist Thorstein Veblen introduced the term conspicuous consumption, he was being sarcastic about the inelegant exhibitionism he detected was becoming part of contemporary society. People were beginning to attach social importance to *things*; that is, products or commodities that could be made, bought, sold and eventually discarded as waste. The products might have functional utility: a tee-shirt is protective clothing, even if it is a baroque print Versace costing $700. But they have additional utility: for display. Veblen sneered at the vulgar manner in which consumers bought things to demonstrate their status, prestige or some other kind of honor. They were showing off. Veblen might not have liked what he saw, but it was an oracular vision: conspicuous consumption became more prevalent in the twentieth century as consumers became aspirational: they constantly sought to upgrade their possessions, indexing their progress, or their progress as they would like others to see it, or as they would like it to be seen.

The Liz & Dick theater would never have made the same emotional impact had the principal players not been such avid, voracious, conspicuous consumers. The jewelry was the most prominent element of a riot of excess that started while Taylor and Burton were filming *Cleopatra* in 1962. The proximity of the Bvlgari store on Via del Condotti to the Cinecittà studios meant that a break from filming often took Taylor and Burton to the high-end jewelry store. On one of their first visits, Burton offered Taylor a gift: it was a ring, which was sized specifically for Taylor. Amanda Triossi, the curator of the Bvlgari Heritage Collection, recounts how they dispatched the ring to the studio: "Then a few days later, a very elegant lady walked into the shop with the same ring on her finger—and it wasn't Elizabeth Taylor. This lady asked to have it resized because it was too big. It was Burton's wife, Sybil," Triossi told Ellie Pithers in 2013.

No one knows exactly what happened: "Within weeks, the ring was back on Taylor's finger, the first of a series of gifts." Burton later said: "I introduced Elizabeth to beer; she introduced me to Bvlgari."

Burton was never a mean man, but, after meeting Taylor, he seemed sucked into a vortex of improvidence, lavishing precious gems on a woman who already had a well-known penchant for expensive jewelry courtesy of Michael Todd, who made no secret of his wish to "spoil" (his word for indulging her) Taylor, as a parent spoils a child. On one of their trips to Paris, she asked him for some earrings, which were costume jewelry and made of cheap paste (imitation gems); Todd bought them and secretly replaced them with real diamonds. Eddie Fisher tried to maintain the momentum: for her thirtieth birthday, Fisher availed himself of Bvlgari and presented his wife with a pair of yellow diamond earrings. Later, when his wife's affair with Burton had become globally known, an irate Fisher sent her the bill.

When making *The VIPs* in London, Taylor and Burton became regular shoppers in Hatton Garden, the jewelry quarter, where Burton bought several baubles. Burton gave Taylor a $200,000 diamond necklace for her birthday. The thing about valuable jewelry is that it is what the British call moreish; so pleasant that one wants more, and more. For Taylor, jewelry was not just a grandiose tribute—though it was certainly that too—but a constituent part of her epicurean persona. She may have been drawn naturally to sensual enjoyment, especially when derived from drink, sex, and precious gems; but she must have, at some point, realized that they were as much part of her public character as her illustrious violet eyes and twenty-two inch waist.

Although, Taylor would not have known it in the 1960s, jewelry would become integral to what some might call the Taylor brand: her affection for precious stones was, to use a term of today, commodified. I will move on to this in later chapters.

Elizabeth Taylor without jewelry was like *film noir* without a *femme fatale* or an Angelina Jolie movie without at least one close-up: incomplete. So Lucy Mangan is slightly off-key when she writes, "Taylor's penchant for jewellery wasn't about avarice, but about mere acquisition" (2012). It was not about *mere* acquisition: it was acquisition for the purpose of satisfying us, rather than her, what Sam Kashner and Nancy Schoenberger call, "fabulousness for the sake of fabulousness."

If she had ever satisfied her craving for jewelry, we would have wondered, "what happened to the real Elizabeth Taylor?" After 1962, her jewelry box expanded from a colossally expensive trove of valuable stones to a nonpareil tableau that approached the world's most opulent collections. Auctioned at Christie's after her death, the collection realized a record $116 million (The complete assembly of jewels, art, and film memorabilia fetched over $156 million, or £100million. I will examine the auctions in more detail in Chapter 18.)

Burton's contributions were among the priciest and many of the pieces he acquired were of historical importance. "The Elizabeth Taylor Diamond," as it became known, was a 33-carat, peach pit-sized, D color, potentially internally flawless diamond set on a ring. It had previously been owned by Vera Krupp, of the famous munitions family. Burton paid Parke-Bernet Galleries $305,000 for the ring and gave it to Taylor on May 16, 1968. It was considered the most iconic of her white diamonds and was the ring she wore nearly every day. After her death, the ring was sold for over $8.8m (£5.7m), as we will discover later in the book. (There are two versions of a meeting between Taylor and Britain's Princess Margaret, who admired the ring and sardonically commented, "How very vulgar." Version 1: Taylor replied, "Yeah, ain't it great?" Version 2: Taylor took off the ring and passed it to the Princess who tried it on. Taylor then remarked, "It ain't so vulgar now, is it?")

Another Burton gift was La Peregrina, a pearl, ruby, and diamond necklace with a 203-grain pear-shaped pearl discovered by a slave in the sixteenth century in the Gulf of Panama: this was part of the crown jewels of Spain. Prince Philip II (1527–98) gave it as a wedding gift to his wife, Mary Tudor, of England, and it later passed on to Spanish queens Margarita and Isabel. It was once painted by seventeenth century Spanish artist Velazquez. In 1969, Burton acquired the sautoir for $37,000 (£23,000). Sotheby's head of jewellery Ward Landrigan hand-delivered it to the Burton's suite at Caesars Palace, where Taylor promptly lost it in the shag pile carpet and eventually recovered it from her dog's mouth. Landrigan has expressed doubt about whether Burton actually earned enough to finance his prodigal gift giving. More likely, Taylor—ever the breadwinner of the marriage—underwrote the expenditure, knowing how much audiences expected her to be the recipient of exorbitantly priced gifts. Being the beneficiary of gifts had become an integral part of the Taylor persona.

The Taj Mahal Diamond, as I noted previously, was Burton's gift to Taylor on her fortieth birthday. The heart-shaped diamond is believed to have been a gift from the Mughal Emperor to his son, who became the great emperor Shah Jahan (1592–1666). This fetched $8.81m (£5.7m). The sale prices were sometimes ten times more than the pre-auction estimates and reflected the premium placed on the association with Taylor. Burton paid only a fraction of the sale prices, of course; but, even so, in the 1960s and 1970s, his purchases were astonishingly extravagant. Burton may have been canny enough to know he was buying more than jewelry. He was buying captivation. Even if he was using Taylor's money to buy it.

Taylor and Burton signified glamour, that exciting and attractive quality that makes certain people, or sometimes things, seem effortlessly appealing.

The Liz & Dick phenomenon was a kind of material manifestation of desirability: everyone wanted what they had, including love, money, happiness, an ability to flout rules, and . . . well, it was harder to think of what they did not have.

"Glamour is a form of secular magic," wrote Nigel Thrift in 2008. "We might see it as a fetish, or as a means of feeling thought and tasting thought. What is clear is that we seek it out" (p. 14). He means that the kind of consumer culture that surrounds and inhabits us has produced a peculiar form of enchantment, part-human and part-thing. We are not only fascinated by, but yearn to be like others who are able to upholster their lives with desirable commodities. In the 1960s, it probably seemed ironic: the more Taylor and Burton distanced themselves from the realm of the ordinary, the more ordinary people were attracted to them. They precipitated the first stirrings of the intimacy at distance that has become so commonplace today.

Should we be surprised by celebrities' extravagance? Being a spendthrift is almost part of the job description today. Paul McCartney blew $3 million on his wedding with Heather Mills in 2002 (the divorce in 2008 cost him even more: £24.3 million in settlement). At the time, this was a breathtaking amount, soon eclipsed by a spate of $3m+ weddings, including the $8 million nuptial festivities of British soccer player Wayne Rooney and his bride Coleen McLoughlin in 2008. Their wedding featured a chartered flight to Genoa, Italy, where guests attended a masked ball aboard a $120-million yacht. The 15-carat Lorraine Schwartz engagement ring Kanye West gave to Kim Kardashian in 2013 cost upwards of $1.6 million. Former Destiny's Child member Kelly Rowland gave Beyoncé's baby Blue Ivy a $5,200 Swarovski crystal bathtub in 2011, when the world was in the midst of an economic recession. These are commonplace events and consumers have been desensitized: there is little or no shock, outrage, or indignation.

Yet in the mid-1960s, there was more disturbance; not just anger—though there was certainly an element of this—but surprise that a pair of film actors would flagrantly flaunt their success, or more accurately, the fruits of their success in such an unrestrained manner. Those who exhibited their wealth shamelessly were typically royals from the mid-East or beneficiaries of vast inheritances, who enjoyed the company of entertainers, but were not themselves in showbusiness. With Todd, Taylor had been like a pampered child, exhibited as the progeny of a father, who declared quite proudly and unblushingly, that, "there is no better way in the world of spending it [money] than trying to spoil Elizabeth."

But, with Burton, Taylor woke up to the idea that she was part of the most glamorous couple in history and that made her more precious than her own or anybody else's jewelry collection. There could be no let-up: the momentum had to be sustained. She and Burton bought a 279-ton, 450-foot, luxury yacht, christened it *Kalizma*, stocked it with rare books and paintings and staffed it with a five-strong uniformed crew and security team.

It cost $200,000 in the 1960s and was described as a "floating palace" after a $240,000 refurbishment. Almost as soon as they bought it, Burton started enquiring about a new mode of transport that had become available in 1964, the six-seater Lear Jet 23. Ostensibly, the yacht afforded the couple a degree of privacy from the media, but, actually, it was a media magnet. The *Kalizma* was usually in range of telephoto lens-carrying paparazzi. Even if it was not, Burton and Taylor invited media aboard. Like the jewelry, the yacht was an extravagance that returned an extravagant reward.

"She spends $1,000 a minute," Burton bombastically reacted to questions about Taylor's prodigal habits, though Taylor herself was more circumspect in her estimates. "Only $100,000" on clothes every year excluding jewelry (of course), according to Kitty Kelley, who repeated Taylor's peerless remark straight from the Marie Antoinette handbook, "We get such pleasure out of spending money" (p. 263).

Kelley acknowledged deliberation in Taylor's studied superciliousness: "Elizabeth enjoyed the extravagant image and helped cultivate it on occasion" (1981, p.264). It seemed more gamble than calculation. The wonder is that, in the 1960s, Taylor and Burton's conspicuous consumption did not attract criticism: from a woman once described as an erotic vagrant and a man who would have sex with a snake if it wore a skirt (according to Joan Collins), their reckless spending might have been popularly perceived as a sign of moral tawdriness, if not downright decadence. It probably was in some quarters; but, for the most part, audiences stood back in awe as Taylor and Burton became the most shamelessly profligate, and ostentatiously glamorous couple in history.

The Liz & Dick spectacle—and I think it can safely be called that: it was a visually striking performance with great impact—maintained a running record of the couple's activities. At a time before *The Real World* (which began in 1992) *The Osbournes* (2002) and *Keeping Up With the Kardashians* (2007), the Burtons offered their own graphic documentary on their marriage through their art. If *Cleopatra* presented a grand, panoramic vision of the passion Taylor and Burton shared, *The VIPs* a narrower, glimpse into one corner of their (at that time) triangular relationship, and *The Sandpiper* an allegory about Taylor's power to disrupt marriages, then *Who's Afraid of Virginia Woolf?* submitted a portrait of marriage as a tense, psychic blood sport.

Many critics regard this film as the apogee of Taylor's artistic life. She was duly rewarded with an Oscar (as well as several other awards) for her role as Martha, a fiercely frustrated wife of a failed history professor, played by Burton. The Mike Nicholls film of Edward Albee's classic 1962 play, satisfied consumers' voyeuristic appetite by exhibiting Taylor and Burton as they might be during a night's drinking. And there were many such nights, of course. In the movie, their marital savagery is conducted through reciprocal humiliation and malicious games. Taylor threw herself into the part with gusto, delighting in her character's malevolent laughter, mostly directed at her downtrodden spouse. Burton responded with pastiche and comic impersonations, but his whimsical geniality masked a devilish character. Albee's play, which is over three hours long, was cropped to 131-minutes, but without any dramatic forfeiture. It remains arguably Taylor's career *tour de force*. It was also a commercial triumph, grossing $40 million. The film cost about $7.5 million to make. Taylor's name on film was an imprimatur. It meant the film would definitely make money. This meant that what was once an exorbitant amount was now a standard fee for Taylor: $1 million, plus the usual 10 percent add-ons. With Burton's package, the couple earned about £5 million.

The film was an unexpected departure for Taylor, who had slid easily into roles of royal enchantresses, nymphets, hookers, and miscellaneous jezebels. Albee's character, Martha, is an older, frustrated, boozy harridan, a ballbreaker, who tries to dismantle her husband's confidence. She was seemingly cast against type. In her 1964 memoir, Taylor called her Martha "a desperate woman," who falsely displays a tough character. "But there are moments when the façade cracks and you see the vulnerability, the infinite pain of this woman inside whom, years ago, life almost died but is still flickering" (p. 156).

Was she hinting that her portrayal of Martha was intended as self-disclosure? Or was this just an effort to tantalize audiences? Was Taylor a vicious bitch once she had sunk a few drinks? And was the sturdier exterior Burton mounted handsomely in every public appearance just that—an exterior? These were the type of questions Warner Brothers, which made the film, wanted audiences to ask. Whatever audiences imagined they had seen added to what was evolving into one of the most lucid, personal, and evocative dramatizations of a love affair in history. As Richard Corliss puts it, they "convinced their huge audience that all these glamorous, embattled characters, especially Edward Albee's George and Martha, were their selves, Liz and Dick, apotheosized from tabloids to tragedy." And one of the most lucrative apotheoses: between 1962 and 1965, movies featuring Taylor and Burton, together or individually, grossed in the region of $162 million.

By 1966, Burton coveted a mid-career *succès d'estime*: his Shakespearean days forgotten amid the excitement of Liz & Dick, he had, for all the world, spurned serious theater and opted to follow the money. So the chance to make proper literature come alive for the delectation of the popcorn-eaters was irresistible. *The Taming of the Shrew* was billed as a Burton-Zeffirelli Production, meaning Taylor and Burton stumped up about $4 million of their own money to make the film and hired Franco Zeffirelli to direct. The running time of the screen adaptation was just over two hours, making it perfect for cinemas.

Again Taylor and Burton were cast as lovers, this time as Petruchio, the gentleman from Verona, Italy, and Katherina, the hot-tempered shrew of the title. As in the previous joint ventures, the Burton-Taylor magic, chemistry, electricity or whatever crowds thought they could create flared and crackled. Also, as in previous ventures, the audiences flocked to the cinema, yielding over $12 million gross. Curiously, this was Taylor and Burton's only production: considering the killing they had made at the box office with *The Taming of the Shrew*, one might assume they would have monetized, to use a term of today, what had by 1967 become, to use another term of today, a brand: Liz & Dick.

As Burton's stock rose, he commanded $750,000 per film. Taylor joined the cast of *The Comedians*, based on the Graham Greene novel, though she appeared for only about twenty minutes in the movie (hence her cut-price $500,000 fee). No sooner had filming on this project finished, Burton dived straight back into English Renaissance theater and retrieved Christopher Marlowe's *Doctor Faustus*. Sourced from legend of the German scholar who made a pact with Lucifer in which he bartered his soul in exchange for knowledge, power, and worldly pleasures, it fitted Burton almost too perfectly. Taylor made her non-speaking appearance as Helen of Troy ("Was this the face that launch'd a thousand ships? And burnt the topless towers of Ilium?"). The film was at the "extremely indulgent" end of the vanity projects spectrum. Burton decided to co-direct, bringing in Nevill Coghill, a professor of English he had met years before at the University of Oxford. "The Burtons, both of whom act themselves as carried over from 'The Comedians,' are clearly having a lovely time," wrote Renata Adler, of the *New York Times*, "one has the feeling that 'Faustus' was shot mainly as a home movie for them to enjoy at home." Adler's 1968 review bore the headline, "Faustus Sells His Soul Again: Burtons and Oxford Do the Devil's Work."

None of the next seven films Taylor and Burton made together made such a critical impact as *Who's Afraid of Virginia Woolf?* Yet they remained adamant that they preferred to live, work, and play together. Even as suspicions grew that they had become a double act, they confirmed their interest in projects that involved both of them. In the 1960s, this might have seemed a crass capitulation: subordinating artistic and creative considerations to their own narcissistic predispositions. Today, it would seem like a perfectly reasonable accommodation of the needs of consumer culture; if you have a multipurpose term and accompanying image capable of adding market value to any conceivable product that was available for purchase, why not work it? Liz & Dick had been insinuated into the popular vocabulary and, even if critics were doubtful about the merits of their collective artistic endeavors, audiences were still prepared to spend money devouring them. Whether preening behind dark glasses as they slid into their awaiting car, phonily demonstrating annoyance at persistent paparazzi or posing lovingly on some immaculate Pacific beach, their seemingly self-replicating image seemed inescapable. Even terrible reviews for *Doctor Faustus* and the modest box office returns for *The Comedians*, did nothing to temper interest in the couple.

The parabola of Taylor and Burton's film careers changed after *The Comedians*, steeply curving downwards with films that are now barely remembered. Considering these actors were in a position to pick-and-choose whatever scripts they wanted, their decision making seemed grotesquely flawed, or informed by ulterior imperatives. For example, the reasoning that underlay their choice of *Boom!* is difficult to discern. Perhaps Taylor was thinking of her role in *Cat on a Hot Tin Roof*, which was written by Tennessee Williams, author of *The Milk Train Doesn't Stop Here Anymore*, the play from which the film was sourced. Her role as the beguilingly slithery Maggie in *Cat on a Hot Tin Roof* was perfect for her; seemingly congruent with her off-screen self. In *Boom!* she was a wealthy writer and widow of six husbands ("I've escorted six husbands to the eternal threshold and come back alone without them"), surrounded by servants and nurses, working on her autobiography somewhere on an unnamed island in the Mediterranean.

Burton's part was equally as unpromising: a poetry-reciting Angel of Death. Noël Coward was also recruited to play "The Witch of Capri." Despite having a quality director in Joseph Losey, the film vanished without trace. It was, to use J. Randy Taraborrelli's phrase, a "creative nadir" for Taylor and Burton. The budget for the film, which was shot in Sardinia, was $10 million, but at the box office, as Burton recorded on page 499 on his diary, it "went BOOM."

The release of the film coincided roughly with the end of Taylor as a box office pull: she slipped out of the top ten in 1968 and never again returned. But, as interest in Taylor and Burton's films sagged, fascination with their unheard of extravagance rose. "I'm glad that I knew the wildness, glamour and excitement when I was in my prime," Taylor reflected on her life in the 1960s, "The parties, the yachts, and the private jets and the jewellery. It was a great time to be young, alive and attractive and to have all those goodies" (quoted in Taraborrelli's 2011 article in the British newspaper, the *Daily Mail*). She and Burton did not so much live as help define what the scholar Christopher Lasch in 1991 called the Good Life, "conceived as endless novelty, change and excitement, as the titillation of the senses by every available stimulant" (p. 520).

Theirs was an existence without want: the only yearning was for even *more* novelty, change, and excitement. They had everything, but, it seemed, could never be satisfied in their eternal quest. Even as her own film career lapsed, Taylor remained aware that her brand demanded excess. So, when she was offered a part in a film version of Frank D. Gilroy's play, *The Only Game in Town*, which is set in Las Vegas, a couple of hundred miles from Hollywood, she insisted that it should be filmed in Paris (France, not Texas).

There was little obvious rhyme or reason behind the demand, which entailed the studio's recreating a complete cityscape in a different continent, a project that would necessitate a budgetary review. But such was Taylor: demands, however arbitrary or preposterous were part of the persona. Her fee was $1.25 million, which was, an objective analyst might conclude, a sweet enough inducement to live apart from her husband for eight weeks. Burton was filming in London (about a 90-minute flight from Paris in the 1960s). The principal reason for relocating the film was probably to test her own marketability: was the Elizabeth Taylor brand so powerful it could induce a major Hollywood studio into a hopelessly irrational and colossally expensive logistical move? It was.

Even more remarkable: the studio in question was 20th Century Fox, which only seven years before had been pushed to the brink of bankruptcy by a combination of Taylor's whims, illnesses, and preternaturally disproportionate demands. The same studio could have realized that the force that almost brought destruction also brought salvation of sorts. Not this time though: the film lost heavily, taking only $1.5 million after an outlay of $11 million. It was not only a catastrophic miscalculation on 20th Century Fox's behalf, but a misunderstanding of Taylor's allure. To put it starkly: by 1970 (when the film was released) she was no longer a box office draw: she was an all-purpose celebrity.

So, when M.G. Lord described the flop of *The Only Game in Town* as a continuation of Taylor's "plunge," she must mean strictly in terms of boxoffice receipts. And she might have pointed out that cinema itself was plunging: receipts dropped dramatically in the mid-1960s, indicating that consumers had assimilated the idea of home entertainment and were structuring their viewing around television, by then a legitimate rival to film; all three major American networks were broadcasting programs in color by 1966. British television started color broadcasts the following year, using a different system.

By 1969, Taylor's film career was effectively over. In other respects, she was soaring. She fired imaginations with her romance, electrified people's lives with her extravagance and recklessness, and piqued their curiosities to the point where they pored over every detail of her private life. Her films were no longer as interesting as her life. Not by a long way. Ironically, Taylor, as she approached forty, was capable of producing performances detached from the glamour-radiating working persona. In the same year, she bombed with *Boom!*, she teamed up once more with its director to make *Secret Ceremony*, an unheralded film, but at least not pulverized by critics. "Miss Taylor, as the role requires, is far more rotund in 'Secret Ceremony' than she has ever been," wrote Renata Adler for the *New York Times* in 1968. She was not the only critic to spot the increasing girth of a woman once known for her wasp waist. But by the late 1960s, Taylor's body was no longer such a prize asset. So when syndicated columnist Rex Reed wrote of

the "disintegration of Elizabeth Taylor," he was failing to grasp how Taylor
had matured not just physically but in terms of her cultural presence. Her
famous looks were once, but no longer, at the center of her status. The
Toronto Star quoted film critic Brendan Gill who wrote that, by the late
1960s, Taylor was "less an actress . . . than a great, natural wonder."

Soon after, she also became a grandmother at thirty-nine. Her son by
Michael Wilding, Christopher, was very much a child of the 1960s and
spurned any chance to follow his mother into showbusiness. Despite hippie
looks, including long hair and kaftans, Christopher succumbed to conformity
when he married in 1970, and presented his mother with her first grandchild,
Leyla.

While tales of Taylor and Burton's wantonness and material promiscuity
continued to captivate consumers, their films together petered out. Burton
played Henry VIII in the acclaimed *Anne of the Thousand Days* (1969), in
which the then up-and-coming Canadian star Geneviève Bujold ("a perfectly
conventional beauty," according to the *New York Times*) played Anne
Boleyn. She was twenty-six at the time of filming. Taylor was ten years older.
The prospect of Burton's renewing old habits made Taylor feel "threatened
and insecure," according to Kitty Kelley. (Incidentally, Bujold was later to
play Cleopatra in a 1976 tv movie *Caesar and Cleopatra*). Taylor petitioned
for a role in the film and got a small, uncredited part. It was around this
time, Burton gave her the Krupp diamond, which ensured his superabundant
gift giving was once more plastered over newspapers. Too much was never
enough.

By this time, an unpleasant but no less interesting theme had irrupted into
the Liz & Dick narrative: quarrels. Perhaps, this understates what often
developed into fullscale slanging matches. Burton's affection for alcohol had
been noted from the time he made his first film in 1949, according to his
biographer, Melvyn Bragg (p. 87). His drinking habits were known to Taylor,
even before they had met. In fact, his hung-over feebleness on the set of
Cleopatra elicited Taylor's first emotion for him. She could have been
disgusted at his lack of professionalism, amused at his comical attempts to
pull himself together or irritated by his lack of respect for her. Instead she
was intrigued. "Her impression of him until then was of a vain, arrogant,
cocksmen full of drunken rodomontade," wrote Gabriel Byrne in his review
of the book *Furious Love* (by rodomontade, he means boastfulness; by
cocksmen, I presume he means a man reputed to be sexually accomplished,
and the plural is just a typo).

There is no evidence that Burton stopped drinking, apart from a few days
here and there, during the first years of their relationship. Later, he gave up
alcohol in the interests of his health; to save his own life, actually. But never
for good: he would always find a way to resume his habit. When they met,

Taylor was a drinker, though not in the same league as Burton. She learned quickly. I will return to this subject later. The repartee between Taylor and Burton was a constituent part of the whole Liz & Dick spectacle: an evening in their company usually meant a kind of impromptu floorshow of badinage, banter, and witticisms. Burton would show no embarrassment in remarking on Taylor's breasts, her skin, and her body size (which varied, of course, prompting him to call her "Lumpy"). Her riposte usually concerned his pockmarked face. Occasionally, alcohol induced them into slightly more vituperative territory and the exchanges grew abusive. There are different accounts of when this began to affect their relationship, most of them speculative.

Burton's diaries are a reliable source and the first evidence of genuine sourness appears in March 1969, when he writes of his "acute unhappiness" and a few weeks later when he recognizes that he is "drinking too much." As Byrne wrote in 2010: "Drink brought surcease, made sense of conflict, for the moment." Whether the conflict precipitated or exacerbated the drinking, no one outside the couple can know with certainty. What is certain is that, by around 1968, their arguments were less private squabbles, more full-blown exhibitions. Ellis Amburn gives an example of altercations. During a 1969 trip to Paris, they stayed at Hôtel George V on Champs Elysées, and, as usual, the media were on standby to record events. "The Battling Burtons" was the sobriquet coined by the Parisian media, according to Amburn (p. 266). *Les Burtons Lutte?* It must have seemed like the ding-dong exchanges audiences saw in *The Taming of the Shrew* and *Whose Afraid of Virginia Woolf?* far from being distortions of the Burton's own harmonious marriage, were actually premonitory visions of what was to come.

Over a relatively short period, Taylor and Burton's relationship seemed to traverse every trial: unraveling the confused tangle of other spouses and children; withstanding the pressures of living, working, relaxing and doing practically everything together; enjoying the shortlived ecstasy and longer term agony of alcohol and the dependency it occasioned; coping with the subtle torment of balancing Burton's artistic predilections with Taylor's zeal for commercial success. Many marriages and civil partnerships navigate similar challenges. But usually not while under constant surveillance. Taylor and Burton had to accept the examination of their every waking moment by the media. Whether they liked it or not, their lives were part of a public spectacle. Neither could simply shrug and say, "That's the end of Liz & Dick. We're closing the play." There was no script, no denouement. Yet, incredibly Taylor herself wrote one. The ingenuity of her strategy was flawless; the audacity unprecedented.

After *Anne of the Thousand Days,* Taylor and Burton made just two more films together, neither of them destined to make a mark in the annals of cinema history. Burton's vanity project *Under Milk Wood* was an instance of his thoughtful showmanship, a film of a "play for voices," as its author

Dylan Thomas described it. Finally, a project that might have seemed like a case of tempting fate: a two-part film called *Divorce His, Divorce Hers*, which dealt with the breakup of a marriage from the perspectives of both parties. Again, this was clever showmanship, with the audience, as ever, granted the opportunity to gaze in on the private lives of Liz & Dick. This time, however, it was not so much a case of art imitating life, but, as Sam Kashner and Nancy Schoenberger reveal, "art *predicting* life, because at the time both Burtons were trying very hard to shore up their marriage" (p. 345).

Cue three hours of babbling, sniping, and grieving over a disintegrating marriage. The resemblance to their own disintegrating marriage was a kind of bonus coincidence, though no one, not even Taylor and Burton, knew until a few months later. The film was never released theatrically and had its US television broadcast premiere on February 6, 1973. On July 4, 1973, Taylor issued what was, even for her, an extraordinary press statement. It was handwritten, probably at the Regency Hotel, New York, where she was staying, and began: "I am convinced it would be a good and constructive idea if Richard and I separated for a while."

Remember, this was a statement specifically intended for the media, not for Burton, or any member of her family, but, basically, for public consumption. "Maybe we loved each too much," the message continued. "I believe with all my heart that the separation will ultimately bring us back to where we should be—and that's together." At this point, modern readers might have interrupted: "Stop! Too much information." Taylor's seemingly heartfelt cry to the media continued: "Friends are there to help each other, aren't they? If anyone reads anything lascivious in that last statement, all I can say is it must be in the eye of the reader." It ended, somewhat bizarrely, with a plea: "Pray for us."

Burton, as far as anyone can tell, knew nothing of this. He was at this stage drinking so heavily that he was probably too stupefied to have been an accomplice in its design or preparation. Taylor may have taken advice from her agent, but the note bore the hallmarks of her own imagination. Think about this again: a Dear John letter, perhaps the most personal of all communications, not delivered by hand or left on a dresser, nor even by mail in a tear-stained envelope; but in a press release. Taylor was never a sentimentalist. Even an act of intimacy could be performed in such a theatrical way that it appealed to popular taste. Playing to the gallery was hardly playing; it was second nature to Taylor.

In recent years, we have become accustomed to reading, for example, "In a joint statement, Robin Thicke and Paula Patton announced, 'We will always love each other and be best friends, however, we have mutually decided to separate at this time'" or "French President François Hollande is expected to announce his separation from partner Valerie Trierweiler on Saturday following a media storm over allegations he is having an affair with an actress." It would be a surprise if, say, Halle Berry tweeted details of an impending breakup independently of her partner. A surprise, though perhaps not a shock. In 1973, it was both. Was it an indiscretion of unspeakable magnitude? Was it the scribbled tantrum of a woman pushed to the edge? Was it a typically Tayloresque revenge, this time served scalding hot? Or was it just what the most glamorous woman does? Wash her dirty linen where everyone can see, as if to confirm she can do what others dare not contemplate. If so, it was another new conjugation of the Taylor brand.

Glamour and romance, suspense and excitement, hedonism and depravity, narcissism and excess, drama and trauma; all these alternated at dizzy velocity for over a decade. It was difficult to believe Liz & Dick, for so long a living breathing, growing phenomenon, was now a corpse. The narrative logic never wavered, however perverse its premise: just when no one expected it, Taylor delivered the killer blow. In a single moment of inventive revelation, she redefined the meaning of "larger than life." Of course, everyone knew she was larger than life, but now they knew she was even larger than they imagined.

Burton was, for the first time in a quarter of a century, a single man. Taylor had headed west to Beverly Hills, leaving him to consider his options. He headed east to Sicily where he was contracted to work on *The Voyage*. Whether the prospect of Burton's playing opposite Sophia Loren prompted her into action, we do not know; but Taylor landed in Sicily for a few days in late July. Shortly after, divorce papers were drafted. The divorce was eventually granted in June 1974. In the interim, questions about Taylor and Burton abounded. She seems to be putting on weight: is she sick again? He seems pale and jaded: is he still on the booze? Are they together again, or are they just finalizing their divorce? When she fell ill, he flew to California to be with her. After recovering, she flew to Italy to be with him. The guessing game continued, giving substance to a kind of Liz & Dick afterlife. A drama conjured purely in the imagination.

In 1970, four years before the divorce, Taylor and Burton agreed to appear as themselves in an episode of *Here's Lucy,* a tv sitcom featuring Lucille Ball. It was unusual but clever: it gave them the opportunity to humanize themselves, gently making fun of their personae. Taylor, for example, remarked that she washed her hair in champagne. Burton grumpily complained about not winning an Oscar. They caricatured popular perceptions of them. Lucille Ball, who also executive-produced the show, was a veteran of television comedy. After working in Hollywood in the 1930s and 1940s, but without too much success, Ball gambled by transferring to television and featuring in a show called *I Love Lucy*. Television was considered a poor relation of cinema though Ball, perhaps more than any other actor, redefined it. The show's extraordinary popularity (it peaked at 44 million viewers) turned Ball into one of the highest-paid actors in the world. She changed the show minimally and changed its title to *The Lucy Show* and then to *Here's Lucy*. In 1953, Ball had been summoned to meet a House Un-American Activities Committee (HUAC) investigator privately to confirm that she never intended to vote Communist and that her association with Communism was only through her socialist grandfather. Many other actors' careers were derailed by the HUAC hearings.

"A monster of staggering charmlessness and monumental lack of humour" is how Burton described Ball. "I loathe her," he recorded in his diaries (p. 352). He reflected that he was not drinking at the time of the program, or else, "I might have killed her." Burton was exquisitely nonchalant in the tv show, playing himself as morose and slightly bitter. He probably was, actually: he had been overlooked for a knighthood, which he desperately craved and believed he deserved at the time. Taylor just mirrored herself: temperamental, haughty, every inch a diva. Yet the very fact that she was prepared to parody herself in a comedy showed her willingness to try to create some distance between her true self and the popular image.

Here's Lucy would last only four more years. Considering its matrix, *I Love Lucy* had started in 1951, it was an incredible run for a sitcom. But, by the time of Taylor's appearance in 1970, the show was slightly out of cadence with the times. Ball's character had remained constant through all three shows: a lovable, well-meaning scatterbrain who enchanted audiences with her unerring ability to create chaos. In practically every sense, she was a stereotype: a simplified, distorted image of a particular type of person, in her case, a woman. Lucy (her characters were always called Lucy) was almost reassuring to those who believed women would never have equality with men—as opposed to other women who believed women were the equals of the men they called "male chauvinist pigs" (a chauvinist, in this sense, was someone who showed excessive, prejudiced support for their own sex). Fortunately for Lucy, there was always a man around to get her out of trouble.

It was not just serendipity that delivered the *Mary Tyler Moore Show*, another sitcom that followed a similar format to Ball's shows, but with a very different lead character. Mary Richards (as with Lucy, the first name remained as the lead actor's) was a young single woman who moves to Minneapolis in the wake of a bad relationship. Originally, the show, which ended in 1977 after a seven-year run, was supposed to be about a divorcée, but since that was a fairly controversial topic at the time, the network decided a broken engagement was more acceptable. Mary Richards was pursuing an independent professional career as a tv producer. This was still 1970: the year in which Germaine Greer's *The Female Eunuch* was published, seven years after Betty Friedan's *The Feminine Mystique*. Tyler Moore's show was built around her, her neighbor Rhoda and her landlady. Her boss was Lou Grant (played by Ed Asner). All three support characters were spun off into their own shows. The CBS network must have realized it was taking a chance with a sitcom that departed from the usual formulae, especially when the scriptwriters introduced themes that reflected social concerns of the day, such as equal pay, gay rights, adoption, and prescription drug dependence. The show was written and produced by women.

Another elbow in the ribs of chauvinism came in September 1973 when Billie Jean King, then the world's second-ranked woman tennis player, won "the Battle of the Sexes" before more than 30,000 spectators at the Houston Astrodome and a national television audience. She had risen to the challenge of 1939 Wimbledon champion Bobby Riggs, who had earlier returned from retirement to beat world number one Margaret Court. King entered the arena carried aloft in a gold platform, presumably in allusion to Cleopatra's entry to Rome. The game had its novelty value, but, in retrospect, is seen as carrying great symbolic weight. King, herself a staunch advocate of women's equality, who challenged tennis' orthodoxy and later revealed she was gay, believed she was freighted with the ambitions of millions; perhaps she was. The responsibility motivated her to a straight sets win, not her most majestic perhaps, but definitely one of her most memorable.

Some writers, M.G. Lord and Camille Paglia included, believe Taylor can rightfully claim a place alongside Greer, Friedan, Tyler Moore, and King: she was a pathbreaker for social progress and women's rights albeit, Lord concedes, an unwitting one. Paglia has called Taylor "prefeminist," believing that she expresses "woman's ancient and eternal control of the sexual realm."

Taylor's films were, in a way that seems subdued by today's standards, subversive. Her first important grown-up role in 1951 was in *A Place in the Sun*, which was about unwanted pregnancy and, tacitly, abortion. It could be argued that Taylor confronted sexism and racism in *Giant*, and *BUtterfield 8* addressed female sexual autonomy. *Suddenly, Last Summer* and *Cat on a Hot Tin Roof* both dealt with homosexuality; and, as we have seen earlier in this chapter, both *The Taming of the Shrew* and *Who's Afraid of Virginia Woolf?* incorporated feminist themes with strong and aggressive female characters. But was her personal life a lesson in empowerment? If one counts material possessions, extravagance and ability to boss successful men, like heads of film studios, about, then yes. When Paglia propounded in *Salon*, "she represented a kind of womanliness that is now completely impossible to find," she is probably right. But it was not the kind of womanliness that would have been recognizable as anything but passé by feminists in the early 1970s. Taylor was not so much riding the waves of change, but swimming against them. I will return to the Taylor-as-feminist argument in Chapter 19.

Taylor was, as everything I have written so far indicates, *sui generis*, literally of her own kind. She was not so much a representative as a harbinger, signaling the approach of others. Taylor married Burton in 1964. By the time of their separation, the Tet Offensive of 1968 had damaged American self-confidence and precipitated the withdrawal of forces from Vietnam, inflicting the nation's first ever military defeat. Confidence at home was also in pieces. An attempt to bug the national headquarters of the Democratic Party, in Washington DC, led to the scandal known simply as Watergate (the name of the building where the HQ was based) and whose legacy we find in "gate," which is suffixed to almost any scandal ("Monicagate," after Bill Clinton-Monica Lewinsky; "Spitzergate," after Eliot Spitzer; "Blagogate" after Rod Blagojevich). The scandal's principal casualty was Richard M. Nixon, who would become the first President to resign from office.

By the time Burton picked up a morning paper and learned that his wife believed "the separation will ultimately bring us back to where we should be," the world was very different from how it had been when they whisked themselves away to Montreal for their first official moment of nuptial bliss. In June 1974, every paper, probably in the world, carried a headline along the lines TAYLOR-BURTON MARRIAGE ENDS AFTER 10 STORMY YEARS. That is how the *Spartanburg Herald-Journal* reported the event on June 27, 1974. The marriage was dissolved in a Swiss courtroom. Burton was indisposed through illness, a bronchial ailment.

The judge said he granted the divorce for reasons of "deep disruption of relations." The ruling took effect immediately. Taylor was awarded custody of Maria, the child she and Burton had adopted and who was in school in Switzerland. The court approved the financial settlement the couple had agreed, but kept private. Prior to the divorce, Taylor and Burton had been together in spring 1974, in Oroville, California, where Burton had been filming *The Klansman*. Taylor had left abruptly after discovering Burton was drinking heavily and had been giving out jewelry as gifts to at least two local women. At forty-two, Taylor was, for the first time since she was eighteen, a single woman, untrammeled by a male partner. But was she a woman liberated?

FIGURE 10 *After Burton, other men were to Taylor what cubic zirconium is to diamonds.*

Photo by Ron Galella/WireImage. Getty Images.

10

Every fiber of my soul

Suzy Miller had spent of her childhood in Southern Rhodesia, as it was called—now Zimbabwe—with her expatriate parents, her twin sister, and a brother. At twenty-four, she had become a successful model in Britain. In the 1970s, models were not supposed to do much: stand around in swimwear or underclothes, look seductive and help draw attention to whatever product they were hired to sell. Very much like today, in fact. In 1974, she met Formula One driver James Hunt, a Brit, who, like Richard Burton, liked to maintain an above-average strike rate with women. So it was a surprise when, after a few weeks, they married. Perhaps, again like Burton, Hunt craved the constancy of a spouse to counter the variability of his other dalliances. So, in October, Suzy Miller became Suzy Hunt. Four months before, Taylor had finalized her divorce. Hunt would have known of Taylor, of course. Taylor would not have heard of James Hunt, at least not unless she had picked up a copy of a British newspaper. He was a prominent celebrity athlete in the 1970s and was famous throughout Europe, though not in the USA. As Taylor tried to re-find her past, Suzy Hunt tried to discover her future and, at the crossroads of fortune and fate, the two women's destinies converged.

At times, Taylor must have felt like Pasiphaë, the Greek mythological character who fell in love with a bull. Burton was a strong, virile, ill-tempered beast, who could be forceful and decisive; he was also difficult to stop. So when he wanted to drink, as Taylor discovered, no power on earth could deter him. The delirium over the first few months of 1973 had not stopped her visiting him on set in California, but the discovery that he was still drinking heavily and had resumed womanizing, must have convinced her that this bull needed castrating.

To no one's surprise, Taylor was soon romantically involved with another man, this time more of a fox than a bull (no more animal analogies from this point, I promise). She met Henry Wynberg at a Los Angeles nightclub in summer 1973. He was a car salesman, born in Amsterdam, living in California. In contrast to the somewhat morose figure Burton had become in his middle age (he was forty-eight in 1973), Wynberg was an enthusiastic, nightclubbing lover of life. All the same, he was an unusual choice of partner for Taylor: with the exception of Nicky Hilton, all of her husbands had been in showbusiness and even Hilton had a showbizzy vibe: he moved in fashionable circles and was fond of social activities with his many friends from the entertainment industry. Wynberg was a business owner, but not in the mold of, say, Richard Branson, Bill Gates or Mark Zuckerberg, all of whom have a media presence. Wynberg soon got one.

The September 5, 1975 issue of *People* magazine described Wynberg somewhat cattily as "Taylor's utility consort," presumably meaning he was useful to have around during this interlude in her life. As Taylor started seeing more of him, the media became more inquisitive and, while Taylor avoided interviews, she was intent on making clear that her relationship with Burton was history. Clocks did not stop for Richard Burton; nor did Taylor. She had an audience to satisfy. Elizabeth Taylor without a man was, well, just not Elizabeth Taylor. So the relationship with Wynberg was conducted in full view of the media. "It was a very public romance, and that was the way Elizabeth wanted it," advised J. Randy Taraborrelli in 2006 (p. 294).

Wynberg was, by far, the least known of her partners, though reporters and photographers began to trail him everywhere in an effort to learn more. He talked only sparingly to the media and, even then, in a way that offered no insight into himself. He may not have welcomed the attention, but he was, after all, seeing Elizabeth Taylor. Actually, for a while, he was living with her: she rented a place in Bel Air, where Wynberg stayed periodically. Ellis Amburn contends that, while he was there, his duties included administering Taylor a daily shot of Demerol, a pain relieving narcotic, and a drug which Taylor would favor increasingly in the years that followed (p. 216).

Any Taylor appearance, regardless of context, was turned into spectacle. Later, in November 1973 when she went to visit actor Laurence Harvey, who was dying of stomach cancer in London. Wynberg accompanied her. As well as promoting gossip about her relationship with Wynberg, the visit offered Taylor the opportunity to emote in full view of the media. On some accounts, she climbed into bed with Harvey; even if this were not true (and it surely is not: would someone climb into a dying man's bed?), the story circulated. At the funeral, she wept exhibitionistically, while Wynberg (who did not know Harvey) comforted her.

Within weeks of Harvey's death (on November 25, 1973), Taylor was admitted to hospital, complaining of abdominal pains and suggested she had cancer (perhaps she thought it was contagious); an ovarian cyst caused her sickness. Wynberg stayed resolutely by her. But he was elbowed out once Burton heard of Taylor's illness. Burton was filming in Sicily at the time and left the set to fly to the US, where he visited her. Almost immediately, Wynberg moved out. There was no scene and Wynberg declined to explain his departure, though it was impossible not to deduce Burton's arrival was the main and probably only factor. For the next few weeks following her recovery, Taylor spent time with Burton in New York, Hawaii, and Gstaad. It seemed Taylor and Burton were reconciled. They were; but only temporarily. Burton's bovine boorishness soon began to grate on Taylor and she was back in touch with Wynberg; they resumed their relationship. At the time, Taylor was still married to Burton: their divorce did not become official until June 1974. But for all intents and purposes, the severance was complete.

Burton was more marketable now than ever: every flurry of activity with Taylor precipitated media speculation and, even a prolonged absence from Taylor warranted guesswork. He announced his engagement to Princess Elizabeth of Yugoslavia, though this was soon forgotten when he began seeing Jeannie Bell, a *Playboy* centerfold model and actor, with whom he shared a home on the French Riviera. He met Bell when making *The Klansman* in California, in 1974. Her name is spelled Jeanie (with one "n") in the cast list.

Hollywood gossip columnist James Bacon exposed the relationship as something of a fraud when he described Burton as "a beard": "A beard in Hollywood lexicon, is a friend or business associate who acts as a front for a married man romancing a young girl," explained Bacon, though the more common definition is a woman who accompanies a gay man to help conceal his homosexuality. Whatever the nature of her friendship, Bell appears to have supported Burton in his efforts to give up drinking.

Taylor and Wynberg became constant companions. What is not clear is how Wynberg earned a living. He dabbled in photography, but the extravagant life Taylor led was way beyond his means, giving rise to the suspicion that he had settled on a kind of parasitic existence.

In spring 1975, Taylor went to St. Petersburg, Russia, where she was to make an improbable US-Soviet picture, a remake of *The Blue Bird*, originally a 1939 vehicle for Shirley Temple. Then forty-three, Taylor had lost 28 pounds after a bout of amoebic dysentery, returning her to about the same weight as she was as a teenager. She arrived at the Leningrad Hotel accompanied by 2,800 pounds of luggage, two Shih-tzu dogs, a Siamese cat, her full staff, including secretary, hairdresser, maid, and Wynberg. It was the kind grand entrance the city might have expected of Catherine the Great. Taylor's suite was scented with lily of the valley and water for both drinking and bathing was imported, as was all of her food (from Fortnum & Mason, of London, actually). Taylor and Wynberg began wearing matching interlocking Russian-style wedding rings from Cartier's, the kind of gesture that Taylor habitually used to tempt rumors.

After completing the film, Taylor flew with Wynberg to Geneva. Burton, by that time, was in the company of Bell at his chalet in Céligny, about fourteen miles (twenty-three kilometers) away. Burton was on what he describes in his diaries as a "health kick" and coherent enough to conduct phone conversations with Taylor, ostensibly about personal finances. In the August 3 entry in his diaries, Burton records a phone conversation with Taylor, after which he writes: "Can't believe it and think of nothing else. What will it be like seeing her again. I'm a little scared. Jeannie Bell desperate" (p. 602).

As they renewed their friendship, Taylor and Burton began to see more of each other. Not covertly; Wynberg was aware that an *entente* of sorts was in the works and was not surprised when Taylor told him she and Burton were ready to give it another shot. Wynberg left, out-of-work, but with a check for $50,000 to keep him on his feet.

On landing at London's Heathrow airport, a gathering of media on the tarmac reminded Wynberg of his fame-by-association (in the 1970s, media could get access to runways and jetways were not in popular use). Still uncomfortable with the press, Wynberg steadfastly refused to give interviews. "I do not want to discuss the affair," he told *People*, before admitting, "I am shattered . . . I still love her." The magazine concluded: "He [Wynberg] is negotiating with a U.S. publisher for the rights to his version of *Life with Liz*" (September 8, 1975). (No such book was published.)

Wynberg's fortunes fluctuated. He kept Taylor's Rolls-Royce and, for a while lived in a luxurious Beverly Hills home. Two years after splitting with Taylor he was tried on charges involving four girls aged fifteen to seventeen. He also launched a news agency, which failed. For a while he was homeless. Whatever he did, his reputation as the man wedged in the middle of Taylor's disjointed relationship with Burton remained.

Yet Wynberg's impression on Taylor's life is actually far, far greater than most imagine. A known wheeler-dealer, he was a businessman with little interest in entertainment, but an appetite for making money. At some point in their relatively short (less than two-year) relationship, Wynberg suggested to Taylor that she market her own fragrance. Obviously aware that intense public interest in her had endured for over a decade and would probably continue through the 1970s and beyond, he thought she could exploit this interest commercially, producing and selling a perfume bearing her name.

This was 1973 or 1974, long before every celebrity, whether an evacuee from a reality tv show or a singer with 10m+ twitter following, had their own cologne. So it was an original and perceptive initiative. Taylor was a friend of Roy Halston Frowick, better known as Halston, a premier fashion designer in the 1970s, who was already preparing to launch his own fragrance on a market dominated by Chanel No. 5. The concept of creating a product closely associated, if not synonymous with, a person and one that could evoke qualities popularly attributed to that person seems commonplace today. In the 1970s, it was almost visionary.

Taylor liked the idea and, in 1975, signed an agreement that gave Wynberg "perpetual" rights to 30 percent of the net profits to perfume and other cosmetics marketed under her name. It could have been a prosperous undertaking, but Burton's return effectively curtailed Wynberg's interest, or at least it would have done if Wynberg had not held on to the signed agreement. Ten years on, in 1985, Taylor would hook up with Cheesebrough-

Ponds Inc. to produce a perfume and she and Wynberg would become involved in a legal contest. I will return to this when considering the post-Hollywood rebranding of Taylor.

On October 16, 1975, page 26 of the *New York Times* carried a story under the headline: ELIZABETH TAYLOR AND RICHARD BURTON ARE REMARRIED. It described how: "A mud-hut village in a Botswana game preserve was chosen by Elizabeth Taylor and Richard Burton for their remarriage last Thursday [October 10]." It happened sixteen months after their divorce. The marriage proceedings were conducted by Ambrose Masalila, African district commissioner, and witnessed by two employees of the Chobe Game Lodge. Note the disparity in the dates of the wedding and the newspaper report: incredible as this sounds today, news of this marriage did not surface for six days. In the context of the overall Taylor-Burton relationship, the second marriage was a disappointing sequel. It lasted only nine months and had none of the anfractuous plot that gave the decade-long original union such appeal—to onlookers, I mean.

Imagine a chimpanzee locked in a room with a bunch of bananas hanging from the ceiling out of his grasp. Also in the room is a chair. The chimp is intelligent enough to realize that, if he (it's a male chimp) stands on the chair, he can release the bananas (I promised no more animal analogies, but allow me one more).

November 10, 1975: it was Burton's fiftieth birthday and his new wife threw a party for him at London's Dorchester hotel, inviting 250 guests and ordering several dozen cases of champagne. Burton's so-called health kick was probably compromised from the outset, and, by the time of the marriage, he was drinking again. The difference this time was that he had occasional spells of sobriety; and, when he was sober, Taylor was usually not. At the time of the party, Burton was in the middle of one his sober passages. He drank mineral water all night, watching his guests drinking themselves into a giggly oblivion. He must have felt like the chimp, except without the chair.

"Elizabeth was drinking enough for both of them," Taraborrelli writes, indicating she had lost none of the *joie de vivre* they shared for much of their first term of marriage. But sober, Burton was a very different character. Gone were the cringe-inducing Shakespeare recitals that probably made guests think, "What a ham!" but which Taylor evidently admired. Gone also was the egotistical loudness that drowned out others. Gone was the bellicose character with whom Taylor, then forty-three, would bicker, argue, and sometimes fight. The bull seemed old, worn-out, and too weary to stand, let alone fight. The birthday party ended without incident.

"You can't keep clapping a couple of sticks of dynamite together without expecting them to blow up," Burton pontificated about himself and Taylor (Francesca Rice, of *Marie Claire* is one of the several writers who has used this quote in her 2013 story). But, without alcohol, Burton was not explosive, and that seemed to disappoint Taylor. Perhaps she had become inured to the devastating repercussions of living with Burton. The more sedate existence offered by a sober Burton may not have appealed.

Within days of the party, Taylor and Burton flew to Gstaad for what they anticipated would be a restful holiday. C. David Heymann quotes a source who reckoned they slept in separate rooms (p. 388). He also suggests Burton started drinking again while in Gstaad. Then, out of nowhere like a downhill skier zipping down the snow-covered Swiss slopes, came Suzy Hunt.

Hunt, then twenty-six, was, like so many other women to whom Burton was attracted, married. In her case, not for long: she was in the middle of a divorce when she ran across Burton, drinking again, but not to the point of incapacitation. He first saw Hunt on a ski lift; they were traveling in opposite directions and Burton turned to his assistant, Brook Williams, and asked if he knew the "vision that has just passed by." Burton would later say of their first encounter: "I turned round and there was this gorgeous creature, about nine feet tall. She could stop a stampede."

A few days later Burton and Hunt met at a party and struck up a friendship that would lead to marriage. Such was the state of his marriage to Taylor that Burton felt emboldened to take her back to the chalet and introduce her to his wife. Taylor, of course, had done worse when she kissed Burton passionately in full view of a houseful of guests and her then husband Eddie Fisher. Unlike Fisher, who slunk away in shame, Taylor counterblasted by escorting a Maltese advertising man named Peter Darmanin, then thirty-seven. With almost indecent haste, Taylor moved Darmanin into her chalet for five nights before he had to return to his day job in Valletta, Malta.

One can imagine Darmanin just about coming to terms with reality and wondering whether his "vacation of a lifetime" actually happened. "Guess what happened while I was in Switzerland?" he teases his friends before disclosing details of "my week with Liz." But then, in a reversal of the precept, fantasy bites. Taylor calls him and asks him to return. Broke, Darmanin borrows the airfare and answers the siren call, picking up a filigree Maltese cross brooch on his way. They resume their carnality for two weeks before the ever-tempestuous Taylor loses her temper, punches Darmanin wearing her 33-carat diamond ring and slices open his eyebrow.

Today, it would be remarkable if someone in Darmanin's position failed to capitalize on their moment of global fame and sold the inside story for several hundred thousand. But the Maltese was no bird of prey and turned down several offers that would have ensured him a comfortable future. In fact, he still spoke fondly of her to the *Times of Malta* after her death in 2011 (available at: http://bit.ly/UfzG64 accessed September 2015).

Burton, though, was more deeply smitten. He left for New York shortly after meeting Hunt to begin preparing for his return to the stage. He was to appear in the Broadway production of Peter Schaffer's *Equus*. Hunt accompanied him. The relative seclusion of Gstaad afforded Taylor a canopy under which to conduct her encounter. Unthinkable as it would be today, she had no Swiss paparazzi to accompany her. But Burton, in New York, was not just putting his head in the lion's mouth, but poking it in the ribs to get a reaction. ALCOHOLIC WOMANIZER AND HUSBAND OF LIZ TAYLOR HITS TOWN WITH FLOOZY 22 YEARS HIS JUNIOR, must have read the headlines in Burton's mind. But, in the event, the media gave him a dignified reception and, when he appeared in the role in late February 1976, the critics warmed to his portrayal of the psychiatrist challenged by a boy who blinds horses. Burton went on to play the same part in the film version of *Equus*. The play was a stunning box office success.

Earlier, Taylor had been infuriated by Burton's summons to New York. She arrived at the Lombardy Hotel, where he was staying, only to be summarily told he wanted a divorce. If Taylor was expecting another attempt at reconciliation, she would have been enraged to discover Burton's intentions: he wished to marry Suzy Hunt. Burton's professional fortunes were different from Taylor's: his pulling power at the box office was undiminished and he would continue to pursue serious acting. Taylor's days as an actor were all but over. Perhaps the media had given her remission for good behavior while in Gstaad, but the throngs of reporters that tracked her every move in New York were reminders that she was still *news*.

And what news she made, even without lifting a finger, on the night she attended a Monday evening preview performance of Burton in *Equus* at the Plymouth Theater. Outside the theater, enraptured crowds chanted "Liz!" as she arrived and reporters laid siege. After the performance, there was a dinner for invited guests at Sardi's restaurant (famed for the hundreds of celebrity caricatures on its walls). Here Burton embraced Hunt in full view of everyone, including his wife.

People magazine, in a story headlined "Liz Un-Burtoned Again" (March 15, 1976) revealed how, before leaving the Plymouth Theater after the preview performance, Taylor had wandered backstage and found Burton's dressing room. Some time, perhaps a week later, Suzy Hunt visited the dressing room to find Burton's mirror daubed in lipstick, "You were fantastic, love." It was unmistakably Taylor's work: she was parodying a scene in *BUtterfield 8*, when her character does something similar. Hunt did not know how long the message had been there, but the mere fact that Burton had left it undisturbed probably meant her man had not fully purified his soul of Taylor.

In his biography of James Hunt, Tom Rubython documents how Burton offered to pay the F1 racing driver's divorce settlement to Suzy: $1m (£627,000). James took the offer without hesitation, leaving Burton with the plaudit, "You've done me a wonderful turn by taking on the most alarming expense account in the country." In June 1976, the divorces of Taylor and Burton, and James and Suzy Hunt, were both formalized in Port-au-Prince, Haiti. Burton married Hunt in Arlington, Virginia in August

1976. Burton's marriage would last six years. Suzy Hunt later married millionaire Jack Cawood and settled in the US.

It seemed an anticlimactic conclusion to what many called "the marriage of the century." After the fighting, the drunkenness, the extravagance and, of course, the scandal, the incendiary partnership had just burned out, leaving only embers. Burton, assisted by his young wife (she was twenty-six when they married, he was fifty), brought his drinking under control and went from strength to strength, though without capturing the Oscar he believed he deserved or the knighthood to which he felt entitled. He came close to the former, being nominated for his central role in Sidney Lumet's film version of *Equus*. But his highest award from the Queen was the Commander of the British Empire (CBE) in 1970. But there would be a coda. In 1983, a sober Burton, by then in a new relationship and ready to take on the role of a lifetime, that of *King Lear*, would receive an invitation from Taylor.

"The different parts of the mind struggle to engage or disengage the clutch pedal of behavior, so bad thoughts do not always cause bad deeds," wrote Steven Pinker in 1999 (pp. 517–18). He was referring specifically to an interview Jimmy Carter gave in 1976 to Robert Scheer, of *Playboy* magazine. In a hugely publicized passage, Carter, at that stage pursuing the American presidency, said: "I have looked on a lot of women with lust. I've committed adultery in my heart many times." But, for all their best efforts, neither the American public nor the media found evidence that he had actually committed adultery. Carter, who had just turned fifty-two when the interview was published in the November edition of *Playboy*, suffered an immediate drop in the polls but recovered sufficiently to win narrowly from Gerald Ford. Carter served as President 1977–81. *Playboy* is, of course, a monthly magazine purveying what it describes as "Entertainment for men"; it mixes high-quality writing with pictures of women, often in lingerie, swimwear, and up till 2015, the nude.

Carter was, indeed is, a Christian: he taught at Sunday School, prayed several times a day, openly cited Jesus as an enduring inspiration in his political as well as personal life, and later, in 2006, helped found the New Baptist Covenant, which sought to embrace 20 million Baptists from across North America. He was one of the most prominent evangelical Christians in the country, often describing himself as "born-again." So an admission that he had committed adultery, even in his "heart" occasioned surprise. Even the choice of word adultery carried connotations, suggesting voluntary sexual intercourse between a married person and someone who is not their spouse. "God forgives me for it," Carter submitted. He—Carter, not God; or maybe both—would not condemn a man "who leaves his wife and shacks up with somebody out of wedlock."

Elsewhere in the 8,000-word article, Carter mused over a range of other issues, domestic and foreign, that affected the USA; though these were completely overlooked. It is possible that, had Carter chosen his words more carefully ("shacks up," for example is coarse and emotive), the passage might have attracted less attention. If the words had dropped from the lips of a less reverent politician (Carter was devoted, though not sanctimonious), they would almost certainly not have prompted a furious reaction. But Carter, at least publicly, was a man of earnest rectitude; his Democrat colleagues were concerned that his humorlessness would hurt him in the polls and probably prayed themselves he would, to use a phrase of today, chill. None could have expected this admission.

The brouhaha that followed was probably more driven by the media than widespread indignation. This was, after all, 1976, fourteen years after the charge of erotic vagrancy against Taylor, five years after the publication of *The Female Eunuch* and three years after the Supreme Court judgment on *Roe* v. *Wade* that made abortion legal. The word adultery would soon be replaced by the altogether less heinous infidelity or "being unfaithful" and eventually by the benign "cheating" (adultery now seems a dysphemism).

The act of having sex with someone other than one's spouse was, in truth, not a big deal: in the same year as Carter's interview, Shere Hite published *The Hite Report on Female Sexuality*, which disclosed the results of a survey of 100,000 women, ages fourteen to seventy-eight, and debunked one of the great myths about female sexuality—that most women should be able to have orgasms through sexual intercourse. Hite's book sold a staggering 20 million copies and is often cited as a catalyst for changing the way people saw women's sexual needs and desires. So the actual content of Carter's revelation was not provocative in the context of the 1970s. The surprise was that a politician with his eyes on the presidency offered full transparency.

It would have much easier to wriggle out of the question or provide a bland reply. But Carter exposed the apparent paradox in his thoughts and behavior, and then all but provided yellow-highlighted grace notes about God's sanction. Ten years before, the interview would have killed his political career. In 1976, it was an almost perfect response to changing sensibilities and perhaps a definition of how politicians were going to have to engage with voters in future: as human beings with human foibles and moral deficiencies. Much like the people they represented, in fact.

The costs of self-fulfillment or egotism (choose your value judgment) were being paid by America. In 1973, US forces withdrew from Vietnam, leaving a death toll of 58,000 US military personnel after eighteen years of conflict. As many as two million Vietnamese soldiers and civilians were killed. It was a damaging blow to the confidence of the nation. Any residual myth of a consensus disappeared. Apparent certainties were stricken. Perhaps communism could not be contained after all; maybe American foreign policy was not so surefooted; it could be that America could not remake the world in its own image after all. The moral fallout from the Vietnam War left the nation with a question: was America always right? Or did it just usually win? And there was another pressing question: could politicians be trusted?

The destabilizing effects of Watergate had left Americans wondering. Richard M. Nixon resigned in 1974, probably the most mistrusted, loathed, but engrossing President in history. For all their hate, Americans could not help be gripped by a man who transgressed every moral and legal boundary necessary in order to secure election. His win-or-die-trying approach may have been uncomfortably characteristic of the nation. Nixon did much to dismantle the conception of politicians as unassailable, irreproachable figures who put the public good before their personal wellbeing.

The investigative journalism that led ultimately to Nixon's resignation signaled a change in the way the media operated: creating or controlling events and situations rather than just responding to them after they had happened, tending to intrude on areas that had hitherto been considered private and outside the permissible range of journalism. The media also became more conjectural in expressing news as an ongoing narrative rather than episodes. One case illustrates this.

On February 4 1974, nineteen-year-old Patty Hearst, granddaughter of William Randolph Hearst, the publishing tycoon, disappeared. For twelve hours, no news of the event was released. Then, with scant information about the disappearance, news organizations around the world broke the story. The problem was: not even the FBI had clues about what had happened. Hearst had just vanished. An audiotape dropped off at a radio station appeared to feature Hearst's voice announcing she was safe and in the custody of the Symbionese Liberation Army, or SLA, a revolutionary Berkeley-based movement. In exchange for her release, the SLA demanded the release of two of its members, who had been arrested in connection with a murder.

This elicited more questions than answers. Why Hearst? She had no record of involvement with radical organizations and, in any case, the SLA was not on anyone's radar. Was she some kind of trophy hostage? And what would happen to her if the police did not respond? All journalists could do was speculate. The demands kept coming: Hearst's parents were told to give millions of dollars to feed California's poor. The Hearst family and Hearst Foundation did so, pouring about $2 million into a food program, but negotiations broke down when the SLA sought an additional $4 million. All the while, the FBI remained clueless.

Then came a staggering blindside: on April 15, a raid on a branch of the Hibernia bank in San Francisco was caught on the bank's closed circuit cameras. The footage revealed a picture of someone holding a rifle while her accomplices stole over $10,000. If, as everyone concluded, it was Hearst, maybe she had been in cahoots with the SLA all along. This theory gained credence when she appeared a month later, again holding a carbine, this time spraying gunfire outside a Los Angeles sports goods store. Investigations led to a house, which became the scene of a shoot-out and, eventually, a fire.

Television cameras captured the whole conflagration live. Every tv channel in the US and hundreds more everywhere carried the news, usually augmented with background stories. Viewers saw six charred bodies pulled from the house. Hearst was not one of them.

Then the guesswork went up a level. All anyone knew about Hearst was that she was in some way involved with the SLA, perhaps enlisted, possibly brainwashed, conceivably subject to the Stockholm syndrome, in which kidnap victims or hostages feel trust or affection toward their captors (the syndrome was named after a case similar to Hearst's in Sweden, in 1973). The SLA drip-fed the media audiotapes of Hearst, one in particular stating that she had *not* been brainwashed, and had assumed a new identity of "Tania," a fully-fledged member of the SLA. No longer a victim, she was now a fugitive.

In the mid-1970s, television channels were few in number compared to today; they featured breaking news, often from 6:00 a.m. till after midnight. In many ways, the Hearst case offered television a test: with hardly any factual data of relevance, the medium rose to the challenge by hosting a mysterious, sprawling drama of speculation, which went on until September 18, 1975, when Hearst was finally tracked down. Defiant images of a handcuffed Hearst, smiling, with the clinched fist of a revolutionary, dominated the news. When asked her occupation during booking and fingerprinting, her response was "urban guerrilla." She was convicted of bank robbery and served three years of her sentence. In 2001, she received a pardon from President Bill Clinton.

For over two years, the case filled broadcast media and induced new ways to frame news-as-drama. In fact, Paul Schrader, in 1988, made the story into a drama in his film *Patty Hearst*. Robert Stone's documentary *Guerrilla: The Taking of Patty Hearst* was released in 2005. Television demonstrated it was capable not merely of carrying news, but creating, shaping, and dramatizing it. When, in 1980, CNN launched its 24-hour news channel it did so in the confidence that news, far from being a tedious interlude between more interesting programs, would be, in the right hands, just as gripping and exhilarating as anything else tv had to offer.

The 1960s is usually defined as the most crucial decade of the late twentieth century, and with justification. But the effects of the 1970s are underrated: they remain with us even today. We think about politics and politicians differently as a result of the 1970s. We were forced into rethinking the value we placed on privacy and whether being free from public attention was a good or bad thing. Changes in the scale, reach, content, and influence of the media pushed us toward accepting its presence not only as part of our lives but as prescription for living those lives.

"He gave a luncheon for her Sunday afternoon, and in the evening, at the wheel of his gleaming Rolls-Royce, he drove her to a party at a Washington in-spot. Monday they dined on caviar at the Iranian embassy. Tuesday he escorted her to the world premiere of her new film, *The Blue Bird*. Wednesday he took her to the harness races in Maryland, where they held hands and she sat in his lap. Thursday night they partied again." Clare Crawford and Parviz Raein, of *People* magazine, could have been Taylor's personal diarists. In June 1976, they chronicled Taylor's every movement, perhaps sensing a romance to rival her epic encounter with Burton. The man concerned was Ardeshir Zahedi, the suave diplomat who was Iran's ambassador to the United States from 1959 to 1961 and again from 1973 to 1979. He was a divorcee.

A spectacular forty-fourth birthday party planned for New York had been shattered by Burton's request for a divorce. Taylor was so upset, she fled to California. Jettisoned by Burton, Taylor fell back to the ever-willing Wynberg with whom she shared a rented home in Los Angeles in spring 1976; they celebrated her birthday together at Wynberg's leased home in Beverly Hills.

While Burton struggled to stay away from the bottle, Taylor made a beeline for it. She went into a temporary exile, surfacing infrequently and refusing to answer reporters' questions with anything but trite statements. This did nothing to quell interest in her relationship with Burton: even while apart, tantalizing questions, such as "are they finished?" and "will they get back together?" continued to circulate. Then, unexpectedly, she reappeared and in the most unusual environment: at a fund-raising gala for the American Ballet Theater in Washington DC's Kennedy Center. Taylor arrived, accompanied by Wynberg, in an outfit specifically designed for the occasion by Halston; her jewelry alone would have probably kept the ballet company going for the next five years. Here she met Zahedi.

Zahedi grew up in England and moved to America in 1969 to study at Georgetown University's School of Foreign Service. "A profligate party-giver," Zahedi, then forty-eight, was "one of the few Washington diplomats to remain in public contact with former President Nixon," according to Crawford and Raein. Nixon was, by 1976, *persona non grata*. Taylor was still very much *persona grata*. Within three weeks of meeting Zahedi, she was on a nonstop flight from New York to Tehran, Iran, accompanied by Zahedi. Somehow, Wynberg seems to have slipped out of the picture. While Taylor was known in Iran, she did not elicit the same kind of response she had become accustomed to in the USA and Europe. On Zahedi's own account, "she chose to dress very simply and wore minimum makeup, which made her unrecognizable and did not attract attention, which made it easy for us to move around" (quoted in Tahiat Mahboob's 2013 article). It was an almost unprecedented strategy: Taylor had never knowingly avoided attention, especially from the media. On one notable occasion she posed for Firooz Zahedi, Ardeshir's cousin who was a professional photographer, wearing a chador and tribal outfits (the *chador* is a large piece of fabric wrapped around the head and upper body, leaving only the face exposed, worn especially by Muslim women. The shot is available as http://bit.ly/1uhUeLK (accessed

September 2015; the rest of the collection is also viewable). Whether anyone bought the idea of Taylor going native, so to speak, is doubtful; even with just her eyes visible, she was perceptibly a Hollywood star.

Zahedi was great raw material for the media, if only by virtue of his lavish hospitality. "The ambassador's soirees, sponsored by the fabulously wealthy Shah of Iran, to whose daughter the ambassador had once been married, left few unfulfilled. Guests were afforded their every desire," wrote C. David Heymann in 1996 (p. 395). "If people like caviar, I give it to them. If they like peasant soup, I give them that," said Zahedi (in Mahboob's 2013 article). Zahedi's entertaining was well known in political circles, though, prior to meeting Taylor, he had largely avoided media surveillance. Outside Iran, Taylor was rarely without media accompaniment and, like her other escorts, Zahedi came under close scrutiny. Even if he grew accustomed to it, the Shah did not approve. In any case, if Zahedi needed reminding: Taylor had converted to Judaism. Prior to the Iranian revolution and the establishment of a theocratic republic in 1979, the Shah had become an ally of the West and instituted many liberalizing reforms. But had Zahedi seriously contemplated marrying Taylor, the Shah would have faced an uncomfortable possibility. Kitty Kelley's diverting, if implausible, theory is that the Shah learned that Taylor wanted to marry Zahedi and immediately put his foot down, reminding him that he "couldn't marry a commoner converted to Judaism and make her the stepmother of the Shah's children" (p. 325).

But Taylor's life was diverting and implausible, so the theory was as good as any other. Apart from her faith, Taylor had another impediment to marriage: she drank, at the time, heavily. Even under the liberal regime of the Shah, a woman who drank alcohol would have not have been considered a suitable spouse for the Iranian ambassador. Zahedi consistently denied he was involved romantically with Taylor, though denials rarely deterred the media. Taylor was non-committal and talked to the media only tersely, confirming that she and Burton were divorcing without providing any more details. The lack of factual information or quotations did nothing to prevent media conjecture, especially when Taylor broke her silence only to utter inscrutably: "I love Richard Burton with every fiber of my soul, but we can't be together. We're too mutually self-destructive" (quoted on p. 20 of Yann-Brice Dherbier's book and in Joey Bailey's "Great love stories" series).

After Burton, other men were to Taylor what cubic zirconium is to diamonds. Even if she did not see it that way, everyone else probably did. Just the sight of her with another man must have sparked curiosity: "Will he ever match up to Burton?" Taylor never compared Zahedi or any of her other partners with Burton, though she would have known the comparisons were understandable, if, for her, odious. Burton was a thrilling, if slightly imperfect, fit for Taylor. Her next husband seemed incongruous beyond belief.

FIGURE 11 *For all the glamour, éclat and showbusiness sensibilities she gave to John Warner, she was a target, just like any other politicians' wife.*

Photo by John Curran/AP Photo. © 2015 Associated Press

11

Facing oblivion

Most people crave the stable, simple life in which events are predictable and futures can be planned with relative certainty. No one in their right mind wishes for crime and killing as a daily part of their lives; yet they flock to movies that feature them. We are terrified of being hijacked on board a plane, but do not mind sitting through two hours of a film like *Non-Stop*. But how do we stand on glamour, extravagance, and debauchery? Would we really trade in our dull, uneventful lives for a Taylor-like cycle of interchangeable husbands, boozing, and shameless self-indulgence? Or are we content with the vicarious experience as filtered through the media?

In the mid-1970s, Americans were drawn to the most reviled man in America. Richard M. Nixon was not especially incompetent, corrupt or sexually promiscuous. Other US Presidents could beat him hands down in these respects. He was committedly anti-communist, though his visit to the People's Republic of China in 1972 was a major step toward normalizing diplomatic relations and opening up trade with China. From the standpoint of the twenty-first century, after the administrations of Ronald Reagan and two George Bushes, his policies seem quite liberal. Yet the Republican statesman's achievements were eclipsed by the Vietnam War and the Watergate scandal, his involvement in the latter precipitating his resignation. He remains a figure of revulsion, mockery, contempt, and hate. And yet: ask anyone to name three presidents in living memory and Nixon is bound to be one of them. He still captivates, as much as he repels. In the 1970s, no conversation about politics could avoid Nixon. Even after his death in 1994, his icon is durable, perhaps indestructible.

Despite his inopportunely frank interview with *Playboy*, Jimmy Carter was elected the first Democratic President since Lyndon Baines Johnson, who had continued the program of reform initiated by John F. Kennedy, but lost popularity by increasing American involvement in Vietnam and left office in 1969. Nixon then assumed the presidency after a landslide victory in 1972, until his resignation, after which Gerald Ford took over. It would have been practically impossible for a Republican candidate to win while Nixon's wrongdoing was still so fresh in the public mind. But Republicans sensed that Carter might have a troubled tenure and that the 1980 election would be an altogether more winnable race. In other words, for Republicans, the 1976 election might be a good one to lose.

John Warner was staid 49-year-old, a former US Secretary of the Navy and aspiring Republican Senatorial candidate from Virginia. He was divorced from Catherine Mellon, daughter of the art collector Paul Mellon; the divorce settlement left Warner $10 million richer. Warner had supported and served under the Nixon administration and became the Director of the American Revolution Bicentennial Administration. As such, he attended Queen Elizabeth II's bicentennial dinner in Washington DC in July 1976. Also on the guest list were President Gerald Ford, Secretary of State Henry Kissinger, and Elizabeth Taylor.

Warner's attraction to famous women who could further his political ambitions had been duly noted when he was friendly with tv presenter Barbara Walters. "A woman like you could probably get me elected senator," he was widely quoted as telling her, presumably as a prelude to a marriage proposal that owed more to calculation than emotion. Even so, it was declined. So, when he was seen escorting Taylor around his 25,000-acre farm in Virginia, journalists began to the join the dots, yet without coming up with a clear picture. Taylor did not seem ideal politician's wife material.

She was foul-mouthed, opinionated, habituated to pharmaceutical drugs, and, if considered by today's standards, a full-blown alcoholic. She talked too much, was prone to accidents, illnesses and more than the occasional scandal. Over the years, she had become as used to lavish gifts as Vikings were used to tributes in silver. Warner's advisors much surely have highlighted Taylor's sweeping range of character flaws and concluded she was, as they might have said, unsuitable. Warner might then have pondered and replied: "Yes, but think of the profile."

In September, Warner flew to Salzburg, Austria, where Taylor was making a film version of the Broadway musical A *Little Night Music*. They married on December 4. *People*'s Garry Clifford recorded the event: " 'It's the strangest romance of the century,' whispered a Washington socialite when love blossomed between the much-married superstar and the wealthy but prosaic gentleman farmer."

In 2008, when French President Nicolas Sarkozy married former supermodel and singer Carla Bruni, less than three months after they reportedly first met (and four months after his divorce from the previous first lady, Cecilia), there was surprise, though not amazement. Celebrity culture, as we know it today, had penetrated every nook of modern society, so a liaison between a politician and entertainer was a kind of elective affinity. In 1976, it was a different matter. The following year Brenda Maddox wrote of Taylor: "By allowing herself to become a public utility, she may have forfeited the possibility of being popularly recognized as an actress" (p. 242). (Bruni continued her singing career and toured after her marriage to Sarkozy.)

Whether Taylor herself had much choice is a moot question: a newly voracious media fortified and sanctioned by inquisitive audiences *made* her into a public utility. Taylor did not pressure fans into poring over her photographs, gossiping about her love life, tut-tutting over her indelicacies. She just went along with them. She did not resist, struggle, fight back or refrain from doing what others wanted of her. Yet she did seem set for a dignified retreat when, in December 1976, she married Warner. "Maybe Taylor now can face oblivion—that is, to escape into a private life and a single identity," surmised Maddox, intimating that "her screen and private worlds" had, up to that point, never been distinguishable, probably not even to her. But, as for oblivion: Taylor would not countenance it. Even without a successful film to her credit for several years, she remained in the limelight. Obscurity would hardly have been a satisfactory option.

On the other hand, Maddox's forecast is understandable. After six turbulent marriages, five divorces, and a death, she could have wished for a more emollient relationship, one in which the anger and confrontation to which she was accustomed was replaced by a calming and conciliatory friendship. Friendship? There is at least what some call inferential evidence (i.e. inferred from interviews) that Taylor and Warner's relationship was based on mutual admiration or fondness rather than adoration, desire, lust, or any of the intense passions that had inflamed her earlier courtships.

"I found her very interesting, fascinating. She is a great conversationalist, and she is just a lot of fun," recalled Warner years later in 2011 when interviewed by Mary Green and Stephen M. Silverman. "We never had any real infractions between us." "Infractions" suggests that there was some sort of agreement that both observed and, on Warner's account, neither infringed. They "managed married life," as Warner put it.

Writing four years after the marriage, Garry Clifford reflected that immediately after the wedding, which took place on Warner's estate, "the smart talk in Washington was that a) It wouldn't last the year, and b) Virginia's aristocratic First Families would snub the legendary Liz." But neither happened. Taylor threw herself into Warner's campaign for the Republican Party's Senate nomination undaunted. She accompanied him on the trail, appearing on the stump and earning her husband the nomination. Actually, Warner lost his bid for the party's Senate nomination, but the winner, Richard Obenshain, died in a plane crash two months later. Warner was then picked to run for the seat.

The Democratic nominee was Andrew P. Miller. Taylor's benefit to Warner was, at this stage, ambiguous; there were no reliable historical guidelines as to how someone as unique as she would influence a major political campaign, especially in the light of Obershain's demise. Miller made a preemptive strike to nullify her, anyway. "I don't think Mr. Warner intends to campaign against my wife and I don't intend to campaign against his," he declared at the outset. It was an inconsequential bromide intended to smooth over what could have been an unmannerly campaign.

Unfortunately for Miller, his wife Doris made sure Taylor was brought to the forefront when she said: "She's [Taylor is] a gorgeous woman and I'm not." In an interview relayed around America by Associated Press, Miller joked that she had led "a dull life . . . with one husband." It seemed a clumsy attempt to burnish her ordinariness. She had been married for twenty-five years. "She's obviously a celebrity, but I honestly don't know if that translates into votes," said the ingenuous Miller (in *Stars and Stripes*, September 1978). Warner eventually got into the Senate by 4,721 votes

He may not have liked his celebrity consort image—Doonesbury cartoonist Gary Trudeau gave him the unfortunate moniker "Senator Elizabeth Taylor"—but it made him known. In 2009, William J. Mann quoted the magazine *New Republic*'s cynical description of Warner, "the Senator from Elizabeth Taylor" (p. 395). Donald P. Baker, of the *Washington Post*, observed how critics referred to him derisively as "Mr. Elizabeth Taylor, the actress' seventh husband." The fame-by-association conferred by marrying or even just being seen with Taylor had brought bounties to several previous husbands, Burton and Todd being the most obvious beneficiaries. It had brought less favorable results to Fisher and Wilding.

Politics in the 1970s had not yet been absorbed into celebrity culture. The absorption would start with Bill Clinton in the 1990s. Taylor, by accident rather than design, discovered the compatibility between the two spheres many years before. "People are always asking her what politics is like," Warner explained to Clifford, "and her favorite answer is that politics and show business are a lot alike, but in politics you use your own script and there are no retakes." Warner's appearances, whether at rallies, conferences or in the media, always drew the kind of crowds he would not dare contemplate without Taylor. David Bret makes the point that, like Eddie Fisher's audiences in the early 1960s, they wanted to catch sight of Taylor rather than the person who was supposed to be the star attraction.

Sex did not exist when Taylor started her acting career; at least as far as Hollywood was concerned. Clean and wholesome teasing was acceptable, but laughs were preferable to carnality, as any number of Doris Day movies underlined. Taylor in the 1960s helped sexualize Hollywood, in those days tightly bound to the Production Code on morality (often known as the Hays Code). By the time Taylor took on her new role as a conservative politician's wife and campaign aide, Jane Fonda had sent a frisson around the world in *Klute,* in which she played a prostitute (1971), Ann-Margaret and Candice Bergen had portrayed sexually uninhibited women in *Carnal Knowledge* (1971) and Debbie Harry was electrifying audiences as lead singer of

Blondie, whose first album *Blondie* was released December 1976, the same month as Taylor's wedding. Compared to these women, Taylor in her mid-forties, seemed sedate, respectable, and—whisper it—unadventurous.

Unthinkable as it would have been ten years before, in 1978, NBC's *Saturday Night Live* lampooned Taylor in its "Bill Murray's Celebrity Corner" feature. John Belushi's burlesque impersonation of Taylor, hideously overweight and munching on fried chicken, parodied a well-reported incident in which Taylor needed nonsurgical medical assistance to dislodge a bone embedded in food from her esophagus. Taylor was with Warner at a campaign rally at a restaurant in Big Stone Gap, in southwest Virginia, in October 1978. Warner canceled his scheduled speech at the annual Columbus Day dinner of the Wise County Republican Women's Club and accompanied Taylor to the hospital. It was a minor incident in a minor town, but this was Elizabeth Taylor, after all. An Associated Press story, headlined in many papers "Elizabeth Taylor Chokes on a Bone," ran widely (for example, *The Times-News*, Henderson, NC, October 12, 1978, p. 6).

It must have been a shock to a woman, who had up to a few years before, been regarded as one of the most sexually desirable women in the world, to discover she could be cruelly ridiculed on national television (and by John Belushi, then about 200 lbs.). It was a reminder that, for all the glamour, éclat, and showbusiness sensibilities she gave to Warner, she was now a target. Just like any other politicians' wife. No: more so. (Belushi died from a heroin and cocaine overdose in 1982.)

Taylor signaled that she was not quite ready to accommodate her new role by maintaining her friendships with Halston and other habitués of New York's Studio 54, including Andy Warhol. Warner, the son of an Episcopalian minister, almost certainly disapproved. Taylor's attempt to combine wifely duties with her by then flagging acting career resulted in a forgettable and spinsterish role in the tv film *Return Engagement* (1978) and an uncredited cameo in *Winter Kills* (1977). But her interest in cinema drifted as she caught sight of an alternative future. Not necessarily in politics.

In 1978, Warner met with Henry Wynberg. Recall that Wynberg had suggested to Taylor, probably in 1974, that she could exploit her status by marketing a fragrance under her name, effectively formalizing the then towering Taylor brand. Taylor's box office appeal had slipped since the heady days of the 1960s, but she was still a powerful presence in Hollywood and her international fame practically assured the venture success. In 1975 Taylor signed an agreement, filed in Superior Court, which gave Wynberg "perpetual" rights to 30 percent of the net profits to any cosmetics marketed under her name. Warner, a businessman himself, must have realized the value of Taylor's brand and scheduled a meeting with Wynberg to discuss the earlier contract. Wynberg had already begun research and development into a product and expressed no interest in halting his project. (By brand,

I mean a name and/or image used to give products or activities a particular identity and imply certain values.)

It barely needs restating that marrying Elizabeth Taylor confers immediate status on a husband. Todd and Burton used theirs to obvious advantage. Fisher seemed weighed down by the cumbrous expectations of the status. Warner managed his—by which I mean controlled its use or exploitation. Perhaps his finest public moment came in July 1980 when he and Taylor attended the Republican National Convention at which Ronald Reagan was nominated as presidential candidate. Taylor sat, with Nancy Reagan, in the VIP box. Reagan went on to become President and, after his inauguration in January 1980, the Warners hosted a ball in DC. Reagan had been a Hollywood actor himself, though nowhere near the level of Taylor. He served as Governor of California prior to his nomination. Reagan's presidency saw the launch of the Strategic Defense Initiative, and cuts in taxes and social services budgets as well as the signing of an intermediate nuclear forces non-proliferation treaty.

In 1979, Taylor gave a typically open and enlightening interview to Judy Klemsrud, of the *New York Times* News Service. It started by declaring Elizabeth Warner was now her preferred form of address, as if consigning Taylor, Burton, and all the other cognomens to history. But, as Klemsrud pointed out, even though she behaved as Mrs. Warner, dutiful politician's wife: "The public reaction was much the same as when she was Elizabeth Taylor, big-time movie star. Necks jerked around with whiplash intensity whenever she walked by."

Taylor—or Warner—was in Richmond for the launch of Virginia's Year of the Child celebration; she was the honorary co-chair. Klemsrud noticed a sharp demarcation between her offscreen sedateness and the more familiar "ebullience" she exhibited when accompanying her husband: "Mrs. Warner went about her duties calmly and unsmilingly, with the jaded look of a seasoned politician."

Taylor/Warner bridled at the suggestion that she might wear any of the jewelry given to her by Burton. "That was a kind of a phase in my life, a kind of camp and fun phase. Maybe my values have matured with my age" (she was three weeks shy of her forty-seventh birthday). Klemsrud asked her about whether she felt "diminished in her new role" and Taylor/Warner responded: "I haven't gone out to pasture. I haven't given up . . . I know my own identity, not as a movie star, but as a woman."

Fifteen years before in the *Life* interview quoted extensively earlier in this book, she had referred to her public persona as a "working commodity" and revealed, "I love not being Elizabeth Taylor" (quoted in Meryman, p. 80). So, when she told Klemsrud, "I have no problems with my identity," she seemed to be separating herself from the publicly owned construction that had fascinated people for the previous three decades—she met Nicky Hilton in 1949. "I'm not going to answer for an image created by hundreds of people who do not know what's true or false," she told Richard Meryman, grossly underestimating the millions who were avid for information about her. Yet in 1979, she seemed to have maturely discarded or alienated herself from "Elizabeth Taylor," as if that being was what Alice Cooper was to Vincent Furnier, or Hannah Montana to Miley Cyrus.

Taylor's dietary problems and habitual use of, if not dependence on, alcohol and prescription drugs, were becoming parts of her personal narrative in the late 1970s. In a book written by Taylor and published in 1988, she revealed that she put on as much as 50 pounds. She later, in 1983, explained this to Marie Brenner as a result of the "terrible boredom I had in Virginia after John and I finished campaigning." She spent her time mostly at home, watching daytime television and eating: "I ate out of nerves, nerves, nerves, and got so fat." Kitty Kelley argued that her husband became concerned about her weight gain and encouraged her to diet. Resolving to get back into fighting shape, Taylor/Warner checked in at a spa in Pompano Beach, Florida and shed about thirty-five pounds.

While Taylor/Warner was secreted away in Florida, Donald P. Baker, of the *Washington Post*, wrote a frontpage article, "Surprising Senator: The new Warner confounds critics" (July 1, 1979, p. A1). "What the Virginia senator hasn't done is about as surprising as what he has done," detected Baker, noting that, after his theatrical senatorial campaign, which included "arm-flailing" and "ego-tripping," politicos in DC expected him to continue in much the same vein, parading Taylor at every opportunity and transforming mundane events into media extravaganzas. This did not happen: instead, Warner, as the headline suggested, confounded critics, establishing himself as an individual; thoughtful and studious enough to establish a political presence in Capitol Hill independently of his wife.

Taylor had not worked professionally since she married Warner and, after his election to the Senate, dissolved into the political background. Baker confirmed this was deliberate, drawing attention to a further surprise: "The Warners have maintained a low profile on the party circuit." Quoting Taylor, he wrote: "His wife, who is vacationing in Florida said in a telephone interview that people are beginning to think of her 'more as Mrs. John Warner and less as Elizabeth Taylor,' which pleases her" (p. A16).

On leaving the Florida spa, Taylor/Warner flew to London to be at the funeral of her former husband Michael Wilding, who died on July 8, 1979, after a fall. She had been divorced from him for twenty-three years, but remained affectionate, as the message on her wreath reflected: "Dearest Michael, God bless you. I love you. Elizabeth." Even in her "low profile" phase, she was still news and her appearance at the funeral in England, looking much leaner than a couple of months before, deflected attention away from the solemnity of the occasion.

Taylor threw herself into the political role with gusto: as well as gracing formal occasions with her regal presence, she attended wives' groups, opened stores, led charity drives, judged pie-making competitions, and baby contests, and even appeared in Warner's stead when he was detained in DC on Senate business. In many ways, she became the perfect politician's wife. Or perhaps she was acting like one. In Taylor's case, it did not seem to make any difference. She was forever acting. Except on one notable occasion.

Warner held to the view that women should not be drafted into the armed forces. This sounds a hidebound anachronism today, but, in 1980, it was not too out of step with changing opinion. Roe v. Wade was 1973 and the Equal Pay Act was ten years before that. Women had been a permanent part of the US military services since 1948, though it was not until 1976 that the first group of women was admitted into a US military academy. As President, Jimmy Carter decided to reinstate the draft after the Soviet Union, as it was called, had invaded Afghanistan. Warner believed Carter's draft should include only men.

Taylor disagreed with Warner and made this publicly known: she delivered a rare but stinging rebuke, leaving Warner embarrassed and unsupported at the Republicans' annual Tidewater conference in Maryland. This was February 1980. It is probable that Taylor might have bitten her lip two or three years before; after all, it was not a subject about which she had previously revealed any strong views. In fact, she was quite ambivalent during the senatorial campaign of 1978: she suggested many women did not welcome the rights guaranteed in the Equal Rights Act she had herself supported in the 1960s.

Perhaps the disagreement with Warner on the men-only draft signaled her intention to re-establish her independent presence after four years of relative docility and (for her) subordination. Certainly sections of the media, especially in Europe, discerned the start of a rift between the Warners. When she married Warner, she may have surrendered any vague hope of returning to acting. Certainly her inattention to her appearance and wellbeing suggested she was out of movies for good.

Just imagine for the moment if Taylor had remained at Warner's side, rather like Hillary Rodham Clinton had stuck with her husband, and eventually emerged as a legitimate politician in her own right. When in 1992 her husband was accused of having a relationship with cabaret singer Gennifer Flowers, Hillary famously declaimed: "I'm not sitting here, some little woman standing by her man. I'm sitting here because I love him and I respect him."

Warner was never in need of such defending by his wife, but it is at least conceivable that Taylor could, like Hillary, gradually have become emboldened to strike out politically on her own. Kitty Kelley reckoned: "She [Taylor] understood her celebrity value and realized her glamour was her husband's greatest political asset" (pp. 361–2). She does not mean that

Taylor radiated, while Warner put across his messages; though she certainly did that. But Taylor did not bring glamour alone. She *could* have just fluttered her eyelashes and sat like a much photographed ornament while her husband worked for his votes. Or just appeared like a warm-up artist while audiences waited for the main event. In fact, she was more like Michelle Obama in the early twenty-first century, involving herself in the political melee, "connecting," as people might say today, with voters. In 2014, in her husband's second term as President, Michelle, at fifty, was rated by *Forbes* as the eighth most powerful woman in the world (see Caroline Howard et al., 2014).

Unlike most other politician's wives of the period, Taylor was never left untouched: she was subjected to rigorous media analysis in every aspect of her being, including her clothes, her weight, her makeup, as well as her political views. Only Jacqueline Kennedy Onassis, wife of John F. Kennedy, who was President 1961–3, had attracted comparable media attention. In fact, Jackie O, as she was then popularly known, was still a favorite subject of paparazzi in the 1970s. Still one assumes, if anyone could withstand the scrutiny, it was Taylor. So it was somewhat surprising to discover, in a book, published in 1988, and extracted for *People* magazine, that Taylor found: "The hardest part of the campaign, a trial not even hot fudge could assuage, was the total lack of privacy" (the text is still available at: http://bit.ly/1vDh3JJ (accessed September 2015)).

Politicians in the 1970s and 1980s tended to steer clear of identity or personality politics. Eventually, they would have to embrace it. Media attention and social influence became watchwords in politics and Taylor had no shortage of these. Maybe she would never have pursued the same route as Rodham Clinton, but, had she stayed married to Warner, how might she have affected his flightpath? Warner was not an extraordinary politician, but he had a decent career and was respected during his long period in politics. He did not leave office until 2009, shortly before his eighty-second birthday. For four years after he married Taylor in 1974, he enjoyed unprecedented attention and interest and, of course, during that period he rose to the Senate.

Once in office, Warner, as we have seen, did not exploit Taylor's status and pursued his own agenda, even when embarrassed by his wife's opposing views. The solecism over the draft question was the first hint of discord between them, but it was enough to crank the rumor mill into life. Both Warners denied a rift and, at that point, there probably was not: just an honest disagreement over gender politics. And then, perhaps unexpectedly, when Warner was in his political ascendancy and Taylor appeared to have contented herself with a comfortable, if less-than-glittering existence, there came news that would set Taylor off on a new tangent.

Taylor resumed acting with a role in a version of Agatha Christie's whodunit *The Mirror Crack'd* (1980). She weighed-in at a slender 125 lbs. When Maddox had written of Taylor's separation of "screen and private worlds" following her marriage to Warner, she could not have anticipated how mischievously Taylor could be in selecting her allegories. In the Christie story, she played a faded film star who is attempting to return to prominence after a fallow mid-career. (The title is from *The Lady of Shalott*, Alfred Lord Tennyson's poem.)

The Mirror Crack'd was shot on location in England in May and June 1980. Warner was occupied on senatorial business in DC. Into the vacuum rushed renewed rumors of a breakup. Another rumor circulating concerned Rock Hudson, who was also in the film. Still handsome in his mid-fifties, Hudson, whom Taylor had befriended in 1956 when they both played in *Giant*, had become the subject of gossip. *Modern Screen* magazine, back in June 1971, published an article on "Hollywood's first homosexual marriage," the newlyweds being an aging, once-major Hollywood star and a tv actor who had just achieved stardom. "It did not take too much detective work," wrote Anthony Slide in 2010, "to identify . . . the film star as Rock Hudson, and the television actor as Jim Nabors" (p. 166). Hudson was forty-six in 1971. Nabors was in *The Andy Griffith Show*, a popular series at the time. Rumors about Hudson continued to circulate, but they received no support or refutation. Neither Taylor nor Hudson gave interviews during their time in England. "When Rock goes out in public women's hearts flutter—just like they did in 1954," recorded *Weekly World News* on February 17, 1981 when *The Mirror Crack'd* was showing, either ignoring the rumors surrounding Hudson's sexuality or trying to stifle them.

As comebacks go, Taylor's was a triumph. *Variety* concluded: "Taylor comes away with her most genuinely affecting dramatic performance in years as a film star attempting a comeback following an extended nervous breakdown." She actually *was* a film star attempting a comeback, though in her case following a prolonged period of tranquility rather than a nervous breakdown. Having wheeled through life surviving marital discord, tabloid assault and, now, it seemed, borderline obesity, the relative quietude of life as a politician's wife must have seemed a tad too placid.

Whether Taylor had grown bored of life as a Virginian farmer's wife and political adjunct is not certain, but the interaction with a proper script and fellow actors appears to have ignited her. Within months of returning to the USA, she appeared on Broadway in *The Little Foxes*, Lillian Hellman's 1939 play about three Alabama siblings (while I am explaining the origin of titles, this one is from the Bible's Song of Solomon, 2:15). She was paid $50,000 per week, confirming the producer's faith in her hardy perennial drawing power.

The origins of this unlikely development lay in a meeting with Zev Bufman, the producer, who was launching a revival of Alan Jay Lerner and

Frederick Loewe's *Brigadoon* in Washington in 1980. On opening night, one of Bufman's friends told him: "I've invited a good friend of mine, a senator's wife, to join us. She is terribly bored here and has nothing to do." When she showed up—late, of course—the senator's wife was Taylor. Bufman's version of events sounds too simple to be true, but he reckons that, at a party after the show, he asked Taylor: "How about doing a Broadway show with me?" She replied straightaway: "I'd love to" (that is the way he told it to *New York* magazine's Marie Brenner in 1983).

A couple of weeks later Bufman procured tickets for a sold-out New York show by dropping the phrase, "I'm bringing Elizabeth Taylor" into the conversation. When Bufman and Taylor arrived at the show, 200 photographers were waiting in readiness. After getting jostled by paparazzi, they eventually got inside, where Bufman anticipated a reprimand, but instead, Taylor, to whom these kinds of situations were as taxing as pushing a cart around a supermarket, was unperturbed and sighed: "I hope that didn't shake you up."

It was comeback heavy with intrigue. As *People* magazine put it: "Liz put on two shows for the price of one: *The Little Foxes* and What Will Liz Do Next?" (December 28, 1981). She developed a 102.5 degree fever before the first curtain went up, but still gave a first-night performance that won money reviews ("charm, grandeur . . . sex appeal . . . tidal force of pure personality"). A week later she collapsed with a respiratory infection, and was later hospitalized with a torn rib cartilage. The play was forced to halt for eight days.

While Taylor had an understudy, producers were mindful that she rather than the play was the attraction, so decided to use the substitute—Carol Teitel—only if Taylor became ill *during* a performance. The media played out the medical narrative and ticket sales reflected the renewed interest in Taylor—Taylor the actor, that is. In the following decades, Taylor's illnesses were to become more severe: she would have viral pneumonia, a fall aggravating an old hip injury, two hip replacements, skin cancer, a brain tumor, and debilitating dependencies on alcohol and pharmaceuticals. *The Little Foxes* was a complete sellout and ran for five months in 1981, transferring to Los Angeles for a two-week spell. Everybody involved in the play, including the playwright, became seriously rich as a result of the show's box office success.

While in LA, Taylor filmed five episodes of the soap *General Hospital*. This seemed a bizarre detour even for the capricious Taylor. She played Helena Cassadine, a vengeful widow. Anthony Geary was a staple of the show, playing one of the central roles. He was fifteen years Taylor's junior. Approaching fifty, the renascent Taylor was formidably glamorous and Geary, almost inevitably, got sucked into the vortex of gossip that typically engulfed Taylor. Neither party said a word to the media, though years later, in 2010, Geary opened up during an appearance on daytime talk show, *The*

Wendy Williams Show (here: http://bit.ly/1k8PnIg accessed September 2015). Of course, Geary, then sixty-three, could have been looking for a late career lift; kissing-and-telling would definitely have worked in 1981 when Taylor was married to a senator. But not nearly two decades later. Even so, Geary's version of events had a superficial plausibility: Taylor and Warner were effectively separated.

She and Warner gave no clue at the time and were often seen and photographed together. But they were effectively living apart, Taylor in New York and Warner mainly in Washington DC. This meant there was little or no opportunity for the kind of public clashes that had made her marriages with Burton such marvelous theater. As Warner's political career prospered, he spent more time in the capital and, eventually, decided to relocate. Taylor had served him dutifully and decoratively for years, but the smell of the greasepaint was irresistible and after the Broadway success, she went with the production to London. Her arrival in London could not compare with Cleopatra's arrival in Rome, but it was not bad: en route to a Chelsea house from Heathrow in a Rolls-Royce (naturally), she stopped by a pub in Chiswick, west London, for a pint of beer. Taylor's West End debut was a predictable success: if her film career had waned, a new career on the boards beckoned.

The London production opened in March 1982 and ran for four months, meaning Taylor had been on stage, with a few interruptions, for almost a year-and-a-half. "Not surprisingly, my marriage did not survive the run of *The Little Foxes*," Taylor later disclosed. "Even before I decided to do the play, John [Warner] and I were aware of our problems, and I think it was clear to us both when I went to New York that we would eventually split" (*Palm Beach Post* March 14, 1988). It was an interesting choice of words, as if two abstractions—the marriage and the run—had collided without human interference. No mention of loving each other too much or destroying each other, as she and Burton had determined the causes of their breakups: Taylor and Warner's marriage was, after all, a managed relationship and, like all managed systems, there are dysfunctions. They divorced on November 7, 1982.

Prior to the official opening of *The Little Foxes* in London, there was a charity preview at the Victoria Palace Theatre. Making a late entry into the theater's Royal Box was Diana, Princess of Wales, who should theoretically have been a greater attraction than anyone on stage. "It seemed impossible that anyone would ever manage to upstage the Princess of Wales, but in the last two weeks, a 50-year-old woman with a turbulent past and an uncertain future has succeeded in doing so," advised R.W. Apple Jr. of the *New York Times* (March 13, 1982).

Diana had married Prince Charles in 1981. She would blaze her way into history, mainly through her charity work and her media appearances, but also because of her troubled, loveless marriage. She was divorced in 1986, the year before her death. Long before that, Diana had reconciled herself to being unique and unrivaled as the paparazzi's favorite subject. In this respect, she was a kind of heiress apparent to Taylor: fame and notoriety overlaid and invaded both of their lives. Taylor created what Dave Kehr calls "a new category of celebrity," Diana became its distillation.

Apple described how Taylor's arrival in London two weeks before the preview "prompted a riot among news photographers" and that her every move from that point had been chronicled by the British media. He was writing for a New York newspaper, of course.

Another visitor to the show was Richard Burton, then fifty-six and, at 140 pounds, painfully underweight; his usual weight was about 175 pounds. He had spent some time hospitalized in Los Angeles, then a period convalescing in Céligny before he needed surgery on stomach ulcers. He and his wife Suzy had split up sometime the previous fall, but they made the separation known only in early 1982. Despite the physical and, one imagines, emotional ravages of the previous months, he accepted a new role in a biopic of Richard Wagner. Also in the five-hour drama were Laurence Olivier, John Gielgud, and Ralph Richardson, all recipients of knighthoods. Filming took place in, among other parts of Europe, Dublin, less than 400 miles from London. When she asked to visit him, Burton consulted his director, Tony Palmer, who probably sensed the disruption poised by Taylor's presence and demurred.

The siren call was scarcely audible to Burton, but he found his way to London, all the same. His purpose was to take first voice in a public reading of *Under Milk Wood*. It was a charity event to raise money for a memorial stone for Dylan Thomas. The event had been arranged for months, so it was coincidence that brought Burton to Taylor on this occasion. From the media's perspective, a heaven-sent coincidence. On February 27, Taylor and Burton stepped out from a Rolls-Royce and into to a London nightclub called Legends where she was holding her fiftieth birthday party.

Burton appeared frail and graying at the sides; or perhaps he was coloring his hair and had just missed a couple of areas. He was on the wagon, as he was on the occasion of his own fiftieth birthday. He fell off it then and he would fall off it again. Taylor, by contrast, was drinking prodigiously and taking Percodan (a painkiller containing oxycodone and aspirin), for sure, and probably other chemicals, including Xanax (a benzodiazepine, which is a central nervous system depressant) and Ativan (which is used to control anxiety).

Apple wrote: "The Welsh actor kept the publicity machine grinding with the confession, during a series of predawn interviews, that he unfortunately loved both Miss Taylor, to whom he has been married twice, and Suzy Hunt, his current wife, from whom he has recently separated." Taylor and Burton danced together; there were Press Association photographers to document the moment (it's here: http://dailym.ai/1xJ91eQ accessed September 2015).

The next day, ABC Television News carried the story, anchor Sam Donaldson advising: "Elizabeth Taylor and Richard Burton may have found each other again. Last night in London, celebrities gathered at Taylor's 50th birthday party. Burton and Taylor arrived together, danced together and later Burton said, 'I still love Liz.' And Miss Taylor said, 'Richard was wonderful.' Although the two have been married to each other twice before, they are at the moment married to other people, but they are both separated" (ABC News, 1982).

"The next few nights, the couple were seen around town, and Burton seemed newly smitten by Elizabeth," write Sam Kashner and Nancy Schoenberger (p. 413). Never slow to jump to conclusions, *People* splashed Taylor and Burton across its March 15, 1982 front cover with the pronouncement, "LIZ & DICK AGAIN!" and, inside, a story headlined, "Two Old Flames Smolder Again."

Burton and Taylor had never been out of audiences' heads. Now, it seemed they were to team up physically again. "After a loving London reunion, Taylor is coy—but Burton still carries the torch," *People* informed readers. For the next several days after the party, they were seen together, dining and socializing, though without ever confirming whether or not they were back together.

When Burton was reading at the charity performance of *Under Milk Wood*, Taylor slipped in and sidled up behind him, dressed casually in jeans and a sweater. She whispered, though not so quietly that the audience could not hear: *Rwy'n dy garu di*. It meant, "I love you," in Welsh. Burton replied, "Say it again, my petal, say it louder." She did and the crowd cheered. Taylor had stormed back from "semiretirement," as *People* referred to her period with Warner, to "the pinnacle," while Burton had experienced a painful period, with back surgery incapacitating him for a while. His marriage to Suzy had broken down. "For some reason," mused Burton when asked about his relationship with Taylor, "the world has always been amused by us two maniacs."

Burton did not keep his diary between October 1980 and February 1983, so there is no clue as to his disposition. William Ivory, who wrote the screenplay of the film *Burton and Taylor*, imagines Burton went back to Taylor's hotel after the birthday party, but expressed no interest in sleeping with Taylor and left her disappointed. There are other interpretations. Of course, that was the beauty of Liz & Dick: everyone could speculate endlessly. Unbeknown to Taylor, Burton had, while filming *Wagner*, met a continuity assistant named Sally Hay, then thirty-four. She and Burton would later marry. In the meantime, he mapped out a couple of projects, both of which fell through, leaving him with a space in his calendar.

The British critics were not kind to Taylor. For example, the *Daily Mail*'s then drama critic Jack Tinker wrote of her entrance in *The Little Foxes*: "Her first appearance in a cottage loaf wig and matching figure (had she by some mischance put on her bustle back to front?) was less than prepossessing."

an old British term for a round bread loaf.) Nicholas de
rdian said that she had "sailed into London like some
1, almost submerging the play which brought her here."
isly, Jenny Rees of the *Express* declared Taylor had made
thy of Miss Piggy, trailing mauve lingerie" (Miss Piggy is,
the Muppets). Despite this, every house was sold out in
Palace Theatre. It was a familiar death-and-resurrection:
wds bring her back to life with new vigor. It would not be
resuscitated her either.

ice said: "When you're in jail, a good friend will be trying
best friend will be in the cell next to you saying, 'Damn,
ivate Lives looked a bad idea from the outside. No one
r's ambition: sneered-at by critics for her apparently
: on stage, she crammed theaters with adoring audiences,
e is more than one kind of success. So when she asked
with her in Zev Bufman's Broadway production of Noël
lay *Private Lives*, he might have advised, in his Welsh
colloquial: "Look, love: you've been skewered by the critics for *The Little
Foxes*, but you've got away with it, probably because of the novelty. Look
at your bank balance! Don't push it anymore on stage. Just find a few nice,
well-paying cameos in the movies." But Burton was not just a good friend
(and he might not have used "skewered").

Taylor, in her fifty-first year, was at the statistical midpoint when women
reach the menopause; so she was in a state of advanced maturation. Having
been lost in the creative wilderness while her husband navigated his way to
Washington DC. She seemed to have found a spot on the landscape. Now,
she wanted Burton to join her. On September 23, 1982, at the Beverly Hills
hotel, Taylor and Burton announced at a press conference that they would
be collaborating together. The next day an ad appeared in the *New York
Times*: it featured a huge heart pierced by an arrow and the words "Together
Again." The image of the golden couple reunited in life as well as on stage
was well and truly set in the popular imagination. *Private Lives* and Liz &
Dick: which was the show and which was the sideshow?

FIGURE 12 *"Do you mean Richard and I should play Private Lives like the audience is looking into our bedroom?" Taylor asked her director.*

Photo by The LIFE Picture Collection/Getty Images.

12

Voyeurs and performers

"They're laughing *at* us," screamed Richard Burton. "They didn't think they were watching a play: they thought they'd had an invite into our lives." The curtain had just fallen on the first performance of *Private Lives* and Burton had listened to the snickering and knowing applause from the packed house. He was fuming: the audience was not, he detected, interested in the artistic merits of the play: the paying customers were indulging in a guiltless voyeurism. Taylor listened to Burton's complaint and just dismissed it, agreeing that there were a few who were more interested in them than the show, but it was a first night crowd, after all. The interaction may or may not have happened. Probably not, at least not in quite the same way. It is imagined by William Ivory, writer of the script for the television film *Burton and Taylor* (2013).

For all his thespian pretensions, Burton had long since exchanged his dramatic purity for hard money. He had not agreed to act with Taylor after nearly a decade because of a fifty-year-old script that was cleverly funny but hardly fresh, original or substantial. He did it for moolah. He would have known just as well as Taylor that audiences were more interested in the players than the play, which was a comedy, after all; so giggling was to be expected. If he had been worried about the audience's confusion of fact and faction, he could have insisted on a pre-play disclaimer, such as: "All characters appearing in this work are fictitious. Any resemblance to real persons, living or dead, is purely coincidental." Come to think of it: this would have been a good marketing ploy.

Taylor had probably first raised the idea of a reunion when Burton was in London. Some time after Taylor's fiftieth birthday party, she probably laid out more detailed plans at her home in Bel Air. The figures mentioned would have sounded like a Welsh male voice choir to Burton: $70,000 per week, an extraordinarily generous fee in the early 1980s. *The Little Foxes* had received mixed reviews, more favorable in the US than in Britain, but the audiences confirmed that, even in her fifties, Taylor still had her magnetic field. Being likened to Miss Piggy did nothing to dent the confidence of someone credited with the phrase, "Success is a great deodorant."

She and Bufman had considered a stage version of *Who's Afraid of Virginia Woolf?* which would have been a safe bet, given Taylor's much-lauded performance in the 1966 film version. Tennessee Williams' *Sweet Bird of Youth* was also a possibility that recalled an early Taylor success; she played Maggie in another film of a Williams' play, *Cat on a Hot Tin Roof,* in 1958. Taylor aspired even higher: she had designs on Shakespeare plays. Yet they decided on a comedy with, as Richard Corliss noted in 2011, "a richly ironic title for a woman who lived every moment in public." *Private Lives* was a play by the English writer Noël Coward, first performed in 1930—two years before Taylor was born. An American film version followed in 1931. Directed by Sidney Franklin, it was a commercial success for MGM. BBC television also turned it into a film, in 1976. The play had been revived at intervals and had actually been on Broadway in 1975 when John Gielgud directed. Taylor and Bufman hired Milton Katselas to direct their first co-production.

So the play had a respectable provenance. Still, it appeared an odd choice. Until the plot became clear: it concerns a divorced couple, who marry new spouses and go on honeymoon in France where they are dismayed to find that they have been booked into adjacent hotel rooms. Over the course of the three-act play, they comb over their tumultuous marriage and gradually arrive at the conclusion that, despite their quarrels, they still yearn for each other. Resolving to rekindle their romance, they take flight, promising not to argue as they once did. They devise a code word to call a truce whenever their conversation gets heated, though this proves ineffective and, in one scene, a physical fight breaks out. "Certain women should be struck regularly, like gongs," is a line that was less controversial in the 1930s than it would be today, when it would be interpreted as an endorsement for domestic violence.

Basically, the couple's renewed relationship recapitulates the same conflicts that drove them apart in the first place. The new spouses track them down and discuss divorce. In the process, new arguments break out and the play ends with an image of marital life as an endless repetition of squabbling. Coward himself was famously gay, although he never came out, living as he did 1899–1993. He was a friend of Taylor's and had appeared with her in *Boom!* He was also in Michael Todd's *Around the World in 80 Days,* though he was better known for his writing.

A couple, divorced after a stormy marriage, who meet up again while honeymooning with their new spouses and realize they are still in love with each other. What could Taylor have had in mind? The logic in her apparent foolhardiness in dusting off an old play became apparent, at least to anyone who had not spent the previous twentysomething years on a solo mission to Mars. Burton, like his character "Elyot," had married again, though he was separated from Suzy Hunt and was now involved with Sally Hay.

Taylor had also remarried, though her divorce from Warner was completed in November 1982. She had started seeing a Mexican lawyer named Victor Gonzalez Luna, with whom she had, in December 1982, flown to Tel Aviv, Israel, to lavish gifts on children living in an area of the Middle East, at that stage gripped by war. One of her stated intentions was to meet the heads of opposing factions, Menachem Begin of Israel, and Amine Gemayel of Lebanon. This did not materialize and Taylor ended up embarrassed by the abortive peace initiative. It would not be her final act as a campaigner: perhaps inspired by her politicking years with Warner, Taylor would spend her final twenty-five years of life advocating reforms. She would not, however, become Mrs. Victor Luna.

If Taylor seemed out of her depth trying to bring peace to the Middle East, she might have wondered if she was also swimming toward the deep end artistically. Burton regarded her as a great actor on film, but not on stage. Never an enthusiast of rehearsals, she was known to be an actor who would come to life only when cameras were rolling. If she messed up, there was always a re-take. Burton, by contrast, had started preparing for *Private Lives* almost as soon as he committed himself. His diary records notes such as "Did three hours or so on *Lives* . . ." and "Back to *Private Lives*. Early to bed . . ." during February 1983. And the preparations continued in March; rehearsals began on March 14 at New York's Lunt-Fontanne Theater. Even by that point, Taylor had not read the whole play. This was not out-of-the-ordinary for her, though one can imagine how the rest of the cast of professionals must have felt.

Director Katselas was in no doubt that the success or failure of this play hinged on whether the actors played out Coward's light comedy or performed a *roman-à-clef*, a story in which actual people are thinly disguised as make-believe characters. "The audience wants to see Elizabeth Taylor," Katselas told the cast, to which Taylor enquired: "Do you mean Richard and I should play *Private Lives* like the audience is looking into our bedroom?" "Yes," came Katselas' answer (quoted in Brenner). Presuming Burton was present at the time, he would have either shared the conceit, or stormed out in protest. The fact that he hung around suggests the opening lines of this chapter were likely to have sprung from Ivory's imagination rather than Burton's lips.

Still, frustrations crept up on Burton. The thespian-turned-self-parodist might have bought into the concept, but his threshold of tolerance for working with Taylor had dropped. His personal feelings about her had also changed. Burton's diary reflects sufferance. Monday 14th March: "ET beginning to bore which I would not have thought possible all those years ago." 15th: "Tells me twice an hour how lonely she is." 20th: "She is such a mess." 24th: "Usual day struggling with ET."

On the wagon himself, Burton regarded Taylor's habitual drinking with disdain. "ET impossibly sloshed all day long," he wrote. "So much she couldn't even <u>read</u> the lines" (p. 651). Burton ceased keeping his diary in early April 1983, so there is no reliable way of knowing how he experienced the run or whether his impressions of Taylor improved. But his observations during rehearsals suggest he approached *Private Lives* as strictly business. He seems to have accommodated Katselas' effort to produce a façade instead of a comedy, or possibly turn his and Taylor's lives into farce. His buffoonery would earn him about $1.7 million.

Taylor, in common with most interesting humans, was chock-full of contradictions, with a few paradoxes and an oddity or two. As she prepared to tantalize audiences with a peek into her and Burton's *Private Lives*, she filed suit against the American Broadcasting Company (ABC) and an independent film company claiming an "old fashioned invasion of privacy, defamation and violation of an actor's right." In October 1982, she sought to stop production and transmission of an unauthorized film biography that would, she charged, exploit her name, likeness, and reputation without her consent or approval. Such biopics had been made in the past and would continue long after this. Gloria Vanderbilt, Prince Charles and Princess Diana, Nancy Viscountess Astor, and the Duke and Duchess of Windsor, among others, had all been subjects for similar film treatments. And Taylor offered irresistible source material. In years to follow, a tv film *Liz: The Elizabeth Taylor Story* would be released while she was alive in 1995. *Liz & Dick* (2012) and *Burton and Taylor* (2013) would be broadcast on tv shortly after her death. But in 1982, Taylor was in fighting mood and ready to oppose an attempt to dramatize her life.

"I am suing ABC television network because they plan on doing a story of my life which is completely fictionalized unless there was somebody under the carpet or under the bed during my 50 years," Taylor told a press conference. "'No matter who portrays me, she will not be me, I will not be she. I am my own commodity. I am my own industry." Tamar Lewin, of the *New York Times*, reported how Taylor had indignantly argued: "That is my industry and if somebody else portrays me and fictionalizes my life, it is taking away from me" (November 21, 1982).

So Taylor was not claiming the film libeled her, infringed copyright or in some way defamed her; these are typically the kind of issues central to cases of this kind. Instead, she challenged the very concept of such a film. It was almost as if she were reinforcing the point she made several years before about her alter-ego commodity, the Elizabeth Taylor that "makes money." Except now, she was sensing that Elizabeth Taylor was slipping out of her grasp and could make money for other people. As Tamar Lewin's headline asked: "Whose life is it, anyway?" It was a question without a ready answer. "Legally, it is hard to tell," Lewin replied.

At about the same time Taylor filed her suit against ABC, the sports car manufacturer John DeLorean was arrested on cocaine trafficking charges. DeLorean's famous car was featured as a time-traveling vehicle in the *Back*

to the Future movies from 1985 to 1990. Rumors immediately began
circulating that Hollywood producers were contacting studios with the idea
of making a docudrama, a dramatized film based on real events. DeLorean
and his wife Cristina Ferrare DeLorean were alarmed: they had not sold
their biography rights and, like Taylor, they did not wish anyone to make an
unauthorized version of a story that might have a solid market value. The
DeLoreans publicly announced they would file suit if necessary to prevent a
dramatization of their story. Two producers contested this, contending the
story was already known through articles in the press and broadcast media.
But the DeLoreans argued their life story was "not public domain and
cannot be dramatized without their consent." Lionel S. Sobel in *Entertainment
Law Reporter* reported the case in 1983. DeLorean was found not guilty on
August 16, 1984. He died in 2005. A biopic went into development, but not
until 2014.

Both cases were milestones of sorts. As Lewin pointed out: "Her [Taylor's]
claims go well beyond those other reluctant media subjects have made. It is
also a classic confrontation between the First Amendment guarantee of free
speech and an individual's right to control what is said about her." The film
was not released and never was: ABC decided against broadcasting it for
"creative reasons," though Taylor's legal action was probably a factor too.
In the years that followed, the confrontation Lewin identified in 1982,
became more of an embrace: the idea of privacy, of actually owning the
intellectual property of one's own life, of being the sole proprietor and
custodian of a personal product customarily called the *self* became hopelessly
compromised. Entertainers first and, later, all forms of public figures who
aspired to be or actually became celebrities were obliged to evacuate
conventional notions of privacy. A similar case instigated by Taylor in 1994
had different consequences and I will return to the legal and, indeed, moral
issues that surrounded both later.

During the 1980s, changes both in the character and operations of the
media and consumers' engagement with figures that populated the media
changed. They changed in a way that brought them into a kind of covenant:
consumers demanded from celebrities something more than the typical stars
of previous eras had been prepared to give up. Only Taylor had surrendered
her private life and, even then, surrendered is hardly the right verb: she
probably never conceived of her life as anything but public. The moneymaking
artifice she valued and protected was, as she called it, a "working thing." But
was it really? Was there ever anything else apart from that Elizabeth Taylor?
As Vincent Canby detected in 1986: "Elizabeth Taylor is the most important
character she's ever played."

Privacy as we know it today is different from privacy as Taylor and her
generation understood it. For Taylor it must have been an abstraction,
anyway: she never experienced the state of being free from public attention.
Canby continued: "She's never had any real, sustained privacy, she's had to

progress from childhood to middle age with what is, in effect, a bird on the top of her head . . . [the bird is] public reputation" (p. 1).

Taylor lived her life in full view of the media and, by implication, everyone else. It seems untenable to imagine she could have existed for more than a few moments unobserved or undisturbed by others. Her sense of privacy was much like the sense of privacy today's celebrities experience.

On the subject of disclaimer (which I was earlier in this chapter), Madonna could have prefixed her entire career with "All characters appearing in this work are fictitious . . ." And no one would have sued. In 1983, Madonna Louise Ciccone established her first character, a prodigal gamine with a taste for tat jewelry and clothes bought from a flea market. Over the next three decades and counting, she advanced through popular culture, like a cortège of metamorphic creatures, wielding post-feminist tropes. All of them, yet none of them was the real Madonna. There was probably no such being. Let me explain.

In a way, the entertainment industry had always treated its stars as consumable products. Taylor learned this early, probably aged eight. The 1964 interview with Richard Meryman I have quoted exhaustively, revealed how clearly she understood the Janus-faced nature of popular entertainment. "The Elizabeth Taylor who's famous, the one on film, really has no depth or meaning to me," was how she described her working product (p. 74). She adjusted to meet the changing requirements of the media over the years, pouring out information like oil into a leaky engine. Her wistful roundelay with Burton in *Private Lives* showed that, even in her maturity, she knew how to excite the popular imagination with insights, no matter how unreliable, into the private life of "the Elizabeth Taylor who's famous."

Gossip columnist Liz Smith reckons Taylor strained to be as different from her fans as she could. "That's part of what excited the public: her vulgarity and her arrogance and the money," wrote Smith in *Australian Women's Weekly*, in 2010. She provided the media with the raw material to portray her as extravagantly different from "ordinary" people as possible: they depicted her as an untouchable being, someone you might stand next to at a supermarket checkout and find yourself tongue-tied.

The multiplicity of television channels specializing in news and light entertainment opened up new opportunities for artists to exploit. But it also set a new question for aspiring showbiz types: are you going to resist the brazen, usually disrespectful, often insidious and always inquisitive media, or meet them halfway when they come snooping into your private affairs? Put another way: you are a consumer product; are you going to be like one of those Rolls-Royces favored by Taylor at around $470,000 (at today's prices) with a waiting list of up to eighteen months, or a Toyota Corolla?

When her first album *Madonna* was released in July 1983, Madonna was a month away from her twenty-fifth birthday. The album was on the *Billboard* chart for over three years and became a bestseller all over Europe and beyond. MTV was then a nascent venture: a 24-hour cable television station that played non-stop music videos, interspersed only by brief news bulletins. When it was launched in August 1981, it was an even more speculative endeavor than CNN, another cable station that started operations the year before and which helped revolutionize broadcast news. Music videos were in the early 1980s a new and untested adjunct to vinyl records (cds came later) and not yet the art form they would become.

The first indication of Madonna's clairvoyance came with her determined effort to foreground her visuals and make them staples of MTV. No artist benefited more from MTV (and perhaps vice versa) than Madonna. The British bands Duran Duran and Dire Straits came close. No artist relied so much on filmed video for the visual promotion of his or her music. Michael Jackson and Kate Bush were her closest equivalents. No other artist gorged consumers in spectacle, sensation, and scandal. Well, maybe one other.

Madonna seems to have decided early on in her career that she would operate outside the parameters of the traditional music scene. Whatever she created would have no obvious musical precedents, but range freely over the whole landscape of popular entertainment. While she never cited Taylor as an influence—she owned up to being "killed" by the sight of her kissing Montgomery Clift in *A Place in the Sun*, but nothing more—Madonna must have realized that the kind of scandals that had been studiously avoided or submerged in the past could have their uses. After the Fisher and Burton affairs, Taylor seemed deliberately to tantalize audiences, raising expectations that she would surely behave improperly, inviting condemnation, approval or some other kind of judgment. And, as if she were encouraging this, Taylor took on roles that required hardly a change of key: the temptation to look inside her world was always dangling. Right up to 1983.

Madonna took her cue: scandalize audiences and they will never forget. Taylor was not just an actor: from the moment she gave Hedda Hopper the fateful "sleep alone" quote in 1958, she was news. Madonna did something slightly different: she *made* news. Mindful of the changes in media, particularly the shift to conjectural news, Madonna realized her career would be at the mercy of an ever-vigilant media in search of stories or speculation on what become stories. It was gamble: scandals would make her news, but probably not for long; and, after the frisson she could have been dispatched to the wilderness, leaving the field clear for contemporaries. Cyndi Lauper and Pat Benatar would be the names on everybody's lips. But Madonna took the gamble.

Madonna thrived on scandal: her flawlessly designed mischief enraged people and sent the media haywire. In the process she discovered that the secret to getting media attention was not hard to discern: shock. The secret to maintaining it was harder, but still discernible: maintain momentum; keep the shocks coming, in other words. So, after appearing on the 1984 MTV awards writhing as if at an advanced stage of a lewd act, while wearing a wedding dress and singing *Like a Virgin*, she shrugged when *Penthouse* and *Playboy* magazines published nude pictures of the star: "So what? I'm not ashamed." Her highly visible wedding to Sean Penn was eclipsed by an even more visible marital breakdown, which at one point involved media helicopters circling above the couple's home (Penn drew FUCK OFF in sand by the house).

Notorious? Madonna had hardly got started. A \$5 million promotional deal with Pepsi—then closing the market gap on Coca-Cola—went sour after the video for "Like a Prayer" frightened the soft drinks corporation into pulling the campaign. The video featured a murder, stigmata, and burning crucifixes. One wonders how Pepsi's market share would have fared if it had stuck with her. Coke remains the market leader. The track and the album from which it was taken were huge successes. Over the next several years, Madonna addressed bisexuality, masturbation, sadomasochism, voyeurism, and probably a few other lubricious activities I missed. Her videos and stage performances (as well as her movies and books) became less theatrical events, more taboo-smashing occasions. When the Pope attempted to ban the Italian leg of one of her tours because of its "blasphemous" content, there were distinct echoes of Elizabeth Taylor. She was pop's *l'agent provocateur.*

Madonna's tireless attempts to remain provocative ensured she would draw condemnation, denunciation, and opprobrium that would have destroyed earlier careers. No other woman, including Taylor, had faced so much vilification and survived. In her 1995 essay on the reaction to the scandalous affairs of Ingrid Bergman and Susan Hayward in the postwar era, Adrienne L. McLean argued that, while Bergman managed eventually to "validate" herself by settling down in a "satisfactory nuclear family," Hayward endured longlasting castigation. "The reaction to the affairs thus reflects concerns about female freedom and transgression," wrote McLean (p. 50). In the same way, Madonna's, and for that matter, Taylor's behavior reflected the way culture viewed the limits of women's autonomy in their respective eras.

Madonna encroached on as many taboos as she could, never leaving them undisturbed, but never hurting herself in the process and always leaving her calling card. She was like the burglar in Siberia who, in 2015, broke into a house and left his photo with a note of apology. Madonna did not get away quite so scot-free; but if there were any stigmas, she wore them like badges of honor. And, when combined with her forays into writing, acting, and talk show appearances, this resulted in a media phenomenon. No one had ever encountered a woman who simply abdicated the role set aside for female entertainers. Taylor had wandered from one unhappy marriage to the next blissful union, then out again into a different liaison with an elegant, seemingly natural grace. It all seemed effortless. Madonna's effort was more determined: as if she were deliberately trying to bring dishonor on herself. (The Siberian burglar story was reported in the *New York Times*, April 3, 2015: available at: http://nyti.ms/1QC6fmC accessed April 2015.)

Yet the media found her compulsively watchable and reportable. They must surely have known how she manipulated them, but could not resist her. To keep them coming, Madonna kept sweetening the bait. She did this in two ways. She swapped personae, sequencing a parade of different guises so that she remained instantly recognizable, but somehow ungraspable, ever-changing. Perhaps more importantly and less visibly, she made what must have seemed in the 1980s a mystifying pact with the media. "I'm going to provoke, surprise, aggravate and generally upset as many people as I can and I'm going to let you watch me do it," Madonna might have promised the media. "In the process, I will disclose more of myself than any pop or movie star in history. My body, my sexuality, my erotic fantasies: nothing is out-of-bounds."

The quid pro quo was simple: Madonna wanted—and got—more saturation media coverage than anyone, present and past. She was operating in an age of global media, when entertainment was becoming the hard currency of tv and when having a video vetoed by the likes of MTV made international news. Compellingly newsworthy in everything she did or said, Madonna was ubiquitous for at least the first half of the 1990s. Thereafter, her presence might have faded, but her influence remained. After her, no one could aspire to becoming a celebrity if they wanted anything resembling a private life. The boundary-blurring that had started in Rome in 1962 was completely obliterated during Madonna's rise, or, as some might have it, diabolically masterminded descent.

Madonna didn't singlehandedly start celebrity culture, as we know it. What she did was realize that Rolls-Royces are desirable, but, for most people, untouchable. Toyota Corollas are accessible, affordable, and sell in multiple countries. Abandoning any vestige of the old public vs. private domains, Madonna made her whole self available for commodification. She became the complete product. The dawning of her era saw the stars' music taking second place to what they looked like, whom they were dating, which diet they currently favored and where they last did a stint in rehab.

Since Madonna's *Like a Virgin* video, scandal has become something of a holy grail for celebrities. From Paris Hilton to Miley Cyrus, artists (I remind readers: Paris has made an album and several films) have sedulously courted controversy, often with agreeable results (for their careers, that is). In 2012, Madonna released her twelfth studio album *MDNA* and, while it sold less than her benchmark 10 million units, it was a commercial success. To promote it, she played to sell-out audiences on an 88-date world tour, her ninth such tour. When Shakespeare wrote, "Age cannot wither her, nor custom stale Her infinite variety," he was referring to Cleopatra (in *Antony and Cleopatra,* 2:2). If he had added, "She makes hungry media appetites Which then she feeds," it would have described Madonna to a T.

The previews of *Private Lives* were at Boston's Shubert Theater and, on first night, "the *paparazzi* were ready to descend," as Marie Brenner put it in 1983 (paparazzi was still considered a foreign word then and so took italics). When the couple arrived in Boston twenty years before, they flew in on the wings of a scandal, newly married after an affair that finished off their previous marriages and, as we have seen, changed the thought and practice of the modern media.

Pickets had held placards plastered with the word "Shame" and angry crowds had accosted Taylor. It was no different from the angry reception they got everywhere in the early 1960s when both Taylor and Burton were in their thirties. Two decades later, a middle-aged Liz & Dick could have become just another doomed celebrity relationship that used to be intermittently amusing but was now dull and repetitive. In fact, the partnership had kept its freshness and retained its sting. Where once Taylor and Burton excited hysteria, they now inspired curiosity. They had shared beds, films, and business enterprises, but never a stage.

Taylor stayed at the Copley Plaza hotel where she had taken twenty rooms. Victor Luna was in her party. Burton was booked into a two-bedroom suite at the Ritz-Carlton hotel with Sally Hay, then described as his secretary-companion. They surfaced from their suite only occasionally, took meals in their rooms and appeared for breakfast only once. Burton and Taylor chose to keep their profiles as low as possible, granting no interviews and confining themselves to their hotel rooms as far as possible. This did nothing to quell interest. As the *New York Times*' Dudley Clendinen observed: "Boston, roused by the voyeur's chance of watching the former Burtons play characters so closely patterned to the play of their own lives, has rushed to the window—the ticket window" (1983). All seventeen performances in Boston were sold out in advance.

At fifty-seven, Burton was weak and, for a while, wore a neck brace. In April 1981 he had undergone cervical laminectomy, which is a procedure to remove a portion of bone from the spine in the neck to relieve pressure. He removed the brace shortly after rehearsals started. He was off alcohol but smoked as many as eighty cigarettes per day. When the previews opened, Burton was sixteen months away from his early death from cerebral hemorrhage. Taylor was still drinking heavily and was just months away from checking herself into the Betty Ford Center for drug and alcohol rehabilitation.

The reviews were lukewarm. *Boston Globe* theater critic Kevin Kelly wrote that Taylor sounded "like Minnie Mouse" and was "weighted down to her ankles in comedic intent," while Burton was "nearly as dour as Titus Andronicus." Both of them, Kelly wrote in 1983, moved through *Private Lives* with "a clumpy hesitation." This might have augured poorly for any other show. But he was panning the play, not the play-within-the-play. Marie Brenner, also in 1983, called it "a canny exploitation guaranteed to turn out the crowds." (Titus Andronicus, in Shakespeare's play, was a Roman general who returns home after ten years of fighting Goths, with the bodies of his two slain-in-battle sons; as such, not a fizzy character.)

Actually, the play was like a *matryoshka* doll, inside the play-within-the-play was yet another drama, this one involving the director who managed to upset everyone, including Taylor. Katselas was wily enough to realize what voyeuristic consumers wanted out of the play, but he was unpopular with the actors, particularly Taylor, and was asked to resign before the show moved to Broadway. The production, however, bore his imprint and, as the *Christian Science Monitor*'s John Beaufort noticed in 1983: "The spectators' response to the revival occasionally betrayed an element of voyeurism," which is exactly what Katselas (and we assume Taylor) wanted.

Private Lives opened to a packed crowd and remained that way for its full eleven-week run in New York. The theater was surrounded by barriers against the nightly hordes of fans, many of them waving biographies of Taylor, presumably hoping (vainly) to get them autographed. When she arrived, she had with her a parrot, which she kept in her dressing room and, later, took on stage, for no dramatic purpose. Sam Kashner and Nancy Schoenberger offer the plausible point that, while many of Taylor and Burton's films had drawn obvious parallels with their own relationship (*Cleopatra, The VIPs, Divorce His, Divorce Hers* and many more), *Private Lives* was not like the others: it was a comedy, not a drama: "Now the parallels weren't dramatic; they were comic" (p. 417). We could also add that, by the 1980s, audiences were cannier than ever. A 1994 study by Joshua Gamson portrayed fans as knowing and savvy participants in the celebrity production process. Gamson concluded: "The position audiences embrace includes the roles of simultaneous voyeurs of and performers in commercial culture" (p. 137).

While Gamson was writing after *Private Lives*, his phrase "simultaneous voyeurs of and performers in" seems close to what Kashner and Schoenberger call the "triple-entendre effect." Audiences were not simply viewing the play as the *roman-à-clef* Katselas, Taylor and probably several others intended: they realized that they were part of Liz & Dick, not the people but the preposterous yet absorbing phenomenon that had worked like magic for two decades. The enchantment was real enough: audiences watched the unfolding of realities within realities, the barely disguised allegory of divorces stuck in a mismatch made in heaven. But they apparently enjoyed untangling the real from the make-believe. Gratification came via a little interpretation. As all artists intuitively know, straight up pictures and stories are the most direct route to a consumer's heart, or brain, but they rarely deliver much satisfaction.

Audiences were connected in such a way that they not only "got" the play, they were also "in on" it. Coward's lines almost begged for reinterpretation. For example, Amanda (i.e. Taylor) says, "I believe it was just the fact of our being married, and clamped together publicly, that wrecked us before," and Elyot (Burton) agrees: "That, and not knowing how to manage each other." Elsewhere in the text, Amanda asks, "How long will it last, this ludicrous, overbearing love of ours?" Audiences knew they were Coward's lines, but were also aware that their own presence breathed new relevance into them. It was not simply the fact that they were spoken by Taylor and Burton: the vitality of the play came from the way the audience read meanings. Social scientists call it reflexivity: taking account of the effect of the identity or just presence of the researcher on whatever is being investigated.

The audience, in this instance, took account of its own effect on the play. This is what escaped and so confounded critics, who slammed the production and the performances and were perplexed by why audiences seemingly enjoyed it. Taylor made matters worse by mugging, blowing kisses from the stage and, on one occasion, threw food into the audience. The crowds loved it; critics could hardly believe it. Ticket sales for the New York run alone ran to $4.5 million. The play went on a brief tour after New York, ending in Los Angeles in November. "Popular entertainment can live despite the critics," Bufman told *People*'s Andrea Chambers, in 1983.

Curiously, Taylor reflected later that the play was "doomed from the start." While it was not an artistic triumph, it was a commercial success and left audiences satisfied. Those may not have been her aims. While writer William Ivory's reconstruction of the production and its backstory is a work of fiction and conjecture, it offers a window. The premise of *Burton and Taylor* is that Taylor, divorced and bored, schemed to draw Burton back into her life. The play, while not simply a subterfuge, provided an opportunity for her to tempt Burton away from Sally Hay before his new love had chance to stake a claim. While, in Ivory's screenplay, Taylor does not succeed in seducing Burton, it is not for want of trying. Burton appears stiff, restrained and full of resolve, a far cry from the hellraising, boozing womanizer, who would—and, once more, I draw on Joan Collins—have sex with a snake if it wore a skirt.

"Sunday 13th, New York, Lombardy [Hotel] ... E's face OK but figure splop! Also drinking ... Became very sentimental. 'Please don't marry Sally'." Burton's diary in March 1983 chronicles his denigration of Taylor (perhaps "splop" is onomatopoeia). At thirty-three, Sally Hay was twenty-four years younger than Burton and probably reminded Taylor of Burton's former wife Sybil. Both were plain looking, homespun types who blended into the background at social events; neither would make heads turn.

Hay was born in Essex, England, and had worked as a production assistant at the BBC before she got a job on *Wagner.* The job demanded she move to various locations in Europe. According to Melvyn Bragg, she was intimidated by Burton at first, but responded without hesitation when he asked her to dinner. "A few days later I moved in with him," she is quoted in Bragg's 1989 biography of Burton (p. 631). Hay assumed the liaison would last until the end of the production, but: "About six weeks in he discussed marriage." This was even before he was divorced from Suzy.

Taylor knew Burton had a kind of default setting: he liked stability, support, and dependability. Sybil had suffered in silence while her sexually incontinent husband took advantage of every opportunity that presented itself. Her stoicism was rewarded: Burton always returned and provided for her and the children. Perhaps Sally Hay functioned similarly: as a mainstay. *Private Lives* opened in Boston less than a month later. If, as Ivory and many other writers suppose, Taylor had set up the play as a stratagem with a reconciliation with Burton as its end, she would surely have known about Hay's presence beforehand. It is probable even that Burton had revealed his marriage plans. Why else would Taylor have implored him not to marry her?

Burton's face and body showed the mileage of foot-down celebrityhood but he remained sober for the whole run of the play, while Taylor binged on alcohol and miscellaneous medications. Dried-out alcoholics tend to be pious about others they suspect are dependent on drink. This may have exacerbated the already fraught relations. At one point, Burton sought an escape route. He was approached to play in John Huston's film *Under the Volcano* and asked Taylor to release him from his contract. As a director of the production company, she denied the request, effectively forcing Burton to complete the run against his will. It was a sound business decision: while Taylor was the primo boxoffice draw, Burton was her foil, though he was in danger of becoming her stooge and he probably realized this. The *Boston Globe* reported that Burton "seemed sadly zombie-like" on stage. There may also have been an element of punishment involved in Taylor's action: she may have resented the contentment and sobriety that Burton seemed to be experiencing.

A variety of ailments affected Taylor during *Private Lives*: laryngitis, conjunctivitis, and bronchitis among them. She missed a total of twenty performances. During one of the illness-enforced interruptions, Burton played opposite Taylor's understudy for four nights, then flew to Las Vegas where he and Hay were married. The media's first stop was, of course, Taylor, who put on a brave face and gave vapid congratulations: "I'm thrilled and delighted for both."

The development would have provided a delectable and unexpected bonus for audiences: Liz & Dick was never a relationship; it was a mediated curio—a rare and intriguing object conveyed to audiences via print and broadcast. After July 3 (the date of Burton's wedding), there was a new addition to the dramatis personae. Soon after, there was yet another: Taylor announced she was engaged to Victor Luna. She flashed a 16.5-carat diamond and sapphire ring by Cartier. Perhaps significantly, no wedding date was mentioned at the party to celebrate the affiancing. Although she did not know it, Taylor was issuing an epilogue of sorts: Burton had finally decided they were all wrong for each other. And maybe she had too. She did not keep a diary, or any kind of record to compare with Burton's, but she must have concluded the ingredients that made their relationship intoxicating actually did include intoxicants. Deprived of them, a clean-and-sober Burton must have seemed colorless and wearisome compared to his former inflammatory self. The truth was known only to Taylor and, for all her confessions, she never let on. Yet there is every reason to believe that, when watching her former devil-may-care paragon of impulsiveness sidle into comfortable domesticity with a mousy production assistant, she realized that he was no longer for her. It was not exactly a noble resignation. But it was a resignation.

Private Lives finally closed in Los Angeles on November 6, 1983. It ended its run a little early because ticket sales slowed down. The reason was probably less to do with the lapsing interest in Liz & Dick and more to do with Taylor's frequent absences, usually occasioned by laryngitis, or, more likely, indifference. Burton returned with his wife to his home in Switzerland. Taylor broke off the engagement with Luna after a year.

The Elizabeth Taylor Theater Company, the production enterprise Taylor started with Bufman, did not outlast *Private Lives* by much. While the company had several productions in the works, only *Private Lives* made money and, even then, not as much as anticipated. HBO had, at one point, wanted to screen the play and was prepared to pay a reported $3 million for the privilege. But the cable television company pulled out. Another production based on the life of singer Peggy Lee folded. Bufman and Taylor agreed to part ways soon after the last performance of *Private Lives*.

Taylor's prodigious drinking, combined with consumption of pharmaceuticals throughout the whole run of *Private Lives* left her in terrible physical shape. Exhausted, overweight, and probably dependent on alcohol, she was warned by her doctor Rex Kennamer that she needed to cut back on the drink. When she did not, Kennamer refused to treat her. Taylor was admitted to Cedars-Sinai hospital in LA after collapsing at home. The illness was, ostensibly, colitis, an inflammation of the lining of the colon. When Taylor came round, she found her brother Howard, who had flown in from New York, three of her children, Christopher and Michael Wilding and Liza Todd, and her friend Roddy McDowall waiting to see her. A doctor was also present. "I was in such a drugged stupor that when they filed into my room I thought, 'Oh, how nice, my family are all her to visit,'" she later told John Duka (in 1985, p. 2G).

"Then they sat down and each read from papers they had prepared, each saying they loved me, each describing incidents they'd witnessed of my debilitation, and each saying that if I kept on the way I was with drugs, I would die" (quoted in Duka, p. 2G). "I was astonished," said Taylor, who was, on her own account, "taking a lot of Percodan" (Percodan is an addictive painkiller, consisting of aspirin and oxycodone hydrochloride, used by, among others, Elvis Presley and Jerry Lewis). She was also drinking heavily. Collectively, they tried to persuade her that a diet of Jack Daniel's, Percodan and other drugs was going to kill her.

Taylor was, of course, a headstrong woman and resistant to the advice of others, even well-intended advice; *especially* well-intended advice. She had plowed her own furrow and always emerged. Not unscathed perhaps; but she had emerged. "Then I realized that that I had to get help."

This was December 1983. At the time, it was unheard of for movie stars, rock singers, politicians or other notables to declare their dependence, or to use the favored term of the day, addiction. Elvis had died five years before, though his habitual use of pharmaceuticals did not become publicly known until after his death. Today, it is no disgrace for celebrities to talk openly about what are often called their demons (i.e. destructive compulsions). But in 1983, a revelation of this kind exposed a celebrity to an abrupt loss of reputation, respect and credibility. No one of note from the entertainment business had voluntarily owned up, let alone taken the extraordinary step of checking into rehab.

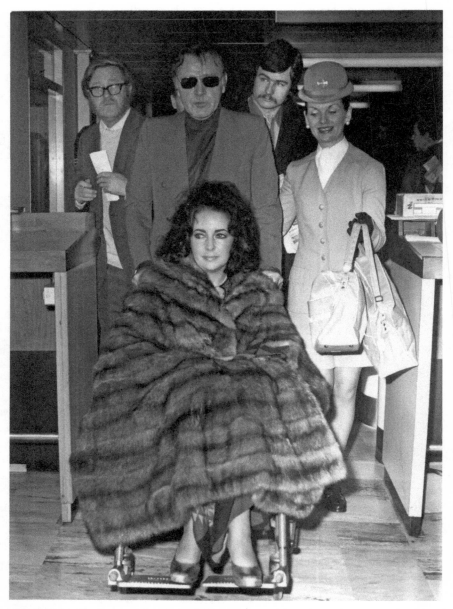

FIGURE 13 *Taylor was the first celebrity to reveal her dependencies to the world and openly seek a means to ending them.*

Photo by Evening Standard/*Getty Images.*

13

Rules of engagement

RICHARD BURTON, 58, IS DEAD. The headline appeared on the front page of the *New York Times*, Monday August 4, 1984. The article beneath it shared space with a report on the first ever women's Olympic marathon, the agreement of Shimon Peres to form a new government of Israel and an explosion in the Red Sea that damaged a tanker. Burton died of a cerebral hemorrhage after complaining of feeling ill; he was taken to a Geneva hospital, where he died. His wife Sally Hay was with him. The *New York Times* writer Maureen Dowd wrote: "He was remembered by friends as 'a monstrous perfectionist' and a 'troubled spirit.'" Dowd quoted John Gielgud: "He was very wild and had a scandal around him all the time" (p. 1).

Eighteen months before, Burton had appeared on BBC television and casually, yet, in a strange way, vulnerably announced, "I am an alcoholic." The admission carried few of the implications it would today: no one congratulated him on his courage or berated him for not resolving to conquer his apparent dependence, seek help or promising not to touch another drop. Burton just followed up the unexpected confession with an unconvincing reminder that he was trying to stay sober, but with a caveat: "I occasionally fall off the wagon and have one or two bottles of vodka a day" (Associated Press, February 23, 1983).

Then fifty-seven, Burton said he realized he was an alcoholic nine years before when he woke up with his first hangover. Considering he had been drinking since he was a teenager and had repeatedly claimed he could always "drink anyone under the table," this seemed implausible. In July 1980, he had prevaricated when US talk show host Dick Cavett had asked him if he considered himself an alcoholic. "It's a dreadful disease and anyone with it has my deepest sympathies," said Burton. "I'm not quite sure I am one, but if not, I'm very near." In perhaps his most revealing and enriching interview, Burton acknowledged to Cavett that he had become an unwitting "representative" of alcoholics and that he approached drinking as a boxer would his opponent, evading punches, trying to land his own (the interview is viewable at: http://bit.ly/1NKyEWD and the subject of alcoholism comes up at 1:27.57, accessed September 2015; Welsh journalist Nathan Bevan reflected on the interview in 2009).

Burton was married to Suzy Hunt at the time of the Cavett interview and credited her with steering him away from drinking, though it seems never for long periods. "Richard could go for maybe three weeks without a drink—and then buckle under," wrote Rob Walters, in his 2010 book, which collected testimonies from people close to Burton. "He would then become a different person, he could be very funny, but also outrageous" (p. 95). This presumably was the face of Burton Taylor knew well, loved and missed. But Hunt and, later, Sally Hay, fought to keep him sober, as did various doctors, who advised that he absolutely had to stop drinking or risk killing himself. This is presumably the reason why Burton tried to break what had been the habit of a lifetime.

Prior to filming *Wagner*, he had revived his role in *Camelot*. The stage run was grueling for a man in his mid-fifties and Burton, in addition to drinking, resorted to as many as ten different kinds of painkillers, antidepressants, and medicines to ease alcohol cravings. In 1981, when he collapsed on stage, causing an abandonment of a performance, audiences presumed he was dead drunk. Walters suggests it was probably the effects of the drugs combined with alcohol. Either way, this seems to have been some sort of turning point.

Even as his debilitation became painfully evident, Burton maintained his habits: in fact, he was drunk the night before he died. Burton was never likely to talk about drinking in the form of a confession, accepting responsibility and promising to make a clean breast of it. He called alcoholism a "disease" and pitied those who suffered, but up to the final few months of his life, never complained. If he thought of it as a disease, it was probably in the way asthma is a disease; most people are aware it causes difficulty in breathing, but few know some sufferers actually die of asthma.

Shortly before turning fifty, eight years before he died, Burton said he liked his reputation of "a spoiled genius from the Welsh gutter, a drunk, a womanizer." In reporting his death Dowd noted the pride Burton took in his capacity: "He boasted, earlier in his career, about being able to drink half-gallons of cognac or 100 proof vodka during stage performances." Chris Williams, who edited Burton's diaries, pointed out: "There are days in some years when the only entry is the word 'booze'" (p. 17). Burton bragged about his drinking. Why would he apologize about something he and his close friends enjoyed so fulsomely?

Far from being his Achilles heel, alcohol was frequently seen as a constituent of Burton's male identity, an adjunct to his film and stage persona. Movie fans never expressed disapproval or distaste: they knew, as *People* magazine put it: "Drinking was always part of his life." Like many of his peers, Burton was seen as a hard-drinking alpha male. Richard Harris,

Oliver Reed, Spencer Tracy, and Humphrey Bogart were among his peers who boasted similarly solid masculine credentials. "I could hold my own with anybody," Burton boasted. "But Spencer could really put it away. Bogie was more civilized. We'd meet at Romanoff's, have a bottle of wine with lunch, then brandy and Benedictine, then home for a nap, then start again at sevenish" (quoted in Louise Lague's 1984 article; Romanoff's was a famous Beverly Hills restaurant, frequented by movie actors.)

It is impossible to conceive of someone like Robert Downey Jr. or Charlie Sheen bragging this way: ". . . and I would start with a few vodkas, then he'd cook up some rock with coke and baking soda and smoke it with a pipe he fashioned from an empty plastic bottle. Then . . . might swing by with some choice crank she gets from her dealer." The difference is not only that alcohol is legal, and cocaine and crystal meth are not: it is us. We might relish the confessions, the more shameful the better, but we simply do not expect celebrities to wear them as badges of honor. We much prefer them to feel mortified, humiliated, shamed and, if need be, crushed by their immoderation. Not proud of it, as Burton clearly was. Richard Harris too. Robert Sellers quotes him: "Burton and I all drank to excess not because we had problems, but because we loved it." Sellers records how Burton, Harris, and other hellraising actors, were unapologetically hedonistic drinkers and laughed at do-gooders and guardians of good taste (2011). Harris joked of having formed a support group called Alcoholics Unanimous that worked this way: "If you don't feel like a drink, you ring another member and he comes over to persuade you."

Alcoholism was simply understood differently in the 1980s: it was a social practice that affected a minority of people who felt or actually were incapable of keeping their drinking within limits. It was not a structural disorder, perhaps genetic in character, which merited the kind of treatment we afford it today. The sight of Burton, Tracy, and Bogart staggering out of Romanoff's mid-afternoon and falling into their cars would have occasioned laughter, not astonishment, pity or consternation; maybe even respect for having the nerve to get smashed at a time when most people were at work, waiting for 5.00 p.m. No professional journalist witnessing the incident would have been self-righteous enough to moralize, as some might do now; though not James Whittaker, who, in 2009, recounted how he was invited by Burton to his caravan, while taking a break from filming *Anne of the Thousand Days* in 1969. "He produced a bottle of Cognac and a bottle of vintage port," recalls Whittaker (2009) "'I've got a cold,' he said, 'and this'll cure it.' It took him an hour to down the lot, drinking a 50/50 mixture of the two drinks. What a man."

Even today, Lieve Gies argues that, "some forms of antisocial behavior appear acceptable . . . even attractive" when celebrities engage in them (p. 351). Antismoking campaigners have railed against celebrities who smoke. Burton did this too, of course—up to four packs per day. Writing in

2011, Gies contended that it is accepted that contemporary celebrities "will break social norms and lead unconventional lives, thus giving them a certain modicum of freedom which non-celebrities, generally speaking, do not possess" (p. 358). Perhaps. But today trespassing celebrities are expected to exhibit (better still, feel) remorse and make spectacular displays of repentance. Burton would have given short shrift to anyone daring to suggest his gratifications were anybody's business but his own.

During his life and even after his death, Burton was not an admitted alcoholic, at least not in a medical sense. We might regard him as such in retrospect, but apart from his offhand remark on BBC, he seems to have taken none of the steps to recovery typically recommended. He did not seek the support of self-help organizations, or rehabilitative care institutions. Indeed he gave the impression that his attitude was: "I'd rather go to hell than listen to interfering, if well-meaning philanthropists." Fans did not express concern at what would today be a serious flaw.

When Philip Seymour Hoffman died in 2014, appreciations of his acting achievements were occluded by both the cause of his death—a mixed drug intoxication of heroin, cocaine, benzodiazepines, and amphetamine—and the revelation that his body was surrounded by seventy bags of heroin and twenty used syringes. Robin Williams' suicide in the same year elicited discussions of both his acting and a dependence on alcohol and cocaine that induced spells in rehabilitation. While obituarists never speak ill of the dead, they rarely Photoshop their faults, blemishes or other undesirable features nowadays. Burton's death did not occasion handwringing over his excessive drinking. No one criticized him for not seeking help or being a poor role model. Burton was not turned into an outcast for failing to publicize his drinking. No one paid much attention to his habit; it was never, to use a term of today, problematized—regarded as problem requiring a solution. He was part of a culture that accepted that private wounds should be privately healed. That would soon change.

(I should, at this stage, clarify the distinction between addiction and dependency, both of which describe the condition of being compulsively attached to a substance or activity. Both also suggest psychological attachments. Addiction often carries with it the assumption that the addict has experienced biochemical changes in the central nervous system and which make him or her reliant on something. Dependency emphasizes the psychological desires to, for example, drink alcohol, use drugs, gamble, etc., without the assumption that there has been a structural change in the chemical processes occurring in the person.)

Burton played no small part in erasing the line between public and private spheres, as we have seen: when paparazzo Marcello Geppetti caught him and an unknowing Taylor embracing, it portended the end of privacy for

Hollywood stars. If Taylor and her consort were not capable of conducting discreet affairs away from prying eyes, who was? Over the next several years, an evermore-intrusive media turned privacy inside out. Madonna read the tealeaves and, as we have seen, surrendered her whole self to the service of the media. Nothing was off-limits; the boundaries traditionally respected by the media were broached so often that they became meaningless. Privacy became a matter of public concern.

We are now used to watching evanescent television celebrities baring their souls, describing often in cringeworthy detail their addictions, illnesses, sex lives, and personal tragedies. Silence and discretion are now seen as obstacles to progress: sharing is therapy. Frank Furedi wrote in 2003: "Disclosure represents the point of departure in the act of seeking help—an act of virtue in therapeutic culture." There was no therapeutic culture in the early 1980s; the boundary between public and private was moving, but not yet gone. So when Taylor herself, in an adventitious acceptance of her need of help, checked in at the Betty Ford Center, it was precisely the kind of act of virtue Furedi has in mind. It was also the first of its kind.

A spell in rehab is almost a qualification for membership to the A-list. Like an endorsement contract and a 5m+ twitter following, it is celebrity accreditation. Any stigma that once attached to bedeviled actors, singers, and politicians who retreated from public view for a while, has long since vanished. Celebrities discuss rehab as if it were a Caribbean cruise: they emerge refreshed, reinvigorated, and purged, at least for a while. It has become so commonplace that no one raises an eyebrow at the news that so-and-so is going into such-and-such clinic to rid him or herself of addictions to gambling, sex, chocolate, shopping . . . the list grows exponentially (and I am not joking about chocolate and shopping: both are recognized, treatable addictions). But this is now. How about in 1983?

Taylor's family had been waiting for her when she woke up in the hospital; they convinced her that she needed help and, on the same night, she checked in at the Betty Ford Center, where her family had reserved her a place. That was December 5. Later, in 1985, Taylor told John Duka, of the *New York Times*: "I became a drunk and a junkie with great determination," adding "and with the same great resolve that got me to that point, I could turn it to work for me" (p. 2G).

The 14-acre complex at Rancho Mirage, California, was founded in 1982 by the former First Lady Betty Ford, who herself experienced problems with her drinking. No Hollywood star had, up to that point, admitted to having dependencies. Taylor was the first to reveal hers to the world. Among later residents at the same Center were Johnny Cash (for drug dependency), Mary Tyler Moore (whom we referred to earlier in the book, for alcohol dependency), Lindsay Lohan (who played Taylor in the movie *Liz & Dick*, for drugs), and Eddie Fisher (cocaine). Every new guest at the Betty Ford Center seemed to validate the effectiveness of reaching out.

Like other patients, Taylor had to share a room with a stranger and was told to wear jeans and casual clothes only. She ate in a cafeteria and went to daily discussion groups. "By the second week, I finally admitted that I was an alcoholic and that I had a drug problem," Taylor told Duka. Burton, at this point, was endeavoring to keep his drinking under control, but resisting the label alcoholic.

Everyone at the Center was obliged to keep a daily diary and in hers, Taylor wrote (and later revealed to Duka): "It's probably the first time since I was 9 that nobody's wanted to exploit me." This could have several meanings, of course; but one them would almost surely involve the constant media "exploitation" of her image, words, and deeds. It prompts a question. One might reasonably be expected to wonder why the media did not miss Taylor: she had been hospitalized, ostensibly for what the hospital initially described as a "check-up," then vanished. By the early 1980s, news reporters were well versed in probing for truth, so it seems hard to believe that they would accept this explanation, even when the reason for her stay was changed to a bowel obstruction.

The fact that she slid unnoticed from the Saint John's Health Center in Santa Monica to Rancho Mirage about 120 miles, or a couple of hours drive, away suggests differences in the speed and vigilance of the media. Ten years later, it would have been inconceivable for a celebrity to enter rehab without fanfare, as Taylor apparently did. Even while she was at the Betty Ford Center, she had nearly a couple of weeks of privacy. Twelve days passed before a curious, but not, it seems, overly inquisitive media sought details of Taylor and tracked her to the Center, where spokesman Cliff Brown declined to elaborate beyond, "much of her trouble stems from prescription drugs administered over a period of years to combat her various medical problems" (quoted by Associated Press, 1983). When pressed he declared: "Under federal and California law, the center is prohibited from making any statement other than that released by the patient."

Elizabeth Sporkin, of *People* magazine, hints at the value of Taylor's willingness to seek support, comparing her response to distress with that of Marilyn Monroe. Taylor "hung onto her nine lives by repeatedly seeking medical help," wrote Sporkin in 1990, noting that rehab was not an intervention available to Marilyn in the early 1960s (though Sporkin overlooks the Synanon residential program, which was started in Santa Monica in 1958 and later closed amid controversy. The Betty Ford Center opened in 1982). Marilyn "privately nursed her pain," wrote Sporkin. "Elizabeth's has been played out on an all-too-public stage."

The other patients might have been amused by the media fascination with Taylor's presence, though administrators at the Center were probably not. "Some photographers came with their telephoto lenses and managed to take pictures of me in the garden and published them," Taylor told Duka. But, almost incredibly, she was left relatively undisturbed. Maybe the declaration that she had a problem suggested a medical problem and editors were more circumspect back then. Whatever the reason, Taylor was allowed to complete a course of seven weeks at the Betty Ford Center. There were no locks on the outer doors and she could, like any other patient, have walked out at any point. When Taylor emerged on January 20, 1984, she was several pounds lighter and apparently sober. Victor Luna was waiting for her and talked about her joining him in Guadalajara, Mexico.

Taylor's spell at the Betty Ford Center was, in its way, a symbolic event. Commonplace as it is to hear actors, athletes, and singers pronounce on their dependencies, it had never been known when Taylor checked in. This goes some way to explain why the media left her alone: they did not know how to respond. Nowadays, the media have ready-made frameworks for interpreting rehab-bound characters. Back then, the idea of a star, and not just any star but Elizabeth Taylor, experiencing something that required an unusual type of non-medical intervention was unprecedented. Then again, much of what Taylor did was unprecedented.

Experiences that would once have been thought normal, such as disappointment, loneliness, tiredness, stress and, of course, depression, have been redefined as syndromes requiring intervention. Counselors now outnumber librarians, firefighters, postmen, and dentists. We are encouraged to search ourselves for vulnerabilities; then share them with others, especially specialists. Taylor presented a jump-off point from older sensibilities: the very act of seeking help from an institutional source endorsed a method of managing emotions. Her confession after two weeks that she was an alcoholic with a dependency on drugs was an acknowledgment that the route to curing both conditions was through structured rehabilitation rather than primitive means such as willpower, self-restraint or determination. In several other respects Taylor had what Cassandra Langer, in 2013, called "a will of iron." Taylor would return to the Betty Ford Center in five years for another spell.

One can imagine news editors' heads swimming with ideas at the prospect of Burton's funeral. The sorrowful widow cruelly robbed of her husband after less than two years of marriage and struggle against his debilitating habits. *The ex-wife with whom the deceased shared two decades of emotional turmoil and the most public love in history.* The earnest, diligent but inner sorrow of a widow. *The hysterical outpourings of a professional actor.* The desire for solemnity. *The inescapable urge to create spectacle.* Editors might have been tempted to assign sports reporters.

Burton's last wishes were to be buried in Célegny's Protestant cemetery. No newspaper, broadcaster or any other kind of news organization in the world would not want a representative on hand to record potentially the most memorable funeral of 1984. Maybe the most memorable funeral of the 1980s. Burton's wife anticipated that it would be memorable but for reasons unrelated to her late husband's demise. She defused what would almost certainly have been an explosive media event by asking Taylor not to attend the funeral in Céligny, Switzerland, about half a mile from the villa she shared with Burton during their thirteen-month marriage Although she relented, she did so too late and Taylor did not show; instead she sent a single red rose.

Taylor's capacity to bewitch was such that her physical presence was not needed: her absence was enough to draw the media to the funeral. The fact that Sally Hay had specifically asked her not to attend (a fact soon picked up by the media) prompted obvious questions. People intuitively knew why. Two years after Burton's death, his niece Siân let slip that Taylor kept a photograph of him under her pillow and, in 2011, revealed to Adrian Lee: "Even when he was married to Sally and living in Switzerland he would talk for hours on the phone with Elizabeth."

The media remained fixated with Taylor's postmortem relationship with Burton, particularly how it continued to haunt Sally Hay right up to Taylor's death in 2011. Liz & Dick never described two human beings: it was a media phenomenon; the death of one of the parties did nothing to quell interest. Two days after the burial there was to be a memorial service at the Bethel Baptist Chapel in Burton's hometown Pontrhydfyen. Further memorial services were arranged in Beverly Hills, New York, and London where Taylor's presence, though unwelcome by Hay, made the event memorable. Burton let an estate valued at £3.5 million ($5.8m), divided largely among Sally Hay and his three daughters, with smaller sums to other family members.

There was no love lost between Hay and Taylor. That much became clear in the years that followed. For all her attempts to remain dignified around the time of Burton's death, Hay let rip years later when she told the *Daily Telegraph*'s Christopher Wilson: "I get pissed off with all the talk of a great love story. Yes, they were in love, but they got divorced twice—that means their marriage didn't work." Twenty-seven years after Burton's death Wilson, in his words, "triggered a Vesuvian reaction" by raising the subject with Hay.

Whatever her feelings toward Taylor in 1984, Hay was right if she thought her presence would have turned what might otherwise be a dignified occasion into a media extravaganza. Taylor unwittingly proved this within a week of the funeral when she made an unscheduled personal visit to Burton's grave. Taylor had flown by private plane from London to Céligny, appearing before dawn August 13. Five years before she might have navigated her way to the graveside unimpeded by the media. *Might*. But this was three years after Diana's marriage to Charles and the media, especially the European media, had developed the faculty of detecting and interpreted the subtlest of signs. Photojournalists were waiting. There is even footage of Taylor's arrival at Burton's grave, indicating the presence of tv crews: see http://bit.ly/1GnuukR (accessed September 2015).Taylor turned back, only to reappear later, this time shielded by security guards and a barricade of umbrellas. Some of her escorts threw dirt at the photographers. Taylor spent ten minutes kneeling at the grave, and was then helped back to a waiting Mercedes, according to wire services (reported in the *Lakeland Ledger*, August 14, 1984, p. 2A).

She then visited Burton's extended family in Wales and, finally, a memorial service in London where she upstaged everyone by throwing elaborate receptions before and after the service and arrived at the church uncharacteristically early in order to find a front row seat next to Burton's eldest sister.

There was even a postscript, though one of dubious validity. When she returned home, she found Burton's last letter waiting for her; it was dated August 2, 1984, three days before Burton's death. She kept it by her bedside. When she died, there were reports that the letter was laid next to her in her coffin (*Daily Mail*, March 29, 2011). Sally Hay denied this: "There was no letter," she told Wilson, who adds: "At the time Burton was supposed to have written it, Sally was nursing him in his final illness." The disagreement suggests Liz & Dick may have outlived, not just one, but both parties.

And perhaps a post-postscript, when Hay, in 1986, unveiled a plot adjacent to Burton's grave, where she would be buried. The implicit warning was, as *People*'s Malcolm Boyes put it in 1986, "If Elizabeth Taylor wants to lay flowers on Richard Burton's grave, she may have to do it over his dead widow's body." There may have been another motive: rumor had it that Taylor and Burton had made a morbid pact to be buried next to each other.

Writing in 2008, Yann-Brice Dherbier revealed Taylor's reaction to the news of Burton's death effectively finished her relationship with Luna. She was so uncontrollably grief-stricken in a way that reminded Luna that, as he put it, "I could never have that special place in her heart she keeps for Burton. For me, the romance was over" (p. 21). For Taylor too, it seems: she was seeing Carl Bernstein, twelve years her junior, in late 1984. The Pulitzer Prize-winning journalist was divorced from screenwriter Nora Ephron. The *Chicago Tribune*'s team of Michael Sneed, Cheryl Lavin, and Kathy O'Malley related how, "when Bernstein told a pal he was dating Taylor, the friend said, 'Remember, you're not the Richard Burton in her life. You're the Eddie Fisher'" (1985).

The friend seems to have been right: by early December, it seems she was giving Bernstein the Fisher treatment. A news report in the *Lakeland Ledger* stated: "Carl Bernstein is gasping, and calling her [Taylor's] answering service every hour, and getting absolutely no response" (December 2, 1984, p. 2A). The report went on: "At this second, her fancy has turned to an ex-jeans manufacturer named Dennis Stein."

Thus started a somewhat curious relationship that quietly intrigued the media, before an unexpected announcement that revved up interest. In December, newspapers carried headlines like, "Liz says 'yes' to New York businessman Dennis Stein" after "a whirlwind one-month romance" (*Miami News*, December 13, 1984). It was five months since she and Luna had broken off their engagement; Taylor called Luna personally to tell him of her new fiancé. Both Taylor and Stein were fifty-two.

Even by Taylor's standards this seemed an impetuous decision. After seven marriages, six different husbands, and cumulative 28-and-a-half wedded years, she had been single for just over three years. Getting engaged after knowing a man for a month seemed overly impulsive for a mature woman, though perhaps there were other motives. Stein numbered Frank Sinatra among his showbusiness friends and operated on the fringes of the film industry.

"You couldn't call him a low-key person," *People* magazine quoted a friend of Stein's, adding that he was "something of a hustler," and had "briefly squired Joan Collins." In the 1970s, his business was in jeans but, by the time he met Taylor he was a consultant to the Technicolor Company, which had been acquired in 1983 by New York financier Ronald O. Perelman. "Stein's apparent function," writes Connie Bruck, "was to introduce Perelman to celebrities" (1989). *Weekly World News'* "Best of Hollywood Gossip" column, on January 29, reported: "Rumor has it that Ron Perelman owner of Technicolor, has been backing his employee Dennis [Stein] with bucks to woo Liz and even promised him a Rolls-Royce as a wedding present." This was apparently contingent on Taylor's agreeing to become a "spokeswoman" for Technicolor.

Warren Hirsh, ex-president of Murjani, the brand developing group, and a onetime competitor of Stein's, described Stein as "very Brooklyn. He's a street guy. He's flashy, very much a seller of himself" (quoted in *People* magazine, 1985). The announcement was in earnest and Nolan Miller, famed for designing costumes for the tv series *Dynasty*, was asked to design Taylor's wedding dress. Stein presented Taylor with a 20-carat sapphire ring; not quite in Burton territory, but not a cheap bauble either.

Stein offered something rather different to the other men in Taylor's life: he did not drink, smoke or take recreational drugs. It was during her announcement to a media, which might have been incredulous had it not been for the subject involved, that Taylor explained: "Every time I fall in love, I get married. My morality prevents me from having adventures" (quoted in De Lafayette, p. 150). Taylor had drawn praise and damnation from critics, politicians, church leaders, "experts," and the public. She had smashed box office records and cultural taboos to smithereens, stretched gossip columnists to their limits and dominated headlines for over two decades. So it probably seemed unkind to contradict her. But: "My morality prevents me from having adventures." Seriously?

An association with Taylor, still one of the most irresistibly newsworthy women in the 1980s, made anyone news, at least for the duration of the association. Stein's profile ascended sharply after the news broke: even if the engagement did not last (it did not) and they did not marry, Stein's status changed in one day. As David Blum described him in the aftermath of the breakup: "Dennis Stein—now and probably forever best known as the former Mr. Elizabeth Taylor-to-be" (p. 41).

Perhaps Stein was over-enthusiastic about his new cognomen. Diana McClellan, of *Weekly World News*, wrote in 1985: "He [Stein] seemed to think it was natural to exploit the engagement" (p. 13). McClellan also speculated that Stein was not "a big enough fish to satisfy the finicky superstar." Taylor described it as an "amicable" split; it was the second time she had broken off an engagement in six months, and her third broken engagement since 1949, when she split up with William Pawley.

"Shortly after Elizabeth Taylor announced that her engagement to Dennis Stein was off, the *National Enquirer* offered him $125,000, he says, for the 20-carat sapphire ring she returned to him." *New York Magazine*'s Sharon Churcher filed an interesting coda to the abbreviated romance. "*Enquirer* president and editor Iain Calder denied having named a price for the bauble but said, 'It would have been a very good news story for us'" (quoted in Churcher). The screen roles offered to Taylor were in minor tv films and her days as a major boxoffice draw were long gone. But she was still news. Anything to do with her, even discarded jewelry, made news. Well, perhaps not anything: not discarded men. After Taylor's departure, Stein's function at Technicolor "became less viable," as Bruck phrases it; after a couple of months in the news, Stein slid out of public purview. He held on to the ring.

Actually, Stein did not completely disappear. Following the breakup and over the next few months, Taylor resumed her friendship with Bernstein. News of the resumption (though gossip columnists suggested the liaison was never actually interrupted) filtered through to Stein, who took umbrage and tracked his erstwhile love rival down. In fall 1985, "Bernstein was involved in a well-publicized confrontation with fellow Taylor suitor Dennis Stein at New York's Palladium disco," wrote Richard Lee, of the *Philadelphia Inquirer* in 1986. The confrontation was Stein's last hurrah on the front pages.

Meanwhile, Taylor was pursuing her post-Warner film career. She had played rulers, sluts, foul-mouthed drunks, and even parodies of Elizabeth Taylor, but Louella Parsons still seemed a surprising choice of roles. In November 1984, she resumed her film career in a television movie called *Malice in Wonderland* (aka *The Rumor Mill*, 1985): the premise of the plot was that Parsons was the nemesis of Hollywood studios with her gossipy stories about the side of the stars they wished to keep secret. So the studios conspired to set up her rival Hedda Hopper, who eventually rose to an even greater level of power (arguably) than Parsons. Remember, Taylor had been

close to Hopper in her early career, up till the fateful "sleep alone" interview.
After that Taylor kept her distance. So the prospect of playing Hopper's
archrival must have been enticing. And, as was customary for Taylor, it was
a surprise; even if the film itself was a letdown.

In November 1985, Princess Diana swept into Washington DC to attend a
gala dinner at the invitation of President Ronald Reagan and his wife Nancy.
She mixed with movie stars and politicians, danced with John Travolta
while Americans watched in rapture. Diana had her critics, but the unseen
emotions she seemed to radiate had powerful effects: to her countless
acolytes, she was a force of nature, animating the spirits of whomever she
touched, bringing vitality to wherever she traveled.

Twelve years later, she was gone. Writing for *Harper's* in the months
following the death of Diana, Princess of Wales, Lewis H. Lapham detected
a secret pact between the media that confer "temporary divinity" on
individuals and all but guaranteed "the gifts of wealth and applause" but in
return for "remnants of his or her humanity" that are made available to "the
ritual of the public feast" (p. 13).

Diana always gave the appearance of "having been granted every wish in
Aladdin's cave—youth, beauty, pretty dresses, a prince for a husband, and
Elton John for a pet." Her fans, who came from all quarters, cherished her
for her neediness, which was, on Lapham's 1997 account, "as desperate and
as formless as their own" (p. 13).

Interest in the British royal family had for long been largely reverential.
Onlookers were exactly that: detached observers, watching as subjects
rather than participants. Only Queen Elizabeth's sister Princess Margaret
induced a more involved curiosity, her trysting occupying the paparazzi,
though without sending them into frenzy as Diana did. As celebrities go,
Diana was *ne plus ultra*: the highest form of such a being. No woman or
man has ever commanded such reverence, respect, and collective love from
such a wide constituency, in her case, the world. Even the most sober account
of her life and death seems like a fairytale that got out of hand. It has the
staples of love and death, as well as liberation, tragedy, and immortality.
Like most great fairytales, its central motif was transformation. As raggedy
servants are transformed into glass-slippered belles of the ball, and sleeping
beauties are awakened by the kiss of handsome princes, Diana was changed
from ingénue kindergarten teacher in a London school to the nearest the
twentieth century had to a Goddess.

Unlike in other fairy stories, Diana's transformation was no magical
affair. It was, as Lapham suggests, a more prosaic business, "Like the making
of sausage or violin strings, the minting of celebrity is not a pretty business."
Both the chow that makes such a tasty breakfast and the twine that produces
the mellifluous sound are prepared from the intestines of pigs, sheep or

horses. In other words, a production in which raw materials are refined into items of taste and grace. Not that Diana herself was without her own immanent elegance. She was one of those "individuals who are defined in the first place as possessing some kind of ineffable 'essence'—an aura that sets them apart from ordinary mortals," as Giselle Bastin captured it in 2009 (p. 36).

Born in 1961 at Park House, the home that her parents rented on Queen Elizabeth II's Sandringham estate, she was the third child of Edward John Spencer, Viscount Althorn, heir to the 7th Earl Spencer, and his first wife Frances Ruth Burke Roche, daughter of the 4th Baron of Fermoy. So, her aristocratic credentials were sound. She became Lady Diana Spencer in 1975, when her father became an earl. Returning to England after attending finishing school in Switzerland, Diana grew close to Prince Charles. They announced their engagement in February 1981 and married later in that year. The wedding ceremony was televised globally. Their first child, William, was born in 1982 and their second, Henry, or Harry as he was to become known, in 1984.

Over the next eight years, interest in Diana went global. Already the most admired and, perhaps, accepted member of the royal family, she contrived to remain imperious while developing a common touch. Time and again, people would testify that "she touched me" even though they might never have met her, or even seen her in the flesh. There was a tangible quality not so much in her presence but in even her sheer image. And this was made possible by exhaustive media coverage that occasionally, in fact once too often, became dangerously invasive.

The image was a cross between Cinderella and Rapunzel: a beautiful, yet lonely princess imprisoned in a loveless marriage with a prince, whose suspected infidelity with an older and less attractive women was the talk of the court. Trapped and with no apparent escape route, she seemed defenseless against a powerful and uncaring royal family. Diana made an enchanting victim, a vision of mistreated womanhood smiling serenely at her millions of faithful followers. And, as Scott Wilson wrote in 1997, there were developments: "Diana's beauty remained indestructible and even blossomed when she became not only the most celebrated 'female victim of a brutal world,' but the patron of victims everywhere" (para 6).

Her popularity seemed to grow in inverse proportion to that of her husband. Diana threw herself into charitable work and aligned herself with great causes, visiting people living with Aids, children in hospitals, and other groups, all of whom responded empathically, as Jane Caputi reflected in 1999: "Those who participated in this flow of identification included people with AIDS, the young urban homeless, the injured, the socially marginalised, the poor, the imprisoned, the depressed, and the unloved" (p. 108).

The "flow of identification" became tidal as people, especially women, from everywhere were drawn to someone, who, in her silence seemed to speak for everyone. Diane Rubenstein, in 1997, highlighted her absence of preconceived ideas or predetermined ambitions as factors in her magnetism; she was "a blank-screen on which women could not resist projecting their fantasies and fears" (para. 2).

The separation was one of those worst kept secrets. When it was finally announced in 1992, both Diana and Charles continued to carry out their royal duties. They jointly participated in raising the two children. Diana continued with her charitable endeavors, attracting battalions of photojournalists wherever she went. If there was a high point during this period, it came in January 1997, when, as an International Red Cross VIP volunteer, she visited Angola to talk to landmine survivors. Pictures of Diana in helmet and flak jacket were among the most dramatic images of the late twentieth century. In the August, she traveled to Bosnia, again to visit survivors of landmine explosions. From there she went to see her companion, Dodi Al-Fayed in France.

Late in the evening of August 30, 1997, Diana and Al-Fayed, their driver and bodyguard left the Ritz hotel in Place Vendôme, Paris and drove along the north bank of the Seine. Ever vigilant, the media were soon alerted and pursued the Mercedes in which the party was traveling. Remember: by 1997, Diana's every movement was closely monitored. Interest in every aspect of her life was genuinely global. Not only was she fêted the world over, she was inspected too. The appetite for news—any kind of news however insignificant—was devoured. "Diana," remarked Lapham, "was a celebrity of the most vulnerable and therefore the most nourishing type, a victim for all seasons."

At twenty-five minutes past midnight, nine vehicles carrying the media and a single motorcycle followed Diana and Al-Fayed into an underpass below the Place de lama. As the Mercedes sped away from the pursuant pack, it clipped a wall and veered to the left, colliding with a supporting pillar before spinning to a halt. There followed a few moments while the chasing photographers paused to consider their options. Inside the wrecked Mercedes were four motionless bodies, including that of the world's most famous, most esteemed, most adored, most treasured and most celebrated woman. Photos of the wreckage would be hard currency. But to delay helping her and her fellow travelers might jeopardize their chances of survival. The paparazzi took their shots.

Diana was still alive when she was freed and rushed by ambulance to a nearby hospital. Attempts to save her life were futile and, at 4.00 a.m., doctors pronounced her dead. Of the Mercedes passengers, only Trevor Rees-Jones, Al-Fayed's bodyguard, survived. None of the others were wearing seat belts. It was later revealed that the chauffeur, Henri Paul, had been drinking earlier in the evening. The media people were cleared.

There followed the most extraordinary expression of public grief ever. This is unarguable: the scale, scope, and intensity of the response to her death distinguished it from any comparable manifestation of sorrow, even those mentioned earlier. The response to Diana's death is usually described as an "outpouring of emotion," suggesting an unrestrained expression of heartfelt grief all over the world. In the days leading to her funeral on September 6, over a million people flocked to pay their last respects, many leaving bouquets at her London home at Kensington Palace. Her funeral attracted three million mourners who cast flowers along the entire length of the journey. A global television audience of 26 million watched the day's events.

Diana's friend Elton John sang and later released a re-written version of his Marilyn tribute, "Candle in the Wind," presumably in allusion to Diana's delicacy; though, she appears to have been much more robust than the song suggests. While John's venture was not borne out of commercial greed, there were plenty of exploitable byproducts to follow. A foretaste of the celebrity value of Diana came when the first issue of *Time* magazine following her death sold 750,000 more copies than usual. Sales of a commemorative issue exceeded 1.2 million. *National Enquirer*, in a somewhat hypocritical gesture, refused to publish pictures of Diana's death scene, despite having headlined a cover story the week before "Di Goes Sex Mad" (the copies were pulled from the newsstands).

Then came the merchandise. A planned comic book featuring Diana raised from the dead and invested with superpowers and entitled (following the Bond movie) *Di Another Day*, was ditched by Marvel Comics amid protest. But less offensive products, such as statuettes, decorative plates and "Cindy"-like dolls began to appear on the shelves within months of the tragedy. The near-inevitable conspiracy theories surrounding the death were equal to those of the moon landing, the JFK assassination, or 9/11. More rational attributions of blame centered on the chasing pack of paparazzi. "I always believed the press would kill her in the end," said Diana's brother, the Earl of Spencer, who is quoted by Jacqueline Sharkey in her 1997 article "The Diana aftermath." "Every proprietor and editor of every publication that has paid for intrusive and exploitative photographs of her, encouraging greedy and ruthless individuals to risk everything in pursuit of Diana's image, has blood on his hands" (p. 18).

Sharkey reflected on how "the public and some members of the press denounced the photographers—and journalists in general—as 'barracuda,' 'jackals,' piranha', and 'vultures' feeding off celebrities" (p.18). If the paparazzi had not been so voracious in their attempts to track down Diana, they would not have pursued her car so heedlessly.

So went the argument. Few wanted to extend that same argument further. If they had, they would have concluded that the paparazzi were motivated by money offered by media corporations that could sell publications in their millions to consumers whose thirst for pictures and stories of Diana seemed unquenchable. In the event, the photographers were cleared of any wrongdoing by a French court in 1999. The fact remains: all parties, from the paparazzi to the fans were connected as if by invisible thread. And then something interesting happened. As Donna Cox put it in 1999: "We became voyeurs to our own displays of 'suffering', playing 'Diana' to ourselves through blinking television monitors" (p. 330).

The audience not only watched the Diana fairytale reach its denouement, but saw themselves as bit part players in that same fairytale. This narrative transformation was both revealing and concealing. The media's part in the death of Diana might have been laid bare, but audiences' complicity, though recognized, was left unexamined, at least not in a deep or critical sense. While audiences might have agreed with the Earl of Spencer and condemned the media, they rewarded them with high sales and record viewing figures. Perhaps transformation overstates the change. Anyone who was aware of Diana—and it's difficult to imagine anyone who was not—was forced to inspect the way in which news values had been subverted by entertainment values. After all, Diana's greatest triumph was not so much in ushering in world peace, or saving the planet, but in offering so much pleasure to so many people.

Yet the inspection was momentary. It did not bring to an end the gathering interest in figures, who, like Diana, offered pleasure while presenting absolutely nothing that would materially alter their lives or the lives of any other living thing. The interest in recognizable people was probably interrupted by Diana's death. Then, after a spell of earnest introspection and critical evaluation of the media, the interest resumed.

During the thirty-six years that separated the Taylor-Burton scandal and the death of Diana, the word paparazzi was inducted into the popular vocabulary, as was "tabloid" and "celebs." "Realty tv" would arrive soon after. Diana had become the paragon of celebrity. Taylor might have been the most famous, most scandalous, and perhaps most revered woman of the 1960s and 1970s, but, by the time of Diana's emergence in the 1980s, the simmering pot of interest in the rich and famous had been brought to the boil. In 1992, when her separation from Charles became official, the pot boiled over. Diana was news: not just what she was doing or saying or even wearing. People seemed to gasp in wonder at the very mention of her name.

In the 1960s, the most adventurous clairvoyant would have been hard pressed to predict the tumult of interest in Diana. Something happened. Not to Diana, but to *us*. We, the living human beings who attributed her with so much celestial power, were the ones who changed. And, after her death, we would go on changing. Following the death of Diana and Al-Fayed, *Time* magazine writer Margaret Carlson observed: "By the time of the couple's dinner at Paris' Ritz Hotel, the rules of engagement sometimes observed between the photo hounds and the princess had gone completely by the board, as the street value of a grainy shot of Diana with al Fayed reached six figures" (p. 46).

Earlier, I used rules of the *game* rather than engagement. Carlson's phrase carries connotations of the principles that bind the actions of parties involved in some sort of conflict or competition. That was not the case here, though the circumstances of Diana's death certainly had the elements of opposition. Carlson's point is that "the run-ins between celebrities and those who take pictures of them are growing increasingly ugly."

The likes of Geppetti and Secchiaroli were not exactly received with open arms by stars of the 1960s, but they became parties to an initially uneasy accommodation, which later became symbiotic, benefiting both. A renowned exception, as we learned earlier, was photojournalist Ron Galella's near-obsessional pursuit of Jacqueline Kennedy Onassis. Incensed by the ceaseless attention, Onassis secured a court order that prevented Galella encroaching on what she considered her private space. In this case, the rules of engagement were enshrined in law—and the well-documented run-ins were truly ugly.

The media were not going to let their subjects appear as if they had come straight from a makeover. Nor were they going to run anemic copy like: "Her favorite recreation is motoring and she is never so happy as when spinning along a country road, the fresh air blowing in her face" (this is actually plucked from the fan magazine *Film Weekly* by Matthew Sweet in his book *Shepperton Babylon*). In September 1997, shortly after Diana's death, *The New Republic*'s Jean Bethke Elshtain wrote: "Diana was no doubt tormented by the monster she herself had helped to unleash. That the celebrity machine will now give her children no peace, even to morn her passing, is the cruelest of ironies" (p. 25).

The "monster" may have tormented Diana, but her children, William and Harry, far from being tormented, learned to live with it, both in their different ways, responding to an environment populated by an expanding number new species of the paparazzi genus.

There were other evolutionary diversifications. For example, the *National Enquirer* and other tabloids with their relentless focus on the exploits of famous personalities were, as Neimark put it in 1995, reducing the scope of world events to individuals (p. 84). We, in turn, became habituated to a softening of news in which entertainment—and I use this in its widest sense: anything that amuses or occupies us agreeably—became an increasingly large staple in our intellectual diets. Our interest in politics took on a personal focus, as we were drawn to politicians as much if not more than their politics.

We started to understand the world through people rather than events, processes, or actions. Interest that, in the 1960s and perhaps 1970s would have been seen as unwholesome or downright salacious became much more commonplace. The scandals precipitated by Taylor's affairs may not have started this, but her epic romance with Burton was the single most important episode in the transition to a culture in which almost everything we knew arrived via the media and everything we did was designed to take us closer to a life of endless novelty, pleasure, and consumption.

A seven-year-old boy in blue pajamas was standing next to his nurse in a seventeenth floor corridor of Harlem Hospital, New York. The woman in a red suit with black velvet sleeve buttons could have walked straight past him; but she stopped and asked, "Are you very heavy?" Then Diana leaned, picked up the child, who had Aids, and hugged him. It was one of those moments when people held their breath and waited for a reaction. The child rested his head on Diana's shoulder for a few seconds before she put him down. Her spontaneous action had a profound effect on a country obsessed with the social unacceptability of Aids. It was 1989.

Aids (or AIDS, as it was known) was first recognized as a medical condition in the US in 1981. It origins were disputed and there were no cures. The first known cases were among gay men and intravenous drug users, leading many to call it "gay plague" and still others to interpret the disease as God's payback for homosexuality.

When Diana, in 1989, attended a new Aids center in London, it was regarded as a typically rebellious act: a member of the royal family disregarding the wishes of Queen Elizabeth—who later declared her opposition to Diana's involvement with Aids—and, in her own way, assisting the erasure of a stigma that attached itself to those who had contracted the disease. The visit precipitated an interest in Aids and Diana became actively involved with the British National Aids Trust. It was one of a number of charities she supported. She worked to dispel myths about the spread of Aids, shaking hands and touching patients to show that it could not be spread through casual contact.

Diana had met Taylor in 1982, at the London premiere of *The Little Foxes*. At that time, there were less than 300 reported cases of severe immune deficiency among gay men. By the end of 1989, the number of reported Aids cases in the United States alone had reached 100,000. Diana and Taylor were by then the most influential figures in the world in the fight against what had by then become a global pandemic.

FIGURE 14 *Rock Hudson's death in 1985 awakened a humanitarian spirit in Taylor and she dedicated much of the rest of her life to Aids charities.*

Photo by Tom Wargacki/WireImage. Getty Images.

14

No life without

Edna Ferber's book *Giant* concerns an oil-and-ranching family modeled on the Kleberg family, who ran (and still run today) the vast King Ranch in South Texas. *Giant* is the story of three characters: a conniving, bigoted oil tycoon-cum-cattle baron, his strong-willed wife, from Maryland, who curbs his Southern vulgarities with her Eastern civility, and a simple cowhand who strikes it rich. Serialized in *Ladies' Home Journal* beginning in the spring of 1952, the book *Giant* was published that fall, making the *New York Times'* best-seller list.

The film based on the novel secretes another story. Warner Brothers, having secured the rights—amid much competition from other studios—to Ferber's work, cast Rock Hudson in the central role of Bick Benedict, the rich Texan. Hudson, then twenty-nine, was what was known in the mid-1950s as "beefcake," meaning he was outstandingly handsome and muscular, emanating heterosexual attractiveness. Montgomery Clift, also possessed of exceptional good looks, was earmarked for the role of Jett Rink, the poor dirt farmer who strikes it rich, thought to be based on Glenn McCarthy, a real-life figure, known as "King of the Wildcatters" (a wildcatter is a prospector who sinks exploratory oil wells). But the producers were suspicious of Clift's drinking habit and opted for a relatively untested method actor, James Dean, who seemed promising in *East of Eden* (1955) and seemed an acceptable risk. Dean was also handsome, though in a different way to Hudson. Dean was, to use a term that originated at the time and has persisted since, *cool*.

Grace Kelly was a natural for the role of Leslie Benedict, Bick's wife. The humble, blonde Philadelphia beauty who became a Hollywood star had not yet fled to become a European princess, and looked perfect. Director George Stevens had briefly considered Elizabeth Taylor, but, at twenty-three, she seemed too young (Kelly was nearly two-and-a-half years older). Hudson, possibly wary that hugely popular Kelly might steal his thunder, argued Taylor's case and eventually got his way. Taylor was not yet the notorious siren she became, though, she had gone through her first unruly marriage and was now wedded to Michael Wilding. But she had not yet taken on a role that was truly mature and demanded that she age an improbable twenty-five years over the course of Ferber's saga.

In Ferber's novel and, indeed, Stevens' film, men are vulgar, patronizing, and misogynistic. But not nearly as extreme as the real people on which the characters were based. "He was a tough man, and the drinking and fight stories are true enough, but he wasn't anything like that character in *Giant,*" one old friend of Glenn McCarthy is quoted by Bryan Burrough, of *Vanity Fair* (2008). "He was a man, and he took a good deal of pride in the fact." Both Dean, who played him, and Hudson were also men and, we assume, proud of it.

Dean (who was born in 1931), like Clift (born 1920) and Marlon Brando (born 1924) was one of those mid-twentieth century screen-rebels challenging a society in the throes of a social, cultural, and psychological adjustment to peacetime. Their political aspirations were captured in Brando's answer to, "Hey Johnny, what are you rebelling against?" in *The Wild One* (1953). "What've you got?" Brando slurred back. Elvis was another pin-up rebel without cause, conviction or purpose. Dean, perhaps more than the others, encoded the mood of his generation. It was a generation that had not yet assimilated changes in the cultural politics of sex: Dean was unequivocally male and that meant his glossy handsomeness was intended to excite young women. It did. But that was just the visible tip of Dean's ultra-cool iceberg.

Hudson was an altogether more conventional character: tall (6 foot 4 inches), classic leading man looks and with none of the renegade spirit personified by Dean. He was straight off the Hollywood conveyor belt, a product for the delectation of women, young and old. There was no ambiguity in his roles, at least not that anyone could discern: he was the very embodiment of what we call today heteronormative; in other words, he promoted the view that heterosexuality is the normal or preferred sexual orientation. Homosexuality was illegal: the USA began repealing its sodomy laws in 1971; Britain had decriminalized homosexual acts between consenting adults earlier in 1967. So it would have been unthinkable for the tightly controlled Hollywood machine to countenance even the quietest whisper about either man's predilections, at least those that did not conform to the heteronormative ideal. And yet whispers murmured softly.

There was never evidence. Hudson strictly avoided Hollywood Boulevard, then the hottest gay cruising area. He is known to have detoured around the area rather than risk being compromised by an amateur photographer, or, worse, a journalist. Hedda Hopper and Louella Parsons were both in their pomp, at the height of their influence in the 1950s. Hollywood actors, male or female, usually kept up a pretense. Those who did not, kept silent, acted discreetly and trusted the industry's sturdy publicity apparatus.

Clifton Webb was an exception. A support player rather than a star, Webb, who played in the 1944 film noir *Laura*, was a lifelong bachelor who lived with his mother (who also managed him) until her death. According to

Leonard Leff, Webb's sexual orientation was known in the film industry, but so tight was the grip of the studios that it never became common knowledge. Despite his mostly supporting roles, Webb actually did star in one big Hollywood movie, the 1953 version of *Titanic*. Leff, in 2008, related an insider gag that circulated at the time: "Did you hear? Clifton Webb went down on the *Titanic*" (p. 22).

Few actors other than Webb were brave enough to allow their sexual proclivities to remain ambiguous. Hudson was not. Stephen Vider, in 2012, argued that some actors, such as Randolph Scott and Cary Grant, in their unusually close friendship, "expanded the boundaries of appropriate and 'normal' male behavior" (p. 550). But this did not undermine their heterosexual credentials during their acting careers.

Between 1946–65, Hudson was precious material in Hollywood: he ranked one place behind Doris Day, with whom he frequently starred, as the tenth most commercially successful actor, with five top 5 films, ten in the top 20, and twenty-five in the top 60. Taylor topped the rankings with ten, eleven, and thirteen in the respective categories, according to John Sedgwick's computations in 2002 (p. 700). As a valuable commodity, Hudson was handled with care. "Universal Studios took an active role in protecting Rock's heterosexual identity," wrote Brian L. Slade in 1996.

The closeness of the studios and the media meant that articles, such as "This is what I like," in which Hudson talked about what he looks for in a woman (in *Movies*, December 1952) regularly appeared. Anthony Slide detects that there was sufficient ambiguity in many of the stories about Hudson that they "could easily appeal to a closeted gay fan magazine reader as well as a healthy red-blooded American female" (p. 168). Slide gives several examples, including one photospread in which Hudson is naked apart for a towel covering his genitals at a bathhouse with other men, including Tony Curtis. And this was not considered homoerotic in the 1950s. At least, not to straight Americans.

While scandal is a proven resource today, its value to the media in the 1950s was uncertain; magazines with readerships that included idolatrous young women were reluctant to risk publishing exposés, even if they had enough proof to defend themselves against libel action. So it was in no one's interest to investigate too deeply.

Despite this, Hudson became the subject of what was, in the 1950s, unwelcome discussion and not only from the gossipy publications. *Life* magazine in September 1955 ran a cover story on Hudson—"Hollywood's Most Handsome Bachelor"—reporting, "Fans are urging 29-year-old Hudson to get married—or explain why not." *Confidential* magazine invited Hudson's agent Henry Willson to comment on rumors about the star's sexuality.

Were Hudson's ladykiller screen persona not so obviously keyed to being straight, Willson might have toughed it out. In the event, he traded. The result was, as Val Holley summarized in 2003: "*Confidential*'s May 1955 issue, with its cover story of actor Rory Calhoun's sordid early years as a car-stealing juvenile delinquent . . . and the November 9, 1955, marriage of Rock Hudson to Phyllis Gates" (p. 29). Calhoun, a lesser star than Hudson whom Willson also represented, was thrown under the bus, though a misspent youth was hardly likely to kill off his career. Calhoun continued to work in Hollywood, specializing in westerns. Hudson's marriage appeared to be a major coup, though, on reflection, it seems a flagrantly, fragrantly lavender arrangement. Not long after Hudson finished work on the movie *Giant,* he and Gates were married in Santa Barbara, with Willson and three friends in attendance.

"Living with Phyllis helped normalize Rock's reputation in Hollywood," Sara Davidson wrote in her co-authored biography of Hudson (with Hudson himself, 1986). But some writers remained unconvinced. Hedda Hopper, for example: in 1958, the same year she broke the "sleep alone" story, she approached *Motion Pictures* for a commission to interview Hudson's wife, who did not ordinarily talk to the media. Slide reports that Hopper confidently told the magazine's editor: "She [Phyllis] won't say he [Rock Hudson] is a fag, and name his lover, but we can hint at that" (p. 168). The interview did not materialize.

In January 1958, Gates questioned Hudson about a Rorschach test he had taken. A Rorschach test is a psychoanalytic instrument consisting of a set of symmetrical inkblots of different shapes and colors that are presented to a subject who is asked to describe we they resemble. "You told me you saw thousands of butterflies and also snakes," said Gates. "A therapist told me in my analysis that butterflies mean femininity and snakes represent that male penis." The interaction was recorded by Stephen Galloway in the *Hollywood Reporter*'s June 14, 2013 issue. According to Galloway, Gates confronted her husband with: "Everyone knows that you were picking up boys off the street shortly after we were married and have continued to do so, thinking that being married would cover up for you."

While Hudson denied this, Gates was apparently not convinced: she filed for divorce in April 1958, charging mental cruelty. Hudson did not contest the divorce, and Gates received a relatively modest alimony of $250 a week for ten years. She later insisted that she married Hudson out of love and not to cover up his homosexuality. She died aged eighty in 2006.

There were few doubts about Dean's heterosexuality at the time he was filming *Giant* though Emily Smith, in her undated "Everything you need to know . . ." book, wrote: "Dean avoided the draft by registering as a homosexual, then classified by the US government as a mental disorder" (p. 5). (Actually the American Psychiatric Association considered it a mental illness up till 1974.) This remains unconfirmed but, even if it did circulate as a rumor, it gained no traction. Several years later, in 2006, Dean's first biographer and friend William Bast stated that he and Dean had an intimate relationship. The 2012 biopic *Joshua Tree, 1951: A Portrait of James Dean* featured Dean in liaisons with other men. According to Jim Provenzano's entry on Dean in *The Queer Encyclopedia of Film and Television*: "Among the men cited as having had affairs with Dean are actors Clifton Webb, Bill Bast, and Jack Simmons, as well as producer Rogers Brackett" (p. 90).

Dean had, at one point, been engaged to a female, the Italian Pier Angeli, but this may have had the scent of lavender, and it did not last, anyway. As Dean died in a car crash on September 30, 1955, shortly after filming *Giant*, he was never able to refute or confirm any of the stories that circulated. He made only three films, two of which had not been released at the time of his death. So the Dean myth was always bound to take on a life of its own and grow new stories.

Today, tabloid writers would run riot, conjecturing the permutations. The cast: Taylor, a renowned beauty, albeit a married beauty; Hudson, not (quite) yet married and one of the most eligible men around; Dean, temperamental and magnetic. It seemed only a matter of time before a relationship or two, or more, were consummated. In the 1950s, the media was more circumspect. Years later, in 2007, Noreen Nash, an actor who played in the film, reckoned Taylor and Hudson wagered which one of them could seduce Dean first. Hudson won the mooted bet, according to Nash, who was widely reported on the LGBT networks (e.g., *PinkNews*, October 30, 2007: http://bit.ly/VN1DD8 accessed September 2015).

Yet Taylor maintained that Hudson and Dean, far from being friends, "didn't get along together" (in Bill Hoffman's *New York Post* interview in 1999). Asked by writer Kevin Sessums in 1997 whether she knew for sure of Dean's sexual status, Taylor replied: "He hadn't made up his mind. He was only 24 when he died. But he was certainly fascinated by women. He flirted around. He and I . . . *twinkled.*" It was obviously intended to tease; Taylor had long since learned not to deny rumors, particularly those concerning her own lack of chasteness. None of these uncorroborated stories surfaced until decades after the film's release and two of its stars were dead. After Taylor's death, Sessums revealed that, in his 1997 interview, Taylor confided that Dean had been molested as a child. She told Sessums not to disclose this until her death and he respected her wishes, publishing the story in 2011.

Hudson found his vocation in a series of three films with Doris Day. The template was *Pillow Talk* in which Hudson and Day played antagonistic neighbors sharing what was used to be called a party line, a telephone line shared by two or more subscribers. Day's portrayal established her as the purest screen virgin of her or, for that matter, any other generation: blonde, wholesome, undefiled, and undefilable. As far as Hollywood was concerned, sex did not happen in 1959, the year of *Pillow Talk*'s release. Two actors could do as much flirting and courting as they liked but they would have to remain strictly pre-pre-coital. Even so, Hudson must have had some misgivings about playing a character who creates an alter ego with effeminate tendencies in order to win the heroine (that is essentially the plot of *Pillow Talk*).

The comedy launched the sparklingly popular Hudson and Day pairing: *Pillow Talk* was the fifth-placed box office film of the year. The follow-up *Lover Come Back* was the seventh highest grossing film of 1961; and *Send Me No Flowers* was seventeenth in 1964. Perhaps they were only fluffy comedies, but they had verve enough to become influential films. "Contemporary romantic comedies can clearly be seen following patterns of both narrative and performance established in these earlier Hudson films," wrote Tamar Jeffers McDonald in 2001 (p. 856).

In the early 1960s, Day was America's number one box office attraction, the first woman to hit that spot since Shirley Temple. "I'd rather have Doris than Liz Taylor," concluded James Garner, who acted with Day in *The Thrill of It All* and *Move Over, Darling*. "Everything Doris does turns to box-office gold," Garner told David Kaufman in 2008. Day acquired the Midas-like power by embodying an image that gave rise to the line, "I'm so old I knew Doris Day before she was a virgin" (usually credited to actor Oscar Levant). Hollywood shaped Day's persona, colluding in presenting her as a sunny young celibate, despite her two failed early marriages and a teenage son, who had been raised by Day's own mother. As McDonald puts it: "She *became* a virgin."

Emmanuel Levy had a hypothesis: "The long-enduring stars have been endowed with particular screen images which were appealing and relevant during the time they were stars" (p. 256). Levy's tests revealed that the longest period of commercial popularity for female stars is ten years and only three women in history have achieved this. Day is one of them. Taylor managed nine years. "The secret of Day's appeal," detected Levy in 1990, "was based on her challenge to society's dominant attitudes towards women in the 1950s, but she did it with a smile, thus appearing to be nonthreatening" (p. 262). Taylor, by contrast, was completely weaponized. Levy's experiment was based on screen personae, not real human beings: Day was no more the Girl Next Door than Hudson was the All-American Heterosexual Male. With Taylor the distinction between screen self and self is not so apparent. Levy's revisionist reference to Day's "challenge" is unusual because she did not appear to issue one: his point is that her roles were often those of professionally ambitious women, who were prepared to face up to men rather than accept their authority.

Hudson's screen status was also "appealing and relevant" to use Levy's terms. Even though his divorce had gone through by the time of *Pillow Talk*'s release, the studio had, as Brian L. Slade suggested in 1996, "fabricated a heterosexual façade for public consumption." Having Hudson play a character only pretending to be gay ultimately was not viewed as a threat. Audiences were hardly likely to see through the apparent irony. Inside the film industry, Hudson's double-life was probably known.

Magazine writers were also privy to the secret, but fearful of legal action. And for good reason. In 1959, the entertainer Liberace sued the *Daily Mirror* British newspaper after it had described him as, "a deadly, winking, sniggering, snuggling, chromium-plated, scent-impregnated, luminous, quivering, giggling, fruit-flavoured, mincing, ice-covered heap of mother love." The publication denied it was meant to imply Liberace was gay, but the jury (in Britain) found otherwise and awarded damages of £8,000, or about £500,000 ($830,000) in today's money (the term "fruit" was and is not used in Britain as slang for gay). This served as a warning shot: entertainers with resources enough to pursue legal cases were prepared to punish publications that crossed them. Liberace was, of course, famously gay, lived with men and actually capitalized on his effeteness. But he denied under oath that he was homosexual or had ever engaged in homosexual acts. He died, aged sixty-seven, in 1987 of an Aids-related illness.

After their screen partnership concluded, Hudson and Day continued to flourish professionally, though Day curtailed her own career somewhat surprisingly. She had been involved in a seventeen-year marriage with Marty Melcher, who managed her affairs and, by many accounts, exploited her. It was more of a business than a conjugal union. Melcher died in 1968. Then Day was offered and turned down the role of Mrs. Robinson in Mike Nichols' film *The Graduate*. It was "the kind of role that could have altered her image as drastically as Nichols' *Who's Afraid of Virginia Woolf* the previous year had changed Taylor's," reflected Dennis Bingham in 2006 (p. 3). Anne Bancroft accepted the role of the mature, urbane seductress, even though, at thirty-six, she was nearly seven years younger than Day and only six years older than her young prey in the film, Dustin Hoffman.

For the next five years, Day appeared in a weekly television sitcom, *The Doris Day Show*. But animal rights became her calling: she heard about a kennel in Burbank, California that mistreated diseased and abandoned animals, so helped mobilize a group to liberate the ailing creatures. David Kaufman calls her disappearance from showbusiness "Doris Day's Vanishing Act" and, while there was no mystery behind it, her withdrawal was unexpected.

Hudson maintained a Hollywood presence through the 1960s, avoiding any inquisitions about his sexuality. His specialty became military roles in war movies like *Tobruk* (1967) and *Ice Station Zebra* (1968). In the 1970s, he featured in *McMillan & Wife*, and in the 1980s, *Dynasty*, both longrunning tv series. As we have seen, he reunited with Taylor in *The Mirror Crack'd*; even in his fifties, he retained the good looks that had been essential to his early success. Like Day, he was rarely short of offers of films and tv roles, but, unlike Day, he welcomed them. He leaped like a salmon when he heard a pitch for a sequel to *Pillow Talk*. This was 1984, twenty-five years after the original, but there is no time limit on sequels: there were almost twenty-three years between 1960's *Psycho* and *Psycho II*, twenty-five years between *The Hustler*, in 1961, and *The Color of Money*.

Day was sent a tape synopsizing the plot, and was interested enough to request changes. But, as with all other projects sent her way, Day, then sixty, passed. Among the other projects she passed on were *Murder She Wrote* and *Dallas*, both immensely successful tv dramas. For a woman who had rejected so many inviting roles, her acceptance of an offer from a cable tv station called Christian Broadcasting Network (CBN) provoked an obvious question: why? The show was centered around animals. *Doris Day's Best Friends* would feature Day chatting to her guests about their pets. The show ran for 26 episodes in 1985–6. Day's first guest on the show was, almost inevitably, Rock Hudson.

A press conference to launch the show was held in Carmel, California, near Day's home, on July 15, 1985. Day arrived at 4.00 p.m. to greet the assembled media and wait for the arrival of Hudson. When he arrived, an hour late, there were gasps. Kaufman explains: "Instead of the gorgeous hunk who had been Day's three-time co-star, the emaciated man who now made his way to her side was cadaverous, his cheeks hollow, with sunken eyes and a gray pallor." Hudson looked unrecognizable from the maturely handsome man who had appeared with Taylor barely a year before. He walked unsteadily on his feet, exhausted, even dazed, as Kaufman puts it, as he bantered with his old friend.

Hudson's appearance at the press conference stoked up rumors about his rapidly deteriorating physical condition. This was a time when the world was still coming to terms with the scale and severity of the Aids pandemic. Sensing the seriousness of his condition, Day implored Hudson to stay with her, but instead he flew to Paris, where he had heard there was a new, experimental drug called HPA-23, which was not available in the USA (the US Food and Drug Administration, or FDA, did not allow the importation of unapproved drugs for persons with life-threatening illnesses until 1988).

In Paris, Hudson collapsed and was taken to the American Hospital of France, where hospital spokesman Bruce Redor explained he was suffering from "fatigue and general malaise." Tests, said Redor, were inconclusive and doctors were still working on a diagnosis. The media in America and elsewhere carried the story of Hudson's "mystery illness," speculating that it may be liver cancer, which was denied by the hospital. In an era of conjectural news, the Aids theory assumed primacy and it seemed just a question of time before an announcement confirmed suspicions. Publicist Yanou Collart, who issued the statement, recalled looking at Hudson as he dictated: "I'll never forget the look on his face . . . Very few people knew he was gay. In his eyes was the realization that he was destroying his own image" (quoted in Christopher Rudolph's 2013 article). Scot Haller, of *People* magazine, maintained in 1985 that even Marc Christian, with whom Hudson shared his home, was not aware of the nature of his illness and, like many of his friends "attributed Hudson's wasted appearance to anorexia."

Collart's confirmation that Hudson had Aids came on July 25 after two days of confusion and speculation. In 1985, Aids was usually a fatal ailment. It was known that it most frequently strikes three groups: intravenous drug users, recipients of blood transfusions and men who engage in homosexual sex. In a statement to Associated Press, published in the *New York Times*, Collart said of Hudson: "He doesn't have any idea how he contracted AIDS."

Today we are accustomed to gay celebrities who are either unabashed about their sexuality or make a public declaration in the reasonably safe knowledge it will do no harm to their career. Anderson Cooper, the television journalist, Jim Parsons, star of *The Big Bang Theory*, and actor Zachary Quinto are among the many public figures who are openly gay. Gillian Anderson, a mother of two and twice divorced (from men) has talked freely about her relationships with women. Lana Wachowski, the filmmaker, and British boxing promoter Kellie Maloney are among those who have declared themselves as transgender. In the mid-1980s, the cultural climate was very different. The historical disgrace accruing to homosexuality was compounded by the Aids pandemic. Paradoxically, it could be argued that Aids, in time, introduced the enlightenment that changed attitudes toward homosexuality.

Hudson died two-and-a-half months later, back in California, on October 2, 1985. The first episode of *Doris Day's Best Friends* with Hudson was broadcast by CBN nine days after his death. He was not the first person to die with Aids, of course. And there were many more prominent Aids-related deaths after 1985: Liberace (1987), Freddie Mercury (1991), Anthony Perkins (1992), for example. The deaths of these figures had enormous impact, though not as great as Hudson's. The disclosure of his sexual identity after so many years portraying a ladies' man forced everyone to recognize the contradictions that abounded in Hollywood. But the disclosure was posthumous: Hudson never publicly came out during his lifetime.

Tracy Ann Oberman's 2012 play *Rock and Doris and Elizabeth* recreates events either side of Hudson's appearance at the press conference in Carmel. Oberman imagines Taylor knew of Hudson's condition and realized he had not got long to live. In the play, she urges him to come out and give a human face to a relatively new disease that is known only abstractly and is still mysterious to many. Day interprets Taylor's plea as a jealously motivated tactic to undermine her attempt to renew her professional relationship with Hudson. She tries desperately to persuade him to stay in the closet. A terribly stricken and conspicuously ill Hudson knows that by appearing on Day's show he will be sending a visual message that he was not the myth that Hollywood created.

Viewed like this, Hudson's was a selfless act; though Sara Davidson's biography advises that Hudson was far less idealistic and had just wanted to die peacefully in Palm Springs, California, citing liver disease as the cause of death. After officials at the American Hospital of France declared he was not suffering from liver cancer, they encouraged him to tell the truth. Hudson remained silent.

But on July 23, 1985 *Variety* columnist Army Archerd revealed that Hudson had Aids and, in the process, incurred the wrath of, among others, Taylor. After he had written his piece, he had an invitation to a press party withdrawn because, as one of the organizers put it: "If I invite you, Elizabeth will not show up" (recalled in 2001 by Archerd). This led some, like Anne Taylor Fleming, of the *New York Times* to conclude in 1989: "Without Army Archerd's column, there is a very real chance that the world might have suspected but never known what killed Rock Hudson" (in Bruce Weber's 2009 obituary).

The implicit argument of the play is that Hudson's Aids experience gave Taylor her future meaning in life, and created a new understanding of Aids. As Oberman told Gareth McLean in 2012: "For me, that was the birth of the Aids awareness movement, and the importance of that shouldn't be underestimated." Hudson's death certainly intensified public, political, and scientific interest in what was then an incurable disease.

There is an additional theme in the play: if Rock Hudson—that virile, red-blooded all-male pinup, the antithesis of the limp-wristed stereotype of gay men—could have Aids, then nothing on silver screen would ever convince audiences that what they were watching had any semblance of reality. Hudson was a persona, not a human being. In other words, Hudson's death defined an end-of-innocence moment, after which audiences became evermore questioning and critical. It is a powerful argument though one that probably underestimates audience's awareness of the film and indeed the entertainment industry prior to the 1980s. But certainly, there were profound changes in the manner in which celebrities engaged with audiences and made them privy to what had hitherto been off-limits areas of their lives.

The day before he died, Taylor visited Hudson at his home. He was receiving nourishment intravenously. Taylor spent only a few moments alone with him in his bedroom. After his death, Taylor helped organize a private memorial service at Hudson's home for fifty of his friends.

Hudson was not the first gay man with whom Taylor had formed a strong and enduring friendship. She was only nine when she was cast with fifteen-year-old fellow Brit Roddy McDowall in *Lassie Come Home* (1943). Years later, they both played in *Cleopatra*. He died from cancer in 1998, aged seventy. She was also great friend of Montgomery Clift with whom she was paired in *A Place in the Sun* (1951), when she was eighteen. Clift and Taylor also played in *Raintree County* the film they were making at the time of Clift's dreadful road accident. Taylor rushed to the scene and saved him from suffocating by prying dislodged teeth from his throat in 1956. Clift died at only forty-five in 1966. "But her first intense relationship with a gay man was with her own father, who was the longtime companion of Adrian, the MGM costume designer," wrote M.G. Lord in 2012 (p. 25). (Adrian, sometimes known as Adrian Greenberg or Gilbert Adrian, but usually just Adrian, was a prominent Hollywood costume designer, who, in 1939, married actor Janet Gaynor.)

Straight women who form deep, affective, and intimate bonds with gay men are known in gay vernacular as fag hags. "If and when we call Elizabeth Taylor a fag hag, we are on relatively safe ground," argued Maria F. Fackler and Nick Salvato in 2012 (p. 71). It may seem an ugly term, but Fackler and Salvato do not intend it as such: "The term has been repurposed by women, gay men, and other queer interlocutors, whose points of view have been powerfully shaped by a reckoning with AIDS" (p. 64). By "repurposed," I take them to mean that the intention or objective of both the term and the women to whom it is applied has changed as a result of Aids.

Paul Flynn, of Britain's *Guardian* newspaper agreed and, in 2011, singled out Taylor: "Taylor's relationship with gay men provided a new model of gay icon. No longer was it enough to be a woman with whom gay men retained a bass-note of empathy, the kind of strung out glamour/tragedy axis that Judy Garland immortalized." He means that, over the years, there had been dozens of female entertainers who enjoyed the appreciation and support of gay men, but without actually giving anything. From 1985, Taylor committed herself to fighting against Aids, making public pronouncements, raising money, badgering politicians and, in her way, changing perceptions of gayness. "Her feeling for camp was not an affectation or strategic marketing device, but something more innate and intuitive," wrote Flynn, who detected a more instrumental approach in Lady Gaga's self-appointment as a gay icon. Madonna and Kylie Minogue are among the many other women who have worked in the effort against Aids. Edwin Bayrd, director of the UCLA Aids Institute, called Taylor the "the Joan of Arc of Aids activism," in allusion to the leader of French armies against the English in the Hundred Years War (1337–1453).

While Hudson's death gave impetus and new purpose to Taylor's campaign, her involvement with Aids began several months before. In January 1985, she and Dennis Stein, to whom she was then engaged, attended President Ronald Reagan's second inauguration. She urged the President's wife Nancy to take an active interest in a disease that was then engendering panic. The previous October, San Francisco had ordered the closure of the city's bathhouses because of the high-risk sexual activity that typically occurs in such establishments. Los Angeles and New York City would follow the example. At this point the cause of Aids had been found in the retrovirus HTVL-III, a term later replaced by HIV (for human immunodeficiency virus). Ronald Reagan was a friend of Hudson's, though, of course, at this point the cause of Hudson's illness was not known. Reagan apparently assumed it was hepatitis, a disease characterized by inflammation of the liver. Taylor broke off the engagement to Stein shortly after the presidential inauguration.

In his 1996 book, Ellis Amburn contends that Taylor did not know Hudson had Aids at the time of his appearance at Doris Day's press conference at Carmel, on July 15 1985, nor even by the time he flew to Paris in search of treatment (p. 467). She, along with the rest of the world, learned only on July 25, 1985, when Hudson's statement was read out by his spokesperson Yanou Collart. Hudson's illness had been diagnosed as Aids in the United States a year before, confirmed Collart. David Bret thinks Taylor realized in January 1985 when she accompanied Hudson to the Golden Globes awards (p. 245).

Even if Taylor had not known the precise cause of Hudson's deterioration, she would have been made forcibly aware of the peril of Aids. Her daughter-in-law Aileen Getty (wife of her son Christopher Wilding) was diagnosed HIV positive. Getty, the granddaughter of J. Paul Getty, was one of the first prominent women to declare themselves living with HIV. She was diagnosed in 1985 and, while, in 2011, she told The Advocate's Jeff Yarbrough that she told her immediate family, it is not known for sure whether she told Taylor. Taylor's friend Halston battled Aids-related cancer for eighteen months before succumbing in March 1990, aged fifty-seven.

A month before Hudson's death, Taylor had launched an organization, which eventually became the American Foundation for AIDS Research, usually abbreviated to amfAR. Its remit was to raise money to finance research into Aids/HIV. In the mid-1980s, Aids/HIV was what might be called an unfashionable cause. Without espousing any debilitating illness, there are some that affect all demographics, which draw an unqualified response and evoke unquestioning communion. Aids was not such an illness in the 1980s. Variously described as the "gay plague" and interpreted by some as God's reparation for sinful behavior, it was controversial, the kind of disease unlikely to attract sympathy. Taylor's decision to champion its cause was that of a woman confident in her own status or ready to gamble with her own popularity.

As amfAR's founding chair, Taylor became progressively involved with the organization and assumed the role of principal spokesperson. In 1986, she appeared in a series of amfAR television spots. She also testified before Congress to ensure Senate support for the Ryan White CARE Act, of 1990, which remains the primary source of federal government funding for Aids/HIV programs in the US (Ryan White was a teenager from Indiana who contracted Aids through contaminated blood products used to treat his hemophilia and, in 1985, was refused entry to his middle school; he died in 1990, aged eighteen). Never shy of crowds, Taylor traveled as a representative of amfAR, attracting huge audiences wherever she went. In the years that followed, Madonna, Bono, Alicia Keys, Annie Lennox, Miley Cyrus, and Rihanna were among the celebrities who lent their support to raise awareness of and help those living with HIV.

Taylor would appear in only two more feature movies, one that was not released theatrically in the United States. She cameo'd in a live action version of the 1960s cartoon *The Flintstones* in 1994. But otherwise, she specialized in television movies. While making one such movie in 1986, she met George Hamilton. Writing in 2011, Joan Collins, a friend of both, believes he wielded quite an influence on Taylor, putting her on a strict diet and suggesting ways she should dress and wear her hair. Seven years Taylor's junior, Hamilton was a jobbing actor, who had never quite made the A-list despite success with a 1979 vampire spoof, *Love at First Bite*. He was rarely short of work and found himself playing opposite Taylor in the modest tv film *Poker Alice* (1987).

There was a time when the mere mention of another man in the life of Elizabeth Taylor would elicit a response from news editors in print and broadcast media. In 1986, Taylor occupied a new position, that of *grande dame*, still a woman of influence, but now a mature woman in a different sphere of influence. One can imagine a journalist calling her editor excitedly to share a juicy piece of gossip she's just heard about Taylor and the roguishly good-looking lothario Hamilton. The editor's response would have been something like: "OK, write it up in 150-words; it's a news-in-brief story for page seven." Pretty much canonized as Saint Elizabeth of California, Taylor remained news, but not as a maneating sexpot: she was by this time part of a new narrative. "I DON'T THINK THE PRESIDENT IS DOING ANYTHING AT ALL ABOUT AIDS," SAYS LIZ TAYLOR was the kind of headline editors wanted. And this is what she gave them.

What really matters is not what you do or say, but how journalists present it. This is not a dictum, or even one of those sayings whose author no one can remember. But it was probably a rule of thumb with Taylor, to whom the media's potency had always been apparent. Even before the Eddie Fisher scandal, she must have realized how crucial the media were in building narratives for public consumption. Her friendship with Hedda Hopper would have been an educative one. The effect of announcing her breakup with Richard Burton to the media must have pleased her, even if Burton had been piqued. So, in 1987, after quietly petitioning President Ronald Reagan without much success, she did something similar. She sent him and his wife Nancy an open letter, inviting them both to a fund-raising dinner staged by amfAR. "I am writing from my heart," she confirmed.

Reagan had, at this stage, spoken publicly on Aids, but shown no depth of commitment to funding research to discover a cure. "Your participation in the dinner would mean a great deal to not only the American Foundation for AIDS Research, but also to people, like me, who are critically concerned about the impact of the ever-growing 'AIDS epidemic,'" wrote Taylor, adding a carefully worded and barely veiled reference to Reagan's well-known hostility to public-sector funding: "AmfAR is solely supported by the private sector and I know that you in particular, Mr. President, believe in encouraging private sector support and involvement in helping to meet our nation's needs." The letter received the desired coverage; as an open letter, it was circulated to all media and its text is still available online at: http://to.pbs.org/1tnpmbE (accessed September 2015). It was handwritten and closed: "P.S. My love to you, Nancy, I hope to see you soon. E."

Of course, US Presidents do not just turn up for dinner without saying something and Reagan, having being practically pressganged into attending, gave only his second speech on Aids, in which he offered what was to date his clearest message on the subject. "Innocent people are being infected by this virus, and some of them are going to acquire Aids and die," said Reagan before adumbrating a package of measures. Reagan was not known as a sympathetic leader in this context, but he was embarrassed by Taylor—abetted by the media—into a speech he must have delivered through gritted teeth.

At fifty-five, Taylor was transforming her persona. Her films were largely ignored and her love life was of little interest to the media, and probably the public. Hamilton dissolved into the background and Malcolm Forbes, the publisher of *Forbes* magazine, came to prominence as her regular escort. Born in 1919, Forbes, like Reagan, was a Republican and stalwart advocate of capitalism; like Taylor, he was a pleasure seeker, spending extravagantly on aircrafts, yachts, art, and hot air balloons. And motorcycles: he had a private collection of about eighty Harley-Davidson, Yamahas and other marques. He gave Taylor one of his prized Harleys.

Taylor was one of a number of glamorous women with whom Forbes was associated, though Stephen McFarland, of the *New York Daily News*, reported in 1996: "There were whispers that the beautiful women were camouflage intended to draw suspicious eyes away from a carefully closeted homosexual private life."

Four years later when Forbes died and unrelatedly Taylor fell ill, a story that Taylor had contracted Aids through Forbes gained currency to the point where Taylor felt obliged to issue a press statement. It was not true.

Taylor's relationship with Forbes appeared to owe more to expedience than passion. He accompanied her to several grand occasions, such as when she received the *Légion d'Honneur*, France's most prized decoration, in Paris in May 1987. She was by his side for his seventieth birthday celebrations in Morocco in 1989.

The exact nature of her relationship with Forbes was of surprisingly little interest to the media. At least, it would have been surprising had it not been for her reinvention. When George Bush took over from Reagan to become 41st President in 1989, he busied himself with arms reduction negotiations with the Soviet Union and international action to expel Iraqis from Kuwait. Bush, perforce, has to contend with Taylor. "I don't think President Bush is doing anything at all about AIDS," she proclaimed to a press conference in Amsterdam at the Eighth International Conference on AIDS. "In fact, I'm not even sure if he knows how to spell 'AIDS.'" As Nancy Collins, of *Vanity Fair*, reported in 1992: "It was the A-I-D-S shot heard round the world, front-page news from Tokyo to Washington."

Could Taylor have thought of a better way to snatch the attention of a global audience? Did she really need sarcasm to make her point? Should she have been a bit more deferential about the holder of the highest office in the country? A sort of answer came when, following her remark, she was pressed by CNN's medical correspondent and informed: "Secretary Sullivan announced the administration will not be browbeaten by movie stars or anyone else on their AIDS policies." Taylor hesitated, thought for a moment and then replied: "Excuse me. Who said that?" The reporter repeated "*Secretary Sullivan*," meaning Louis Wade Sullivan, who was the Secretary of the US Department of Health and Human Services. "Well, I wasn't addressing my remarks to him," riposted Taylor. "I was addressing my remarks to the president."

"When you're as famous as Elizabeth Taylor, when a single utterance can command world-wide media attention, you are, almost by definition, political," concluded Nancy Collins. Taylor did not even have to earn her political spurs, nor even learn the ground rules. Without even trying, she seemed to become a political force, judging the exact distance she needed to keep away from mainstream politics: not too close to appear cozy, not too far away to be appear detached, the middle zone where her compassion could unite with her carping.

It seemed an undignified conclusion to an otherwise quite distinguished movie career, though Taylor was, by 1987, pursuing more idealistic goals. Her final full-length feature film *Young Toscanini* or *Il giovane Toscanini* to give it its original title, was based on an episode in the teenage life of the Italian conductor Arturo Toscanini. Taylor played an aging soprano who vies with a younger woman for the affections of Toscanini. Franco Zeferelli directed the project, which was panned after its premiere at the Venice Film Festival and gained only limited theatrical release. The film was probably just a paycheck. There were a few tv films to come and a notable comic cameo; but essentially Taylor's days as a movie star were history.

She was now a traveling fundraiser, making appeals, embarrassing politicians, and pricking everyone's consciences. The Live Aid concert of

1985 had started with the bright idea of Bob Geldof, Bono, and a few other rock musicians, but became a reminder of the universality of compassion. Taylor, like the rock musicians, was drawing audiences who wanted a performance in exchange for their sympathy. In addition to her Aids campaigns, she had also brokered a deal that would eventually become the source of her personal fortune; we will come to this shortly. And she had also written a new book.

People magazine's pre-publication extract was headlined with A STAR IS REBORN (still available at: http://bit.ly/1vDh3JJ accessed September 2015). *Elizabeth Takes Off* was a memoir mixed with prescriptive text on how to lose weight. In the early 1980s, "she [Taylor] was inspiring cruel jokes about her burgeoning weight, and in response she was only guzzling more booze, gobbling more pills, gorging more calories," reported *People*. But: "Today, at 55, having shed nearly 60 lbs., she is once again a startling figure, the envy of women of any age."

The Elizabeth Taylor narrative never became predictable; if audiences could guess what would come next, they might have started to anticipate Taylor's next move. No sooner were they getting to grips with her newfound vocation, the latest men in her life, and her film catastrophes, than Taylor published a book. It was not her first: way back in 1946, when a child star, she wrote *Nibbles and Me*, an account of her and her pet chipmunk. In 1964, there was her *Elizabeth Taylor: An Informal Memoir*. And years later in 2002, she would write *My Love Affair with Jewelry*. While *Elizabeth Takes Off* was not a biography, there were plenty of aperçus on her recent history, particularly her phase with John Warner, when she relates how she escaped her film star persona and threw herself full tilt behind her husband's political campaigns, usually to the detriment of her appearance. "As the physical strain mounted, I kept on eating. Junk food. When you're on the road before dawn, you grab anything you can and it's usually dripping with grease and slapped in a bun," wrote Taylor.

It was a plausible explanation of how she piled on the pounds. Around the same time, Taylor gave a televised interview to Barbara Walters in which she offered another angle: she claims that her segue out of showbusiness into politics afforded her the opportunity to take control of her own body. "I've worked since I was nine," she reminded Walters, suggesting that other people had been instructing her on how to look ever since. So, when she had chance of taking a measure of control of her own appearance, she took it. She summarized her response: "If I want to be fat I'll bloody well be fat." She weighed about 122 pounds at the time. (The interview is viewable at: http://bit.ly/1CiNP4A accessed September 2015.)

The two explanations are not entirely incompatible, but the former appeared more plausible after Taylor had completed an extensive promotional campaign to publicize her book. In a way, the endeavor could be compared to the kind of whistle-stop touring she had done with and for Warner. By the time she had finished the promotion, "she was exhausted, overeating, and drinking alcohol," according to biographer Ellis Amburn (p. 383).

She was also taking painkillers to numb the effects of various ailments, including osteoporosis, a condition in which bones become brittle and fragile from loss of tissue. Taylor spent time in a wheelchair, when she was out of public purview. When she appeared in front of the media, she was as professional as ever: polished, dazzling, and full of bounce. It was typical Taylor: a theatrical performance. To worsen matters, her mother, then ninety-two, was ailing.

In the fall of 1988, Taylor, fatigued and disabled by the compounded effects of the touring and osteoporosis, had to consider that she had spent the previous several months telling consumers how she had brought her diet under control and, to use common parlance, cleaned up her act. All the time, she was ratcheting up her use of painkilling medication. It was a show of bad faith: she had been issuing advice on how to avoid the kind of temptations to which she had herself succumbed.

Several years later, in 2009, Gerald Posner, an investigative journalist for the *Daily Beast*, disclosed that, in the mid-1980s, having spent one period in the Betty Ford Center, Taylor realized she had conquered one habit, but was surrendering to another. After drinking for almost her entire adult life, she had brought a practice that, like her passions, grew wilder during her years with Burton, under control. But her physical conditions ailed her and the release from pain brought by medication was in itself intoxicating.

After efforts to wean herself off painkillers and various other pharmaceuticals, Posner concluded: "She [Taylor] abandoned the pretense of wanting to be drug-free and instead asked for Dilaudid and Ativan." Diladud is a narcotic, typically prescribed for severe pain; Ativan is a drug often used to treat anxiety disorders. They were just two of several kinds of pharmaceutical products Taylor habitually consumed in the 1980s.

Three of Taylor's physicians were, in 1987 and 1988, treating Taylor for her painful back and other conditions but in a manner, that "fell below the accepted standard of medical practice," according to Los Angeles's Deputy District Attorney Daniel Feldstern. The doctors in question were Michael Roth, William Skinner, and Michael Gottlieb, the immunologist who reported the first Aids cases in the US. All were on staff at Saint John's Health Center in Santa Monica, where Taylor was hospitalized. Skinner served as the director of the hospital's chemical dependency unit. In addition to her doctor-patient relationship, Taylor shared with Roth and Gottlieb a dedication to the Aids movement.

Associated Press reports in spring 1990 disclosed how the doctors "overprescribed" narcotics to their "demanding famous client" (*Sun Journal*, Lewiston, Maine, April 21, 1990, p. 8). The case reached California's Medical

Board and, while Taylor was not identified in the accusation, her name was revealed during legal discovery (i.e. the process in which parties are required to disclose information essential to a case). In the mid-1980s, the doctors had ordered for Taylor 1,000 prescriptions for twenty-eight controlled substances, including Percodan, Xanax, Preludin, and Demerol, the strong narcotic analgesic I referred to in Chapter 10. Charges, totaling about 80 pages, include an exhaustive list of drugs prescribed in various combinations, both by tablet and by self-injection.

In 1994, Roth, Skinner, and Gottlieb received state reprimands for trying to hide dosages by falsifying patient records (*Seattle Times*, August 11, 2004). It was a relatively minor punishment, interpreted by their attorneys as "an exoneration of three dedicated physicians who were trying to control Taylor's pain and kept inaccurate medical records only to protect the actress from the prying eyes of reporters for tabloids such as the *National Enquirer*," as Claire Spiegel and Virginia Ellis, of the *Los Angeles Times* reported it in 1994. The allusion was to the habit of tabloid journalists of paying hospital orderlies, who are responsible for the non-medical care of patients, for information on Taylor, including her medical charts.

Skinner's attorney Donald Goldman suggested the doctors' efforts in not accurately recording the full list of drugs she was taking were designed to protect Taylor's reputation: "You see what comes out in the tabloid press these days and you can see very clearly why they (the doctors) did it." It was an ingenious and, in its way, insightful argument: by the mid-1980s, the Diana era was underway, and tabloid writers cheerfully dispensed cash payments to anyone with information relevant to a celebrity.

By further way of mitigation, the lawyers pointed out that Taylor, with her long history of back and neck pain, and several surgeries, needed more drugs than most patients to control pain. "Liz Taylor is a different patient, with intractable, long-term, untreatable pain," advised Gottlieb's attorney Harland Braun. The drug dosages would have been excessive for most people, but were appropriate to combat Taylor's discomfort and allow her to function. "She has no life without painkillers," Braun concluded dramatically (quotes from Spiegel and Ellis' article).

Posner's investigative story was published fifteen years after this case and added a new name to the medical practitioners who had treated her in the 1980s. Posner cited an unnamed doctor who, while treating Taylor, refused the Dilaudid and Ativan she requested and asked her to reveal the full extent of her medication history. Taylor supplied the doctor with the list of drugs she was taking. "A source close to the doctor said that when she was pressed about who was prescribing such a wide mix of drugs, she said it was Dr. Klein," reported Posner. The anonymous medic promptly advised her to check back into rehab.

"Dr. Klein" was Arnold Klein, a dermatologist who worked in UCLA's School of Medicine. He was, with Taylor, a founding member of amfAR.

Other founders included David Geffen, creator of Dreamworks and Asylum Records, and Mathilde Krim, a doctor who practised at New York's Memorial Sloan-Kettering Cancer Center. Taylor's work for amfAR brought her into frequent contact with Klein. Taylor later introduced Klein to her friend Michael Jackson, to whom we will turn shortly.

Of all the aspects of Taylor's life that had been turned inside out and made available to her audience, her dependency on pharmaceutical drugs was arguably the least glamorous. Even her drinking excesses had a certain exciting, irresponsible, even rebellious quality that made them seem appealing in the 1980s. Taylor could hardly disguise her drinking, but she approached drugs with understandable delicacy. Later, she would make a short but honest declaration.

"I had the arrogance to think I could be a social drinker," Taylor told Nancy Collins in 1992, "and I was addicted to painkillers." Taylor had exited the Betty Ford Center in January 1984. In October 1988, she returned.

Gossip sounds more authentic when it has some association, however tenuous, with empirical evidence. The evidence was: Taylor was the most charismatic Aids campaigner in the world. By the late 1980s, any mention of her name automatically elicited the word Aids in the mind. Over the years, Taylor had given new meaning to all manner of words in the popular lexicon: Burton, Cleopatra, Oscar and, of course, Sex. And now Aids. After completing her second stint at the Betty Ford Center in 1988, she resumed her fund-raising activities and set off on a tour to promote her book, seemingly refreshed, sober, and freed from her reliance on pharmaceuticals. So when she was suddenly hospitalized, the word Aids almost naturally sprung to people's lips.

One near-death experience is more than enough for most people. Taylor was always prone to excesses. Having pulled through the life-threatening viral pneumonia when filming *Cleopatra* in 1961, Taylor had grown accustomed to persistent sicknesses and, perhaps, more bedeviling, to the medications prescribed to allay the pain they brought. In March 1990, she caught what she thought was a sinus infection. By April 9 she was in the Daniel Freeman Marina Del Ray Hospital. A week later she was transferred to St. John's Hospital and Health Center, where she stayed, hovering between life and death with a pulmonary virus, for the next three months.

Taylor claimed doctors asked her to go on a life-support machine and, when she balked, they told her, with or without her permission, they would, if necessary put her on the equipment. She reckons a doctor confronted her with the uncomfortable prospect: "You are a dying woman. Now sign this paper [the permission document]." Taylor told Collins she called her lawyer and made out a living will, stipulating that if she was unconscious for two weeks somebody had to pull the plug. They went on to perform a lung biopsy. Catheters were placed in her chest and it was discovered that as well as the pulmonary virus she had contracted candidiasis, a yeast-like parasitic fungus that can cause thrush. Perversely, this is an illness often associated with Aids.

On April 23, Taylor's doctors issued a rather premonitory statement that included the phrase, "She is seriously ill." Taylor's publicist Chen Sam assured an expectant media: "She's not well. She's not on her deathbed or anything" (both statements are covered in, among other publications, the *Tuscaloosa News*, April 24, 1990). The announcement probably had the effect of a boxing manager's affirmation that his man will have no trouble making the weight for an upcoming fight. Journalists instantly assume the opposite is true. Taylor's personal doctor, the previously-mentioned Roth, happened to be an Aids specialist. Rock Hudson had died from an Aids-related illness five years before. Only weeks before Taylor fell ill, her close friend, the designer Halston had died from Aids. A month before that, Taylor's companion Malcolm Forbes had died of a reported heart attack and, following his death, there were confirmations of rumors about his predilections for gay sex. Sam's denial "She's not on her deathbed" all but guaranteed that creative minds would be exercised over Taylor's condition.

Stories of doubtful factuality flourish with both conjecture and refutation, of course. Even hard evidence does not always have a crippling effect on perfectly good hearsay. Taylor probably knew this when she issued, through Sam, another statement that began: "I would like to dispel the plethora of rumors." Journalists must have buckled their safety belts; what on earth was coming next? "That I have an Aids-related condition," perhaps? Chen continued to recite Taylor's actual words: "I feel it is important that people should not be afraid to be tested for Aids. I have an annual physical and have been tested for the disease, and the test results are negative."

Taylor had a well-known tendency to mess with the media, of course. She had been doing it in one way or another since she was a teenager; perhaps there was something in the spaces between the words. She was quashing Aids rumors, not denying that she could be dying from some other terrible disease. In Taylor's universe, many things were susceptible to different laws of corroboration and falsification. She had been out of the Betty Ford Center barely a year, but, for Taylor, that was ample time to reattach herself to old favorites, like Jack Daniel's and Demerol. This was 1990, remember: conjectural news, which had its origins in the mid-1970s (as we discovered earlier) had become the norm: journalists speculated legitimately, surmised defensibly, gave license to their imaginative power.

Taylor had already acknowledged a dependence on painkillers and sleeping pills in 1983, when she first entered the Betty Ford Center, partially at Skinner's request. She recognized that dependencies had progressed over several years. Since then she had returned for treatment at the Center, again, it seemed, to no avail. Now she lay in a hospital bed, in stable condition, but still apparently stricken by pneumonia, surrounded by the 400 "get well" cards and floral gifts she received every day. Perhaps it was just another of those coincidences that fate had dropped on Taylor; but the timing of the story added grist to the mills of doomsayers.

It took until June 1990 before the rumors were put to rest. Taylor was discharged from hospital, underweight and weak, but still very much alive and almost ready to resume her charitable work. She convalesced at a rented beach house in Santa Monica in the company of a relatively new man in her life.

FIGURE 15 *By 1991, when White Diamonds was launched, Taylor's persona was so well established that she could put it to any service she wanted, including the creation of her own brand.*

Photo by Jim Smeal/WireImage. Getty Images.

15

Everything is for sale

January 14, 1987. Helmsley Palace Hotel, New York. It was a news conference, though it was run more like a Scholastic Aptitude Test, according to Michael Gross, of the *New York Times* (January 15, 1987). On entering, journalists were asked to wear name tags and instructed that the person they had all turned up to see and hear would answer only questions that related specifically to her announcement. She would not discuss her health, her love life, her films or other creative projects, or even the Aids campaign on which she was spending the majority of her time. So what was the subject? All the media knew was that they had received invitations marked TOP SECRET a few weeks before and Elizabeth Taylor would be center stage. What she intended to talk about was anybody's guess.

Once the 500 or so journalists, including members of seventeen overseas film crews, were assembled, the doors of the hotel's Versailles Room were closed and folders were distributed. The first clues: the purple colored booklets were embossed with what looked like a bottle of cologne, or eau d' toilette. Inside, information packs about Parfums International Ltd, the prestige fragrance group of the Prince Matchabelli division of Chesebrough-Pond's Inc. An American version of the 1974 Italian movie *Profumo di Donna* maybe? No: *Scent of a Woman* would not appear until 1992. Cynical journalists could probably guess what was coming.

Celebrities today are a little like those Gruffalo hand puppets: we see *them*, but not the corporation's hand inside that manipulates them. One of the greatest triumphs of celebrity culture is that it offers satisfaction without actually delivering much apart from commodities. Back in the 1980s, corporations like Chesebrough, which came to power with its near-universal Vaseline and merged with Pond's Creams in 1955, were beginning to understand that famous actors were not just for selling box office tickets: they could sell anything. Sophia Loren had crossed the street that divided craft from commerce when she struck a deal with Coty, allowing the cosmetics company to produce a fragrance called Sophia, which she promoted. The product was launched in 1981. "Wear it with a passion," Loren prescribed in one of the tv commercials. Even the strapline evoked Loren's voluptuous, seductive, sensuality.

Coty was encouraged sufficiently to innovate with unisex fragrances, this time with the clothes designer *du jour* Calvin Klein. This hugely productive partnership started in 1985. From today's vantage point one wonders why it took anyone so long to approach Taylor. She had shown an almost superhuman capability for arresting and keeping the attention of consumers, not just for a year or so, but for over two decades. Why not use some of that power to sell a product, in this case perfume?

Celebrities had leased out their names and images to advertisers for years. Endorsements were proof that artists with no expertise or qualifications apart from being consumers themselves could sell products. Larry Hagman appeared in ads for Cannon Mills beds, Ted Danson endorsed Aramis cologne, Bill Cosby fronted several advertising campaigns for Jell-O pudding. Taylor herself had appeared, with Michael Todd, in ads for TWA airlines; and way back in the early 1950s, she endorsed Whitman's chocolates (framed posters of the advertisement are still available for purchase).

The Parfums International/Chesebrough-Ponds venture, however, was more than a straightforward endorsement: "Elizabeth Taylor's Passion," as the product was known, incorporated not only her name but her identity and all the qualities radiated by Taylor over the years. As Rafer Guzman and his colleagues wrote of Taylor in 2011: "Her name continued to symbolize beauty, wealth, luxury and a distinctively Hollywood brand of excess long after her film career faded" (p. A3). Taylor's film career may have faded, but she was still effulgent. The fragrance played no small part in this.

"There are, by latest count, six people in the world who cause a fuss simply by moving around. They are the Pope, President Reagan, Michael Jackson, Jacqueline Onassis, Frank Sinatra and Elizabeth Taylor." So wrote the *Chicago Tribune*'s Jon Anderson in 1987. The extensive marketing of the new product involved Taylor's traveling to nine department stores and launches to augment the $10 million television and print ad campaign. She held private audiences with selected customers at stores, at first in the USA, then across Europe. At Neiman Marcus in Dallas, 10,000 people turned up, not to meet but just catch sight of Taylor. At other stores, thousands of customers turned up. Those who were privileged enough to get close enough seized the opportunity to become inquisitors. "They often ask brutally direct questions about her sex life and dress size, and she provides charming nonanswers," reported Charles Leerhsen in 1996.

Every effort was made to unify the product with Taylor's persona. "I don't know of any brand that revolved around the personal positioning in the mind of the consumers in the same way," reflected Michael O'Connor, president of marketing and brand consultants Style & Substance Inc., to *CNN Online*'s Lisa Respers in 2011. "Elizabeth Taylor was probably one of the first entrepreneurial celebrities who was able to turn her celebrity into a commercial proposition." Monetize is the word we use today.

The concept was to convert Taylor's manifest cultural value into hard currency. The Taylor brand recognition index was as high as it had ever been. As part of its research and development, Parfums International commissioned research on 5,000 participants in the US and several thousand more abroad, and discovered 100 percent name recognition; this was hardly surprising; who had *not* heard of Elizabeth Taylor? "The emotional response to her was positive," reflected Sherry Baker, who was responsible for the market research. "People respect her because she's a survivor," Baker told Anna Sobkowski in 1989. They also identified her broad appeal to affluent, mature women who "understand quality, are fascinated with fantasy and possess an eye for luxury," according to Jon Anderson, of the *Chicago Tribune* (writing in 1987).

Six French *perfumiers* worked for six months to develop fragrances and presented Taylor and Baker a hundred samples from which they drew the eventual product. Taylor's opinion always got priority. The manufacturers maintained they sought Taylor's authorization at every phase: "She put her signature and sign-off on everything," until her death, according to Lorna Koski, of *WWD: Women's Wear Daily*.

As the movies died away so the Aids campaign flared into life. This is not a cynical interpretation and in no way casts doubt on Taylor's motives. The fact remains: she was by 1987 synonymous with the fight against Aids and this effectively repositioned her in the wider market. The Passion venture was designed to turn this into sales of cologne. And the results suggested a different type of chemistry, one in which bottled scent could be transformed into the promise of being a bit more like Elizabeth Taylor. While he does not call it chemistry, Grant McCracken has argued that companies that pay celebrities to advertise their wares are aiming at "meaning transfer," in the sense that they want consumers to identify certain meanings in the "source model," while screening out others.

Taylor, as we know, signified all manner of attractive qualities. Her dependencies, poor health, and wrecked marriages were not among them. The marketing seemed calibrated in a way that screened out negative aspects of Taylor's persona, allowing consumers to associate her more conspicuously positive qualities with the product. "Meaning then moves to consumer goods and finally to the life of the consumer," wrote McCracken in 2005 (p. 104).

This is an orthodox approach to marketing theory, but one which may have missed the point: Taylor's devotees and the potential customers of her product were no doubt aware of her tribulations as well as her other more lauded properties. Taylor was unmistakably imperfect; this reminded consumers that despite her otherworldly beauty and impossibly exotic lifestyle, she had the same kind of foibles as everyone else. As Joseph Ronchetti, an executive with Elizabeth Arden, put it in 1991: "Liz Taylor is an individual that a lot of people will relate to. We've all known people with drinking problems, we've all had weight problems, and she coped so beautifully" (quoted in Duffy).

Taylor's travails were constant reminders of her flawed humanness, and this was the quality that, to use McCracken's formulation, transferred to the product, then into consumers' lives. "Her [Taylor's] ups and downs are positive for business and have not hurt us," confirmed Clare Cain, Elizabeth Arden's vice-president of marketing development for fragrances, quoted by Sharon Edelson in 1991. "People want her to win, they want her to be well, they want her to be thin." Cain was referring to Taylor's various illnesses and weight control problem.

Some predicted disappointment. "The way things are going, industry analysts say, Passion will have considerable difficulty making a splash," warned Timothy Kalich in 1987. The highest priced bottle of cologne was $200 and came complete with a personal message from Taylor herself. The entry-level bottles retailed at $25. In the first four months after launch sales of the product hit $36 million. Within two years, Elizabeth Taylor's Passion reigned comfortably over the celebrity cologne market with annual sales of $70 million. Emboldened by this, she introduced Elizabeth Taylor's "Passion for Men" and, in 1991, "White Diamonds," a product that would eventually become market leader. Between 1991 and 2011, when Taylor died, her products would generate over $1 billion in sales, according to *The Hollywood Reporter* (in 2011).

White Diamonds was launched under the rubric of Elizabeth Arden, then a division of Parfums International. The above-quoted Ronchetti was Chief Executive of Elizabeth Arden at the time of the launch. The House of Taylor was the cognomen bandied around to suggest a segment of the company that would accommodate products associated with Taylor. White Diamonds was a slightly upmarket of Passion, with prices 15 percent higher. For clarity: in 1986, the British-Dutch corporation Unilever acquired Chesebrough-Pond's, and two years later negotiated a buyout of Elizabeth Arden and its sister company Fabergé. Arden then took over Taylor's line. From 1989, Arden became the fastest-growing company in what was a stagnant prestige cosmetics market.

Taylor may not singlehandedly have changed the character of the market, but, by 1990, there were 800 perfumes jostling for space on department store shelves, with about sixty new scents added every year. The attrition rate was phenomenal: six out of every seven new products failed to make an impact and were withdrawn (that is an 85.7 percent failure rate). Taylor's went from strength-to-strength, as did "California by Jaclyn Smith" (Smith was "Kelly Garrett" in the tv series *Charlie's Angels*), "Moments by Priscilla Presley", and Mikhail Baryshnikov's "Misha" (the nickname of the famous dancer). Among the backfires were Cher's "Uninhibited," Joan Collins' "Spectacular", and Catherine Deneuve's "Deneuve," suggesting that the chemistry was still experimental.

Baryshnikov, like Taylor, claimed to have creative control over many details concerning packaging, marketing, and the fragrance itself. Other celebrities merely negotiated a deal that allowed the corporation to associate their names with the products. Baryshnikov's more immersive approach earned him $250,000 plus an annual fee. Details of Taylor's initial contract were never declared.

At this stage Henry Wynberg re-entered the picture. Taylor's onetime escort had not been part of Taylor's life since 1976, when the couple had a brief interlude. Taylor was rebounding from her second marriage with Richard Burton. Wynberg had originated the idea of a Taylor-endorsed scent in the early 1970s, and had the contract to prove it. Taylor's romance with Wynberg was an on-off affair that lasted no more than two years, but Wynberg was like the Richard Gere character in the 1993 film *Sommersby*: missing presumed dead, he returns from the Civil War a transformed character. When Taylor was preparing to launch her Parfums International product in 1986, she became aware that Wynberg was clinging to the valuable agreement bearing her signature and dated 1975. Since then he had stuck with the project. Recall how John Warner, when married to Taylor, tried but failed to persuade Wynberg to nullify the deal. Wynberg, unlike the Gere character, was a nice guy first time around, but he returned, again unlike the Gere character, a combative foe.

Hoping to squeeze any legal life out of the contract, which entitled her former beau to 30 percent of net profits deriving from any cosmetics marketed under her name, Taylor sued Wynberg, claiming his failure to follow through on the project violated the contract and rendered it invalid. Predictably, Wynberg fired back claiming breach of contract, fraud, and misappropriation; he contended that the new Passion product was actually just a copycat of his concept. As Carol McGraw, of the *Los Angeles Times*, reported in in her article "Liz Taylor Stars in Battle Over 'Passion' Fragrance": "Wynberg, 56, says that he presented the fragrance in a purple heart-shaped bottle to the movie star in 1985, two years before Passion was introduced in the marketplace." While the fragrance market had taken a slight downturn, it was still worth about $4 billion per year in the US alone. Taylor's product was already a success and was set to return $70 million a year in profits.

The legal spat lasted four years and became in itself an advertisement for the fragrance. "Indeed, the dispute over who got what profits and just who concocted the floral scent seemed as if it could have been devised by a diabolically clever advertising team," joked Denise Hamilton in 1990. She made a valid point: every media mention of the legal case carried namechecks for the product that lay at the center of the case. There was also a synchronicity of timing: the legal arguments were heard in November and

December, when thoughts of Christmas gifts were beginning to pop into the heads of consumers.

Observers readied themselves for an epic Los Angeles Superior Court court case in which the lavish lifestyle, loves, and illnesses of Taylor would be aired in court and the past indiscretions of Wynberg would return to haunt him. Screen Legend vs. Used Car Salesman. Then, in December 1990, it came to a stunningly sedate conclusion. The ex-lovers just dropped their cases against each other. Taylor would retain control of the Passion perfume line, and the two agreed never to take any other action against one another regarding the legal issue. No further details were disclosed, though it was thought a cash settlement persuaded Wynberg to abandon the contract, which had been so bothersome to Taylor.

A second legal case was initiated by Annik Goutal, a French former model who had created and sold a collection of skin care and cosmetic products, including the perfumes Eau d'Hadrien and Gardénia Passion, both available on the American market. The case involved the rights to the word Passion: Goutal complained, asking for Taylor's product to be banned from sixty-nine American stories, including behemoths Bloomingdale's, Macy's, Lord & Taylor, and Neiman Marcus. In December 1987, a New York federal judge ruled that Taylor's perfume could not be sold at fifty-five stores for six months. It was a limited injunction and Parfums International took it in its stride claiming, according to a 1987 UPI report, that the ban would have "little if any impact on sales of the fragrance, which they call the most successful celebrity perfume ever launched."

"Tropical beach, blazing sun, men in white suits, winsome native children. A horse gallops along the shore as a light plane lazes overhead. A beautiful woman sits in a convertible, adored from afar, drenched in diamonds, caressed by a soft-focus camera." This is how Martha Duffy, of *Time* magazine, described the *mise-en-scène* in 1991. The plane lands, a group of men disembark and start up a poker game. The stakes get high and one of the men folds, "I'm a little short." At which point the woman interrupts. "Not so fast," she cautions, tossing one of her diamond earrings onto the gaming table. "These have always brought me luck."

Cinema, like all visual art, is an expression of creativity and imagination, work to be appreciated primarily for its beauty or power to evoke emotion. Ads have just one function: to promote sales. Yet no one rushed to condemn Taylor for trading in what was left of her acting career for a job as a pitchwoman for scent. She was all but canonized, anyway. Taylor's most significant film of this period of her life was not the 1989 tv film *Sweet Bird of Youth*, based on a 1959 Tennessee Williams play, in which she played a wasted, drug-dependent movie star, a role that did not tax the audience's credulity. It was *White Diamonds: The Movie, Starring Elizabeth Taylor*.

This was the official title of what Martha Duffy called a "semi-surrealistic video," though others might have just called it a commercial. It was shot in a somewhat arty monochrome, ran for two minutes and forty-five seconds and screened in full only at department stores' fragrance counters; a sixty-second cut was shown on television. But imagine how many people saw it.

By the early 1990s, consumers were inured to being treated as, well, *consumers*. Advertising used all manner of tricks, tropes, and devices to pass as art. Some of it actually is indistinguishable from art; art is always an act or recognition rather than an essence. *Michael Jackson's Thriller*, directed by and co-written by John Landis, was a thirteen-minute music video, which premiered on December 2, 1983. The following year, David Bowie's *Jazzin' for Blue Jean*, directed by Julien Temple, was twenty-minutes long. Received appreciatively, the videos bridged the domains of art and advertising without leaving consumers with the impression they were being manipulated. But both videos were, like all other videos, designed with one purpose: to sell records. MTV, in those days, screened only music videos. The ostentatiously youth-oriented channel succeeded not only because it entertained viewers, but because it induced them to spend money on records, as well as on the other products it advertised more covertly. Perhaps I was wrong when calling art and advertising indistinguishable: identical is more accurate.

Taylor did not sell-out, rebrand or metamorphose: her persona was now so well established that she could put it to any service she wanted. Think of Taylor as one of those electronic passes that allow drivers to bypass the booths on to toll roads: in her case she could use her image to shortcircuit shoppers' considerations about products. They did not have, nor even need to believe Elizabeth Taylor actually tested, approved, less still, wore the scent she peddled. They almost instinctively thought they knew her. So Taylor's mere association with the product was enough to send shoppers speeding to the stores to watch the video then buy the cologne. After the Aids work, Taylor was probably due a mercilessly commercial venture.

Launched in 1991, four years after "Elizabeth Taylor's Passion," the new White Diamonds fragrance was produced by Elizabeth Arden, by then a division of Parfums International. Stuart Elliott, writing in 1991, estimated the launch campaign to have cost $20 million. The video of less than three minutes would make her more money than *Cleopatra*. The comparison is flawed, of course; the point behind it is not. This was the first woman to earn $1 million for a movie; the woman who won an Oscar; the wealthy politician's wife; the woman with homes around the world and one of the most expensive personal jewelry collections. Surely, she was *already* rich before she started advertising cologne.

Perhaps. She was also a prodigious spender with a large staff, and, by the mid-1980s, needed to work in small budget tv movies, her box office power dissipated. By the time of her death, she had had a net worth of about $600 million; the $77 million per year she earned from her fragrances, contributed appreciably to this, according to *Gawker*'s Brian Moylan, in 2011. This is probably exaggeration: annual global sales of her best seller White Diamonds were $75 million. But Taylor still earned more money from her perfume deals than from her films combined. Inconceivable as it seems, were it not for her fragrances, Taylor would probably have spent her final years in comfort but not in financial splendor.

Despite her creative endeavors, particularly her highbrow theatrical ventures with Burton and her imaginative enlivenments of Tennessee Williams, Taylor owed her wealth ultimately to bottles of scent.

By the mid-1990s, the launch of a new Taylor fragrance was comparable to the premiere of one of her movies in the 1960s and 1970s: "Much anticipated," as Hollywood publicists would put it. Or, as the industry magazine *Drug & Cosmetic Industry* opened an article in 1996: "The long-awaited debut of the Elizabeth Taylor's Black Pearls fragrance will finally happen this April." As movie stars attend premieres of their own films, so Taylor once more toured the nation, making appearances at the likes of Bloomingdale's and Macy's. By then, as I noted earlier, Chesebrough-Ponds had become part of Unilever.

The marketing of Black Pearls was ingenious or, to repeat Denise Hamilton's phrase, diabolically clever, depending on one's perspective; it was inventive, for sure, but fiendishly so. CBS television ran four sitcoms on Monday nights. *Murphy Brown, The Nanny, Can't Hurry Love*, and *High Society* aired consecutively between 8:00 to 10:00 p.m.

Executives at the network apparently came up with an idea: bring in a big name diva to appear in a narrative spanning all four shows. Taylor was first choice, though Cher and Barbra Streisand were also in the mix. At this stage, Taylor was known largely for her Aids work and, of course, her travails with weight/pills/alcohol/divorces/all of the above. Taylor agreed on the condition that CBS made a donation—of an undisclosed amount, described by CBS as "a sizeable sum"—to amfAR. CBS ventured that the thread in the plot would involve a $300,000 string of pearls owned by Taylor, but which goes mysteriously missing.

By a coincidence of colossal proportions, Taylor's new fragrance was due to be unleashed on the market and by a further coincidence, this time of cosmic proportions, its name described the stones set in the plot's missing necklace. The coincidence could only have been more serendipitous if Fox had decided to re-release a director's cut of *Cleopatra* that included hitherto unseen scenes of the Egyptian queen wearing an ornamental string of dark grayish spheres taken from the shell of a bivalve mollusk. Some people do not believe in coincidences, of course. Not CBS though: the television network, "denied to *Advertising Age* the existence of a promotional tie-in with the perfume," confirmed Pat Sloan, a journalist on that trade magazine in 1996. "CBS sources say the idea was theirs" rather than Elizabeth's (Arden's or Taylor's).

Taylor made brief appearances on the first three shows, although only her voice featured on *High Society*. In the *Can't Hurry Love* appearance, she was seen in a department store en route to an in-store promotion for the new fragrance. Disclaimers at the end of each show explained "'Black Pearls' is the trade name of a fragrance owned, in part, by Elizabeth Taylor." Each comedy's ratings got a boost by between 15–20 percent, according to Chuck Ross. "Black Pearls" got namechecked, though in a way that purported to be entertainment. Taylor was seen on primetime tv in a way that did her no disservice. In sum, a win-win, with only skeptics, like Jennifer Weiner, of the *Philadelphia Inquirer*, grimacing at the brazenness of what was, on her account, "most assuredly a stunt." How should we describe it? Think of word beginning with "a" and ending with "sing." Amusing? Advertising? "We're already well along, toward a future in which everything is for sale," wrote Weiner in 1996."Not just the commercials that appear during the shows; not just the actors and actresses, in character and out; but the shows themselves."

The *Baltimore Sun*'s tv critic Chris Kaltenbach probably captured the question in the heads of viewers at 10.00 p.m.: "You mean we've just sat through a two-hour perfume commercial?" Readers will, I hope, excuse me for comparing full-length feature films with commercials and, by implication, art with advertising earlier in this chapter. In a sense though, advertising percolated into so many aspects of popular culture from the 1990s that ads and art became like Tweedledum and Tweedledee.

Watch any film today and you will be bombarded with images of branded merchandise. Sports events are multi-hour exposures to logos and strip hoardings. Art exhibitions are always sponsored by companies. So, when Peter Marc Jacobson, executive producer of *The Nanny* (the third of the four sitcoms featuring Taylor) declared, "It's not a commercial at all," most rational viewers would have nodded in agreement, then added, "in the same way *American Idol* was not a commercial for Coca-Cola."

A "stunt" such as Taylor's might today pass without too much comment. Taylor herself was unapologetic, though Weiner notes that she issued a statement claiming that she would have participated in the four shows regardless of her fragrance product. But Taylor sounded more opportunistic when she told Dana Wood in 1996: "I could get a plug in for Black Pearls—in prime time," as if it were a bonus rather than a condition of the deal (p. 3). It would have been interesting to learn how Streisand or Cher, both of whom had endorsed fragrances, would have reacted. Streisand's movie and soundtrack album *The Mirror Has Two Faces* were released in 1996, so she might have been receptive; but Cher was two years away from her highest selling, Grammy award-winning album *Believe*, so would have little to gain.

In a sense the 120-minutes of primetime tv in 1996 defined the way we would enjoy popular entertainment for the decades to follow. Weiner was right when she proposed: "It's not the end of the world as we know it, nor is it the beginning of an era." But it was a moment when viewers were forcefully reminded that entertainment—and I use this in its widest sense: anything that amuses or occupies us agreeably—is never *just* entertainment. It is an opportunity to sell to while consumers' sensory guards are down and they least expect a pitch. The distinction between promotional material and entertainment was smudged if not erased by MTV. By the mid-1990s, the cable channel was well established and the traditional distinction seemed passé.

So the question: *Cui bono?* Who were the beneficiaries of the hitherto unprecedented and, so far, unrepeated televisual feat? Taylor, obviously: she received a sizable donation for her charity without any damage to her credibility. CBS's viewer ratings spiked and, as the shows were screened during a sweeps week (when a survey was carried out to determine advertising rates), it stood to profit in monetary terms. Elizabeth Arden, according to all accounts, did not pay a penny to the networks, though Black Pearls was prominently featured and, despite what everyone claimed, the exposure was tantamount to advertising of the finest order—"the kind of exposure money can't buy," as Weiner puts it. Advertising that does not seem to be advertising at all, in other words.

How about consumers? This is trickier. American tv viewers have been reared on advertising. Unlike in Britain and some other parts of the world, there are no networks funded by government (and, in turn, by license-fee-paying audiences). So viewers enjoy television shows in exchange for the constant intrusions of commercials on the major networks. In the 1950s, subliminal advertising was one of those scary prospects: advertisers were sneaky enough to send out commercials that affected consumers without their being aware of them. The Federal Communications Commission took it seriously enough to issue a statement, in 1974, declaring subliminal advertising to be against the public interest. In 1993, just three years before the CBS-Taylor initiative, Martha Rogers and Kirk H. Smith revealed between 75 to 80 percent of Americans believed in the existence and efficacy of subliminal advertising. The CBS shows would not equate to conventional understandings of subliminal advertising, but a case could be made: ostensibly, they were pure entertainment with no undue prominence given to a branded item. Yet Taylor's presence and her close association with a product that shared the same name as the McGuffin meant that the commercial potential of her appearance slipped under the conscious guard of audiences. "McGuffin" was Alfred Hitchcock's term for an object in a film that serves merely as a trigger for the plot.

Taylor would eventually become the face and name of a total of twelve fragrances, the final one of which was Violet Eyes, introduced in 2010. After

Taylor's death, Nia Long replaced her at the fore of marketing campaigns. White Diamonds held steadfastly to a top selling spot for over two decades and, as I noted earlier, passed $1 billion in sales. It was the most commercially successful celebrity fragrance in history. The likes of Jennifer Lopez, Sarah Jessica Parker, and Beyoncé were among the elite of celebrities, all seeking to emulate Taylor in the congested fragrance market of the twenty-first century. Lopez et al. would typically demand up to $3 million upfront plus a percentage of gross sales (say, 6 or 7 percent; similar to the kind of film deals Taylor preferred). JLo, by 2012, had assumed hegemony of the market, putting her name to eighteen different fragrances for Coty and earning, what Deborah Arthurs, in 2012, worked out to be $933 (£570) per hour for her labors. Lopez was forty-two at the time. Taylor was fifty-nine when White Diamonds launched, suggesting that the approval of female celebrities who retain their allure into their maturity counts in the marketplace.

The global fragrance industry is valued at over $25 billion a year. Taylor is frequently credited as a pioneer in film and a defiant flouter of social mores. Rarely as a lifestyle expert, or forerunner of the countless celebrities who used their fame and reputations to create a range of branded products and turn their names into a profitable business. Martha Stewart took her first steps to becoming a lifestyle brand in 1982 with a cookbook. After that she introduced all manner of products bearing not just her endorsement but *her*.

Elizabeth Arden set up a dedicated House of Taylor business and, in 2004, expanded the fragrance's concept into color cosmetics, including lipsticks and pressed powder, though, surprisingly, not eyeliner or mascara—surprisingly because eye makeup was something of a trademark for Taylor herself. The packaging was predictably Taylor-esque: silver, adorned with diamond-like crystals. The idea was presumably to expand Taylor's range of products. But, as in all other aspects of Taylor's life, chutes were never far away from ladders and her brand, while sound, was not infallible. She could dare to front the sale of a special edition of White Diamonds in a hand-blown pear-shaped bottle featuring an 18-carat gold stopper and flowing ribbons set with 403 pave diamonds totaling 17.16 carats and retailing at $100,000. But the cosmetics range was sold over the counters of stores such as Kmart and Walgreen's. (The one-of-a-kind bottle of perfume went on sale in 1991.)

In fact, the high profile launch of Black Pearls masked a near-disaster. "Some of the country's toniest, most powerful department store chains had earlier bowed out of the running following a dispute over financing," reported Dana Wood in 1996. *People* writer Charles Leerhsen paraphrased Taylor's response: "Taylor didn't want to lend her name to the product only to have Bloomingdale's salespeople saying, 'Black Pearls? Sorry, no, but you'll find it stacked next to the Power Rangers pj's at Kmart'" (1996). Taylor also objected to what she called, "the cheap-looking bottle they [Elizabeth Arden] were planning to use."

Elizabeth Arden responded by brokering an exclusive deal with Sears and JC Penney. The upscale stores backed-off, prompting Arden to delay the debut. The CBS hook-up brought them back to the bargaining table and, by the time the product was ready for the market, Sears and Penney were out of the reckoning again.

Taylor, in 1989, founded a business engaging in the design, manufacture, and sale of jewelry. Headquartered in West Hollywood, House of Taylor Jewelry was a partnership between Taylor and Kathy Ireland, then a 26-year-old model, best known for her abundant appearances in the *Sports Illustrated Swimsuit* issues. Approaching the end of her modeling career, Ireland diversified into business. As well as her venture with Taylor, she launched clothes and home goods businesses, all bearing the Kathy Ireland brand. She became a lesser known, but still successful, Martha Stewart type. House of Taylor Jewelry Inc. sold its products through specialty couture jewelry retailers, independent jewelry stores, and chain jewelry and department store retailers. The other major shareholders of the company were Jack and Monty Abramov, of a company called Mirabelle Luxury Concepts.

In 2005, House of Taylor Jewelry merged with Nuruscell Inc., a publicly traded holding company. The jewelry products ranged from $3,000 to over a million. At the merger, Taylor announced: "I wanted to share the passion and joy that jewelry has brought to my life with other people." PR Newswire carried the story in 2005. "This new organization is committed to that effort. Something wonderful is about to happen." The company folded in June 2008, more than $11 million in debt.

Taylor's late career expansion into branded goods was what might be called a slightly-qualified success. But it was far from a question of her approaching a company with an offer: "Here's my name, here's my image. I'll show up at department stores, sip tea and answer questions. Here's the address I'd like you to send the check to." Today, anyone in showbusiness who can turn a penny, does so: no one stays in their channel. The likes of Jay-Z, Gwyneth Paltrow, and Heidi Klum have created lifestyle portals online to dispense advice, but more importantly, sell their own branded goods. Taylor was not the first artist to broaden her business and she was not even the most successful, though, of course, she did make plenty of money. But, as with so many of her other actions, it was congruent with, and possibly slightly ahead of her times.

FIGURE 16 *As her film career faded, Taylor divided her time between promoting her products and campaigning for Aids charities. She was a co-founder of amfAR, The Foundation for AIDS Research.*

Photo by J. Vespa/WireImage. Getty Images.

16

Other people's lives

It was a marriage made in heaven, but the happy couple soon shifted to the perfumes counter of a department store. Less than four hours after she had said, "I do" for the eighth (and last) time in her life, Taylor spirited away to do a mini-tour promoting White Diamonds. More than 3,000 shoppers showed up at Robinsons-May in Del Amo Fashion Center in Torrance, Los Angeles County. "A hundred paid $300 for a limited edition bottle of perfume, entitling them to have tea with the actress," according to Rose-Marie Turk, of the *Los Angeles Times* (October 11, 1991).

Only after honoring that commercial obligation, was Taylor prepared to resume nuptial protocols and take off on honeymoon. It was October 1991 and the wedding clashed or coincided—depending on your perspective—with the launch of a second perfume, a product that would eventually outsell Elizabeth Taylor's Passion.

Taylor met her final husband not on a film set, or at cocktail party, or through a mutual friend. She met him in rehab. Her elective imprisonment at the Betty Ford Center was hardly a life sentence; in fact, for her it was something of a release from a media that had monitored practically every waking hour of her life and more. Not that she had ever seemed uncomfortable with her destiny. Her first interlude at the clinic was forced on her by her family and close friends who whisked her straight from her hospital bed in Santa Monica to the renowned alcohol and drug rehabilitation clinic in Rancho Mirage, California, on December 5, 1983. She checked out six-and-a-half weeks later on January 20, 1984. By the time she returned in October 1988, she had turned two new story cycles to her life, one as an Aids campaigner, the other as a brand of perfume. The story of her dependence on painkillers was still going on. And, as she later disclosed, she considered herself a "social drinker," which probably meant she was dependent on alcohol too.

Larry Fortensky found himself at the Betty Ford Center after being convicted for driving while under the influence of alcohol. Police had found him behind the wheel in a parking lot in San Clemente, California. At the time, he was living in Stanton, where he worked in the construction industry.

Fortensky was thirty-six when he checked-in. He was twice divorced and had one daughter.

"Maybe I should have fallen for a busboy, then the whole thing wouldn't cause so much attention," Taylor told Bob Thomas, of Associated Press, for the *Daytona Beach Morning Journal,* in March 1949, when news of her romance with Glenn Davis broke and she became the center of more press interest than she, then seventeen, had anticipated (for non-American readers: a busboy is someone, usually a young man, who clears tables in a restaurant—this author was once such an operative). "Its no fun to conduct a courtship with 150,000,000 people looking on," observed Thomas, alluding to the total population of the USA at the time (he was probably underestimating interest abroad).

Even as a teenager, she had become accustomed to the pop of camera flashbulbs and the incessant questions of journalists. Davis was a noted football player, making himself and Taylor what we today call a celebrity couple. Fortensky was not a busboy, but he was a paid-up member of the same artisan class, blue-collar workers. His working days were spent with bricks, concrete, and plaster.

Think for a moment about Taylor's previous husbands and fiancés. William Pauley, son of the American ambassador to Brazil, to whom she was engaged for three months. Conrad Nicholson Hilton, better known as Nicky Hilton, a member of the Hilton hotel dynasty, and great-grandfather of celebrity socialites, Paris and Nicky Hilton. Taylor was only eighteen when she married him in 1950. Michael Wilding, a respected British actor, with whom she had two children. Michael Todd, the film producer and showman extraordinaire, whose penchant for extravagance left an indelible mark on Taylor. Eddie Fisher, a recording artist, whose relationship with Taylor caused the media equivalent of carnage; they married in 1959. Richard Burton, known for both his acting in theater and on screen, and his serial womanizing, whose scandalous liaison with Taylor occasioned even greater outrage than her relationship with Fisher. John Warner, the wealthy Virginian landowner and politician, whom Taylor helped in his successful campaign for the US Senate in 1978; they were divorced in 1982. Dennis Stein, the New York businessman, Mexican lawyer Victor Luna. Wealthy publisher Malcolm Forbes, and Carl Bernstein, the author and journalist, were both escorts. Even the men who did not possess vast wealth, had reputations as alpha males.

Perhaps Fortensky was also an alpha male, but he had no reputation to speak of beyond his own locale and he certainly had no money. His fees for the Betty Ford Center were paid by his Teamsters Union insurance. Taylor's thought seems to have been: forget showbusiness types, wealthy politicians, and powerful entrepreneurs; a life less ordinary is overrated; normal is the new normal.

Fortensky was twenty years younger than Taylor. They met in the group therapy sessions that are designed to assist patients in describing and discussing their problems at the Betty Ford Center. "We were at our most vulnerable," Taylor later reflected. "They [the counselors] knock you down [in therapy], kick the shit out of you, then give you the tools to build yourself up," she told Nancy Collins, of *Vanity Fair* (1992). "Larry felt very protective toward me. He told me later there were times he wanted to kill the counselor."

That effectively defined the nexus of the relationship: Fortensky's protectiveness: Taylor apparently felt secure in his presence. She never claimed to have fallen for him in the same way she did Burton or Todd. "He's very deep—listens, watches, sucks everything in. He wants to learn and he's always asking me questions. But he's very private," Taylor told Collins, inadvertently hinting that she was drawn to him in much the same way she was to Fisher, who brought comfort and support to Taylor after the death of Todd, though never enraptured her in the way Burton apparently did.

Rehab is a great leveler: no matter what station a patient starts from, once the recovery starts, everyone is equal. For all her wealth and fame, Taylor was on the same level as an anonymous, penniless construction worker, who had dropped out of school, been discharged from the military (for undisclosed reasons) and was on three years' probation. She had heard the word "want" but never understood its meaning: she had been earning practically since she was old enough to stand and had lived every second of her life free of the kind of irksome little irritants that affect most people, like paying bills, saving for a down payment, or finding monthly dues. Fortensky's familiarity with all of these gave him second sight as far as Taylor was concerned: "Larry sees through the world of bullshit I live in. He's very protective."

For all his apparent sagacity, Fortensky seemed an unlikely partner for Taylor. Rehab buddies, perhaps, cast on the same rocks by different circumstances but bonded by a common aspiration. But lovers? Fellow patients at the Betty Ford Center were expressly told not to form intimate attachments, anyway. If patients remain attracted to each other, the recommendation is to wait twelve months before making commitments. Taylor and Fortensky paid no heed to the second piece of advice and, probably not the first either: after leaving the center shortly before Christmas 1988, he and Taylor continued to see each other, and, by the end of February 1989, Fortensky had become a regular stop-over visitor at Taylor's Bel Air home. Apparently sober and healthy, he resumed his work as a heavy-equipment operator, presumably determined not to become known as a kept-man. His resolve soon weakened, however. Fortensky's days of mixing with common folk at an end, he moved in with Taylor and became a good, old-fashioned househusband.

Fortensky was ever-present during Taylor's dramatic brush with death in spring 1990. He also stayed with her during her rehabilitation. And when she was well enough to return to her schedule, he accompanied her on her promotional tours of the department stores. He also assisted her work on amfAR. The popular perception of Fortensky was that he was a man Friday, or, to dignify his role, an *aide-de-camp*, rather than marriageable material. Taylor remained friendly with Malcolm Forbes, with whom she was regularly seen. In fact, when she went to Forbes' seventieth birthday party in Tangiers, on the northern coast of Morocco, Fortensky was not present, apparently at Forbes' specific request. In 2011, Katy Sprinkel contended: "Forbes was maniacally jealous of Fortensky, saying he was 'not the sort of fellow you would expect to be with Elizabeth'" (p.115).

There are all types of research on what attracts women to men. An Australian study reported in the APN Newsdesk in 2014, for example, found that a sense of humor is the feature that attracted most (29 percent) women to their partners. An earlier study in 2010 by a seven-strong research team led by Andrew Elliott indicated that simply wearing red was enough to grab a women's initial interest. We cannot be sure what color shirt Fortensky was wearing when he first met Taylor at the Betty Ford Center, though she cited his ability to make her laugh as a powerful attractant, according to M.G. Lord (p. 165). Whatever the source of attraction, it bloomed during 1991 and Fortensky's status converted from buddy to fiancé.

When Taylor introduced Fortensky at a New York press conference in September, she was supposed to be promoting the then newly launched White Diamonds. Journalists were less interested in the fragrance than the news that wedding plans were afoot. "Why is Taylor taking the plunge for the eighth time?" was the query from the floor. Taylor's answer was typically honest, yet unrevealing. "I haven't been married in ten years," she declared, in case any journalist was not already aware. "I'm never one to say never . . . I want to grow old with someone." She was fifty-nine, Fortensky was thirty-nine. Some, like journalist Emma Forrest, called it "the triumph of hope over experience." Never reticent about plugging her products, Taylor confirmed that she would wear both White Diamonds and Passion at her nuptials. Despite her best efforts, her perfume was of less interest to the media than her man and the headlines typically read: TAYLOR WHISKS IN FIANCÉ TO MEET THE PRESS HOUNDS (*Spartanburg Herald-Journal*, September 13, 1991, p. A2).

Less than a month later, Taylor and Fortensky stood under a gazebo altar at Michael Jackson's Neverland ranch in Los Olivos, California. Taylor had befriended Jackson in the 1980s and had an unusually and, for many, unfathomably close relationship with him until his death. As we will see shortly, Taylor became a redoubtable defender of Jackson in his famously troubled period. In 1991, Jackson was three years away from his indictment for molestation. He footed the bill—estimated at over $1.5 million—for Taylor's wedding. Taylor wore a $25,000 Valentino gown, though this was probably a gift from her designer friend.

In addition to the 160 invited guests, there were, 500 feet or so above the ceremony, fifteen helicopters carrying airborne paparazzi, all eager to capture a picture. One especially innovative freelancer wearing a helmet camera parachuted into Jackson's estate, falling to earth within 100 feet of Taylor and Fortensky as they prepared to take their vows. Security guards promptly moved in, handcuffed the journalist, Scott Kyle Harris, and escorted him from the scene, thus depriving him of what could have been one of the most famous paparazzi coups of all time. The incident is actually quite revealing.

Taylor had granted exclusive media rights to cover the ceremony to photographer Herb Ritts and gossip columnist Liz Smith. Ritts was an early Aids advocate and helped Taylor start her foundation. The deal he struck with Taylor was to contribute $1 million to Aids research in exchange for the wedding photographs. Ritts died in 2002; he was HIV positive and died with "complications from pneumonia," which was something of a euphemism for Aids at the time (Ritts had photographed and directed videos for Jackson, Madonna, and several other prominent showbusiness figures).

Syndicated newspaper columnist Liz Smith, who claimed to have followed Taylor for twenty-six years and traveled with her and Richard Burton, was the only journalist invited on site. The report she filed in 1991 opened: "Cynics say that Elizabeth Taylor planned her eighth wedding to coincide with the launch of her new perfume." Whether or not Smith was obliged to pay for her access was never made clear, though she was later criticized by Ann Gerhart for "serving as a flack" for Taylor. Flack is slang for publicity agent. Smith, in 1993, emceed a press conference at which Taylor introduced three new fragrances. Smith is still writing.

Exclusivity deals such as these became commonplace at celebrity weddings. *OK!* magazine paid David and Victoria Beckham $1.5 million for the sole rights to their wedding photographs in 1999. The following year, the same publication struck another $1.5 million deal with Catherine Zeta-Jones and Michael Douglas, only for gatecrashers from rival publication *Hello!* to smuggle cameras into the wedding and take photographs. So, while the aerial interloper at Taylor's wedding was unusual, his mission was probably guided by good sense. "I want to make one thing real clear—I am not a fruitcake," Harris emphasized to Greg Braxton, of the *Los Angeles Times* in 1991. "I'm a commercial photographer. I'm not a particularly big fan of Liz Taylor's . . . I was just amazed at how much money was being offered by the tabloids for a shot. They were offering in excess of six figures." Think about it: $1 million for unofficial pictures of Taylor's wedding. In 1991. "For that kind of money, I'll do anything, as long as it's reasonably safe and reasonably legal," confessed Harris.

Necessity is the mother of invention. Avarice is a decent surrogate. Tough problems demand resourceful solutions. The emergence of Princess Diana made pictures of her the most valuable currency of paparazzi. From 1981, when she married Prince Charles, she had become the most sought-after woman in the world, from the media's perspective. Every effort she made to shield herself from the media occasioned a redoubled effort to capture an image of her. Days before her death in 1997, she spent time aboard a $20 million yacht moored off Portofino, Italy. The photographer who captured them earned over $1.6 million for his work. The parachuting wedding crasher at Taylor's wedding was, on his own account, not a fruitcake, but a rational, risk-taking journo in seek of a big payday; he was also a harbinger. In the years that followed, every celebrity wedding would have uninvited guests, if not quite as daring as Harris, as creative in their efforts to snag the money shots. The notable exception was Beyoncé's marriage to Jay-Z in 2008, which wrong-footed the media; the couple had a private wedding ceremony at Jay-Z's New York apartment.

A couple of months after Taylor's wedding, in December 1991, Fortensky had his first solo brush with the paparazzi, and had to sneak into a courthouse in Corona, California, through a private entrance (and exit the same way). As celebrity court cases, this was not in the same class as the Mike Tyson rape trial (1992), or the O.J. Simpson murder case (1994): it involved a few cans of Coors and a breathalyzer reading of 0.11, just over the legal limit. But it also involved the husband of Elizabeth Taylor, so, when Fortensky's lawyer declared his client "wants his privacy," one can guess the media's counter: "Then he shouldn't have married Liz Taylor."

The *National Enquirer*, on March 30, 1993, ran an article headlined "Liz & Larry Force Neighbor to Flee His Home in Fear." According to the tabloid, Fortensky drove Max Hoshahn out of his $5 million home in a dispute over a property fence. The story quoted Hoshahn as saying Fortensky threatened to break his legs. It was dismissed as "absolute fiction" by Taylor and Fortensky's attorney. The *Enquirer* stood by its story. The couple charged that the article damaged their reputations and invaded their privacy, though the court did not agree, and they lost the suit against the tabloid. The case dragged on for three-and-a-half years before Taylor and Fortensky were ordered to pay $432,000 in legal costs to the publication. By this time, they had split up.

"Two things are certain about Taylor: if she marries she'll get divorced, and if she's seriously ill she'll recover." Emma Forrest wrote this in 1997, no doubt musing on events of the previous few decades and, in particular, the previous three years. In 1994, Taylor entered hospital to undergo a left-hip replacement; only fifteen months later, she returned for a similar operation on her right hip. She and Fortensky slept in separate beds at that point. The two announced a trial separation in August 1995, Taylor stating, "We both hope this is only temporary." It was not. Taylor filed for divorce citing irreconcilable differences in February 1996. By Taylor's standards, it was a normal length marriage, though, again by her standards, it lacked the highlights ordinarily associated with her partnerships.

Unlike the volcanic marriage to Burton, or the perpetual motion marriage to Todd or the politically engaged marriage to Warner, her marriage to Fortensky seemed uneventful. Perhaps because she announced shortly after the wedding that she no longer classed herself as an actress (her term), as they would say in the 1990s.

"I'm a housewife," she told Liz Smith. A housewife who started each day with a massage and beauty treatment, received her daily consignment of fresh flowers, spent a few hours on the phone, ate meals prepared by her staff and, unless she was on tour, watched television. Fortensky had, by this time, ceased his work on construction sites and organized his life around Taylor's. Her time was divided between promoting her fragrances and her Aids charity work. Demand for her in Hollywood had dropped, though not completely: she played a small (7 minute) part in *The Flintstones*, a live action version of the 1960s cartoon tv show.

"Everywhere we went there were cameras," Fortensky explained to Caroline Graham, of Britain's *Daily Mail*. (April 24, 2011). "Elizabeth would put lipstick on constantly because she said she never knew when she was being photographed. I found it hard. It wasn't my cup of tea, those cameras everywhere. Elizabeth was used to it. I never got used to it." Some might argue that, in return, he lived like a Hollywood celebrity and wanted for nothing. Perhaps Fortensky had no interest in a life of privilege and preferred an honest day's labor for a fair reward.

After the estrangement, Fortensky possibly harbored thoughts that he could skulk back into anonymity. If so, he would have been disappointed. In September 1995, he featured in the lead story of several evening newscasts after police took him into custody for suspected illegal drug use. By now, Fortensky was used to headlines, file footage, and the close attention of journalists; he was probably used to being constantly on the brink of notoriety too; he was certainly accustomed to smears that he was a moneygrabber. On this occasion, authorities declined to pursue charges against Fortensky; his drugs test returned a negative result.

Fortensky's scrapes with the law continued: he was convicted in 1996 of carrying a loaded handgun in the saddlebag of his motorcycle after being pulled over for not wearing a helmet. He did not have a valid driver's license. Fortensky was fined for the violations and placed on two years' probation. His troubles escalated in 1999 when he suffered a serious head injury after falling when intoxicated. He also made a few bad investments and, on several occasions, asked Taylor for money.

Taylor was worth around $200 million at the time of the divorce, according to Caroline Graham. Fortensky had signed a prenuptial agreement, entitling him to a maximum of $1.25 million. But Taylor, through her lawyers, offered him $1.25 million plus add-ons, including stock, a beach house, per diem expenses and a couple of Harley-Davidsons; a package worth comfortably over $2 million (later she started sending him an extra $1,000 per week). Somewhere in the settlement there may have been a non-disclosure agreement, often known as an NDA, or confidentiality clause. This is a contract through which parties agree not to release information covered in the contract to third parties. The third party most people feared was the media. Even without an NDA, Fortensky had shown little, if any, interest in the media and, eventually, seemed averse to them. When his sister Linda sold a story to the *National Enquirer*, he was so angry, he refused to speak to her again.

So there is no evidence that he would have fled to the nearest tabloid and offered to sell his story, nor even if he had anything of interest to sell. Taylor's life was a matter of public record, anyway. All the same, even in her maturity she remained a figure of great fascination and Fortensky would almost certainly have found a buyer for an "inside story" if he had been inclined to seek one. In the 1990s, interest in other people had become something akin to an obsession. I use obsession to describe a state when thoughts of others continually preoccupy or intrude on us. In the second decade of the twenty-first century, this sounds unremarkable: twitter, Facebook and other kinds of social media, reality tv shows that put others under surveillance, and publications that specialize in material that would have made Hedda Hopper and her contemporaries blush, are staples of our daily media diets.

Taylor, as we know, played no small part in ushering in an age when privacy was less hallowed, but she was part of an era in which libel, slander, invasion of privacy, and intentional infliction of emotional distress were parts of showbusiness *realpolitik*, a system of principles based on practical considerations that impinged on the way people conducted their lives. But principles change. Privacy was turned inside out.

"The 1997–98 season will, no doubt, be remembered as Jerry Springer's year," wrote Marc Berman, of Seltel, a tv-research firm in a memo to client stations. He is quoted by *New York* magazine's Barbara Lippert, who, in 1998, pointed out that, at that stage the *Jerry Springer Show* was the fastest growing program in syndication ever. In the unlikely event that any reader has never witnessed the show in question, I should outline the format. Ostensibly, the show tries to repair dysfunctional relationships by inviting the parties to said relationships to talk through their "issues" (to use the term most people seem to prefer to problems, troubles or harmful situations). The parties involved are often members of homo-, hetero-, and bisexual tri- or rectangles. Transsexuals and hermaphrodites share space with others who regard themselves as straight. But the cast of characters is less important than the method of resolution.

Springer, the ringmaster, directed with a light touch, inviting his guests to divulge information that would make most people squirm. Yet, far from being inhibited by the tv cameras and the prospect of being watched by 11 million viewers (at its 1998 peak), the participants just poured it out. Imagine pitching this idea to a tv executive in, say, 1986. "You have to be kidding. Who on earth would want to watch a bunch of losers bitching with each other about who's been screwing with whom?" would have been an initial response. "Anyway, where are you going to find someone who will sit in front of cameras and fess up to millions that his wife has been giving oral sex to men for money in hotel rooms then spending the money scoring oxy for her and her girlfriend?"

Springer had answers to both questions. He launched the show five years after the fictitious conversation, in 1991, and soon became a lightning rod, attracting criticism as the champion of sleaze tv, while deflecting attention from a serious question—why would anyone watch the show? By 1997–8, the show had surpassed Oprah Winfrey's all-conquering daytime talk show and become a paradigm of what many called confessional culture. This has nothing to do with an enclosed stall divided by a screen in which a priest sits and listens, and everything to do with our willingness to reveal private thoughts, especially ones about which we feel (or should feel) embarrassed. There also have to be others who are gratified to hear such thoughts. "A confessional culture critically depends not just on subjects who are willing to tell all, but also on the presence of an audience that regards revelations as entertainment," wrote Juliet Williams in 2006 (p. 116).

Springer's show was a kind of Rorschach test. Critics said it was just an unwelcome splotch on the networks: crass, foul-mouthed, unutterably mortifying, and an all-round disgrace. Others—and I count myself among them—saw a pattern. The show presented a coherent picture of a society in which no one felt inhibited by the presence of strangers and, in fact, probably felt empowered by the opportunity to share their thoughts. No matter that others' curiosity edged toward the prurient: by the 1990s, voyeurism had become respectable. So, when Frank Furedi establishes, "The act of 'sharing'—turning private troubles into public stories—is now deeply embedded in popular culture," he implicitly recognizes our appetite for consuming those stories.

From the moment Marcello Geppetti focused his lens on two unsuspecting lovers secluded, so they thought, off the coast of Ischia, and squeezed his camera's shutter button, privacy changed. The membrane separating private and public life became permeable. It would not have seemed that way in 1962. Nor even in 1982. But in 1992, there were signs that popular notions of privacy were in flux. The private sphere was opened up for public scrutiny. If the likes of Elizabeth Taylor could not preserve and protect her own space, no one could. And why should they? The question did not seem relevant in the 1960s. But it was asked persistently and with increasing urgency, not just by the media, but by the audiences and the celebrities they followed. This was why Springer's program was powerful: it gave a loud, emphatic answer.

Every show provided affirmation that what previous generations had considered personal and no one else's business was not necessarily privileged and confidential information. It might be intimate and, in some cases, secret; but this was no reason to incarcerate it. Releasing it was, in its way, therapeutic; as well as deliriously entertaining for others, as the shows frequently dissolved into violent melees, broken up by security guards.

Oprah had fashioned a way of presenting privacy in a public way; she had accomplished this by becoming a presenter who seemed to share the same kinds of vulnerabilities and problems as her audience. An interview with her was more like a confidential disclosure. Springer pared away any pretense: any therapeutic benefit was coincidental; the aim of his show was to entertain. Springer himself acknowledged this. "People enjoy it and it has absolutely no redeeming social value whatsoever, other than escapist entertainment," he told Greg Braxton in 2010. True or false? It depends what he meant by value. Perhaps Springer knew sex, violence, and drugs were already in one zeitgeist and he was just turning over a stone to reveal another. Or maybe he accidentally kicked a stone that had already been dislodged. Either way, the show made a spectacular blur of the line separating privacy from public exhibition. Social value? Maybe not. But as a social metaphor, it was unbeatable.

Everyone who appeared on the show enthusiastically imparted knowledge about themselves and others that, in another era, would be restricted to confidantes. Audiences were rather like the crowds that gathered at the stocks in medieval England to watch criminals exposed to public ridicule or assault. The difference was that the criminals were secured in a wooden structure, while the guests on Springer volunteered for the experience. There was an additional difference: in all probability, any member of the audience watching Springer's guests publically denude themselves of their secrets would have swapped places.

Nowadays, we think nothing of watching, listening, and reading about celebrities, who, in turn, think nothing of imparting information on their illnesses, addictions, sex lives, and personal tragedies. In fact, we expect it; we feel entitled to know. And if it is not forthcoming, we either consign the reticent celebrity to obscurity or simply make up what we suspect. Once shared, it takes on the status of legitimate gossip and spreads like the contents of a leaking tank truck.

Springer delivered a lesson: his show demonstrated how privacy could be relinquished without any corresponding loss of modesty, self-worth or even self-respect: participants (and I include the observers) experienced no evident destruction of pride or human dignity as they brazenly unfolded their tales, often while convulsive starts of laughter broke out among the live audience. Do not be misled into dismissing Springer's show as a grotesque freakshow for the masses: it was cunningly representative of changing sensibilities, indexing a modification of our values. The shock was that it was not just the people in the show who were surrendering their privacy. We all were.

Privacy, *noun*, a state in which one is not observed or disturbed by other people; the state of being free from public attention.

First Amendment, *noun*, an article of the US Constitution that protects the right to freedom of religion and freedom of expression from government interference.

He might have been stating the obvious: "Everyone is interested in other people's lives, especially famous people's lives." But Roger Gimbel, the president of EMI Television, was talking in 1982, before anyone had accepted that voyeurism was, if not respectable, acceptable. Gimbel was responding to the *New York Times'* Tamar Lewin. "I think that's obvious," he continued, "or there wouldn't be so many gossip magazines." An awful lot more were to follow.

Lewin was analysing the implications of Taylor's law suit against ABC Television, which was, at the time, working with David Paradine Television, Inc., on the production of a film tentatively titled either "The Elizabeth Taylor Story" or "Liz." Lewin discerned that Taylor's attempt to block the proposed film involved a clash of "the First Amendment guarantee of free speech and an individual's right to control what is said about her."

Today, we are accustomed to all manner of biopics (biographical films) or docudramas (dramatized television films based on actual events) that seem to escape any individual's control. In 1982, Taylor's life presented filmmakers with an *embarras de richesses*, though they would have been naïve to assume she would ignore, give her tacit approval, less still rubberstamp a television film from which she stood to earn nothing. Maybe ten years later when she had her own fragrance on the market, she might have considered offering her consent in exchange for generous product placements (the practice in which brand products are featured in films and tv shows). But Elizabeth Taylor's Passion was still five years away, so the producers had little to offer in return.

Films based on the lives of famous figures meet two demands: the first for a good yarn; the second for an inside track on someone's life. Though she would never openly admit it, Taylor must have known how the world devoured tittle-tattle about her; so she served up more, not just off screen either. She all but invited audiences to see in her film roles a reflection of her private life. So the idea of formalizing the entire narrative independently of her occasioned not just indignation but fury: "The film is an outrage. This docudrama technique is simply a fancy new name for old-fashioned invasion of an actor's rights."

Taylor did not spell out exactly what rights she had in mind, nor what specific rights actors, as opposed to other variants of the human species, had. ABC had in the works a movie on Princess Grace of Monaco, made without the approval of the Palace of Monaco. The tv movie was broadcast in 1983, with Cheryl Ladd in the title role of *Grace Kelly*. The death of Kelly in a 1982 road accident, a scene not included in the film, probably gave the network more latitude than it might otherwise have enjoyed, though Rita Hayworth was still living when *Rita Hayworth: The Love Goddess*, with Lynda Carter as Hayworth ("an inadequate impersonation," according to the *New York Times,* November 2, 1983) was screened by CBS television in November, 1983. This was another hybrid, based on actual events but with fictionalized dialog and dollops of imagined sequences.

Traditionally, legal attacks on films featuring real people, living or dead, have been predicated on defamation; in other words, the person is depicted in a way that damages his or her otherwise good reputation. The producers of the 1967 movie *Bonnie and Clyde,* for example, were sued by relatives of Frank Hamer, a Texas Ranger who was portrayed in the film. It was settled out of court. Legal actions of this kind still persist: former International Monetary Fund (IMF) chief Dominique Strauss-Kahn threatened to sue the makers of *Welcome To New York,* a 2014 film allegedly based on events in his life, which depicts a "Mr. Deveraux" taking part in several alcohol-fueled orgies involving prostitutes. (Incidentally, Gérard Depardieu, who played Deveraux, might have been a kindred spirit to Richard Burton: boasting he drank on average six bottles of wine a day, Depardieu insisted he was not an alcoholic because, unlike him, "alcoholics never get drunk.")

Taylor's approach was different to the orthodox legal challenge. "I am suing ABC television network because they plan on doing a story of my life which is completely fictionalized unless there was somebody under the carpet or under the bed during my 50 years," she said at a press conference in October 1982. "No matter who portrays me, she will not be me, I will not be she. I am my own commodity. I am my own industry. The way I look, the way I sound, that is my industry and if somebody else portrays me and fictionalizes my life, it is taking away from me" (quoted in Lewin's 1982 article).

Taylor insisted ABC was exploiting her name, likeness, and reputation. This is known as the right of publicity and refers to a law designed to protect the public use of name, image, and identity for commercial purposes. *People* magazine quoted attorney Renee Golden, who agreed with Taylor fulsomely: "How dare ABC take Elizabeth Taylor's life story—worth up to $250,000 if she sold it to TV—and appropriate it without paying her for it?" (November 8, 1982). The magazine concluded presciently: "Clearly, the outcome of the Taylor case will have repercussions."

As we learned earlier, ABC abandoned the entire project, citing creative problems, and Taylor's suit was dismissed. It is by no means certain whether the courts would have supported her. The television company's capitulation spoiled what would surely have been a spectacular court case fought over the question: do individuals' have the rights to their own lives, or are we all public property?

In 1982, the question was left unsettled, though, in 1994, it was asked again when Taylor became aware of another, similar project, this time planned by NBC television. The tv network had, in 1993, announced its intention to turn an unauthorized and then unpublished biography of Taylor into a four-hour miniseries. The biography in question was C. David Heymann's *Liz: An intimate biography of Elizabeth Taylor*, which Taylor tried, unsuccessfully, to block. Taylor sued NBC in the California Supreme Court to prevent it from using her image and likeness or using an actor to play her in a miniseries about her life, again invoking the right of publicity. But this time the court rejected Taylor's argument, stating that the right of publicity could not be used to stifle comment on the lives of "public people." John T. Aquino interpreted this ruling in a 2005 book: "An injunction against NBC would constitute an unconstitutional prior restraint against First Amendment-protected expression" (p. 34).

"This is some form of lunacy," declared Taylor's lawyer Neil Papiano to *Entertainment Weekly*'s Dana Kennedy at the time of the case. "You don't have the right to protect yourself from these vultures?" he asked. Kennedy clarified: "The vultures in question are the TV producers and writers who have been circling over celebrities in search of fodder for TV movies and miniseries." The answer to Papiano's apparently rhetorical question was clear enough.

"What could Ms. Taylor have to fear?" Anita Gates asked in 1995, raising what many probably regarded as the most relevant question to emerge from the whole imbroglio. "At the age of 63, she is a veteran of six divorces, one widowhood, three Caesareans, innumerable hospitalizations, the untimely deaths of close friends [Clift, Hudson, Halston et al.], two stays at the Betty Ford Center and," adds Gates, pausing to remind readers of the Eddie Fisher scandal we covered in Chapter 1, a brief period "as the most hated woman in North America." This leads Gates to conclude: "It would seem she can take it with the best of them—and then some."

But Gates had probably not divined Taylor's changing state of mind. In the period between the two cases, Taylor had launched her branded merchandise: she was earning millions from her fragrances, White Diamonds in particular. So there was more at stake than before. Her name, image, indeed, her whole identity was now associated with products that could be bought over a counter. "Elizabeth Taylor" had been monetized. The movie would become part of that process (for a start, consider the advertising space sold for every screening of the four-hour film), though Taylor stood not to benefit financially from it. She probably feared nothing, apart from the potential impact on sales of her commodities.

In 1982, Taylor might conceivably have had the backing of the courts. We will never know because ABC was, it seems, intimidated by the remonstrations of a high-powered celebrity. Any faint hopes that NBC would also back off, seeking to curry favor with Taylor soon disappeared and the series aired in March 1995, with Sherilyn Fenn in the Taylor role. The following year when Taylor appeared in four consecutive sitcoms (the Black Pearl narrative covered in the previous chapter), it was for NBC's network rival CBS.

The film itself was bland. *Variety*'s John P. McCarthy described it in 1995 as "a tame version of Taylor's personal life," and suspected "exec producer Lester Persky let the NBC legal department have its way too often." NBC won its legal fight to make and screen the film, but it would have been vulnerable had it calumniated Taylor, that is, screened false and defamatory scenes or statements. (The film is viewable online at: http://bit.ly/1w6twCF accessed September 2015.)

So perhaps NBC was more circumspect when it came to the final edit (the nearest the film got to injuring Taylor's feelings was probably in featuring Fenn so bulked up with prosthetics that she resembled Gwyneth Paltrow in *Shallow Hal*). In spite of this, the import of the case remained: in 1994, celebrities were not so untouchable and godlike as they were earlier in the twentieth century; and they certainly carried less weight with the media than they did in the 1980s. Television companies, or, for that matter, any other media corporations, were not spooked by expressions of outrage or legal threats. They probably realized that the media's role was no longer to report, monitor, and faithfully record the public life of stars; now, they had the power to create, maintain, and annihilate. The celebrities' right to privacy was no longer sacrosanct. Quite the opposite: their privacy was, paradoxically, a public concern.

Think of the films either centered on or featuring living people since the NBC decision. These include: *The Fighter* (2010), with Mark Wahlberg as boxer Micky Ward (b. 1965), *Moneyball* (2011), in which Brad Pitt played baseball coach Billy Beane (b. 1962), *The Fifth Estate* (2013), with Benedict Cumberbatch as WikiLeaks founder Julian Assange (b. 1971) and *The Queen* (2006), for which Helen Mirren won the Oscar for Best Actress for her portrayal of Queen Elizabeth II (b. 1926). Diane Werts, of the *Los Angeles Times* quoted producer Lester Persky: "Whether the person is alive or dead doesn't influence the performance, which is its own entity."

The statement captured the confidence of the media and its willingness to risk upsetting its subjects. Around the time of the Taylor-NBC case, two biographies of Roseanne Barr were screened despite her objections and Mia Farrow's relationship with Woody Allen was the subject of another film. Later, Facebook founder Mark Zuckerberg criticized his depiction in Columbia Picture's *The Social Network* (2010), but to no avail. The late Brittany Murphy's father said he would sue Lifetime over its *The Brittany Murphy Story* (2014), a film made without his or his wife's permission. But people, living or dead, pose fewer problems to media corporations than they used to. As Tom Jicha concluded in 1995: "It is almost impossible for public figures to prevent dramatizations of their lives."

Surprisingly, the NBC miniseries was the only docudrama or biopic made on Taylor during her life. *Liz & Dick* was released in 2012, followed by *Taylor and Burton* the following year. Her life almost offered itself as raw material for scriptwriters. *Beautiful Ruins*, the Jess Walter novel, was published in 2012, its title taken from Louis Menand's description of Richard Burton in 1980, "fifty-four at the time, and already a beautiful ruin" (this is from Menand's article in *The New Yorker*, November 22, 2010). Water's story integrates fiction with fact, supposing that a young female actor playing a small part in *Cleopatra* has a tryst with Burton. BBC's radio play *Rock and Doris and Elizabeth*, which I covered earlier, was broadcast in 2012. Dhanil Ali's *The Liz and Dick Show* debuted at the Edinburgh Festival in 2013. Taylor's estate has not protested to any of these creative works.

Taylor helped shape a culture possessed with the spirit of enquiry; enquiry, that is, into other people's lives (to use Gimbel's phrase again). In 1960s America where Hollywood adjudicated on what became known and what remained hidden, Taylor became a sort of third force: a woman who lived so close to the intersection where public crossed private, that she offended, enraged, astonished, and, of course, fascinated. And she seemed to do it effortlessly. But it was a time when a glimpse into the private lives induced frisson. By the 1990s, Taylor *l'agent provocateur,* had become Taylor *la grande dame*, still able to captivate, but not in a revealing, challenging or arousing way.

Biopics and docudramas like NBC's were parts of diet supplied by the media to satisfy consumers' appetites for evermore-prurient details. Audiences became Peeping Toms, lusts intensified by the inchoate internet age. The browser Netscape was released in 1994, as was the portal Yahoo! Google began in 1998. Later, Web 2.0 revealed the true capacity of the net for producing and reproducing, what became known as generativity. Once blogs, podcasts, and video sharing started, a new type of grapevine burgeoned. Rumors, gossip, and the word on the street circulated via sites like Facebook (launched 2004) and twitter (2006). Complementing these were tv shows, not just Springer's, but MTV's *The Real World*, which started in 1992, on the audacious premise that observing ordinary people doing run-of-the mill stuff in everyday settings would be interesting. *Big Brother* was created in 1997, at first in Holland, premiering in the USA and Britain in 2000 and eventually spawning fifty-two editions internationally. All were part of the same diet, satisfying our appetite for information on other peoples' lives, no matter how closely they resembled our own.

Taylor might have been surprised when she was rebuffed by the courts and had to join millions of other tv viewers watching her life unfold over

210-minutes. But when she looked around her, she would have realized that surveillance was the new norm. She had once been the subject of one of the most outrageous pieces of close observation in history. Now, every celebrity, every person who aspired to be a celebrity, and many more who wished simply to remain unknown, fell under the scrutiny of everyone else.

A new Taylor romance in the 1990s may not have occasioned the fevered media hyperactivity it would in earlier decades. All the same, hearsay involving amours, no matter how farfetched, registered with the media. One especially intriguing tidbit surfaced in June 1990 and involved a purported romance between Taylor, then fifty-eight, and a 23-year-old man from Detroit named Julian Lee Hobbs. The bomb-disposal duties, as usual, fell to Taylor's publicist Chen Sam, who could defuse as expertly as she could engineer any story about Taylor. She described the story as "a hoax and a sick one to boot," though why it was sick (unpleasant, offensive, perverted?) was not clear. A woman had gained access to Sam's answering service (a business that receives and answers call for its clients, popular before the rise of cellphones) using a secret code (obviously not secret enough) and returned calls to the media, giving out information to the likes of United Press and Associated Press agencies. The woman told reporters that Hobbs had flown into LA from Detroit and spent the weekend at Taylor's side, helping with her recovery from a near-fatal bout of viral pneumonia, the hugely publicized illness we covered in Chapter 14. Taylor was still in the Santa Monica hospital at the time. Hobbs was set to fly with Taylor to her home in Switzerland, said the woman. Even more intriguing, the woman added that Taylor had undergone an abdominal biopsy. Taylor had been linked with Forbes who had recently died and, of course, Fortensky, then thirty-five. So the prospect of an even younger man appearing from nowhere to become a new love interest was compelling. The story was nixed and Hobbs faded from view, at least for a few of years: in 1993, Julian Lee Hobbs, twenty-six, also known as Rory Emerald, was charged with trying to steal $10,050 in goods by posing as Mia Farrow's personal shopper in the Ralph Lauren store Rodeo Drive. Associated Press' Lee Siegel covered the story in 1993.

Chen Sam, as usual, fashioned an elegant, if somewhat unbelievable, denouement for the Taylor end of the story (how was the whistleblower woman able to get the code and persuade experienced journalists, well-versed in handling Taylor stories?) Sam herself was once described as the "mystery lady who gate-keeps for Liz Taylor." Like Taylor's other aides, she was quietly, sometimes invisibly and steadfastly supportive of her efforts to promote Aids causes. So there was potential embarrassment in the manner Sam reacted to a 1991 tabloid report that she had been diagnosed with cancer. A stalwart spokesperson, organizer, and publicist for Taylor since the early 1970s (when she first met Taylor and Burton in southern Africa), the

Egyptian-born Sam moved to the US in 1981 and started up her own agency Chen Sam & Associates Inc. While she represented other celebrities, like Donald Trump and Karl Lagerfeld, Taylor was her most prominent client and, most people assumed, confidante: "We're like sisters," she told Ellen Stern in 1994.

In August 1991, the *National Enquirer* reported that Sam had been diagnosed with cancer. When, in 1992, Sam filed a lawsuit her lawyer argued that the report was libelous because cancer is a "loathsome disease" associated with Aids and that the story injured Sam's business, it seemed an extraordinary act of inconsistency. A false statement that a person has a "loathsome disease" can be found defamatory without evidence that the statement harmed the person's reputation. Sexually transmitted diseases are generally considered to fall within the category of loathsome diseases. New York's state Supreme Court's Appellate Division disagreed with the allegation when it declared in January 1996: "Cancer is not a loathsome disease and it cannot be said that society as a whole views it . . . as a sexually transmitted disease" (the case was *Sam v. Enquirer Group, Inc.*) It went further in rejecting Sam's argument: "Under [Sam's] analysis, pneumonia or colds would fall into the same category because of their association with Aids" (as chronicled by the Reporters Committee for Freedom of the Press, January 29 1996; http://bit.ly/1PVVkCm accessed September 2015). Taylor, at the time deeply involved in her Aids work, managed to avoid becoming entangled in what could have been an awkward predicament.

After Sam died at Taylor's Bel Air home in 1996, the reason for death was announced as "complications from an illness" with no elaboration. Most publications followed this, though *USA Today* reported that she had cancer, according to *New York* magazine (September 16 1996, p. 14). Her age was not revealed, presumably at her own request. Litigation continued after her death with Sam's executors, though the courts found no defamation (as the Reporters Committee for Freedom of the Press conveyed on July 14, 1997; http://bit.ly/1EX9rkT (accessed September 2015).

Sam was a quiet but important presence in Taylor's 'professional life, though little has been written about her, Norma Libman's 1993 *Chicago Tribune* story and Ellen Stern's profile for *New York* magazine in 1994, being minor exceptions. A specialist in managing publicity, she kept her own affairs and, indeed, worldviews out of reach from the media and disclosed only some of them when she felt provoked.

FIGURE 17 *Taylor called Michael Jackson "the least weird man" she had ever known. Her friendship with him mystified many, though Taylor hinted its source lay in their comparable childhoods, or perhaps absence of childhoods.*

Photo by Steve Granitz/WireImage. Getty Images.

17

On dangerous ground

Larry King: But didn't you think, Elizabeth, Dame Elizabeth, I'm sorry, that it would look strange to people to have someone who is in his forties spending a night with children? I mean, just on the face of it.

Elizabeth Taylor: All right. I'll answer that, because I've been there, when his nephews were there, and we all were in the bed, watching television. There was nothing abnormal about it. There was no touchy-feely going on. We laughed like children, and we watched a lot of Walt Disney. There was nothing odd about it.

Larry King: So you think they were out after him?

Elizabeth Taylor: I do.

Larry King Live, CNN, May 30, 2006
(Transcript at: http://bit.ly/1lSTgCs accessed September 2015.)

They called him the "King of Pop." Some say Taylor herself christened him this when she awarded him with the Soul Train Heritage Award in 1989. Like Taylor, Michael Jackson was a performer practically as soon as he was old enough to stand. Childhood for him was like a petri dish: he had a rare and conspicuous talent that needed to be grown and contained. The methods of encouraging growth were hardly gentle though: he was cajoled or coerced into singing and dancing with his four brothers. Seven years separated the ages of the Jackson 5, Michael being the youngest. Managed, often dictatorially, by father Joe, the brothers, in 1969, signed with Motown Records. Influenced by the success of the assembled-for-television band the Monkees, Motown boss Berry Gordy initially wanted to create a black version, complete with cartoon series and a range of merchandise. He launched the Jackson 5, using established stars such as Diana Ross and Sammy Davis Jr. as endorsers. In fact, the band's first Motown album was *Diana Ross Presents the Jackson 5*.

Father Joe, however, was dissatisfied with Gordy's handling of his sons' careers and, in 1976, negotiated a deal with CBS's subsidiary label, Epic. For contractual reasons, the band became known as the Jacksons, its first album being released in 1977. While both the band and Michael continued to sell records, progress was unspectacular until 1979 when a collaboration with producer Quincy Jones yielded Michael's solo *Off the Wall*, which sold 8 million copies—and continues to sell. The album spawned four hit singles. Around this time, the facial changes that were to become the stuff of myth began: two rhinoplasty operations followed an accident in which Michael broke his nose.

Despite his commercial success, MTV was impervious to Michael Jackson for a long while. In 1983, the 24-hour all-music cable tv channel rejected Jackson's *Billie Jean*, giving rise to the suspicion that the station wanted only "safe" acts that appealed to white youth; and, for this reason, concluded that black artists were not good for business. CBS threatened MTV with a boycott by all its artists, forcing a change of heart. In a way, MTV's decision may have been an historic one, providing a black artist with a genuine mainstream showcase. The track was taken from Jackson's album *Thriller*, which turned him into the bestselling recording artist of his time. The album sold 50 million copies worldwide and continues to sell. The title track's video, a state-of-the-art horror movie pastiche, was made into an extravagant tv event, receiving a premiere in December 1982. It helped usher in the music video age.

Around this stage, Jackson's private life began to overshadow his music. He was far from the only performer to find his life the subject of public inquiry. Princess Diana and Madonna were both figures of fascination, the latter being instrumental in changing the rules of engagement that governed showbusiness performers' relationships with the media. By the mid-1980s open season had arrived and Jackson found himself the unwitting prey of journalists who found his personal habits almost as, if not more, interesting than his music. Jackson would remain in the public eye for the rest of his life, though it would not be his music that kept him there.

In many ways, Jackson prefigured the emerging cultural dissatisfaction with fixed identities and the strictures they imposed. For example, Jackson's sexuality seemed indistinct to the point of being unclassifiable. So too his ethnicity: black, white or something altogether different? He was, to use the *New York Times'* Guy Trebay's phrase "the literal embodiment of identity in flux."

In 1984, the Jacksons were to give the final performance of what was known as the Victory tour at Los Angeles' Dodger Stadium. Taylor requested seats for herself and her entourage of fourteen, and was granted a VIP box. Always the diva, Taylor was dissatisfied with the position of the box, which was some distance from the stage. It was at a baseball stadium after all. So she upped and left before the end of the concert. When news filtered back to Michael, he was horrified to think one of his idols had been inconvenienced; so he made sure he issued a personal apology. Taylor, then fifty-two, had been seeing Victor Luna earlier in the year, but they had broken off their engagement; she was days away from announcing her betrothal to Dennis Stein.

Jackson, at twenty-six both a solo artist and a member of the Jacksons, called Taylor to express his regret that she had been disappointed, though it was several months before they met face-to-face. When they did, it started a friendship that perplexed all but child abuse counselors. "One of the reasons I think Michael Jackson and I are so close [is] because neither one of us had a childhood, and we can relate to that and wonder at how we got by," Taylor once tried tactfully to explain the unusual symmetry that brought and kept them together.

Taylor had met plenty of other child prodigies, of course. She befriended and remained close to Roddy McDowall, for example; though she never seemed to have formed close bonds with others, such as the like of Angela Lansbury and Mickey Rooney. Jackson had a history of friendships with luminary women: as well as his muse Diana Ross, there was Brooke Shields, Sophia Loren, and Liza Minnelli. But, as Harriet J. Manning detected in 2013: "Jackson's longtime fondness for Taylor is particularly well known but as well as fondness it would seem there was also a strong identification" (p. 149).

Like Taylor, who was making movies at eight and became a star at twelve, Jackson had no period in which to mature from childhood to late adolescence: both their lives were controlled to a degree rarely experienced by other children. Both had their childhoods, indeed their youths, traded by demanding, ambitious parents. In exchange, they had glittering theatrical careers. While Taylor refrained from criticizing her mother directly, she famously compared her own experiences with Jackson's notoriously harsh upbringing. "He had one of the worst childhoods ever. I think I had the second" became Taylor's near-canonical verdict on Jackson (this has been quoted extensively; for example by *forbes.com*: see http://onforb.es/1IFJOfg accessed September 2015).

Of course, Taylor was probably laboring with a somewhat idealistic conception of normal childhood. She may not have been familiar with parental tensions, peer pressures, and bullying at school, the awkward experimentations with sex, drugs, and cures for acne; perhaps not even a first love, at least not in the sense most of us experience it. Taylor was fourteen when her book about her pet chipmunk, *Nibbles and Me,* was published. She was fifteen when she started seeing Glenn Davis, though practically every moment they shared was monitored by the media. To repeat journalist Bob Thomas's observation from 1949: "Its no fun to conduct a courtship with 150,000,000 people looking on."

Jackson, to be sure, had an extraordinary non-childhood. He was shy of his ninth birthday when *I Want You Back*, the Jackson 5's first hit record, made him a star. Even then, he was something of a showbiz veteran, having been performing on stage since aged seven. He was whipped by his father, who also taunted him over his looks. Despite this and the incessant rehearsals, Jackson later acknowledged that his father's discipline played a huge part in his success and ultimately forgave him.

There seems to have been a celebrity equivalent of Newton's law of universal gravitation at work: Taylor and Jackson were attracted to each other by a powerful force. Both whizzed past their childhoods, avoiding the calamities and misadventures that typically assist maturation. Neither repined. At least not until middle age. Memories of lost childhood tormented Taylor and the prospect of an endless adolescence blighted Jackson. There seemed inevitability about the way both succumbed to the allure of narcotics.

They called him the "King of Lips." Taylor called him "the most brilliant doctor in the world." Arnold Klein, the son of an orthodox rabbi in Michigan, graduated from University of Pennsylvania in 1967, earned his doctorate in 1971 and served a residency at UCLA, specializing in dermatology. His practice was at Riverside, California, but he moved upscale to Beverly Hills, at first doing "a lot of pimple popping and light treatments," as he put it, then diagnosing and treating a variety of skin disorders for members of the A-list. One of his clients was Merv Griffin, who was impressed enough to invite him onto his syndicated tv talk show. He went on to appear several more times, boosting his status as a celebrity skin doctor. By 1981, Klein, then thirty-six, lived in a 30-room mansion in Hancock Park, a palatial area in central LA. He co-authored *The Skin Book* (with James H. Sternberg and Paul Bernstein) in 1982.

In 1982, *People* magazine's Suzy Kalter called him "skin doctor to the stars" and even that might have been an understatement: in 1985, he was granted an audience with Pope John Paul II, who had a skin condition his own doctors could not heal. Klein claims he cured it.

In the early 1980s, many of his clients were young men who consulted him over rashes, sores, and lesions. Klein claimed to be the first physician to diagnose Kaposi's sarcoma, or KS, which is a cancer-like disease occurring in people with weakened immune system. The most common cause of KS is HIV; it was a sign of Aids, of course. Klein was one of the co-founders of amfAR, which he helped establish in 1985 with Taylor, Mathilde Krim, and David Geffen. He also worked with Taylor to start UCLA's Elizabeth Taylor Endowment, and elicited $1 million from Doris Duke, the socialite and philanthropist.

Taylor would later swear: "He has helped save my life." Taylor said this of the Beverly Hills dermatologist in February 2003, when speaking at a benefit for Aids Services Foundation Orange County and the Laguna Art Museum. Ann Conway, of the *Los Angeles Times* covered the event. Taylor lauded Klein further: "He's supposed to be a dermatologist, but he's so much more. I cannot tell you how many times he has seen me and said, 'Elizabeth! Off to the hospital!'" Taylor became one of Klein's stalwart supporters. Her endorsements suggest he was more than a personal dermatologist, though he appears to have become that too.

Why "King of Lips"? Because Klein's specialty was plumping up lips. "In 1984, after a woman walked into his office complaining her lips were disappearing into her mouth with age, Klein made his first injection of a newly developed collagen substance," reported Dave Gardetta, of *Los Angeles Magazine* in 2002 (p. 48). "A decade later, upon hearing about a common toxin that would later be marketed as Botox, he made up his mind to become an expert in the forehead's muscle groups" (the US Food and Drug Administration approved the purified form of botulinum toxin Type A we call Botox in 2002).

There were occasional bumps in the road: in 2003, he and Allergan Inc., which sold Botox, were forced to defend themselves against a glamorous Hollywood fund-raising wife who alleged that Botox shots caused her to develop hives and become bedridden with fatigue; her movie-producer husband contended he had been denied her companionship. Klein emerged intact.

Jackson had been a patient of Klein's since April 1983. Jackson was anxious about a rash that had appeared on his face and scalp. Gerald Posner, of the *Daily Beast*, suggested in 2009: "It was Taylor who endorsed Arnold Klein, the cosmetic dermatologist to Hollywood's A-list, to Jackson." She certainly appreciated Klein's work and praised him wholeheartedly; so it is conceivable that she endorsed him, though Jackson did not need an introduction. Klein diagnosed lupus (which refers to a group of diseases marked from inflammation of the skin) and, more controversially, vitiligo. Klein's diagnosis in itself was not controversial, but vitiligo is a condition in which pigment is lost from the skin, leaving whitish patches and was often cited as the reason Jackson grew paler as he matured. Some suspected he deliberately used skin-whitening agents and yearned to be white.

In January 1984, Jackson, then twenty-five, was filming a commercial for Pepsi in LA. He would sing *Billie Jean*. There were to be all manner of pyrotechnics involved. During the third take, Jackson's hair caught fire; he continued dancing oblivious to this, until someone ran onto the stage and smothered him. His hair had been badly burned and his scalp was damaged. Jackson was taken to hospital and treated for second-degree burns (that cause blistering but not permanent scars).

After the hair-burning accident, Klein visited Jackson in the hospital. At the time, Jackson was, with Madonna, one of the two biggest singing stars in the world, so being his personal consultant carried with it significant kudos, as well as unexpected burdens, as Klein and, more famously, Dr. Conrad Murray later discovered. Jackson had used Dr. Steve Hoefflin, a well-known plastic surgeon who had transmogrified, among others, Joan Rivers, Ivana

Trump, and Taylor, for the rhinoplasties that resulted in a conspicuous change in his visage. But Klein gained Jackson's trust. Posner advances the theory that the habits that ultimately killed Jackson had their origins in the aftermath of the Pepsi shoot incident: "This was around the time Jackson first began using some of the same pain and sleeping pills as Taylor."

When she first spoke to Jackson, Taylor had recently emerged from her first visit to the Betty Ford Center. She would return in 1988, of course, again undergoing treatment for alcohol and painkiller dependencies. Taylor was unembarrassed about this and spoke openly about her habits. Within eighteen months of her leaving the Center, the California state attorney general's office with the assistance of the Los Angeles County district attorney, investigated several physicians and eventually in 1994 reprimanded three doctors "for prescribing huge amounts of drugs to Elizabeth Taylor: more than 1,000 prescriptions in five years for 28 different drugs including Demerol, Percocet (painkillers), Valium and methadone," according to the Citizens Commission On Human Rights in 2008 (p. 6). I covered this in the previous chapter, but it is worth bearing in mind in the context of Taylor's friendship with Jackson.

Jackson's manchild goody-two-shoes image in the 1990s was a far cry from the creepy malefactor he became—at least in the eyes of many. He seemed infantile, puppyish, as tame and lovable as one of Taylor's Maltese terriers. And lest we forget: he was an African American, who, through a quirk of nature or a trick of nurture, was getting whiter. Maybe that was part of his appeal to white fans: he had talent, money, the adulation of millions and the world at his feet; but the one thing he seemed to crave, but could not have, was to be white. We must hold that argument (though for interested readers: I explore it in my *The Black Culture Industry*).

Jackson was a wondrously gifted prodigy, a consummate showman, a misunderstood genius, and a malignant, destructive, and deceptive freak. Maybe all of these, depending on your point of view. Everyone started by marveling at his astonishingly precocious talent. But as Jackson matured, so his audiences began to glimpse less palatable facets of his character. Jackson spent his thirty-fifth birthday with Taylor and his sister, Janet Jackson. They were not celebrating. Instead, they were closeted away from the media in a Singapore hotel. Days before, Jackson had performed to 50,000 fans in Bangkok. But any triumphalism was tempered by an allegation that he had sexually abused a thirteen-year-old son of a Beverly Hills dentist.

In August 1993, the news was dumfounding: the most celebrated male singer on earth, partner (and future husband) of Lisa Marie Presley (daughter of Elvis) and erstwhile squire of Tatum O'Neal and Brooke Shields, Jackson was considered callow but eligible. There was nothing in his past to suggest he was gay, less still that had any tendencies that could be construed as abusive. Surely, this was a hysterical shriek from some kid who had mistaken the soft-spoken Jackson's kindness for something more sinister. Jackson was reclusive and had some unusual practices; but global icons are allowed eccentricities.

In any case, Taylor had been on *Oprah* a matter of months before and called Jackson "the least weird man" she had ever known. Actually, from Taylor that was an ambiguous commendation. At the time, Taylor had completed two spells at the Betty Ford Center and the benefits of them were not immediately apparent. She was drinking again and mixing tranquilizers with painkillers, though maintained enough objectivity to see that Jackson's response to the allegations was the equivalent of self-harming. "He wasn't aware of what was happening," Taylor told ABC News' Diane Sawyer in 1995. "He was dulling his pain, but it really frightened me, because I have been there and I know how easy it is to get there when you're in mental or physical pain" (quoted in Ian Halperin's 2009 book, p. 157).

The resemblances with Taylor were underscored when she interrupted the tour after a concert in Mexico and insisted Jackson checked into rehab. "Elizabeth takes us aside and says to us, 'We're going to get him out of the country after the show. He's going to go to London,'" recalled Jackson's personal assistant Frank Cascio, who was also a longtime friend, when talking to Alice Gomstyn and Chris Connelly in 2011.

Jackson issued a short statement in which he referred to "what has become an addiction." He attributed his dependence on drugs to his anguish over the accusations: "The pressure resulting from these false allegations, coupled with the incredible energy necessary for me to perform, caused so much distress that it left me physically and emotionally exhausted" (in "Michael Jackson Ends Tour, Citing Addiction" in *New York Times*, November 14, 1993). Jackson, then thirty-five, said the drugs had been prescribed after recent reconstructive surgery on his scalp, presumably part of the ongoing treatment for the injuries incurred while making the Pepsi video nine years before. Pepsi had remained sponsors of Jackson but canceled the contract immediately after Jackson's drugs admission. Years later, Dr. Stuart Finkelstein, who treated Jackson on the 1993 tour, reflected that Jackson appeared to have a high tolerance for morphine and had on a patch that administered another opiate drug.

The allegations against Jackson were in a social worker's report on Jordan Chandler, who described how he had visited Jackson at his ranch several times. Jackson, said Chandler, became progressively intimate and tried to kiss him on the mouth. America's broadcast media gave extensive coverage to the story, though the more cautious press, presumably mindful that Jackson had not been charged with any offense, paid little attention. Still, there were questions. Did 35-year-old Jackson have the kind of sexual feelings associated with a man of his age? If so, how did he express them? With whom?

In May 1994, Jackson married Lisa Marie Presley, who, when asked (repeatedly), always insisted that her relationship with him was both genuine and sexual. A more popular view was that it was designed to deflect attention from his bizarreness and toward his normalness. If so, it was not effective.

Jackson agreed to talk about the charges on a "live" satellite hookup from his Neverland ranch. He complained that the police had subjected him to a humiliating inspection and taken photographs of his genitalia. In 1994, Jackson agreed to pay Chandler, by then fourteen, an undisclosed sum, thought to be more than $25 million, to stop a sex abuse lawsuit ever reaching court. Jackson was never put under oath for a civil deposition, which could be used in a criminal trial. The deal was negotiated on Jackson's behalf by his lawyer, Johnnie Cochrane Jr.—later to represent O.J. Simpson— and Larry Feldman, who was retained by Chandler's parents. Part of the agreement reached was that the payment did not constitute an admission of guilt by Jackson. After the charges, Jackson was forced out into the open and made to defend himself, whether he liked it or not. In the process, the qualities that were once integral to his appeal were turned into instruments of torture. He was no longer just unusual: he was odd, and not necessarily in a likable way. Everyone by then knew he was weird but there were additional questions: was he cutely weird, unusually weird or a weird sicko? The answers were seemingly forthcoming in February 2003.

The effects of the accusations combined with the acknowledgment of dependencies dented Jackson's hitherto global popularity and his album *HIStory: Past, Present and Future* sold a modest (by his standards) 1.7 million copies in the US and 8.5 million worldwide. In 1995, he agreed to make an HBO special concert to be filmed at Manhattan's Beacon Theater. During rehearsals Jackson collapsed and was rushed to a hospital. The suspected condition was cardiac arrhythmia, a potentially serious condition in which an irregular heartbeat impairs blood flow. Later, the official diagnosis was "viral infection." The concert was canceled.

Jackson and Presley divorced in 1996. If, as Presley claimed, theirs was a genuine marriage, then the same could not be said of his second. Arnold Klein's nurse Debbie Rowe had grown to know (and presumably like) Jackson over the years. She knew that Jackson wanted children and, after the failure of his first marriage, made him an offer: she would bear his children. She became pregnant in 1996, and she and Jackson married the same year. The following year, she gave birth to Prince Michael Jackson, and in 1998, to Paris-Michael Katherine Jackson. Although Jackson maintained his first two children were produced through intercourse, Rowe later acknowledged that both her children by Jackson had been artificially conceived. The marriage lasted till 1999, after which Rowe granted full custody rights to Jackson and walked with an $8 million settlement, plus a Beverly Hills house.

In 2013, Klein invited speculation that he was the sperm donor for and thus biological father of Prince by comparing pictures of himself as a teenager and the then fifteen-year-old on Facebook. A third child Prince II, better known as Blanket, was borne by an unknown surrogate mother in 2002.

It took place on September 7, 2001. The audience filled New York's Madison Square Garden, paying up to $2,500 a ticket to see Jackson's first performances since 1989 in the continental USA (his world tour included Hawaii in 1997). It was nominally thirty years after he separated from his brothers to make his first solo single, so it was billed as a "30th Anniversary Celebration." It was not a concert per se: as well as live numbers, there were videos and encomiums from the likes of Chris Tucker, Samuel L. Jackson and, of course, Taylor, who described Michael Jackson as "my closest friend." She had not been on stage since *Private Lives* in 1991. Liza Minnelli and Marlon Brando also made contributions. Jackson's previous album had been released in 1995. *HIStory: Past, Present and Future* was poorly received. The concert was intended to launch his next album *Invincible*. There was a second performance on September 10. The timing was less-than-perfect.

The day after the second performance, attacks on New York's World Trade Center incited panic in the city and a lockdown on all flights. Jackson considered an evacuation via a private plane, but even these were grounded. He, Taylor, and Brando were all intent on heading west to the presumed safety of their California homes. Tim Mendelson, Taylor's former personal assistant, told *Vanity Fair*'s Sam Kashner how the three improvised by renting a car and driving 500 miles to Ohio, where they boarded a plane. The unlikely road trip is surely the raw material of a future movie: Brando, then seventy-seven, and at his most corpulent; Jackson, fresh from his concert and probably jacked up on painkillers, and Taylor, no doubt discomforted by having to travel in something other than the backseat of a Rolls or a private plane. Brando, on Mendelson's account, aggravated his fellow riders by intermittently stalling at KFCs and other fast food outlets. Whether they took turns driving is not known. It is a delicious story nonetheless. And one that intuitively everybody wants to believe.

All the same, Dan P. Lee, of *New York* magazine, in 2011 quoted Brando's lawyer: "That story's all bullshit." He suggests instead: "Like everyone else, the three indeed found themselves temporarily stranded in Manhattan. Taylor evidently decided to stay on, busying herself with charity work, while Brando and Jackson flew later, separately, on private jets to Los Angeles."

Kashner also pours cold water on the tale, quoting an anonymous aide of Taylor's who reckoned she did not join her two companions and instead went to church, and then to Ground Zero, where she talked to reporters. This is a more plausible rendition of events, or at least it would be were there any newspaper stories to corroborate it. It is difficult to imagine any editor spiking a story on Elizabeth Taylor's impromptu visit to the scene of the cataclysm in the aftermath of 9/11. The apocryphal story, like so many other Taylor stories, became part of the folklore that surrounds her.

Kashner's *Vanity Fair* story contains an aperçu about Taylor's relationship with Jackson, whom she visited regularly at his Neverland ranch. Jackson had hosted her wedding in 1991, of course; the one when a paparazzo descended from the sky. Taylor learned that Brando's son Miko, who worked as a bodyguard for Jackson, was rounding up children for sleepovers at the ranch. "She knew it wasn't right," wrote Kashner in 2011. "Even if they *were* the innocent little sleepovers Michael claimed, he was still on dangerous ground."

It was probably more to do with unworldliness than resolution, but Jackson refused to budge from the *terra periculosa*. He enjoyed the company of children and welcomed them to his estate where they played and enjoyed themselves. Often, they stayed the night, fueling stories that some even shared a bed with Jackson. With barely believable ingenuousness, Jackson, his persona already mutating from pop genius to infantilized freak, agreed to an interview on British television in February 2003, which later aired on ABC's *20/20*. Journalist Martin Bashir's earlier interview with Princess Diana had won her enormous sympathy; Jackson presumably deduced he could repeat the trick. It was a risk. But consider Jackson's position: in his mid-forties, he was not selling records as he used to, was reliant on painkillers and morphine-like analgesics, and was once more the subject of rumors about his arcane sexual proclivities. The second two are common features of modern celebritydom; but he wanted to arrest his declining sales.

During the interview, Jackson confirmed that, despite his 1993 out-of-court settlement over abuse allegations—which he continued to deny—and the fog of rumors that enveloped Neverland, he still let children sleep at his home, sometimes in his bed. Jackson called it a loving act and proposed it had nothing to do with sex.

After the telecast, Jackson moaned that his interviewer had betrayed him, so filed a complaint with British media watchdog groups. Then, he helped produce a rebuttal entitled *The Michael Jackson Interview: The footage you were never meant to see*, which was shown on Fox two weeks later. Meanwhile, stories that Jackson had money troubles were supported by the multiple lawsuits filed against him. Worse was to come. Far worse: in November, Jackson was arrested for allegedly molesting a twelve-year-old boy, who was, at the time undergoing treatment for lymphoma.

Jackson surrendered to the authorities and prepared to defend himself against ten felony charges, including four counts of "lewd acts on a child under fourteen," one count of an "attempted lewd act on a child under fourteen," four counts of administering alcohol to enable child molestation, and one count of conspiracy to kidnap a child, false imprisonment, and extortion. The offenses were alleged to have taken place in February and March 2003; the alleged victim was anonymized as "John Doe" (later revealed as Gavin Arvizo). Jackson repudiated the charges and, on a website dedicated to denying them, called them "a big lie." Fans around the world showed their support by staging all-night vigils and, at Neverland, about 600 people, including showbusiness and sports celebrities congregated to affirm their faith in Jackson's innocence.

Taylor flexed her own celebrity muscles in November 2003, issuing a press statement in which she proclaimed: "I believe Michael is absolutely innocent and that he will be vindicated." She was partly right: Jackson was declared innocent, though, if, by vindicated, she meant cleared of suspicion as well as blame, she was wrong.

In June 2005, after a trial that dominated headlines for four months, Jackson walked from the Santa Maria court a free man. He said nothing to the media or to the hundreds of fans thronging the courthouse, leaving his lawyer to confirm: "Justice was served. Michael Jackson is innocent." Perhaps he should have added, ". . . in the eyes of the jury."

Over the previous nineteen months (he had been arrested in November 2003, remember), Jackson's life had been opened to the kind of microscopic scrutiny he had conscientiously tried to avoid. Intentionally or not, Jackson had presented himself as a much frailer, less confident and, if possible, weirder character than anyone could have imagined (one day, he turned up in court wearing a suit jacket and a pair of pajama bottoms). This did his popularity no harm.

Within a month, his record company Sony/BMG released *The Essential Michael Jackson* compilation double-cd, which became an instant best seller. So Jackson at least stopped the rot in sales. But at what cost? Lurid if inconclusive testimony about Jackson's hitherto secret bedroom activities seemed to authenticate suspicions of at least twelve years standing. True or false, the stories first aired in 1993 warped the course of the rest of Jackson's life and damaged his legacy.

In 2006, Jackson disappointed fans in his first appearance since being cleared, by singing just a few lines of *We are the World* at the World Music Awards in London. There were suspicions that Jackson's dependency on prescription drugs was now affecting his normal functioning.

All celebrities thrive on gossip, no one more so than Taylor, as we have seen. But for Jackson, gossip must have sounded like that buzzing noise when a mosquito is nearby: flailing arms do not deter the insect, and the droning noise persists. Jackson was similarly helpless: his sexuality and drug habits had fed endless rumors and, in 2000, talk of his debts became louder and more incessant. Declining record sales combined with increasing legal bills placed pressure on Jackson to meet the $3 million per year cost of running Neverland. So, in March 2009, when Jackson announced plans to perform a 50-date residency at London's 20,000 seat O2 Arena, the motivation was transparent: Jackson stood to earn $400 million ($283m) for the shows, which sold out in minutes. It was an astonishingly ambitious undertaking for a fifty-year-old who had not performed live since the pre-9/11 New York concerts.

By December, reports that Jackson was suffering from a newly revealed ailment were greeted with as much cynicism as concern. Roger Friedman, of Fox News, was among the cynics. "Over the years, Jackson's illnesses have been identified as vitiligo, Lupus, addiction to prescription pain killers, and laziness," wrote Friedman in 2009, dismissing news of a serious illness as "totally hokum" and adding cryptically: "He's also a publicity hound who thinks that news of illness will make him sympathetic to the public. He learned this from Elizabeth Taylor, his one-time best friend."

Friedman seemed to be suggesting that Taylor had advised Jackson to milk his audience for compassion and solicitude. Illness could be a resource. The implication was that Taylor herself had exploited her public's kind-heartedness by dramatizing her several infirmities over the years. This is a view worth exploring in more detail and I will return to it shortly. For now, let me just note the skepticism that seemed to be emerging among a media inured to stories of Jackson's perpetual sickness.

The "whys" proliferated: apart from the obvious "why does the world's bestselling recording artist need money?" there was "why is he looking so thin, even emaciated?" "why is he always wearing an oversize fedora?" and, most arrestingly, "why is he wearing a surgical mask that covers his nose and mouth?" With three months to go before the opening performance in London, Jackson cut a curious figure. (Actually, the surgical mask was not such a new innovation: he had worn one intermittently since at least 2002, when he showed up in a Santa Maria courthouse to defend himself in a $20 million breach of contract and fraud case.)

The promoters of the London concerts, AEG Live tried to put a lid on the rumors. President and CEO Randy Phillips claimed: "He's as healthy as he can be—no health problems whatsoever." Responding to British tabloid stories that he was consulting "a dermatologist in Beverly Hills" [presumably Klein] and had treatable skin cancer, Phillips, in 2009, told CNN's Denise Quan Jackson "had passed a stringent physical exam' before contracts were signed." "And he'll have to take another before the shows start."

Jackson did not take the second medical: on Friday, June 25, Dr. Conrad Murray found Jackson unconscious at his home and called paramedics. Two hours later, Jackson was pronounced dead at UCLA's medical center, the initial cause of death thought to have been cardiac arrest. Murray, a cardiologist, who had befriended Jackson in 2006 after treating one of his children, had been hired by AEG Live at Jackson's request. His salary was $150,000 per month (it was later discovered that Murray's debts were more than \$780,000). Eight months later Murray was charged with manslaughter after Jackson's death was ruled a homicide by the Los Angeles coroner. In November 2011, Murray was sentenced to four years' imprisonment. Jackson's mother, Katherine, and three children later sued AEG Live for wrongful death, arguing the firm negligently hired and supervised Murray. A jury found in favor of AEG Live, concluding that the firm had no reason to question Murray's judgment.

Several drugs were found in Jackson's system, though a lethal amount of Propofol, the fast-acting anxiety-reducing drug that slows the activity of the brain and nervous system (and is typically used to help patients relax prior to surgery), was identified as the cause of death. Murray's lawyers' defense claimed that Jackson injected himself with the lethal dose and that Murray had been trying to wean Jackson off Propofol (popularly known as "milk of amnesia"). He prescribed it, lawyers said, to combat Jackson's insomnia, which, the defense said, was a side effect of Jackson's prior dependence on Demerol. This is the trademark for Pethidine, the compound used as a painkilling drug I have cited earlier in the book. According to Mark Seal, Frank Cascio had become concerned that Jackson was exhibiting symptoms that indicated "addiction to the narcotic pain medication" as early as 2000.

Seal recounts how in that year: "[Jackson] dialed his Demerol dermatologist, Dr. Klein. He put the doctor on speaker and asked him to verify that the quantity of Demerol he was taking was safe and appropriate." Whether Taylor actually recommended the drug to Jackson is uncertain, though this possibility has been aired, for example in the book by Victor Gutierrez (1997). And, following Jackson's death, when Murray was on trial, the defense team argued that Klein provided Jackson with vast amounts of Demerol "for no valid medical purpose," thus inducing an enfeebling dependency. The judge said it was "not relevant" and Klein was spared an appearance. No Demerol was found in Jackson's body after his death.

Despite escaping involvement in the legal case, Klein was soon submerged under an avalanche of litigation, accusations and, ultimately (in January 2012), bankruptcy. The relative influence of Klein and, for that matter, Taylor on Jackson's habits is unknowable, though all accounts indicate that both she and Jackson were habitual users of Demerol and that Klein prescribed and administered the drug to both. Klein's intentions are opaque: he conceivably might after all have urged Taylor to spend a purgative second spell at Betty Ford; and he could resist being blamed for Jackson's eventual escalation to the various other drugs found in his system at his death. It seemed an outrageous perversity of fortune, but the two prodigies from different generations were united at first by common childhoods and later mutual affection, but also by debilitating "shared dependencies," as Gerald Posner calls them. Perhaps even more perversely, there was one more unity, but I will cover that in the next chapter.

It was more a postscript than a sequel, but the triadic drama had one further act when Taylor, having praised Klein fulsomely for almost thirty years, turned on him sharply. Klein brought this in on himself in 2010 by telling TMZ.com, the celebrity gossip website, that Jackson was gay. There was more: Klein said that his own office manager, Jason Pfeiffer, had been "the love of [Jackson's] life." The syndicated tv newsmagazine *Extra* aired an interview with Pfeiffer, who declared, "I just assumed that he [MJ] was probably bisexual" (in *Extra*, April 29 2010; here: http://bit.ly/12YQ8wi accessed September 2015).

Apart from the angry reaction of Jackson's family, there was a four-part outburst from Taylor's twitter account: "Dr. Arnie Klein declared on May 2 that he did not betray Michael Jackson by saying publicly that he had a homosexual relationship with someone in Arnie's office. It seems he supplies not only women (Debbie Rowe), but men too . . . how convenient." Klein explained, again to TMZ.com, that his declaration was meant "to shoot down rumors that Jackson was a pedophile" (TMZ staff, May 3, 2010: http://bit.ly/1suHElk accessed September 2015.) He also tweeted: Dearest Elizabeth Michael CHOSE whom he loved; I only SUPPLIED medical care. May God bless you and Michael. Your friend Arnie."

The *Los Angeles Times'* Harriet Ryan, in January 2012, wrote: "Jackson's family blasted the report, which Pfeiffer now concedes was 'embellished,'" and Taylor castigated her longtime pal publicly. "I thought doctors, like priests, took an oath of confidentiality. May God have mercy on his soul," Taylor tweeted. Did she still regard Klein as a friend? Almost certainly not, though the reasons for her fury are slightly puzzling. Even if Jackson was gay (and we still do not know), so what? Taylor was hardly homophobic. Perhaps she was affronted that Jackson might have been in the closet and never confided in her; or confided in her and assured her that, apart from sexual partners, she was the only person who knew; or made her swear she must never tell. No one will ever know. Then, straight out of left field, came a recantation: Klein issued a statement on his Facebook page (no longer available), in which he denied Jackson had been involved in a relationship with Pfeiffer. TMZ.com again reported this, as did *Vanity Fair's* Mark Seal: "Klein took back his statement about the purported affair, posting on Facebook, 'Allegations about . . . Jason being Michael Jackson's lover are ridiculous. That story was made up.'" Klein died in 2015 after suffering abdominal pains.

In the aftermath of Jackson's death, the full extent of his money problems became known: he left debts of $500 million. Ironically, his earnings leapt immediately after he died: his estate received a $60 million advance for the film *This Is It*; sales of a Jackson-themed videogame, memorabilia and a re-released autobiography brought in an additional $50 million; and a significant spike in radio play and album sales produced nearly $50 million in rights. Other sources of revenue effectively wiped out half his debt within twelve months of his demise. He also owned a publishing catalog that would ensure a colossal income for his estate for years to come, reported Zack O'Malley Greenberg for *Forbes* in 2010. It sounds crass, but Jackson was worth more in death than he was in life. Five years after his death, Jackson was still the highest earning dead celebrity.

And if he had lived? Jackson may not have completed the hugely ambitious fifty concerts scheduled for London. Several medics speculated his drugs intake so was so formidable, it would have killed him. Many have prognosticated similarly about Keith Richards, of course. Perhaps he would have pulled a sickie or two, missed a few dates and somehow managed to get through; in which case it is possible he would have gone on to perform 260 shows as part of his planned "This Is It" world tour. The movie *This Is It* showed him rehearsing with his customary perfectionism for the tour. There were plans for further films. Whether he would have remained at Neverland after the scandal is another question: perhaps he would have found Europe more congenial. Taylor and Burton both found a kind of sanctuary in Europe and Mexico, though today's media have global surveillance.

Jackson's eldest son Prince Michael was twelve when his father died. His daughter Paris-Michael Katherine was eleven. Debbie Rowe was their mother. Prince Michael II (Blanket) who was born to an unknown surrogate mother, was seven. So it is probable that Prince Michael would have gone to college, leaving the others with their father.

Of course, legal action never seemed far away from Jackson, even after his death. Had he lived, no doubt allegations would have flared up as they typically do once famous figures are accused of impropriety. This would ensure he stayed in the public consciousness, as much for his suspected sexual proclivities as his showmanship. Taylor would no doubt have continued to defend him unflinchingly, as she did before his death. But, of course, he would have been robbed of one of his most vigilant allies within two years. Taylor's loyalty was matched by Jackson's fans, who literally worshiped him—and I stress *literally* because they expressed their adoration and devotion as worshipful followers of deities often do. Even five years after his death his Facebook page had 75 million "likes," more than Justin Bieber's, Katy Perry's or Lady Gaga's (though not as many as Shakira's 100m+). So Jackson's tribulations would have hardened the resolve of his followers, not deterred them. What seems certain is that Jackson would have become an even more polarizing character than he was in the 2000s. Those who loved him were unshakable; those who despised him were equally unshakable. He was a misunderstood, sweet-natured and unfairly maligned genius, who dispensed his love generously to some, a fiendishly devious pervert who exploited others' kindness to others.

Taylor was obviously in the former camp. And, if she ever remotely suspected his dangerous tendencies, she forgave him his trespasses. She was one of the first to arrive at Jackson's funeral at the Forest Lawn Cemetery in Glendale, California. She arrived in a wheelchair, which was placed at the end of a row of seats at the private service. Days before, there had been a memorial service but Taylor had declined to attend and deliver a eulogy, her reason being: "I just don't believe that Michael would want me to share my grief with millions of others. How I feel is between us. Not a public event." She tweeted this to her 320,000 or so followers.

There may have been another reason for her absence. According to Stacy Brown, of the *New York Post*, Jackson's mother, Katherine, "hated Taylor" and often said: "She's stolen my son away" (October 13, 2013). But, let us assume Taylor's version reveals her true motivation: she did not want her intense sorrow displayed to countless others by the media.

Recall the transcript in this chapter's preamble:

Larry King: So you think they were out after him?
Elizabeth Taylor: I do.

King asked for a clarification of who "they" were. "The authorities and the like?" he prompted. Taylor answered haltingly: "I think the paparazzi started—not the paparazzi, the press." It was a slightly hesitant reply, but its import was clear enough: Taylor believed the media waged a campaign to undermine and, ultimately, destroy Jackson. Others have argued similarly. Julian Vigo, a professor at Université de Montréal, wrote in 2010: "The paradox of Michael Jackson is that all parts of his life were rendered public" (p. 31) Why is it a paradox? There appears to be nothing absurd or self-contradictory about this proposition. Unless Vigo means that, despite having gone to enormous lengths to conceal his private life and lived as a virtual recluse, he was the subject of some of the most invasive and perhaps aggressive media surveillance and conjecture in history. There seemed no aspect of his life that was not made transparent to everyone. That symmetry again: Jackson, like Taylor, was obliged to engage in confessionals, acknowledging and denying to the media, if only to manage the condemnation creep. Between the announcement of the child molestation charges in 2005 and his death in 2009, Jackson was not a singer, an actor, even a star: he was, as was Taylor, *news*.

In the 1960s and for most of the 1970s, the media was responsive and so amenable to a degree of control. In Jackson's era, media had become creative and slippery, hence making them practically unmanageable. For the final sixteen years of his life, Jackson seemed to be battling adversity, hysteria, and unconstrained opprobrium. His fans' staunch allegiance was no doubt a direct reaction to this. Struck with the seemingly impossible task of redeeming him, fans attached themselves to him with a fidelity probably never before witnessed. "It was not sufficient to worship Jackson as a great entertainer," wrote Paul Hollander in 2010, "he had been also transformed into a veritable saint and tragic figure" (p. 147). Even after his death, fans kept vigils, commemorated his life and paid homage to him, and will continue to do so for decades to come.

In 1990, with Taylor fighting for her life in an intensive care unit in a Santa Monica hospital, inundated with well-wishing cards and flowers, Elizabeth Sporkin commented on the public exhibition of Taylor's "47 years of health crises." Every development of the latest scare, from her 104-degree fever to her eventual recovery had been minutely monitored by the media, as had every other development been for almost all of her life. Taylor's medical history had been "played out on an all-too-public stage." It is an unusual way of describing someone's health problems and one that finds a partner in Neeraja Sundaram's phrase "the performance of Jackson's illness."

Writing in 2011, Sundaram describes the popular representations of the many ailments that affected Michael Jackson. She is not referring to the sicknesses themselves; she means their projection and circulation through images and texts. In other words, how the media presented or portrayed the infirmities and incorporated them into the Jackson icon—and I am using icon in the sense of a symbol worthy of veneration, rather than a human being. I will extend Sundaram's phrase: both Jackson and Taylor had theatrically spectacular performances of illness that beguiled audiences in an almost ghoulish way. Lurching from one near-death, or near-near-death experience to the next or to an enervating incapacity became part of a performance. This is not a heartless interpretation of others' suffering: it is a candid understanding of the media's penchant for making that suffering entertaining.

I am taking liberties with Sundaram's term and she does not intend to depict Jackson's serial sicknesses as a form of entertainment. I do. Consumers enjoyed learning about the various diseases, afflictions, indispositions, or just complaints. They might even have suspected some of them were not genuine; just pretenses to engender sympathy. There is no way of knowing whether Roger Friedman was right in mischievously raising the possibility that Jackson had taken a valuable lesson from Taylor when she told him illness could be a resource. Even if she did, she would not have been the only celebrity to exploit public compassion. In any case, would she have been right?

Sympathy is not the only emotion audiences feel when they see or hear of a celebrity's incapacitation: there is also an indeterminate emotion that lies somewhere between *schadenfreude* and assurance. Daniel Harris provides a steer: "We use the media 'vultures' we profess to despise to amass incriminating evidence that our idols aren't immortal after all, that their bodies fall apart just as ours do, that they get fat, go bald, shrivel up, and, most importantly, die" (p. 617).

Harris was writing in 2008 and was not proposing we take pleasure from celebrities' misfortunes exactly; he was not even claiming we need the confidence and certainty that famous figures, for all their apparent powers, are eventually going to shuffle off this mortal coil. Harris was specifically interested in the deaths of celebrities, but, if I can modify his argument without distorting it, it seems to offer a way of understanding our fascination with the health of Jackson and Taylor and why we found their ailing physical conditions entertaining.

Taylor was probably stricken with the same kind of illnesses as any other child in the Western world. But, when she broke her foot while filming *Lassie Come Home,* it became the first entry in what was to become an epic register of health problems, compounded, of course, by her own predilection for alcohol and her reliance on painkillers to mute the effects of other ailments. The **+** symbols on the timeline on pages 1–17 indicate the major incidences of ill health, at least as reported by the media.

Jackson's infirmities were not features of his childhood or adolescence for that matter. He was twenty-five when his accident on the set of the Pepsi commercial made headlines around the world. The burns alone were big news, though Pepsi's $1.5million compensation payment, which Jackson donated to a Californian medical center, underscored the seriousness of the pyrotechnical mishap. There were doubts about whether vitiligo was the cause of his apparent loss of pigmentation, though his autopsy confirmed he suffered from this skin condition. Klein had diagnosed lupus, probably as early as 1983, though this was not disclosed to the media at the time. His response to illness, like Taylor's, created as many problems as it solved and, while he did not drink alcohol (at least, not until the period immediately before his death when he drank wine to help him sleep, according to Fay Strang's 2013 report), his drugs habits contributed to his physical fragility.

In Jackson's case, media speculation on his health took on a life of its own. If he had suffered from all the afflictions attributed to him by the media, it would have been a miracle if he had seen forty, let alone fifty—the age at which he died. These included cancer, anorexia nervosa, lung disorders, and various mental health problems, especially body dysmorphia (which makes people conscious of their perceived physical deficiencies). Jackson's physical seclusion and reluctance to engage with the media with regularity, effectively handed the media a blank patient chart.

Death may be, as Harris called it, "the ultimate democratic epiphany," but sickness has democratizing reverberations. It reminds fans that celebrities are susceptible to exactly the same kinds of illnesses as everyone else; their bodies are vulnerable, unprotected, and always at risk, no matter how much they try to guard against sickness and how much access they have to medical facilities. "Our contact with celebrities is so limited that we view them as mirages until the one event that restores them their real physical presence," wrote Harris, with death in mind (p. 619).

Prolonged ill health and, in the cases of Taylor and Jackson, life-threatening conditions, have much the same effect: they serve as reminders of their fleshly mortality, at the same time enhancing the feeling of intimacy. Their wealth, glamour, and pizzazz often obscures how close celebrities are to everyone else. But the performance of illness brings them into range.

FIGURE 18 *"My body's a real mess," Taylor told* W *magazine in 2004, when aged seventy-two. "I've become one of those poor little old women who's bent sideways." She was largely confined to a wheelchair at the time.*

Photo by Kevin Winter/Getty Images.

18

Only the custodian

Sometimes, it is difficult to know whether people have an endless capacity to forgive and forget, or just suffer from poor memory. In 1964, with Taylor married to Richard Burton and Debbie Reynolds married to businessman Harry Karl, the women made peace after a chance meeting on the *Queen Elizabeth II* cruise ship. Six years before, Taylor had swept like a harpy into Reynold's life, taking her husband and wrecking her seemingly perfect domestic life. Had Reynolds completely forgotten? Hardly. Even allowing for her profound, if perplexing forgiveness, the chances of her actually working with Taylor would have been remote. Yet she did, though not until 2001. They both played in an ABC television film *These Old Broads*. The film proved that Reynolds was capable of forgiving a calamitous betrayal. It also proved that Taylor was capable of encircling herself and taking pot shots at someone she used to be.

Perhaps it was not such a surprising pairing: Taylor had for decades distanced herself from "the Elizabeth Taylor who's famous . . . a totally superficial working thing," so reflecting on her own *succès de scandale* seemed at least consistent. In the film, Taylor's and Reynolds' characters exchange sardonic stories about a man who had come between them years earlier. His name in the film is Freddie Hunter, the family name suggesting a pursuer of wild animals, rather than fish. He is the butt of several jokes, some about his limited sexual prowess. Carrie Fisher, daughter of Debbie and Eddie wrote the script.

The film also featured Joan Collins, then sixty-seven, who had been put on standby to play Cleopatra in 1961, when it was feared Taylor would not survive her illness. Shirley MacLaine, then sixty-six, was also in the film forty-five years after her breakthrough role as Princess Aouda in *Around the World in 80 Days*, directed by Taylor's third husband, Michael Todd. Taylor and Reynolds did not play themselves in the film, though their alter egos were visible. Reynolds' character is shown in a struggling casino; she actually did have a Las Vegas casino that failed in 1997. Taylor played a Hollywood agent (based on Sue Mengers, who represented several prominent artists, including Collins). She performed most of her scenes seated or in bed. By 2001, Taylor's osteoporosis combined with other ailments meant she could walk unassisted for only limited periods. She had surgery in 2004 to correct seven compression fractures in her spine. In the same year, she declared to Christopher Bagley of *W* magazine: "My body's a real mess." And she was largely confined to a wheelchair from that point. "I've become one of those poor little old women who's bent sideways." Taylor was seventy-two at the time of the interview.

The film with Reynolds was hardly an artistic highpoint for Taylor, who would announce her retirement from acting two years later. She would never act on screen again, though she voiced over a role for the animated series *God, the Devil and Bob*. Much of her productive time was spent on Aids charities or promoting her fragrances. Seven months after the television premiere of *These Old Broads*, Taylor attended the Michael Jackson 30th Anniversary concert at Madison Square Garden and, according to urban myth, tried to escape from New York with Jackson and Marlon Brando. I provided an alternative account of her post-9/11 activities in the previous chapter, though a third option comes from David Leafe, who, in 2013, contended that Taylor spent the days following the concert with—of all people—Reynolds, for whom she had procured a concert ticket, and, in desperation, called her ex-husband John Warner (they had divorced in 1982), who arranged for a private jet to take the two women to Los Angeles.

Over the next several years, Taylor receded from public view. One of the reasons was physical: by 2004, the back pain with which she had lived for many years combined with the effects of three hip replacement surgeries made walking too uncomfortable to bear and Taylor relied on a wheelchair. She resented being written-off, however. "There's some resilience in me that makes me keep fighting," she told Bagley in 2004. And, in 2006, with rumors about her apparently deteriorating health widespread, she went on CNN's *Larry King Live* and asked her host and, by implication, the viewers, "do I look like I'm dying? Do I look like or sound like I have Alzheimer's?"

While she maintained an interest in promoting her fragrances, which were her primary source of income, charity work remained close to her heart. Toward the end of 2007, she made what was to be her final dramatic appearance to raise funds for mobile Aids units. She was assisted on stage in a wheelchair to read her role in the epistolary play *Love Letters*. The play is a two-hander and requires little memorization as the characters read letters, cards, and notes.

Earlier in the year, Taylor, then seventy-five, had taken a vacation in Hawaii. Accompanying her was Jason Winters, an executive of Sterling/Winters, a management agency owned by Kathy Ireland, with whom Taylor had formed House of Taylor Jewelry in 2006. The agency represented Janet Jackson, Michael Jackson's sister. Taylor had first met Winters in the aftermath of her divorce from Larry Fortensky in 1996. Winters became one of Taylor's closest confidantes: he was a frequent visitor at her home and an escort whenever she appeared at public events.

Almost inevitably, stories of a new romance surfaced. Seven thousand miles away from Hawaii, the *London Standard* newspaper was reporting Taylor's "very public display of *amore*" (September 28, 2007). Actually, similar stories were circulating in the USA, though the *London Standard* and other British newspapers seemed confident Winters, then forty-seven, would become husband number nine. Neither Taylor nor Winters managed, or even tried, to quell the rumor, which gained momentum over the following years, culminating in an *Us Magazine* report of their engagement in 2010 (April 9).

News of an Elizabeth Taylor engagement may not have had the thunderclap resonance it had in the 1970s or 1980s, but it still reverberated. She had not been linked with a man, at least not in an amorous way, since 1999 when she was often sighted in the company of Cary Schwartz, a dentist with a practice in Santa Monica. Nothing developed then. But the Winters' association seemed to have more purchase. There was no "official comment," but the absence of a denial was sufficient. Confined to a wheelchair, fighting constant pain and barely a year after heart surgery, Taylor appeared to be ready to tie the knot again.

The news seemed particularly interesting for the African American media. By then Taylor's fathomless and, for many, unfathomable friendship with Michael Jackson had lost its mystery. But a superficially more conventional friendship with another black male offered a different kind of teaser. Smokey Fontaine's story for *NewsOne for Black America*, the online news source was headlined ELIZABETH TAYLOR ENGAGED TO BLACK MAN (April 2, 2010). There were ninety readers' comments, one of which mentioned, ". . . word on the street is homie is gay as can be, has a boyfriend." Many of Taylor's closest friends had been gay, of course; some of them had been linked romantically with her. Winters, it seemed, was the latest.

Usually not one to spoil a spiraling rumor, Taylor broke the habit of a lifetime by issuing a denial. "The rumors regarding my engagement simply aren't true," she tweeted in the spring of 2010. "Jason is my manager and dearest friend. I love him with all my heart." Maybe Michael Jackson's death in 2009 had robbed her of the sense of mischief that had for long been part of her character. She had used twitter to convey her thoughts: "I loved Michael with all my soul, and can't imagine life without him."

While it might have seemed a tad platitudinous, Taylor had been a close friend of Jackson's since 1984, when she famously walked out of his concert, and, for a quarter of a century, she had bonded, defended, and, at times, fought for him. So her prolonged distress was surely sincere. Perhaps his death robbed her of more than a friend.

By 2010, it seemed like every actor, pop star, and reality tv star was hawking a signature perfume. Taylor had, of course, set the template in 1988. Since then she had launched eleven fragrances, which had collectively yielded nearly $200 million in sales. In 2010, Taylor superintended the introduction of Violet Eyes, a product she initially wanted to call Follow Me. "So I put it to a vote, on twitter. Violet Eyes won, hands down, so my twitter followers [of which there were about 300,000] actually chose the name," Taylor told Genevieve Monsma, of *More* magazine in 2010.

Kathy Ireland insisted Taylor pored over the development of the product. "It's like being part of military strategy, [seeing] the way she [Taylor] handles every detail," Ireland told Emili Vesilind, of the *New York Times* in 2009. Despite her health problems, Taylor, on Ireland's account, found time to oversee the launch of the new perfume and provide copy for journalists. Even in her decline, she continued to brand what was effectively her own identity.

"I'm in London at the moment doing product research," Taylor informed Monsma. "I was able to meet with Prince Charles at Buckingham Palace for the naming of the Richard Burton Theatre building at the Royal Welsh College of Music & Drama." It was April 2010. Five years before, Taylor had agreed to help raise funds for the theater in Cardiff after being approached by Burton's brother, Graham Jenkins. She appeared at the ceremony dressed in red, the color of Wales' national symbol, the dragon. From her wheelchair, she presented a bronze bust of Burton to Prince Charles. The bust was destined to stand in the foyer of the new theater in Cathays Park, the civic center of Cardiff.

It was to be Taylor's last trip to the UK. As in the past, she stayed at London's Dorchester hotel, the scene of many exceptional moments in her life. She had stayed here with Burton at the height of the scandalous affair that made them the world's most infamous lovers. It was here on March 3, 1961, she had a near-death experience. As always, Taylor stayed in the hotel's most expensive 1,647 square feet Harlequin Suite, which had a pink marble bathroom installed at her request in the early 1960s.

Shortly before leaving for London, Taylor had posed for what turned out to be her final photoshoot. Her friend Firooz Zahedi took her portrait. Firooz was the cousin of Ardeshir Zahedi, the former Iranian ambassador, Taylor's onetime suitor from the 1970s. She had known Firooz since he accompanied her on her trip to Iran in 1976. (Zahedi has published widely since and is credited with several outstanding images, such as the one of Uma Thurman languishing on a motel bed for *Pulp Fiction*.)

After returning to LA, Taylor was seldom seen, save for the occasional sighting at The Bel Air hotel restaurant on Stone Canyon Road, or the Abbey, a gay bar in West Hollywood. Otherwise, she became more reclusive than ever, discouraging house calls from family and friends, relying on the companionship of a coterie of medics, walkers, and her dog. Taylor kept up communications with her still strong audience via social media. "I like the connection with fans and people who have been supportive of me," she told Kim Kardashian in an interview written up by Laura Brown for *Harper's Bazaar*. Published in March 2011, the story carried the title "Kim Kardashian: Cleopatra with a 'K'" and consisted of pictures of Kardashian in outfits that could have been part of Taylor's wardrobe when she played the Egyptian queen, and a Q&A featuring Kardashian and Taylor in which Taylor—without intending to be ironic (presumably)—concluded: "I think we know too much about our idols and that spoils the dream."

Taylor wasted no time in publicizing the interview, using twitter to pump up interest. "Our interview in Bazaar came out!" she tweeted, complimenting Kardashian, "You look like a princess in Egyptian robes, love!" At some level, it seemed like she was granting a permit; as if no one else could actually play the queen, but Kardashian had the looks to carry off the lesser role adequately. Taylor retained her moral authority to own the role of Cleopatra, but was gracious enough to acknowledge epigones.

The tweet was destined to be her penultimate public address. She was, at the time, preparing for another occasion, the twenty-fifth anniversary of amfAR gala, set for February 2 in New York. Taylor was to be honored for her longstanding charity work. Bill Clinton and fashion designer Diane Von Furstenberg were also due to receive awards. Taylor intended to wear a Badgley Mischka caftan she bought especially for the occasion and had briefed her team to write her an acceptance speech.

Taylor was preparing for the event when she was taken ill and admitted to the Cedars-Sinai Medical Center. Any event in Taylor's life was almost immediately the subject of scrutiny by the media, so a precipitate response from the tabloid media was hardly a surprise. The *National Enquirer* was first off the mark with a February 10 report that Taylor had been taken to the hospital, suffering from intense abdominal pain. Sally Morrison, Taylor's publicist issued a statement, playing down the seriousness of the situation and explaining Taylor's decision to withdraw from the amfAR event: "Unfortunately, the combination of the unstable weather conditions and the fact that she was feeling under the weather forced her to make the decision not to travel."

Morrison addressed the emerging conjecture: "It seems that the combination of her non attendance last night, combined with the fact she was photographed last week leaving her dentist's office in a wheelchair, has caused a lot of negative speculation."

The speculation may not have been completely accurate but its import was correct. Taylor was treated for symptoms caused by congestive heart failure, a condition she disclosed she had in November 2004. The initial expectation was that she would stay in the hospital for the next several days as a precautionary measure. An announcement on February 12 prompted no alarm. "With her history, they're going to want to keep her in for a while just to make sure they've fixed what they needed to fix," announced Morrison. It sounded almost nonchalant.

At the amfAR event, Sir Elton John accepted Taylor's honor on her behalf and passed along a message from her: "I am there in spirit and I join you in saluting my fellow honorees and all these extraordinary leaders. I am inspired by their example, exhilarated by their vision, and encouraged by their compassion and love. And I love them in return." This was her final address.

"She had a pretty good day Saturday, and a good night," announced Morrison the Monday following Taylor's hospitalization, indicating that Taylor was resting comfortably and was likely to spend a few more days in the hospital. A week after Taylor's admittance to the hospital, Morrison issued what sounded a hopeful statement: "There has been steady improvement in her condition . . . it is hoped and expected that this will continue over the next few days. For now, she will remain under their care in the hospital for continued monitoring." On February 27, Taylor spent her seventy-ninth birthday at the hospital. A further statement from Morrison made it clear she proposed a postponement rather than cancellation of her annual celebration: "Elizabeth Taylor will spend a quiet birthday this year as she continues to rest and recover at Cedars-Sinai. She plans to watch the Academy Awards with family and close friends and will be rooting for *The King's Speech*. A proper birthday celebration will be planned for when she returns home." Her birthday wish came true when *The King's Speech* won the Academy Award for best picture. It was a solitary good omen.

Taylor's condition took an unexpectedly dramatic turn for the worse and, as her condition deteriorated in early March, she was placed on a respirator, an apparatus used to induce artificial respiration. It was not her first encounter with such a machine: in April 1990, when suffering from pneumonia and with her health deteriorating, she was ventilated to assist her breathing, while at the St. John's Hospital and Health Center in Santa Monica. She was then fifty-eight and strong enough to recover from what was her second "near-death" experience; her first was when she was making *Cleopatra* in 1961.

This time, she would not recover. On March 15, 2011, a number of newspapers, including *USA Today*, ran an Associated Press story: "Elizabeth Taylor has entered her second month at Cedars-Sinai Medical Center in Los Angeles, where she is being treated for symptoms of congestive heart failure." Morrison confirmed that she continued to receive treatment but did not elaborate on Taylor's condition or prognosis.

Surrounded by her four children, Taylor died of complications from congestive heart failure at 1:28 a.m. on March 23 at the age of seventy-nine. She had been in the hospital for six weeks. Morrison made a brief announcement, stating that she had died peacefully in her sleep. Her son Michael Wilding issued a longer statement. It read:

My Mother was an extraordinary woman who lived life to the fullest, with great passion, humor, and love. Though her loss is devastating to those of us who held her so close and so dear, we will always be inspired by her enduring contribution to our world. Her remarkable body of work in film, her ongoing success as a businesswoman, and her brave and relentless advocacy in the fight against HIV/AIDS, all make us all incredibly proud of what she accomplished. We know, quite simply, that the world is a better place for Mom having lived in it. Her legacy will never fade, her spirit will always be with us, and her love will live forever in our hearts.

As well as Wilding, Taylor's other survivors included her daughters Maria Burton-Carson and Liza Todd-Tivey, son Christopher Wilding, ten grandchildren, and four great-grandchildren.

Even in death, Taylor provoked controversy: within days of her demise, members of the Westboro Baptist Church revealed plans to picket her funeral. The Topeka, Kansas-based congregation disparaged Taylor and stated its intention to demonstrate at her funeral. Opting to send out its message on social media, the church tweeted: "No RIP Elizabeth Taylor who spent her life in adultery and enabling proud fags. They cuss her in hell today. #Westboro will picket funeral!"

Since 1991, under the leadership of Fred Phelps (who died in 2014), the church, which espoused a rigid and unforgiving Calvinist ideology, and specialized in homophobic rhetoric, had picketed many funerals, its protesters sometimes holding placards displaying "God Hates Fags" and similar messages. The church had picketed the funeral of Michael Jackson in 2009. So its response to Taylor's death was, in many ways, predictable. Phelps's daughter referred to Taylor as a "serial-adulterous fag hag."

It was the last sign, statement, or expression of disapproval. Taylor had become inured to opprobrium so it seemed perversely appropriate that she should be condemned even in the immediate aftermath of her dying, a time typically reserved for mourning and gracious appreciation. Transgression, passion, drama, and unpredictability followed Taylor in life. It would have been fitting—if regrettable—if her funeral had been convulsed by fanatical hellfire-and-brimstone protesters. In the event, it was not and the dignity of the private funeral was left intact.

The funeral was held the day after her death in keeping with the Jewish faith to which Taylor had converted in 1959 before her marriage to Eddie Fisher. About forty-five friends and members of her family attended the ceremony at Forest Lawn memorial park, where many celebrities including Jean Harlow, James Stewart, Clark Gable, Errol Flynn, Humphrey Bogart, Nat King Cole, and Spencer Tracy were buried. Michael Jackson was also there. Taylor was interred in the great mausoleum but in a different wing from Jackson. The service ended speculation that Taylor might be buried alongside Burton. Although Burton and Taylor had made plans when they were married to be buried together in Pontrhydyfen in South Wales, he was buried in the Swiss village of Céligny, near Geneva. Members of the Burton family declared they would honor her wish to be buried near his home village in South Wales if that desire was included in her will, though, as I noted earlier, Burton's widow, Sally, had bought the adjoining plot and placed a large headstone across the two graves possibly to ensure that Taylor could not be buried next to him.

The service began 15 minutes after its announced start time in observance of Taylor's parting wish that her funeral start late, Morrison said, informing the media that Taylor had specifically left instructions asking for a tardy start and had requested that someone announce, "She even wanted to be late for her own funeral." The proceedings were watched at a respectful distance by a phalanx of the world's media, including circling helicopters.

A bigger event attended by nearly 400 family and friends was held in October on the Warner Brothers studio lot. Actor Colin Farrell hosted the memorial. Taylor had struck up an unlikely friendship with the Irish actor in the months leading up to her death. Farrell had been at the Cedars-Sinai Medical Center for the birth of his son in 2009. At the time, Taylor was having treatment at the facility.

No one knew precisely how much Taylor was worth on her death. Her earnings derived primarily, perhaps almost exclusively, from the fragrances, though there were residuals, these being royalties paid for repeats of movies on television (she still collected money from *Cleopatra* and from Todd's *Around the World in 80 Days*). Elizabeth Arden reported that her fragrances had generated $1 billion in sales since 1991, leading speculators to conclude that her wealth was somewhere between $600 million and $1 billion. At the time of Taylor's death, White Diamonds was the bestselling celebrity perfume ever and sales were bound to bounce in the aftermath of her death as fans sought to validate their relationship at the department store counter. The value of her personal jewelry collection became a topic of speculation. Taylor herself had once said: "I feel as though I'm only the custodian of my jewelry. When I die and they go off to auction I hope whoever buys them gives them a really good home."

Taylor left behind a cornucopia of personal effects, including 269 individual jewels, an haute couture collection of 400 outfits, and paintings by Degas, Renoir, and Van Gogh. In a sense, they offered an index of an extravagant life lived in the public sphere. There was a black velvet evening cape, emblazoned with giant silver scorpions that Taylor wore to the fortieth birthday party of Princess Grace of Monaco. A silk chiffon wedding dress served as a reminder of the first of her two marriages to Burton. Her jewels formed a narrative in their own right. The various items were integrated into an exhibition that moved around the world, stopping in London, Paris, Dubai, and Hong Kong before the grand auction in New York.

In December 2011, with public interest in Taylor showing no signs of diminishing, her jewelry went under the hammer at Christie's in New York. The auction was preceded by a ten-day showcase that sold 25,000 tickets at $30 each and included a highlight reel, showing excerpts from her major films and clips from home movies. The sale of eighty items from Taylor's jewelry collection had been expected to raise between $35m and $40m but this was based on a market prices and took no account of the Elizabeth Taylor premium, the sum added to the ordinary price by its provenance: being once owned by Taylor conferred added value. The auction of the jewels alone took in $116 million, more than double the record for a single-owner collection. The previous highest was in 1987 when the Duchess of Windsor's jewels sold for just over $50 million.

From the very first item, a charm bracelet estimated at about $30,000, it was clear the Taylor cachet would deliver way beyond expectations. The bracelet fetched $326,500. Among the other gems sold was La Peregrina, the 50.6-carat natural pearl, given to Taylor by Burton as a Valentine's gift in 1969; this was once owned by Mary Tudor of England on her engagement to Spain's Philip II in 1554, and belonged to a succession of eight Spanish kings, after being discovered by a slave in sixteenth-century Panama. Taylor had commissioned Cartier to design a ruby-and-diamond necklace mount for the piece. The item sold for $11.8 million, almost $9 million more than expected and the single most expensive item in the collection.

The famed Elizabeth Taylor Diamond (also known as the Taylor-Burton Diamond, and formerly the Krupp diamond) sold for $8.8 million to a South Korean entrepreneur. The 33.19-carat ring, also a gift from Burton, who bought it in 1969 for $300,000, was originally estimated at $2.5 million to $3.5 million. The Taj Mahal ruby and gold chain, with a heart-shaped diamond, by Cartier, sold for $8.81 million to an anonymous buyer. The diamond is believed to have been owned by Emperor Shah Jahan (1592–1666) and given to his favorite wife, Mumtaz-i-Mahal. The emperor's grief at her death four years later inspired him to commission the majestic Taj Mahal in her memory. The necklace was a fortieth-birthday gift from Burton. It was estimated at $300,000 to $500,000. (The diamond's provenance was subsequently disputed by the buyer, who demanded the cancellation of the sale.) A diamond tiara, Michael Todd's 1957 gift to Taylor sold for $4.2 million, a staggering six times the estimate. Kim Kardashian paid $64,500 for three diamond and jade bracelets, which had an estimated price of only $8,000. Only two items sold within auction estimates, making it record-breaking.

"This truly is one of the greatest jewelry collections in the world," Rahul Kadakia, head of jewelry for Christie's Americas told Chris Michaud, of Reuters in 2011. "But in my wildest dreams, I did not think we would outsell the estimate by five times." The estimates were based on what François Curiel, Christie's Asia president and head of Christie's jewelry department called the items' "intrinsic value" and took no account of the value of Taylor's status.

The second day of the jewelry auction was less spectacular, bringing the overall sale to more than $137 million. A portion of the proceeds was earmarked for the Elizabeth Taylor Aids Foundation.

Taylor's haute couture, artwork, scripts, and other items were sold separately, some in London. While the New York jewelry auction is well documented, the artwork auction at Christie's in London in February 2012 is often overlooked. Yet is presents a reliable guide to Taylor's tastes. The three most significant works were Edgar Degas's *Autoportrait*, Pissarro's *Pommiers d'Eragny*, and Van Gogh's *Vue de l'asile et de la Chapelle de Saint-Remy*. An appreciation of art ran in Taylor's family: her father, Francis, and great-uncle Howard Young were dealers, of course. In fact, Francis bought the Van Gogh on her behalf at an auction in 1963, paying £92,000 ($140,500). At the London auction, this fetched £10.1 million ($15.5 million), the highest price of any item in the entire Taylor portfolio. The Degas self-portrait and the Pissarro landscape sold for £713,250 ($1.1 million) and £2.9million ($4.5 million) respectively. This meant the combined total of the three artworks realized more than double the £6.2 million estimate, highlighting the efficacy of the Elizabeth Taylor premium across sectors. As with the proceeds from the New York auction, a portion was donated to Taylor's Aids foundation.

The total amount accrued from the auctions was $184 million, or over £120 million. When added to the $75 million from the sales fragrances, money from property disposals and the movie residuals, Taylor's earnings for the twelve months after her death reached $210 million, giving her the somewhat ambiguous distinction of being the top-earning dead person for 2012, according to *Forbes*'s Dorothy Pomerantz. In previous and, indeed, subsequent years, Michael Jackson occupied the top spot, largely because of sales of his music and his ownership of a 50 percent stake in Sony's ATV music publishing catalog (which includes the likes of Taylor Swift and Lady Gaga, as well as the Beatles). His estate earned $145 million in 2012 and comparable amounts in the following years. This is the perverse link I alluded to earlier, the one that united Taylor and Jackson after death: they were, for a while, the top-earning dead celebrities.

After the one-off auctions, Taylor's revenue stream depended on her other interests, which brought her estate about $20 million per year. (After Jackson, Elvis Presley is consistently the next highest-earning dead celebrity, with an annual income of about $55 million, then Charles Schulz, the creator of "Peanuts," before Taylor; Marilyn Monroe usually lies behind Taylor, her seemingly everlasting brand yielding about $17 million annually.)

There were no unseemly family feuds over Taylor's money; no probate filing, no copies of her will published on the web, and no high-profile court battles. In fact, very little was, or is, publicly known about her estate, apart from its worth. After her death, it became known that she had created The Elizabeth Taylor Trust and funded it with her assets (including her publicity rights, to manage her name, likeness, and image). According to some reports, she started this in 1998, when she fell and fractured her lower back. There were unverified reports that the Trust left most of her assets to her children, grandchildren, and charities, including her own foundation; but the document supposedly confirming this was not made public. The reason there is so much uncertainty about these matters is that Taylor's trust was and is still a revocable living trust, which means, unlike a will, which is a public record and thus open to scrutiny, it can remain private. Only the trust's beneficiaries and trustees, and their respective legal representatives and accountants were privy to the contents. (A revocable living trust is a legal arrangement created by a person effectively to own his or her assets. After death the assets transfer to the beneficiaries. It is called a revocable trust because, unlike an irrevocable trust, it can be amended or discontinued at any time.) After living so much of her life in public, she opted to make the dispersal of her money a secret affair.

"Always a progressive and savvy business woman, she [Taylor] established The Elizabeth Taylor Trust with specific instructions to develop and grow the business ventures she established during her lifetime," states the Elizabeth Taylor webpage (http://bit.ly/1zFNs28 accessed September 2015). It goes on: "The mission of The Elizabeth Taylor Trust is to honor Elizabeth Taylor's life by creating products and experiences that transform a passion for beauty into a world with more compassion," and is signed by the Trustees, Barbara Berkowitz, one of Taylor's lawyers, Tim Mendelson, her longtime personal assistant, and her son Christopher Wilding.

De mortuis nil nisi bonum. Roughly translated, it means speak no ill of the dead. It seemed untimely and more than a little disrespectful when, just nineteen months after Taylor's death, an exposé purporting to reveal hitherto unknown evidence of Taylor's sexual incontinence was published. Consider for a moment: this was Taylor, the girl who played with fire, a woman whose colossal reputation was built, in large part, on her sexuality; not just her sexual activity, but her capacity to fascinate, captivate, charm, seduce, beguile, entice and, generally, make men's mouths water. Even the solemnity of her charitable work and political sorties did not erase memories of those couple of decades when she redefined female sexuality.

What more was there to say about her? Maybe something like an account of the time she walked in on her first husband Nicky Hilton (who died in

1969) to find him in flagrante with Marilyn Monroe (d. 1962)? Or how, as a fifteen-year-old, she seduced future US President Ronald Reagan (d. 2004)? A description of her threeway liaison with another President, John F. Kennedy (d. 1963), and actor Robert Stack (d. 2003), perhaps?

These—often lurid—details, were in a book by Danforth Prince and Darwin Potter who argued that Taylor also had affairs with, among many others, Peter Lawford (d. 1984), Errol Flynn (d. 1959), Tony Curtis (d. 2010), Paul Newman (d. 2008), Frank Sinatra (d. 1998), and Swedish heavyweight boxing champion, Ingemar Johansson (d. 2009). The authors were clearly not interested in producing a hagiography. They claimed that, after Taylor's affair with Sinatra petered out, she tried to trap him into marrying her by claiming she was pregnant with his child. This story had circulated several years before in Kitty Kelley's 1987 tell-all biography of Sinatra. On this account, Sinatra scoffed at the idea and arranged for an abortion. Taylor had also been linked in some way with all the other men cited as her lovers. One of the self-evident reasons for her notoriety in the 1950s and 1960s is that she was portrayed as Hollywood's premier femme fatale: any man with whom she acted, or even met was potential prey for Taylor. Indeed, her well-earned reputation as a playmaker rather than a plaything earned her the respect of many—as we will see in the next chapter.

Taylor was a careful and able curator of her own commodity and, presumably, understood that the scarlet woman image was a defining resource after 1958. Far from challenging popular conceptions, she encouraged them. Rumors of her affairs with gay men or men suspected of being gay were sensational grist to the Taylor mill. She never explicitly denied relationships with Rock Hudson or James Dean, and tantalized journalists with allusions about their penchants. Much younger men were also useful material, which is why she nurtured hearsay about her friendship with Anthony Geary, with whom she played in *General Hospital* in the 1980s and who was fifteen years her junior, but who did not appear prominently in the exposé. He is still alive.

Once asked somewhat sarcastically by *People* magazine's Charles Leerhsen, "are you proud of your taste in men?" Taylor answered: "Oh yes. I wish I could bottle it like my perfume." She was acknowledging that they were both saleable items. In the same interview in 1996, when she was sixty-four and having divorced Larry Fortensky, Taylor declared: "I'm through with marriage, but I'm not through with men."

This is one probable reason why the book by Porter and Prince (who was also the president of the book's publishers) made less impact than a biography of this kind might otherwise have made. It was too predictable. How was it possible to shock consumers by disclosing supposed secrets about her sexual partners? The most pertinent question about Taylor would have been: what man, straight or gay, would not or had not succumbed to her? (Peter O'Toole's death in December 2013, became an occasion for tabloids to speculate on his supposed dalliance with Taylor). It meant that, instead of delivering a delicious feast of clandestine *bonnes bouches*, the book served up scrapings from the bottom of the pan to diners who had just polished off a five-course meal and were enjoying their cognac.

Another reason is that uncomplimentary books on celebrities frequently follow their death. In American law, there is no liability for defamation of dead people, either to the deceased or to the deceased's defendants or relatives. The law is much the same in the UK. This was tested quite rigorously in the aftermath of the death of Princess Diana: several claims about her purported relationships (including one with John F. Kennedy Jr.) were published. Neither Taylor nor Diana could be libeled, so neither of their families could sue.

No matter how outrageous the claims of authors, their impact is invariably lessened by posthumous publication. Libel laws are designed to protect only the living against unjustified attacks on their reputation. The impact of Porter and Prince's book was further dissipated by their subject's reputation, which had been under attack of one kind or another for at least the previous half-century. Taylor reveled in the *causes célèbres* she enkindled; without the attacks, she just would not have been Elizabeth Taylor, at least not the one we know.

FIGURE 19 *"Ms. Taylor managed the role of sex object effortlessly as if it too were just part of the job," wrote Manohla Dargis, of the New York Times.*

Photo by MGM Studios/Archive Photos/Getty Images.

19

Nobody can hurt her

Suppose Elizabeth Taylor had retired from acting in 1955. Already an established Hollywood star with twenty films to her credit, the 23-year-old explains: "I've just had my second baby and I want to be able to share fully in both of my children's lives. I'm happily married to my second husband, Michael Wilding, and he will carry on with his acting career, while I spend more time at home. I've been acting since as long ago as I can remember, so I think I'm due an early retirement."

The decision would doubtless have met with a lively reaction from her mother Sara, then sixty: "Are you going to walk away from everything we've been working toward? Everything we've built together since you were a little girl? This wasn't in the plan. Now that blonde skank will dominate. She has a new Billy Wilder movie out later this year: *The Seven Year Itch* will make her, you wait and see."

Hedda Hopper was a confidante as well as chronicler of Taylor's early life, and, as such, occupied an influential position. She too would have been dismayed, though probably not as angry. "My predictions don't always come true," she might have reminded Taylor. "But I still say you could have been the biggest Hollywood star in history. You have the world at your feet." She might also have admitted through gritted teeth: "That damn talent show host Arthur Godfrey wasn't far off the mark when he said you would quit showbiz to become a nun. He could still be right." (In her *Chicago Daily Tribune* column of June 22, 1962, Hopper recited Godfrey's outlandish forecast, on page 2, part 3, see http://trib.in/1xdc4iw accessed September 2015).

In 1947, when fifteen, Taylor told off her boss, MGM studio head Louis B. Mayer, arguably the most powerful man in Hollywood, for talking brusquely to her mother. She left the mogul's office crying, fully convinced she was going to get fired. Mayer had been deposed by 1955, but would probably have fumed: "The world outside Hollywood might be in awe of stars, but I regard them like worker ants. You're employees of the film studio, that's all. Studios are what really count. Remember what your friend Howard Hughes told Kate Hepburn: 'Actresses are cheap in this town.'"

(Actually, it was what Martin Scorsese imagined Hughes said to Hepburn, in the film *The Aviator*.)

But, let us assume Taylor ignored the reactions and walked away from the movies. What would be the consequences of her non-metamorphosis from child star into the world's most infamous woman? She would not have met Michael Todd and become one half of one of the most flamboyant and ostentatious couples in history. Todd was brash, perhaps even vulgar in his theatrical displays of wealth and indulgence. Taylor was complicit in his exhibitionism. Without him, she would have been a film star, though not (to repeat Rock Hudson for the final time) news. In this parallel reality, Hollywood actors would have remained, well, actors: not all-purpose celebrities.

There would be other glaring consequences too, the main one of which is: she would not have met Eddie Fisher and scandalized audiences in America and beyond. The world would have been deprived of an event that effectively invited, even demanded, everyone's opinion. There were no polls, though it seems reasonable to speculate retrospectively, her deeds registered mostly disapproval. No one would have seen the image that perfectly visualized the crux of the affair; it was not of Taylor, nor even her new man, but of the wronged woman, Debbie Reynolds.

The photograph of Reynolds, standing alone on her front lawn, diaper pin affixed to her shirt—as if reminding the world of her infant son—was the image that spoke volumes of Taylor. Reynolds, then twenty-six, had just been discarded by her husband for another woman. Taylor was not just another woman, of course: she was the world's most beautiful woman, a woman many thought could have any man she desired. It just happened that the man she desired at that time was married to one of the most popular, wholesome and endearing females in America, and father of her two children. Taylor just took him, as a child might take a schoolfriend's homework and claimed it as her own.

When the media tracked the scent of guilt to Taylor, she seemed untouched or at least unperturbed, her Marie Antoinette-like response practically challenging the media to do their worst. "Never before had celebrity scandal pushed so far into global consciousness," wrote David Kamp of *Vanity Fair*. It annihilated Fisher's career. It created Taylor's. The once child star and radiant adolescent who had charmed audiences was reborn as Jezebel incarnate.

What about the cultural changes that were to follow? Would our appetites, our sensibilities, our sheer receptivity to gossip, rumor and idle talk have changed without this event? We became avid consumers of news about others' lives, not just their outwardly available lives, as presented in the magazines and newspapers: but their so-called private lives, the parts the Hollywood machine kept away from all but the best informed columnists, like Hopper and her confederate-cum-rival Louella Parsons. Our tastes changed or were perhaps changed for us in the early 1960s when Taylor surpassed her previous outrageous wrongdoing with behavior that attracted the opprobrium of no lesser institution than the Vatican. In 1949 and the early 1950s, Rita Hayworth and Ingrid Bergman prompted scandals, having highly publicized affairs with Prince Aly Khan and Roberto Rossellini respectively. But whereas the landscape of the 1950s was disturbed, it remained fundamentally unchanged.

The same could not be said after Liz & Dick: elements of culture changed discernibly as a result. In particular, the media became sharper, proactive and more conjectural. Audiences wanted to make their own pronouncements on stories; in other words, become judgmental. Consumers in the 1960s did not just gaze awestruck at stars as if they were brightly-colored cephalopods swimming in an aquarium; they discussed the creatures' sexual proclivities or their self-destructive urges; later they would wonder whether some of them needed a spell outside the aquarium to rid themselves of unwanted habits; later still they would try to clamber into the tank to explore said creatures in greater detail, or even take up residency behind the glass.

Is it possible that paparazzi, that well-worn term of Italian origin that is now such a staple of our vocabularies would still be just an item in phrasebooks were it not for Taylor? *I paparazzi ci aspettano fuori?* /Are the paparazzi waiting outside? The word gained more currency with the emergence of Princess Diana in the 1990s, but it first slid into popular use during the *Cleopatra* scandal, and, of course, it has been there ever since.

Even after the scandals had subsided, Taylor commandeered the media, usually to her own advantage. She might have seemed as if she were constantly trying to escape reporters, if not impose some order on their pursuit, but she took time to take notes. It is difficult, if not impossible, to imagine another person so well versed in dealing with the media in the 1980s. And whether she turned her attention to Aids campaigns or peddling her own brand of fragrances, the results were the same: dramas. Whatever she did was dramatic. And, of course, the media responded instantly and unfailingly.

Would Aids have received the support it needed without Taylor and the tsunami of interest she created? Eventually perhaps. But remember: in the early 1980s, the "gay plague," as it was often called, was defined by some as retribution rather than disease. It was not a sickness likely to engender compassion from those who regarded it as a payback for promiscuous sodomy. Aids was regarded as much a moral pestilence as a treatable medical condition. Taylor's gift for embarrassing politicians, pressganging movie stars and, most importantly, ensnaring the media served the purpose of medicalizing the disease in the public mind.

It is a wonder more of us do not suffer repetitive strain injury through incessant clicking on the "Check out with PayPal" button. Celebrities seem to urge us to buy something or other every time we open a newspaper or glance at a screen of some kind. Taylor cannot take blame or credit for this, though, in 1987, when the product Elizabeth Taylor's Passion entered the market, the idea of integrating person and product had not been fully realized. Taylor probably owed the concept of a fragrance bearing her name, signature and image to her onetime suitor Henry Wynberg. Certainly, the years-long legal dispute suggests he had a legitimate claim that she eventually pried from him. Taylor could not even claim the distinction of becoming the first film star to launch a product that was marketed in a way that promised to convey the drama, sophistication and, as its name suggested, passion that were integral to her persona. Sophia had done this in 1981 with her self-named fragrance. There is still a product called Sofía on the market, but it bears the imprimatur of Ms. Vergara, not Señora Loren.

The brilliance of Taylor's enterprise was that it made her image and her purple perfume, bottled and boxed in purple and selling for a top-priced $200 (in 1987) ubiquitous: she occupied the counters of department stores everywhere dressed in white and (of course) purple, accessorized in her inimitable jewelry, her eyes flashing through advertising materials. She signed autographs and drank tea, chatting about anything her public wanted her to chat about.

Today, when someone like Beyoncé has enough merchandise associated with her to fill a mail order catalog and every aspiring celebrity needs to re-engineer themselves as marketing instruments as well as performers, the concept of perfume bearing someone's name sounds almost passé. But in the early 1980s, using someone who excited envy and desire to excite more envy and desire was more than a clever marketing ploy, it was a *tour de force*.

Still hypothesizing that Taylor had retired in 1955, let me raise another question: where would women be without her? It seems an unnecessary question with an obvious answer: same place as they are. Yet there is a strong argument that, without Taylor, feminism would have been robbed of one of its most powerful representatives and the changes feminism wrought would have been slowed without her encouragement. Let me be clear: Taylor was not affiliated to any wing of any organized feminist movement; nor did she align herself with feminist causes in the same way as, say, Jane Fonda or Lee Grant. This has not deterred some writers from appraising her importance to women.

Taylor, for all her seductive glamour, was no sex-prey. The opposite in fact: "Elizabeth Taylor could control men." That is the conclusion of Camille Paglia, one of a number of women who see in Taylor a rebuke to "a long feminist attack on the Hollywood sex symbol as a sex object, a commodified thing, passive to the male gaze" (p. 3).

Paglia was being interviewed in 2011 by *Salon* magazine, which asked her to reflect on a 1992 essay, in which she wrote: "Through stars like Taylor, we sense the world-disordering impact of legendary women like Delilah, Salome, and Helen of Troy." This is an unexpected evaluation of Taylor as a "pre-feminist." Readers will no doubt be familiar with Delilah, betrayer of Samson, and Helen of Troy, beauteous wife of Menelaus, whose abduction led to the Trojan War. But Salome is less well-known, at least to those not versed in the New Testament: a dancer extraordinaire, when granted a reward for her celebrated performance of the Dance of the Seven Veils, she asked for the head of St John the Baptist and so caused his beheading.

"Hollywood's Pagan Queen," as Paglia called her, represented a new kind of womanhood, not vulnerable or quiescent, but tough and questing, venturing into taboo areas but without ever being turned back. "There was a robustness about Elizabeth Taylor, compared to the vulnerability and emotional train wrecks that were Marilyn Monroe and Rita Hayworth," argued Paglia in the *Salon* article (p. 3).

Taylor "wields sexual power that feminism cannot explain and has tried to destroy ... the femme fatale expresses woman's ancient and eternal control of the sexual realm," Paglia claimed in the original 1992 essay (p. 17). She meant that, in the 1970s and 1980s, feminists were in a state of agitation over the objectification of women, particularly in the media: women were degraded to the status of objects, they argued. But Paglia disagreed: "For me, sexual objectification is a supreme talent," she wrote, citing Taylor as its quintessence.

Taylor was aware of public expectations and regarded her own objectification as obligatory. As Manohla Dargis, of the *New York Times*, put it in 2011: "Ms. Taylor managed the role of sex object effortlessly as if it too were just part of the job. In contrast to so many other actresses, she seemed as desiring as desirous, with the gift of a thrillingly unladylike appetite." (I presume Dargis means Taylor made her own yearnings conspicuous in the secure knowledge she was the object of *others'* yearnings.)

She is "like a goddess," advised Paglia, whose idolization of Taylor has to be understood in the context of her more comprehensive critique of feminism. Sexual objectification, for Paglia, is indistinguishable from the "art impulse," by which she presumably means the urge to produce work of creativity and imagination in visual form, such as a painting or sculpture. Taylor accomplished something very much like this, a point she occasionally acknowledged herself, particularly when referring to the commodity she originated. Of course, Taylor regarded her artifice as more of a moneymaking than an artistic creation.

But there is arguably a more fundamental way in which Taylor altered the course of women and one not fully realized in Paglia's analysis. Taylor became "the pariah of the American press," after the Fisher scandal, and, while Paglia does not amplify the importance of this, being treated as a social outcast surely contributed to Taylor's objectification. To use a philosophical term, she was Othered, that is, viewed as intrinsically different from and even alien to respectable society: a sign of what is not virtuous. So, when Paglia writes of Taylor's emergency tracheotomy in 1961, "This brush with death seems, in some strange mythic way, to have divinized her," she does not quite grasp her own argument: it was not strange, less still mythic: Taylor was already regarded as distinct and perhaps even the opposite of most women. The miraculous recovery, if not, resurrection, confirmed this status, but prompted further questions.

Writing in 1967 for *Esquire*, Lee Israel paraphrased media pronouncements and public opinion in the early 1960s: "She must pay for her transgressions in some important way ... all the sensational Liz-Burton stories reflected that imperative." Sinners suffer. Taylor did not suffer. She was rewarded with enhanced status after her first near-death experience. Maybe she was not a sinner after all. This is how Israel unscrambled the logic. "Taylor, no matter how you looked at it, wasn't suffering" (p. 345 of the 1970 re-publication of the article).

The implication of Israel's argument is that Taylor's apparent transgressions with Fisher and Burton served to expose the "inherent contradictions of marriage and romance ... feminine desire and practice with the cultural construct of romantic love and with the legal institution of marriage." She was not just breaking rules; she was disputing their legitimacy. The title of Israel's article expresses her assessment, "The Rise and Fall and Rise of Elizabeth Taylor."

Israel did not interpret Taylor's acts of defiance as driven by impetuosity or childlike recalcitrance, but by courage. She likens her to one of the medieval women suspected of being a witch and thrown into the river so parishioners could "judge them according to whether they sank or swam." Taylor, as Israel puts it, "made it to the shore."

Susan McLeland has written about much the same issue in her 1996 PhD thesis: "Unlike Marilyn Monroe, whose sexuality was a function of her desire to be the object of desire ... Taylor demanded the (heretofore masculine) right to desire as well, sometimes with tragic results" (p. 124). Taylor's strength was not her ability to tease, but her inclination to take. Like Paglia and Israel, McLeland believes Taylor's serial transgressions were crucial in instigating changed conceptions of what it means to be a woman. As she observes: "For at least a decade, Taylor, as the erotic woman, continued to threaten the status quo by breaking the rules of acceptable female behavior without being punished" (p. 143).

Taylor was castigated and reviled after her relationship with Eddie Fisher became known in 1958, but McLeland argues that the "aggressive desire" that at first drew censure was later construed as a source of strength and a measure of her fighting spirit—which were admirable qualities for a woman in the 1960s and 1970s. Taylor became—indeed remains—"the personification of desire and female grotesque." By grotesque, McLeland does not mean repulsive or distorted, but inappropriate to a shocking degree (as in, for example, "enjoyed a lifestyle of grotesque luxury").

Taylor was not just a potent, dangerous star in the 1950s and 1960s: she was invulnerable. As Debbie Reynold's mother, Maxine told the *Chicago Tribune*'s Seymour Korman in the midst of the Fisher scandal: "Liz won't get hurt because nobody can hurt her" (September 13, 1958, part 1, p. 4). Read that again: *nobody can hurt her.*

Taylor never just sat there and waited to be judged: she pressured people to make pronouncements on her indiscretions. Were they catastrophic or propitious? In a 1999 essay that extends her thesis, McLeland examined how the media were caught in a state of shock by Taylor's brazenness. Reynolds offered herself as a natural example of what Taylor was not. "Women were officially encouraged (or forced) to leave their jobs to marry and raise children," wrote McLeland of the 1950s. "Reynolds was a model: marriage was posited as the satisfaction of a woman's desires." The media idealized Reynold's young love, even in the years leading to the split, when there had been murmurs of trouble in paradise. The popular media had opted to ignore these. Even by the time of the Fisher scandal, Taylor at twenty-six had been married three times, so she was hardly normative, as McLeland puts it, meaning her behavior strayed far from the standard set for marriageable young women.

Before she met Michael Todd, Taylor was much closer to the norm, but this Taylor disappeared and "in her place, a reenergized erotic charge emerged unencumbered by domestic duties," as McLeland put it in her 1999 essay (p. 231). It was a symbolic transition, though one that had different meaning when it occurred. Today, argued McLeland in her thesis, Taylor's role as a "sexually and socially free woman" might look attractive, but in the 1950s, without the availability of birth control and the punitive nature of the legal system to women known to be sexually active outside marriage, the role was "a virtually unthinkable option for any woman wishing to maintain her status in bourgeois American society" (p. 232).

Taylor once appeared to have bought into the dream of domestic happiness and, for a while, she was a perfect distillation of the privileged, white woman-who-has-everything. If she had retired, as I have fantasized, Taylor might have stayed that way: well bred, likable, perhaps admirable, but not threatening.

Taylor's most subversive act coincided with the publication of Helen Gurley Brown's infamous handbook-cum-manifesto *Sex and the Single Girl*, which announced unapologetically that unmarried women not only had sex but actually enjoyed it. The book effectively told them how to enjoy it even more. Published in 1962, the year before Betty Friedan inspired modern feminism with her *The Feminine Mystique*, Gurley Brown's book instructed unmarried women how to look their best, have rewarding affairs and ultimately snag a man for keeps. It was celebrated and castigated in about equal measure. As *Cosmopolitan* magazine's editor from 1965 until 1997, Brown was often credited with introducing frank discussions of sex into magazines for women. Women could "have it all" was her message. Taylor seemed resolved to offering confirmatory evidence.

In particular, "her well-publicized 'lust for life' narrative," as McLeland calls it, was a performance befitting a hedonistic, philandering male—a Robert Mitchum or a Steve McQueen—but not a female, at least not in the natural order of things. This is McLeland's point: she uses a Greek term *doxa* to describe common beliefs and opinions in any period. Taylor's scandals damaged the prevailing *doxa*. I would go further and argue that, in shaking the entire doxastic world, Taylor raised questions about whether behavior considered unacceptable for women, was acceptable after all. Should women be denied engaging in acts from which they derive pleasure? Why is male sexuality openly discussed, but female sexuality suppressed?

Interpreters of the artist Kathe Burkhart have made almost the same point. Burkhart began painting images of Taylor in 1982. "Burkhart elaborates a complex persona who knows that the pleasure of heterosexual women come in sharing the pleasure of men," observed G. Roger Denson, of the *Huffington Post*, in 2011 (April 9). "The Burkhart Liz . . . is found defying the conventions laid out for her by men and early, single-minded feminists alike." (Denson calls Taylor, as Burkhart visualizes her, a "proto-feminist.")

McLeland believes Taylor surprised and perhaps confused the inchoate women's movement of the 1960s and confounded herself: "For the second-wave feminist, Taylor remained an avatar of old Hollywood in which a women's value was determined by her 'to-be-looked-at-ness'." For Taylor herself, her life was the saga of a traditional woman who continued to seek romantic fulfillment through marriage" (p. 248).

Despite this, McLeland believes Taylor, or more specifically, the Taylor portrayed in the media, became the raw material for a "new conceptualization of women's sexuality" that broke the traditional domestic vs. erotic division: in other words, women need not aspire to be either a maternal, housebound wife or a glamorous, erotic siren: like Taylor, they could want it all. Were Taylor to have suffered inordinately, have her reputation crushed by the weight of public condemnation and her professional career wrecked by censorial studios, then the longterm fallout might have been different. But, and here McLeland concurs with Israel, Taylor was actually remunerated, decorated and so rewarded for her transgressions. "This denotes a significant shift in public representations of feminine sexuality," writes McLeland.

McLeland concludes that Taylor emerged from her scandals loaded with "symbolic capital." She means Taylor had non-financial assets such as style, dress, physical appearance and, most importantly, a formidable reputation that gave her influence, prowess or leverage. When she did something, people took notice; when she spoke, people listened; when she did nothing, they still paid attention. Most other women in the public sphere who used their influence to promote change acquired their symbolic capital from men. Jacqueline Kennedy Onassis, Lady Bird Johnson and Betty Ford, for example, became famous and influential because their husbands were well-known politicians. Even Jane Fonda inherited a portion of her puissance from her father. Taylor built her own pile of symbolic capital, arriving in the public sphere as a sweet and virginal girl before developing an appetite for mischief that turned her into an unnerving and fearless personage.

Gloria Shin likens Taylor to her most famous historical role. "Like Cleopatra, she stands unafraid of the cabal of men who want to control her or her image," wrote Shin, using the present tense to picture Taylor in the early 1960s. Like McLeland, Shin based her doctoral thesis on Taylor (listed in the bibliography under Shin, 2012a). "She defies the heads of film firms which have made billions of dollars through their unyielding control of the representation of femininity often at the women performers' expense," Shin continued (p. 181).

Shin agreed with Paglia, Israel and McLeland about Taylor's seamless integration of film roles with her own life. McLeland argues that Taylor "fleshed out" a persona that was not easily reconciled with existing images of women. Taylor's selection of film roles that resembled her popular image was almost certainly a deliberate strategy. But did she actually intend to challenge shibboleths? Possibly. Was she making a principled stand for liberated womanhood? Not according to M.G. Lord.

Lord called Taylor "the accidental feminist" and subtitled her book "How Elizabeth Taylor raised our consciousness and we were too distracted by her beauty to notice" (2012a). Taylor's feminism from 1985 was hardly accidental, of course. While her Aids campaigning may not have been part of the feminist remit in the 1960s and 1970s, it was certainly part of a wider, global movement for justice, fairness and righteousness that feminism of any era would embrace. Lord believed Taylor, "like the beautiful somnambulist in Harold Lloyd's movie *High and Dizzy* who sleepwalked onto an upper-story ledge—strode unconsciously into risky territory, unaware of just how 'out there' she was" (quoted from her article "I am Liz, Hear Me Roar"). Whether she knew it or not, she was a pathbreaker for social progress and women's rights.

In many of her roles, from *National Velvet* onwards, there is "a sly critique of gender discrimination" and an assertion of feminist principles like womens' right to control their own bodies and sexuality (in the film, she is barred from riding in an important horse race because she is a girl and poses as a male jockey). Had Taylor preached women's liberation, as it was called in the late 1960s and 1970s, she could have suffered ruinously. But secreted in her films are themes and motifs that transmitted gestures to those who sought them and left those who did not agreeably entertained.

In 1959's *Suddenly Last Summer*, for example, Taylor "portrays the callousness of the male medical establishment toward women patients"; in *Who's Afraid of Virginia Woolf?* (1966), she dramatizes the destructive effect that having to live "through her husband's career" can have on a thinking woman. Taylor confronted sexism as well as racism in *Giant* in 1956. This is why she was an *accidental* feminist: she seemed unintentionally to take on roles in films that had subversive themes and that, on reflection, were lucky to escape greater scrutiny from the Hays Code censors, who expurgated American films between 1930 and 1967, and who ordered revisions of some of Taylor's work, though without erasing the themes Lord highlights. But the fact remains, in these and later films, in which she played more overtly sexual roles, Taylor addressed issues that were to take on greater visibility with the onset of feminism. Taylor became adept at playing a kind of artistic hide-go-seek with audiences and filmmakers as well as censors.

Evaluations such as this are, as Liesl Schillinger pointed out, "in the eye of the beholder." Schillinger, in reviewing the accidental feminist argument in 2012, wrote: "Lord maintains each [film] serves as a cinematic Rorschach of social changes percolating through postwar society, in which Taylor stars as the protean blot." Someone squinting at the films from a different angle could conclude that Lord's overall argument is weakened by her disregard of the many films in which Taylor played traditional female roles. *The Last Time I Saw Paris* and *Ash Wednesday*, to name but two. Susan Smith argued in 2012 the "fiery, independent femininity" she exhibits for much of *BUtterfield 8*, is complicated, perhaps undermined, by the script's rooting the independent impulse in "an experience of sexual abuse she suffered in childhood" (p. 79).

Censors under the auspices of the Hays Code were responsible for cuts and changes in the script that might have declawed the whole film. "But Taylor's performance subverted what the censors had intended," claimed Lord (2011). "The [Hays] Code ordered women to revere marriage and authority." Taylor's character "spits at the men around her, curling her lip in contempt."

Taylor did not personify feminists' ideal, or a world in which gender equalities reigned. She was not a paragon of feminism. And, despite Lord's theory, she did not even pretend to try to disguise her motives: she had no feminist agenda in her choice of films; which is not to say there was no agenda at all. But, if it existed, it seems one of her personal design.

To judge by the varied and slightly dissonant voices extolling her feminist virtues, Taylor, was an inspiration and perhaps a key inspiration at that. No one could mistake Taylor for a man's plaything or a woman without agency—she was her own woman and acted to produce the results she desired. She pursued her own interests and protected them with whatever means she could and, if this meant forming coalitions with men, so be it. She may have used men; they may have used her; but she was never subordinate to them. This made her, in many ways, an ideal emblem for womanhood. Not the womanhood that embodied the qualities assumed to be natural to women, but a new conception of what it meant to be a woman.

McLeland and those who champion Taylor see in her the epitome of a new type of woman, independent of thought and mercurial of taste. Shin calls her "an unstoppable woman who intoxicates men and turns them into her successive husbands during the decade in which women first begin to experience the new sexual agencies tied to the commercialization of the birth control pill" (under Shin 2012b: para. 34).

Catherine Bennett lent force to this, in envisioning Taylor's lifestyle and appearance as an attack on "the received wisdom about female sobriety, sexual continence and not letting yourself go." In Taylor's times, as today, female imperfections provided the media with fodder for ridicule and chastizement. Taylor's food indulgences were almost legendary. Joan Rivers joked, "Her favorite food is seconds." One of *Saturday Night Live's* most famous sketches, in 1978, featured John Belushi impersonating a corpulent Taylor gorging herself and nearly choking on a chicken bone, as she famously did while campaigning for John Warner. Taylor was ardently unapologetic about her eating and drinking habits, let alone her other indulgencies. At a time when women are persuaded by wispy models, couturiers' prefer gracile body shapes and thinness is *sine qua non*, Taylor seems like a reminder of a bygone age when women were voluptuous, curvaceous and immune to enforced eating disorders rather than "boys in dresses," as Bennett put it (she was writing in 2011, before the likes of Christina Hendricks and Kim Kardashian made their presence felt).

Bennett saw in Taylor someone who embodied feminist psychoanalyst Susie Orbach's postulate: "Fat expresses a rebellion against the powerlessness of the woman." Taylor's own book *Elizabeth Takes Off* quotes women's rights activist Gloria Steinem and airs thoughts on body image first advanced in Orbach's 1978 anti-diet text *Fat Is a Feminist Issue* (2006). Orbach's theory is that, while fat women may think that they are desperate to lose weight, they unconsciously harbor the "desire to get fat." Referring to Taylor, Bennett writes of "the sublime, apple-tumescing appeal of a plump, lustful, self-destructive alcoholic, whose excesses make top femme fatale Angelina Jolie look like a much tattooed Milly-Molly-Mandy" (Milly-Molly-Mandy is a character in British children's books, a girl in a pink-and-white striped dress who lives on a farm in the English countryside).

For these writers, Taylor is, for want of a better term, a feminist-without-feminism. Silently, she made statements; without motioning she sent out signals. But it seems a stretch: after all, Taylor, for all her independence, power and symbolic resources, insisted on some very traditional and, for many, hidebound patriarchal protocols. One of them was receiving gifts from men. Being the recipient of lavish gifts, particularly jewelry, became part of her persona. When, as some suspected, Richard Burton could not afford the extravagant jewelry she desired, she probably underwrote the purchases herself, just to keep up appearances. Every man who romanced her was bound to proffer tributes, usually in the form of precious stones.

Suzanne Leonard, in 2010, discerned other more reactionary qualities in Taylor herself and the media's treatment of her. Once processed by the media, the image of Taylor emerging in the 1960s reflected an "antiquated model of femininity, one that patronizes sexual women as 'not knowing any better'" (p. 86).

Leonard offered a layered understanding of both Taylor and the media's response to her trysts with Fisher and Burton. She pointed out that, in Taylor's case, the threat that she, as an "adulterous *woman*" posed was defused by the media's emphasis on her girl-like demeanor, even though she was twenty-six when she started her affair with Fisher: it was as if a child was being scolded rather than a mature woman being persecuted. This had the effect of portraying her behavior as that of a miscreant rather than a rebel.

Then there was the question of Taylor's rush from one marriage to the next as if singlehood was about as welcome as acne. At the time of the Fisher affair, there was no debate between opposing viewpoints about the desirability of marriage or whether it suited the interests of patriarchy. These arguments emerged in the 1960s. Today various partnership arrangements populate the cultural landscape and the idea of a married woman co-habiting with a man, who is married to another woman, is hardly likely to register a reaction. In the 1950s and for at least the first half of the 1960s, it was a major contravention of the codes set out for women: the decent were herded into homes, their destiny to keep those homes spick and span and have children. Only the indecent rebelled. Taylor's apparently selfish and possibly capricious striving for gratification seemed like the first stirrings of independence to some. Yet her zeal for marriage—or, her failure to learn from mistakes—took her into marriage time and again, eventually, eight times. If there was challenge in her behavior, it was not aimed at what Leonard calls "ideological norms or heterosexual organizations." Serial bride that she was, Taylor violated codes, but without ever suggesting the codes themselves were wrong and was ever-ready to recommit to "the sanctified institution of marriage" (p. 86).

Brenda Maddox, in 1976, wrote of Taylor's "indomitable faith in marriage and her Man," the capita M presumably an allusion to Taylor's uncritical acceptance of the need for a man, who was or would become her husband, in her life (p. 246). No doubt, Taylor, from age eighteen, wanted to be married: even her brief interludes as a single woman were packed with relationships that carried matrimonial potential. No doubt, too, that she wanted to free herself from the tedious and restrictive routines of traditional married life. She seemed endlessly seduced by a conception of conjugal bliss, when her every experience of married life suggested this was just an ideal, not an attainable reality. Whether this was the first glimpse of a new kind of womanhood striving for satisfactions comparable to those traditionally enjoyed only by men, or a naïvely conservative Utopianism is a matter of perspective. Taylor as a feminist hero, or a patriarchal patsy? She fits both bills.

She did *something* for women, but whether it advanced them along the road to the kinds of freedoms realized in the form of the Equal Pay Act (1963), *Roe* v. *Wade* (1973), the Family and Medical Leave Act (1993) or the cultural shifts that transfigured the condition of women in modern society is not certain.

Taylor has been credited with many praiseworthy accomplishments, several of which she would probably not have not acknowledged. She has less creditable achievements on the other side of the balance sheet, though even these have been interpreted in a way that emphasizes her cultural impact.

Shin is convinced Taylor was an effective activist, albeit an unknowing one, in at least one sense. "Elizabeth Taylor and Richard Burton's open pursuit of pleasure is best signified through spectacular sexualized consumption and organizes the public lives and codifies the personas of the duo as not only erotic legends but exemplars of postcolonial whiteness. They demonstrate that whiteness after the end of colonization can remain," writes Shin in paragraph forty of an online essay based on her doctoral research (listed as Shin 2012b).

This is a heady passage and one that requires unpicking. Shin noticed the coincidence of Taylor's rise to global prominence and the decline of colonialism. The postcolonial era was one in which many states in Africa and Asia gained independence, leaving uncertainty about the West's political and cultural dominance. The Hollywood film industry remained a kind of cultural mainstay amid the instability and, while audiences were not panicked by the end of colonialism and the loss of traditional white power, the sense of doubt was subtly pervasive. Movies allowed a kind of assurance of the supremacy of whiteness. "Taylor became an exemplar of postcolonial whiteness," Shin proposed. In her films, particularly *Cleopatra*, and her "affective adventures," as Shin called her romances, Taylor supplied a model of a possessive white individual, who owned herself and owed nothing to society, who sought satisfaction through acquisition of luxuries, who was absorbed in a sybaritic lifestyle, perhaps reminiscent of the old colonial masters, and who issued reminders of "the stability of white authority." (Incidentally, Rouben Mamoulian, who was originally hired to direct *Cleopatra*, intended to populate the film's cast with African American actors and wanted Dorothy Dandridge for the title role, according to Nichelle Gainer, writing in 2014.)

With her days of conspicuous consumption and the relentless pursuit of pleasure behind her, Taylor became an unwavering humanitarian, making her even more "ideologically powerful," as Shin argued. She means that Taylor became part of melodrama that colored "American whiteness with a sense of largess that becomes globally recognized as a most legible form of good white citizenship." Again, this requires unpicking: Shin argues that, when Taylor became the most renowned and effective fund raiser for Aids, she revealed the compassion, benevolence, and infinite magnanimity of white society when faced with a problem experienced by disenfranchised groups, particularly gay men and populations of Sub-Saharan Africa.

Shin was interested in Taylor as a motif or a symbol of a particular quality rather than a functioning human being and, as such, imputes no motives to Taylor herself. This is, of course, a singular interpretation of Taylor, but an effort to understand her impact has to consider her multiple effects, no matter how obscure. She seems an improbable figure to symbolize whiteness, as Shin propounds. Perhaps that is the whole point. Shin may appear to grasp at every possible inference to establish her argument. Some of Taylor's qualities are so flagrant they cannot be missed; others are so elusive that only imaginative deciphering reveals them.

"This time it's personal." The phrase was splattered across posters for *Jaws: The Revenge*, when it was released in 1987. Taylor could have trademarked it years earlier when the media suspended its customary practice of observing the purdah dividing the public lives of stars from their private affairs. Her relationship with Fisher was unexpected and unbelievable; this is why it caught everyone by surprise. Once initial disbelief subsided, the media went in search of a story that promised to eclipse the Bergman and Hayward scandals, and quickly did. The quest necessitated venturing into domains traditionally considered off-limits to the media. In common with other Hollywood actors, Taylor probably felt entitled to a personal life. If she did, she learned that it was a conditional entitlement.

"Just when you thought it was safe to go back in the water," Taylor did it again (no more *Jaws*-themed expressions, I promise). The Burton affair all but sent out gilt-edged invitations to the media. Cue proactive reporters. Cue conjectural news. Cue gradual obliteration of traditional notions of privacy. Cue celebrity culture. By now, we are used to being in the hearts, minds, and lives of people we do not know. McLeland wonders whether this loss of privacy—at least, privacy in the way it was once understood—has implications specifically for women.

Women once had little or no presence in the public sphere: they were culturally coded as private beings, responsible for having and rearing children, running a home, doing laundry, cooking the meals and caring for the sick. This was how they were meant to find self-fulfillment. For Paglia and Israel, Taylor anticipated concerns later voiced by feminists. As with the accidental feminist theory, there is no reason to impute motives: whether or not Taylor intended to strike out for women is of less importance than the tangible changes she instigated. McLeland would presumably point to the several issues that were once considered private; for example, domestic abuse, including marital rape, mental cruelty and treatment of children. These are no longer private issues, but matters of public interest and, possibly, concern. Changes in our conception of privacy extend beyond social media, gossip and the voyeurism implied in celebrity culture: they involve everyone in the affairs of others, but in a way that is anything but trivial. In McLeland's phrase, culture no longer *codes* women as private; this means the set of conventions or moral principles governing women's behavior in the private sphere has been modified.

In the putative scenario I offered to start this chapter, Taylor professes a wish to relinquish her fame, glamour, money, and the other accouterments of Hollywood and, instead, pursue more conventional gratifications of the home; conventional, that is, in the pre-sexual revolution 1950s. Taylor would not be missed. The world would be not have been scandalized fascinatedly by her. But it would have been only a matter of time before another famous entertainer or perhaps politician shook or horrified the media and public with a real or imagined violation of propriety or morality. The 1960s were years of great cultural change and the so-called family values to which women were supposed to cleave were under attack from several quarters. Almost inevitably, a woman would seize the attention of everyone by challenging accepted truths about womanhood. Jane Fonda perhaps, Janis Joplin, if she had not died from a heroin overdose in 1970; or a European firebrand such as Jane Birkin, Charlotte Rampling, or Elke Sommer, all of whom in some way subverted conventional ideas about the place of women. It is difficult to imagine any of them doing it with quite the same combination of provocation and renegade sexuality as Taylor, however. Because of this, none of the others would have made such a deep impact.

The story begins as a fairy tale about a girl not unlike *Frozen*'s Elsa, who was inspired by Hans Christian Andersen's *Snow Queen*, the fairy with the killer looks, who beguiled every man. Elsa has the power to create and control ice and snow, a fantastic but perilous magic. Retreating to her castle after accidentally hurting her sister, nearly fatally, she tries to suppress her scary potential. Elsa meets a handsome prince who may become her savior but who, instead, becomes her evil accomplice, though with ideas that elevate and ultimately condemn him. All right, I have changed this part of the story, but let us pretend the girl loves endlessly, always in vain, breaking hearts and having her own broken until she metamorphoses into one of the world's greatest do-gooders. The story climaxes in an Apocalypse in which bombs and aerial fighting-machines assail a misunderstood friend whom she seeks to protect. My mashed-up version hardly sounds promising material for a film. But stories are not just the pictures we see on screen, or the words in books: they are what our imaginations make of them.

In a sense there was more than one Elizabeth Taylor. Of course, there was a human being named Elizabeth, movie star, temptress, philanthropist and *parfumeur extraordinaire*. There was also an Elizabeth Taylor who existed, and still exists, beyond time and space and who resides in our minds. In other words, the Taylor we imagine her to be. Loved and hated, probably, in varying proportions that changed over time, she was able to fascinate audiences. By audiences, I mean all of us; by fascinate I mean draw our attention and interest to the point where we felt unable to resist.

"Yet the character 'Elizabeth Taylor' cannot move completely independent of the real Taylor," Lee Israel once argued. Not *completely* perhaps. But the latitude consumers had in imagining Taylor was so considerable, she may just as well have been a fictional character. The media made sure of that. Israel coined the term "para-fictive character" to describe the version of Elizabeth Taylor audiences consumed. We will never know whether media and the consumers they served actually engaged with Taylor's private life, or their *surmise* of that life. Even today, consumers never know, though, in a sense, it is of no consequence: the natural order of things demands that fans think through the lives of others for themselves. The media supply the raw material, the brio and the trivia; but the consumers conjure the lives into a coherent narrative. They, that is we, responded to practically every thing Taylor did, said, and all those things she probably did not do or say, but were reported somewhere, anyway.

She was, for two or possibly three decades, the most publicized person in the world. For good reason: audiences were consistently entertained by Taylor; this does not diminish her artistic accomplishments or her many other endeavors because entertainment should not be understood as just amusement, distraction or a diversion from important matters. It is, as Stephen Bertman propounds, "a way of life, occupying interstices between periods of work" (p. 123). We find events, performances, and other activities entertaining when they prompt us to think about something in a way we find agreeably engaging, perhaps occasioning laughter or deeper reflection. Taylor was living entertainment. Which leads us to the final and most central question asked, but perhaps not yet fully answered by this book: would celebrity culture have happened without Taylor?

"Surely" will be the answer of many. "One individual could not singlehandedly cause the kind of cultural shift that has affected practically every aspect of modern life." But wait. If Julius Caesar had not crossed the stream called the Rubicon that marked the boundary between Italy and Cisalpine Gaul in 49 BC, would there have been *Pax Romana*, providing peace across the Roman Empire from Spain to Persia? Bearing in mind Taylor's most illustrious film role, I cannot resist this comparison. More to the point, we could ask whether the Jazz Age would have happened without Clara Bow (1905–65), the "It Girl" who was synonymous with the period characterized by hedonism, wealth, freedom, and youthful exuberance in the 1920s. Would rock 'n' roll have become such a cultural force without a white artist to sing music written by black musicians? And, if not Elvis Presley (1935–77), was there another singer who could have filled his role? Those who still maintain "Surely," should stay mindful that the individuals just mentioned were not like characters in *The Simpsons* or *South Park*, who could be made to behave and appear anywhere their creators pleased. They had minds of their own and willfully instigated changes that grew into transformations.

Drop Elvis, Clara Bow, and even Julius Caesar into different places at different times and they would change nothing, at least nothing that we would be thinking or writing about today. People connect with their social and historical contexts, by which I mean circumstances that form a setting, the times in which an event takes place.

Taylor, as I have argued throughout this book, was a product; but there was nothing synthetic about her. She was an original: a headstrong young woman with no formal acting training, nor even a childhood in the way we conventionally understand it. She made decisions that would have had calamitous consequences for many others and would almost certainly have destroyed her Hollywood career had she made them ten years before she did. Taylor's life is a narrative of intersections: of biography and history, of spiritual and carnal, of acceptance and taboo.

They converged and, on occasion, collided in the life of a determinedly calculating yet suggestible woman who simply refused to obey rules. By doing so, she exposed those rules as redundant. They would probably have unraveled, anyway, with or without Taylor. Probably. But her presence helped accelerate many of the changes of the 1960s, 1970s, and beyond.

The defining feature of Taylor's life was not her acting, nor her serial marriages, not even the epic Liz & Dick liaison; it was not her pestilential ill health nor the seemingly endless struggles against dependencies; and it was not even her metamorphosis into the world's most famous and probably most effective charity worker. She was the centrifuge of an emergent celebrity culture.

Whether by design or intuition, Taylor personified the worlds she envisioned in both her pictures and her life. She allowed us to see the mess of her personal life, the unkempt love affairs, the ugly dependence on drugs and alcohol, and the reckless extravagance of her consumption. She had a private life but only in the way Madame Pompadour (1721–64) or Giovanni Jacopo Casanova (1725–98) had private lives. They too were real people, but became enshrined in operettas, books, plays, and movies to the point where their myths outgrew their persons. Taylor's myth is already immeasurably bigger than the woman. Who knows? Three hundred years from now, Taylor might occupy a status comparable with that of the scandalous mistress of Louis XV, or the notorious sexual adventurer.

There may be trace memories of Cleopatra, Gloria Wandrous and Velvet Brown, but, to repeat David Germain and Italie Hillel from 2011: "Her defining role, one that lasted long past her moviemaking days, was 'Elizabeth Taylor,' ever marrying and divorcing, in and out of hospitals, gaining and losing weight, standing by Michael Jackson, Rock Hudson and other troubled friends, acquiring a jewelry collection that seemed to rival Tiffany's." Assembled from memory, biography, and media reportage, and embellished by whatever we want to think, our image of Taylor will be exactly that—an image, a product of our imagination.

The scenario I described at the start of this chapter prompted a question: suppose Elizabeth Taylor had retired from acting in 1955 ... how much different would life be? I have likened her relationship to today's celebrity obsessed culture to Clara Bow's to the Jazz Age and Elvis' to rock 'n' roll. Some readers might think of more apposite comparisons with someone else who happened to be in the more or less right place at exactly the right time.

With hindsight, we can see that every famous figure credited with playing some role, however large or small, in a cultural movement is in the right place at the right time. Some revolving doors turned in a way that opened for them, others had to be pushed, and still others were jammed and needed to be smashed through. But there had to be someone and there had to be a revolving door. Forgive this obscure metaphor: the door is a continuous opportunity to change; some people, for all sorts of reasons, choose to step into it, while others stand back.

We can be reasonably sure Taylor, prodded and promoted by her mother, had every intention of becoming a major Hollywood star and would have been disappointed had her status waned as she matured. Surely though, she would not have envisioned herself at the center of not one but two scandals, nor to have stumbled on the philosopher's stone I referred to in Chapter 1.

Neal Gabler, in an attempt to uncoil the twisted history of celebrity culture, argues that audience interest is typically initiated by newspapers or tv. Our first brush with figures who are destined for celebritydom is through the media, though not necessarily the traditional media Gabler has in mind; social media have become increasingly vital since 2009. But there is a reason why those figures, whether entertainers, athletes, politicians or anything else, were publicized in the first place: as Gabler points out, "they received publicity because they provided narratives for us." A narrative is an account of connected events, such as a story, a history, a record or a chronicle. It can convey a moral or a lesson in what is right and prudent, or bad and foolish.

And it is always open to interpretation: interpreters who search narratives usually reveal hidden meanings.

If we understand her in this way, Taylor was not so much a character in a drama: she *was* the drama. Her life was turned into one vast script.

Analyzing the exploits of Britney Spears, a woman with a Taylor-esque predilection for scandal, Kathryn Lofton makes a similar point, though abstractly: "The converted human also becomes a composite sketch, with parts and pieces and accessories easily redacted and packaged, remembered and satirized" (p. 348). She means that we, the audience, once in possession of the raw material, edit (redact and package) to our own requirements. The authors of "Britney's stories," as Lofton calls them, are the very people who are enraptured by them.

When, in 2011, Cindy De La Hoz listed at #127 of "the reasons why we love Elizabeth Taylor," because she was "just like us," she was only partly right. Taylor shared the same kind of human fallibilities as everyone else: she used up her quota of excusable errors and then kept making more; she learned from mistakes but continued to make them. Just like us. But Taylor was quite unlike us too: not just because she was wild and willful, resisted codes, broke rules and, in her own way, framed new ones. She was unlike us in the sense that her history is our present.

Celebrity culture would have materialized without Taylor, just like feminism would have without Betty Friedan, or rock 'n' roll without Elvis, or any of the cultural movements mentioned in this book without key individuals. They just would not have materialized in quite the same way. This sounds a cheap answer to an expensive question, but I am not trying to rewrite the verities of history and culture. Taylor's influence on today's culture is felt and thought every time we pore over a lovable or hateable character's love life, gaze compulsively at a reality tv show, gossip about someone we believe we know, but have never met, and index our own lives to people making theirs public.

Players

PANDRO S. BERMAN 1905–96. Film producer from Pittsburgh, who worked at Universal in the 1920s, then at RKO. He played a key role in Taylor's professional development from child roles in *National Velvet* (1944) to an adult part in *Father of the Bride* (1950). He also produced *BUtterfield 8* (1960) for which Taylor won an Oscar.

CARL BERNSTEIN b. 1944. Investigative journalist and author famed for his reports (with *Washington Post* colleague Bob Woodward) on the Watergate scandal of the early 1970s, and subsequent book on the subject. He had a relationship with Taylor between her engagements to Luna (broken May 1984) and Stein (announced December 1984). In 1985, Bernstein was involved in a well-publicized confrontation with Stein in a New York club.

RICHARD BURTON 1925–84. Son of a Welsh coalminer, Richard Jenkins, as he was christened, bootstrapped his way to an Oxford scholarship to study acting, distinguished himself on stage and, later, in film. The scandal occasioned by his romance with Taylor, whom he first married in March 1964, reverberated around the world and, in many ways, changed the way media and audiences engaged with Hollywood figures. After ten years of marriage, Burton and Taylor divorced, but remarried in October 1975; their second marriage lasted less than a year and they divorced in August 1976. While his death from cerebral hemorrhage at fifty-eight was sudden, Burton's health had been in decline for a number of years and, as early as 1970, he had been diagnosed with cirrhosis of the liver and kidneys due to his prodigious drinking.

VICTOR CAZALET 1896–1943. The wealthy British Conservative politician who befriended Francis Taylor and Sara Sothern (Taylor's parents) and became Elizabeth's godfather was a benevolent acquaintance during the family's time in England. Cazalet was a friend of Hedda Hopper and her ex-husband and introduced Sara to the gossip columnist. Several stories surround his close friendship with the family. One suggests he had a gay relationship with Francis; another that he, Francis and Sara engaged with others in group sex and that he was, in fact, Elizabeth's real father. He died in a plane crash when a converted bomber in which he was flying plunged into the sea while taking off from the short runway in Gibraltar.

MONTGOMERY CLIFT 1920–66. Born in Nebraska, Clift had a brilliant start to his acting career, playing in *A Place in the Sun* (1951), with Taylor, and *From Here to Eternity* (1953). Rumors of a relationship with Taylor were wide of the mark: Clift was, as Taylor knew, gay. They both played in *Raintree County* (1957); during filming, Clift had a car accident and Taylor rushed to his rescue. Clift was badly injured and never fully restored himself. He drank heavily, used prescription drugs and faded from public view. He died from a heart attack, aged forty-five.

PETER DARMANIN b. 1938. Advertising agent from Malta who met Taylor at the Olden Hotel, Gstaad, Switzerland, in 1976 when Burton, to whom she was married (second time), was away. Darmanin spent what he called "five days of wondrous bliss" with Taylor before returning to his Mediterranean island home. Taylor entreated him to return, which he did, borrowing money to do so. But a violent argument ended the brief romance. Darmanin refused all media offers for his story.

GLENN DAVIS 1926–2005. Born in La Quinta, California, Davis won the Heisman Trophy in 1946 and helped lead the Army to three national football championships. While on Army leave in 1948, Davis, by then a celebrated athlete, briefly dated Taylor attracting a clamorous media and prompting Taylor to remark: "Maybe I should have fallen for a busboy, then the whole thing wouldn't cause so much attention." After military service, Davis spent most of his career as an executive in the promotion department of the *Los Angeles Times*. He died of complications from prostate cancer, aged eighty.

STANLEY DONEN b. 1924. Known best for his co-direction of *Singin' in the Rain* (1952), the South Carolinian had a brief romantic interlude with Taylor in 1951. "Elizabeth's mother, Sara, did everything in her power to call it off," according to Donen, who was, at the time, married. Taylor was nineteen. It was thought that Sara petitioned Louis B. Mayer and he responded by assigning Taylor a project in England, where she met (and later married) Michael Wilding.

EDDIE FISHER 1928–2010. Born in Pennsylvania to Russian migrants, Fisher became a best-selling recording artist in the 1950s. He became part of a celebrity couple when, in 1955, he married popular singer and actor Debbie Reynolds. After the death of his close friend Michael Todd, he became embroiled in a hugely publicized scandal when he began an affair with and, later (in May 1959), married Todd's widow, Taylor. The affair stigmatized both parties and Fisher never recovered professionally. They divorced in March 1964. Fisher died after complications following hip surgery, aged eighty-two.

MALCOLM FORBES 1919–90. Born in Englewood, NJ, the chairman and editor-in-chief of *Forbes* magazine and one of the US's most flamboyant multimillionaires was an enthusiast of yachting, motorcycling, and ballooning. He also had a collection of sixty-eight motorcycles, most of them Harley-Davidsons. He was often seen in the company of glamorous women, including Taylor, especially between 1987 and 1990 when he was rumored to be planning to marry her. There were whispers that the women were what are known in the gay vernacular as "beards"—intended to draw suspicious eyes away from a closeted gay private life. After his death from a heart attack, aged seventy, the whispers grew louder and he was retrospectively outed by several sources.

LARRY FORTENSKY b. 1952. The construction worker from Stanton, California, whom Taylor met at the Betty Ford Center, was an unlikely match for Taylor: twenty years her junior, from a solid working-class background and with no celebrity credentials whatsoever. He had a daughter from a previous marriage. Fortensky was thirty-nine when he married Taylor in October 1991 at Michael Jackson's Neverland ranch; paparazzi circled in helicopters above the ceremony. The couple divorced in October 1996. Taylor reputedly gave him a lump sum in the region of $1 million and a $5,000 monthly allowance, later reduced to $2,500. Following the divorce, Fortensky spent weeks in a coma after a fall at his home; as a result of the injury incurred in the fall, he was unable to work. In 2015, he was reported to be living in a trailer home.

KURT FRINGS 1908–81. The German-born ex-boxer was Taylor's agent, who negotiated her history-making contract for *Cleopatra*. Frings was working as a ski instructor in France when he met his future wife Ketti Hartley who became a Pulitzer Prize-winning author. After marrying her in 1939, he moved to Mexico and then to Beverly Hills, California where, in 1956, he established the Kurt Frings Agency. An agent's business is to represent clients, to procure employment, negotiate on their behalf and provide advice, for which they receive a percentage of earnings, typically about 10 percent. Once her MGM contract was complete, Taylor became one of Frings' clients; he also represented Lucille Ball and Marlene Dietrich, among others. Although, it was less publicized than Taylor's *Cleopatra* contract, the *My Fair Lady* (1964) deal Frings negotiated for Audrey Hepburn in 1962 was equally lucrative. He died aged eighty-two.

VICTOR GONZALEZ LUNA b. 1927. Mexican lawyer to whom Taylor was engaged. In August 1983, Taylor, then fifty-one, announced she and Luna were affianced and thus he would become her eighth husband. He had four children and an ex-wife to whom he was married for twenty-eight years. They officially announced they had broken off their engagement the day after Taylor had attended a memorial service for Burton in July 1984; it was assumed the split was precipitated by Taylor's grief.

HALSTON 1932–90. Roy Halston Frowick, better known as Halston, was a leading fashion designer; in fact, the *New York Times* believed he "personified American fashion in the 1970s." Born in Des Moines, Iowa, he began as a hat designer. In 1961, Jacqueline Kennedy wore one of his signature pillbox hats to her husband John F. Kennedy's presidential inauguration, and Halston's reputation grew. He established his own company to make couture clothes and lines to be sold at department stores. In the 1970s, Halston became a noted figure at New York's Studio 54 club where he would meet Taylor, among other celebrities; Taylor's husband of the time, John Warner, cautioned her about frequenting the club. In the 1980s, Halston became undependable and his own company fired him. He died of Aids-related complications in San Francisco, aged fifty-seven.

DICK HANLEY 1908–71. Originally from LA, Hanley worked for MGM and then as Michael Todd's secretary's assistant; after Todd and Taylor's marriage, he became a sort of Man Friday to the couple. When appearing on the tv show *What's My line?* in March 1960 (after Todd's death) he was described as "Elizabeth Taylor's Secretary." He and Rex Kennamer were the people who broke the news to Taylor about Todd's death. It is believed that Taylor used Hanley's rented apartment in Rome when conducting her affair with Burton during the making of *Cleopatra*.

CONRAD NICKY HILTON 1926–69. When he married Taylor in May 1950, the 23-year-old Texan was already wealthy and a top executive in his father's hotel business; he was Taylor's first husband; they were divorced in January 1951. Hilton was a known gambler and drinker. He suffered a heart attack and died aged forty-two.

HEDDA HOPPER 1885–1966. Born in Pennsylvania, Hopper left home to seek work on Broadway before moving to Hollywood where she picked up acting roles, though without ever scaling significant heights. The contacts she made in Hollywood proved invaluable when she started writing an entertainment column for the *Los Angeles Times* in 1938. The column, "Hedda Hopper's Hollywood," gained national syndication as Hopper's reputation as a purveyor of high quality tittle-tattle grew and she was offered her own radio show specializing in gossip. She was an outspoken sympathizer with HUAC (House Un-American Activities Committee), which was established in 1938 to investigate subversives and which became notorious for its interrogations of alleged Communists. Her reputation as top gossip maven was rivaled only by Louella Parsons. Hopper was complimentary about Taylor and influenced her early career, but the infamous "sleep alone" interview when Taylor was seeing Eddie Fisher forced a wedge between them, Hopper disapproving of Taylor's behavior and Taylor believing Hopper had betrayed a confidence. Ironically, the scandal Hopper's story incited, enhanced both women's reputations. Hopper died of pneumonia.

ROCK HUDSON 1925–85. Born Roy Harold Scherer Jr. in Illinois, he lived through the Great Depression before joining the US Navy in 1944. Discharged in 1946, Hudson touted for work as an actor and was spotted by Henry Willson, who rechristened him and placed him in minor film roles. In the mid-1950s he found fame in a number of starring roles including that of Bick Benedict in *Giant* (1956); also in the film were Taylor and James Dean. Hudson's defining roles were opposite Doris Day, in movies such as *Pillow Talk* (1959). His marriage to Phyllis Gates in 1956 was, on reflection, an attempt to kill off whispers that he was gay. Were this to have become common knowledge it would have undermined his ladykiller film persona and effectively ruined his career. The lavender marriage (as such liaisons were known) lasted three years. In 1984, after a successful transition to television, Hudson complained of an irritation on his neck, which turned out to be a sign of Kaposi's sarcoma, a tumor that affects people living with Aids—then a disease causing alarm and about to become a global pandemic. Hudson never recovered and, when he died, aged fifty-nine, he became the first celebrity Aids victim. His suffering and untimely death became the inspiration for Taylor's charitable work for Aids.

KATHY IRELAND b. 1963. Santa Barbara model-turned-entrepreneur-turned author, who, with Taylor, formed the House of Taylor jewelry company—which went bankrupt in 2008. Ireland owned the Sterling/Winters agency, of which Janet Jackson, sister of Michael, was a client.

MICHAEL JACKSON 1958–2009. A child prodigy from Gary, Indiana, Jackson sang with his brothers in the Motown group the Jackson 5, before branching out as a solo artist. His *Thriller* (1982) became the best-selling album in history. After meeting Taylor in 1984, he became a close friend. Jackson's rising fortunes were accompanied by a multiplication of idiosyncrasies and his later years were beset by his substance dependencies. The stigma left by abuse allegations never disappeared and, when Jackson died from cardiac arrest, the response was ambivalent. In 2010 an official coroner's report detailed the cause of death as acute propofol intoxication. Jackson's personal physician, Conrad Murray, was convicted of involuntary manslaughter and sentenced to four years in prison.

REX KENNAMER 1920–2013. Physician from Pittsburgh, whose clients included many Hollywood names, such as Rock Hudson and Frank Sinatra as well as Taylor, to whom he broke the news of Michael Todd's death. He also accompanied and comforted her at Todd's funeral.

ARNOLD KLEIN 1945–2015. Born and raised in Michigan, Klein studied medicine at UCLA and went on to become a prominent plastic surgeon in Hollywood, known particularly for his work with Botox. Among his most celebrated clients were Taylor and Michael Jackson. He divided his time among three homes valued at $22m+, decorated with a $7.2m art collection. Klein was a pioneer in Aids treatment and, in 1985, helped found amfAR. While Taylor lauded him initially calling him "the most brilliant doctor in the world," she later turned on him. One of his assistants, Debbie Rowe, married Jackson. Klein became involved in several financial scandals, declaring bankruptcy in 2011. He died aged seventy, cause of death not announced.

MATHILDE KRIM b. 1926. Born in Italy and educated at the University of Geneva and Cornell Medical College, Krim pursued biomedical research before, in 1983, establishing the AIDS Medical Foundation. Two years later, she helped amalgamate the organization with Taylor's National AIDS Research Foundation to form American Foundation for AIDS Research, or amfAR.

JOSEPH L. MANKIEWICZ 1909–93. American film director, producer and writer, who was enlisted by 20th Century Fox to direct *Cleopatra*, after the studio dropped Rouben Mamoulian. It was thought that Mankiewicz's experience directing Taylor, whom he had directed in *Suddenly, Last Summer* (1959), would equip him well. He was paid $1.5 million for his effort, but the stressful conditions under which he worked—he directed during the day and wrote the script at night—took their toll on his health. What he thought was his final cut of the film was edited again without his involvement, reducing what Mankiewicz thought to be two films to a single movie. He died from a heart attack, days before his eighty-fourth birthday.

LOUIS B. MAYER 1884–1957. Born in poverty in what is now Ukraine, Mayer migrated to the US to avoid the pogroms and rose to become arguably the most powerful man in Hollywood. In 1947, the MGM founder and owner was famously told off by a fifteen-year-old Taylor for being rude to her mother. Mayer died of leukemia in 1957.

KEVIN O'DONOVAN MCCLORY 1924–2006. County Dublin-born screenwriter, producer and director who worked on Michael Todd's *Around the World in 80 Days*. He lived a varied life: serving in the Navy, and working as a tin prospector, before he was engaged by director John Huston on a series of films. McClory became involved with Taylor, who eventually left him for Todd. McClory is credited with adapting Ian Fleming's character James Bond for the screen and for producing *Thunderball*, the third Bond movie. He later became involved in a legal conflict with Fleming.

WILLIAM PAULEY 1920–2012. The decorated US Army pilot was twenty-seven when he proposed to the then seventeen-year-old Taylor; but his proposal carried the implicit condition that she would have to abandon her Hollywood career and, after a short (June–September 1949) engagement, she decided against this. Pauley met Taylor when she visited Miami Beach accompanied by her mother. They exchanged a series of over sixty love letters later auctioned online, fetching $47,672. He died aged ninety-two.

HERB RITTS 1952–2003. Los Angeles photographer who captured the emergent sensibility of the 1980s with gay-inspired, fashion plate shots that honored the statuesque body and the beautiful face. He helped Taylor start her Aids foundation, donating $1 million from the shots he took of her 1991 wedding to Larry Fortensky. Died suddenly at fifty.

CHEN SAM 1927–96. Taylor's long-time publicist. Sam was born in Cairo to an Egyptian father and an Italian mother. She studied in Rio de Janeiro and London, her intention being to specialize in pharmacology. Her grandparents left her a house in Morocco and, up to meeting Taylor, she divided her time between there and South Africa. She first met Taylor and Burton (then her husband) in 1974 when they were promoting black theater in southern Africa: Burton contracted malaria and Sam treated him. After, she became the couple's business manager and spokesperson, moving to New York in 1981. Initially, she represented Taylor exclusively, though later she had other clients, including Karl Lagerfeld and Donald Trump; she formed Chen Sam & Associates Inc. in 1982 for this purpose. Sam planned Taylor's charity work and her perfume product promotions. Neither Sam's age nor cause of death were announced, though seven months before her death, an appeals court in New York dismissed a libel suit Sam brought against a tabloid which reported in 1991 that she had been diagnosed with cancer.

SPYROS SKOURAS 1893–1971. He was one of three brothers who arrived in the USA from Greece in 1910 and formed a film theater company. In 1942 he became president of 20th Century Fox and tried to rescue a studio that was challenged by a series of failing films and the rise of television. Skouras introduced CinemaScope in *The Robe* (1953), in which Burton appeared. Skouras was in charge when the *Cleopatra* project was conceived and oversaw the hugely expensive folly. In 1962, he was reassigned to a less influential role in the organization. He died of a heart attack, aged seventy-eight.

LIZ SMITH b. 1923. Texas-born gossip columnist who worked as entertainment editor under Helen Gurley Brown at the US edition of *Cosmopolitan* in the early 1960s, and then wrote an internationally syndicated column for the *New York Post* where she stayed until 2009. She got married in Texas at twenty-one, and moved to New York when she was twenty-five. Smith was openly gay. She cultivated friendships with several Hollywood actors including Taylor and Burton in the 1960s, claiming: "They trusted me and eventually I became the only journalist who could get to them." When Taylor died, Smith wrote: "She was only 79, but had lived a thousand years, had fired up and exhausted endless fantasies for herself and the millions who watched her."

SARA SOTHERN 1895–1994. Arkansas-born Sarah Viola Warmbrodt, as she was christened, was an aspiring stage performer in the early 1920s, appearing in a few Broadway shows, before marrying Francis Taylor and moving with him to London, where he ran an art gallery owned by her uncle. Here she had two children, Howard and Elizabeth. The family moved back to the USA in 1939 and she concentrated her energies on promoting the acting career of her daughter. In 1946, she had an affair with Michael Curtiz, who was directing a film in which Elizabeth had a part. She was ninety-nine when she died.

DENNIS STEIN 1933–2003. The Brooklyn-born entrepreneur made his name manufacturing and selling designer jeans; he numbered many showbusiness celebrities among his friends. On December 12, 1984, Taylor announced plans to marry the 52-year-old Brooklyn-born businessman, only a month after meeting him (reputedly on a blind date arranged by mutual acquaintance Frank Sinatra) and five months after breaking off her engagement to Victor Luna. On February 4, 1985, she announced an amicable split with Stein.

FRANCIS TAYLOR 1897–1968. Born in Illinois, Taylor's father moved to New York City to work as an art dealer for his in-law Howard Young. He married Sara Warmbrodt in 1926 and the couple moved to London where they had their two children, Howard (b. 1929) and Elizabeth. The family returned to the USA in 1939 in anticipation of the Second World War, and opened an art gallery in Beverly Hills. In the 1940s, he became a companion of Gilbert Adrian, often known as just Adrian, a costume designer with MGM costume designer. He died after a stroke, aged seventy.

MARIA TAYLOR BURTON b. 1961. Taylor began adopting the two-year-old girl from Germany, Maria, while married to Fisher but the adoption was not processed until after they divorced and Burton adopted Maria, who became a clothes designer. She had over twenty surgical procedures to correct a genetic defect in her hips. In her teens and twenties, she tried out modeling and fashion design, and later started a talent agency with her first husband, Steve Carson. Their marriage lasted until 2000. She married again, but filed for divorce in 2014.

MICHAEL TODD 1909–58. Often known as Mike Todd, he was a stage and film producer, born in Minneapolis, whose best known production was a film version of Jules Verne's *Around the World in 80 Days*. After meeting Taylor, whom he married in February 1957, he lived flamboyantly in the media's gaze, exploiting every opportunity to display his conspicuous consumption. Many attribute Taylor's penchant for exhibitionism to Todd's influence. He died in a plane crash in March 1958.

LIZA TODD-TIVEY b. 1957. Taylor gave birth to Elizabeth Frances Todd, to use her original name, by caesarian section. Following the troublesome birth, Taylor had a tubal ligation, meaning she could have no more children. Liza never knew her father Michael Todd, who died in 1958. She went to a boarding school in Gstaad, eschewed the entertainment industry and became an equestrian sculptor, remaining protective of her privacy. She married the artist Hap Tivey in 1984.

WANGER WALTER 1894–1968. The man who persuaded 20th Century Fox to make the then most expensive film in history was born in San Francisco, served in the US Air Force in the First World War and worked at Paramount Studios after the war, later starting his own film production company and working for practically every studio. His reputation was that of a socially conscious intellectual with a penchant for epic dramas. Such a penchant first led him into trouble when his ambitious 145-minute version of *Joan of Arc* (1948) flopped. Wanger also landed in prison for four months after shooting a man he suspected of having an affair with his wife. On the other hand, his *I Want to Live* (1958), a drama with an anti-capital punishment subtext drew acclaim and brought Susan Hayward an Oscar. Wanger—pronounced like stranger—believed *Cleopatra* would save a then struggling 20th Century Fox, but, in the event, it almost ruined the studio. Wanger died from a heart attack, aged seventy-four.

JOHN WARNER b. 1927. Warner, from Washington DC, was a veteran of the Second World War who later became a Republican politician, serving as Secretary of the US Navy during the Richard Nixon Administration, 1972–4. He was appointed in 1974 to head up the federal government's American Revolution Bicentennial Administration. He met Taylor on the diplomatic circuit and married her in December 1976. It seemed an improbable alliance, but Taylor threw herself into his ultimately successful campaign to become a Senator. The couple divorced in November 1982, after which Taylor returned to acting and other pursuits.

CHRISTOPHER EDWARD WILDING b. 1955. Born in LA, Taylor's second child with Michael Wilding, Christopher worked as a photographer and assistant film producer. He married oil heiress Aileen Getty in 1981 and had two children; in 1985 Getty was diagnosed HIV positive after an extra-marital affair; they divorced in 1989.

MICHAEL WILDING 1912–79. Taylor's second husband, whom she married in February 1952, was an English actor who made his screen debut in 1933, a year after Taylor's birth. He followed Taylor to the USA but struggled professionally. She left him after meeting Michael Todd and they divorced in January 1957. Wilding died after a fall following an epileptic seizure.

MICHAEL HOWARD WILDING b. 1953. Taylor's first child was born in London, his father being Taylor's second husband, Michael Wilding. He became an actor (mainly in the US soap *Guiding Light*, now off-air), and then formed a rock band. He fathered two children by two different women.

JASON WINTERS b. 1961. In April 2010, Taylor, then seventy-eight, felt obliged to dismiss rumors that she was engaged to Winters, referring to him on twitter as her manager and dearest friend. Winters worked for Sterling/Winters Company, an LA-based artist management firm owned by Kathy Ireland.

HENRY WYNBERG b. 1935. Dutch entrepreneur who had a relationship with Taylor in the mid-1970s. In 1990, he and Taylor were thrust back together, this time in a courtroom: according to a 1977 agreement, Taylor had given Wynberg "perpetual" rights to 30 percent of the net profits from any cosmetics marketed under her name; she later alleged that Wynberg had not lived up to his part of the contract. Wynberg then sued her for breach of contract, fraud and misappropriation, triggering a four-year legal battle. The case was settled amicably.

BIBLIOGRAPHY

Books and articles

ABC News (1982) *World News Tonight*, ABC News Transcripts, February 28. Available at: http://bit.ly/1sfk51Q (accessed August 2014).

Acuna, Kirsten (2014) "The 30 most expensive movies ever made", *Business Insider UK*, June 18. Available at: http://bit.ly/1CvFo90 (accessed March 2015).

Adler, Renata (1968a) "Screen: Faustus Sells His Soul Again: Burtons and Oxford do the devil's work", *New York Times*, February 6. Available at: http://nyti.ms/1kmm7IK (accessed July 2014).

Adler, Renata (1968b) "Screen: 'Secret ceremony'", *New York Times*, October 24. Available at: http://nyti.ms/1oHb1lI (accessed July 2014).

Allan, John B. (2011, first published 1961) *Elizabeth Taylor*, Los Angeles CA: Blackbird Books.

Amburn, Ellis (2011) *The Most Beautiful Woman in the World: The Obsessions, Passions, and Courage of Elizabeth Taylor*, New York: Harper.

Anderson, Jon (1987) "Elizabeth Taylor sells Mystique with a passion", *Chicago Tribune*, September 27. Available at: http://trib.in/1uvOw5Y (accessed September 2014).

APN Newsdesk (2014) "Sense of humour tops relationship shopping list", *Sunshine Coast Daily*, October 1. Available at: http://bit.ly/1mUX1r9 (accessed October 2014).

Apple, R.W. Jr. (1982) "Elizabeth Taylor: London's big news", *New York Times*, March 13. Available at: http://nyti.ms/1pCdIpf (accessed August 2014).

Aquino, John T. (2005) *Truth and Lives on Film: The Legal Problems of Depicting Real Persons and Events in a Fictional Medium,* Jefferson NC: McFarland.

Archerd, Army (2001) "Rock Hudson's AIDS disclosure stunned Hollywood and the World", Reuters/*Variety*, June 5. Available at: http://bit.ly/XXzjQ7 (accessed August 2014).

Arthurs, Deborah (2012) "Sweet Smell of Success! Jennifer Lopez's perfume sells more than any other celebrity fragrance", *Daily Mail*, June 29. Available at: http://dailym.ai/1vb03Ig (accessed September 2014).

Associated Press (1983) "Elizabeth Taylor in drug program", *Chicago Tribune*, December 13, Section 1, p. 14. Available at: http://trib.in/1NWIra9 (accessed April 2015).

Associated Press (1985) "Hudson has AIDS, spokesman says", *New York Times*, July 26. Available at: http://nyti.ms/1CPGuJJ (accessed April 2015).

Associated Press (1990) "Doctors overprescribed drugs for Elizabeth Taylor, DA says", *Sun Journal*, Lewiston, Maine, April 21, p. 8.

Austerlitz, Saul (2010) "Public eye: The celebrated celebrity of Elizabeth Taylor", *Filmcomment*, vol. 46, no. 3 (May–June), p. 78.

Australian Women's Weekly (2010) "Liz Taylor's secret love letters", *Australian Women's Weekly*, July 28.

Babb, Francesca (2010) "'She liked being pursued': Ron Galella on Jackie Onassis", *Daily Telegraph*, November 25. Available at http://bit.ly/1x6Uk7Q: (accessed June 2014).

Bacon, James (1958) "Todd's wife begged him to delay trip one day", *Pittsburgh Post-Gazette*, March 24, p. 5). Available at: http://bit.ly/Rs31so (accessed May 2014).

Bacon, James (1975) "Black actress Jeannie Bell lives with Richard Burton", *Sarasota Journal*, May 20. Available at: http://bit.ly/WeAzgx (accessed July 2014).

Bagley, Christopher (2004) "Elizabeth Taylor: La Liz", *W*, December. Available at: http://wmag.co/1zk9VQq (accessed April 2015).

Bailey, Joey (2012) "Great love stories no. 4: Elizabeth Taylor and Richard Burton", *This is Glamorous*, April 22. Available at: http://bit.ly/1iJgx97 (accessed September 2015).

Baker, Donald P. (1979) "Surprising senator: The new Warner confounds critics", *Washington Post,* July 1, p. A1, A16–17.

Ballard, J.G. (1990) *The Atrocity Exhibition*, San Francisco: RE/Search Publications.

Ballard, J.G. (2008) *Crash*, London: Harper Perennial.

Bast, William (2006) *Surviving James Dean,* Fort Lee NJ: Barricade Books.

Bastin, Giselle (2009) "Filming the ineffable: Biopics of the British royal family", *a/b: Auto/Biography Studies*, vol. 24, no. 1, pp. 34–52.

Beaufort, John (1983) "Animated trio of one-acters—and some not-so-private lives", *Christian Science Monitor*, May 15. Available at: http://bit.ly/1un8guz (accessed August 2014).

Beer, David and Ruth Penfold-Mounce (2009) "Celebrity gossip and the new melodramatic imagination", *Sociological Research* Online, vol. 14, no. 2, paras 1–5. Available at: http://bit.ly/-BeerCelebGossip (accessed May 2014).

Bennett, Catherine (2011) "The strange case of Liz Taylor as a 'real woman' role model", *Observer*, March 27. Available at: http://bit.ly/1AsTxi9 (accessed December 2014).

Bergan, Peter (2011) "She was the most incredible vision of loveliness I have ever seen", *The Age*, News section, March 25, p. 17. Available at: http://bit.ly/1lIfJOP (accessed May 2014).

Bertman, Stephen (1998) *Hyperculture: The Human Cost of Speed*, Westport CN: Praeger.

Bethke Elshtain, Jean (1997) "Mourning in America", *The New Republic*, vol. 217, no. 13, p. 25.

Bevan, Nathan (2009) "Richard Burton tells of booze battle in forgotten interview", *Wales Online*, October 14. Available at: http://bit.ly/Vyqqu7 (accessed August 2014).

Bidini, Dave (2013) "Elizabeth Taylor and Richard Burton's 1964 visit to Toronto sent the city into chaos", *National Post*, March 29. Available at: http://bit.ly/1qKtxwy (accessed June 2014).

Bingham, Dennis (2006) "'Before She Was a Virgin . . .': Doris Day and the decline of female film comedy in the 1950s and 1960s", *Cinema Journal*, vol. 45, no. 3, pp. 3–31.

Bishop, Ronald (1999) "From Behind the Walls: Boundary work by news organizations in their coverage of Princess Diana's death", *Journal of Communication Inquiry*, vol. 23, no. 1, pp. 90–112.

Blum, David (1985) "The shy stripper", *New York Magazine*, 18 November, pp. 38–43. Available at: http://bit.ly/1AA3OJB (accessed August 2014).

Born, Matt and John Steele (2014) "Tape reveals how Diana challenged Camilla over her affair with Charles", *Telegraph*, March 12. Available at: http://bit.ly/1omTiQi (accessed May 2014).

Boston Globe staff (1984) "Richard Burton", *Boston Globe*, August 7, p. 1.

Boxer, Sarah (1998) "Tazio Secchiaroli, the model for 'Paparazzo,' dies at 73", *New York Times*, July 25. Available at: http://nyti.ms/1l5eYji (accessed June 2014).

Boyes, Malcolm (1984) "While Liz Taylor mourns Burton, she and Victor Luna lament the end of a romance", *People*, vol. 22, no. 12. Available at: http://bit.ly/1F8wYj5 (accessed April 2015).

Bragg, Melvyn (1989) *Rich: The Life of Richard Burton*, London: Coronet.

Braxton, Greg (1991) "Wedding crasher famous, not rich", *Los Angeles Times*, November 2. Available at: http://lat.ms/YWBenH (accessed October 2014).

Braxton, Greg (2010) "'Jerry Springer': 20 years of fights, bleeps and sleaze TV", *Los Angeles Times*, October 27. Available at: http://lat.ms/1ncRvAv (accessed October 2014).

Brenner, Marie (1983) "The Liz and Dick show", *New York*, May 9. Available at http://nym.ag/1qy5kpJ (accessed August 2014).

Bresler, Robert J. (1997) "The death of Hollywood's golden age and the changing American character", *USA Today Magazine*, vol. 125, no. 2622, March 1, p. 64. Available at: http://bit.ly/QyYDHU (accessed April 2013).

Bret, David (2011) *Elizabeth Taylor: The Lady, the Lover, the Legend—1932–2011*, Edinburgh: Mainstream Publishing.

Brisbin, Richard A. Jr. (2002) "Censorship, Ratings, and Rights: Political order and sexual portrayals in American movies", *Studies in American Political Development*, vol. 16, no. 1, pp. 1–27.

Brodsky, Jack and Nathan Weiss (1963) *The Cleopatra Papers: A Private Correspondence*, New York: Simon & Schuster.

Brown, Laura (2012) "Kim Kardashian: Cleopatra with a 'K'", *Harper's Bazaar*, no. 3591 (March), pp. 405–12. Available at: http://bit.ly/1K6cZsO (accessed June 2015).

Brown, Stacy (2013) "Katherine Jackson called son Michael a homophobic slur", *New York Post*, October 13. Available at: http://bit.ly/1QdEsdh (accessed April 2015).

Bruck, Connie (1989) *The Predators' Ball: The Inside Story of Drexel Burnham and the Rise of the Junk Bond Raiders*, New York: Penguin.

Burrough Bryan (2008) "The man who was Texas", *Vanity Fair*, October. Available at: http://vnty.fr/1tAIPmO (accessed August 2014).

Byrne, Gabriel (2010) "A review of *Furious Love* by Sam Kashner and Nancy Schoenberger", *Huffington Post*, July 27. Available at: http://huff.to/1lWPxgf (accessed July 2014).

Canby, Vincent (1986) "Elizabeth Taylor—her life is the stuff of movies", *New York Times*, May 4, Section H, p. 1. Available at: http://nyti.ms/1t5Da7W (accessed January 2014).

Caputi, Jane (1999) "The second coming of Diana", *NWSA Journal*, vol. 11, no. 2, pp. 103–23.

Carlson, Margaret (1997) "Blood on their hands?" *Time*, vol. 150 (September 8), p. 46.

Caro, Mark (2011) "How Elizabeth Taylor changed the face of fame", *Chicago Tribune*, March 23, pp. 1 and 15.

Celeste, Reni (2005) "Screen Idols: The tragedy of falling stars", *Journal of Popular Film and Television*, vol. 33, no. 1, pp. 29–38.

Chambers, Andrea (1983) "Zef Bufman", *People*, vol. 19, no. 20. Available at: http://bit.ly/1IqGLUw (accessed April 2013).

Churcher, Sharon (1985) "Bid for Liz's ring", *New York Magazine*, 11 Mar 1985, p. 12. Available at: http://bit.ly/1BFf4pB (accessed August 2014).

Citizens Commission on Human Rights International (2008) *When Prescribing Psychotropic Drugs Becomes Criminal Negligence: Cases and convictions—a public interest report and recommendations*, Los Angeles, CA: CCHR international.

Clendinen, Dudley (1983) "A public 'Private Lives' for Taylor-Burton fans", *New York Times*, April 18. Available at: http://nyti.ms/1kZg6HY (accessed August 2014).

Clifford, Garry (1980) "So happy in love", *People*, vol. 14, no. 16, October 20. Available at: http://bit.ly/1tVKVgx (accessed July 2014).

Cohn, Art (ed.) (1956) *Michael Todd's* Around the World in 80 Days *Almanac*, New York: Random House.

Collins, Joan (2010) "Bring back the brawn!", *Daily Mail*, March 23. Available at: http://dailym.ai/T2XtFq (accessed June 2014).

Collins, Joan (2011) "My wickedly funny friend Liz Taylor", *Daily Mail*, March 27. Available at: http://dailym.ai/1wNKl9R (accessed August 2014).

Collins, Nancy (1992) "Liz's AIDS odyssey", *Vanity Fair*, November. Available at: http://vnty.fr/YeR9OF (accessed September 2014).

Cones, John W. (1997) *The Feature Film Distribution Deal: A Critical Analysis of the Single Most Important Film Industry Agreement*, Carbondale IL: Southern Illinois University Press.

Conway, Ann (2003) "A benefit, a chopper and arrival by La Liz", *Los Angeles Times*, February 16. Available at: http://lat.ms/1ugmzwd (accessed October 2014).

Corliss, Richard (2011) "Elizabeth Taylor, 1932–2011: Hollywood's star of stars", *Time*, vol. 177, no. 13. Available at: http://ti.me/1wwLjUp (accessed June 2014).

Cox, Donna (1999) "Diana: Her true story: post-modern transgressions in identity", *Journal of Gender Studies*, vol. 8, no. 3, pp. 323–38.

Crawford, Clare and Parviz Raein (1976) "The Charming Zahedi Ponders: Can Liz Taylor be a diplomatic incident?", *People*, vol. 5, no. 23. Available at: http://bit.ly/UuBXKx (accessed July 2014).

Crowther, Bosley (1960) "The Screen: Elizabeth Taylor at 'BUtterfield 8'—film based on O'Hara novel in premiere", *New York Times,* November 17. Available at: http://nyti.ms/QU6rEr (accessed April 2014).

Crowther, Bosley (1963) "The Screen: 'Cleopatra' has premiere at Rivoli: 4-hour epic is tribute to its artists' skills", *New York Times*, June 13. Available: http://nyti.ms/1pPBb8T (accessed June 2014).

Daily Telegraph (2011) "Dame Elizabeth Taylor", *Daily Telegraph*, March 23, p. 33.

Dargis, Manohla (2011) "Lust for Life: Movies, men, melodramas", *New York Times*, March 23. Available at: http://nyti.ms/17kRoeN (accessed February 2015).

David, Lester and Jhan Robbins (1976) "Springtime in Rome, 1962 . . . gossip", *Miami News*, June 15, p. 1A and 12A.

Davis, Victor (2002) "The father of scandal", *British Journalism Review*, vol. 13, no. 4, pp.74–80.

De La Hoz, Cindy (2011) *Elizabeth Taylor: A loving tribute*, Philadelphia PA: Running Press.

De Lafayette, Maximillien (2010) *Hollywood Most Beautiful, Exclusive and Rarest Photos Album of the Silver Screen*, 3rd ed., New York: Times Square Press.

Denson, G. Roger (2011) "The Liz Taylor Paintings of Kathe Burkhart: Picturing the trials and tribulations of a proto-feminist", *Huffington Post*, April 9. Available at: http://huff.to/1EdUvC4 (accessed March 2015).

Dherbier, Yann-Brice (2008) *Elizabeth Taylor: A Life in Pictures*, London: Anova Books.

Dowd, Maureen (1984) "Richard Burton, 58, is dead; rakish sage and screen star", *New York Times*, August 4, p. 1.

Drug & Cosmetic Industry (1996) "Taylor to go 'on the road again' for Arden", *Drug & Cosmetic Industry*, vol. 158, no. 2 (February), p. 8.

Duchesne, Scott (2010) "Stardom/fandom: Celebrity and fan tribute performance", *Canadian Theatre Review*, vol. 141, no. 1, pp. 21–7.

Duerden, Nick (2005) "Beyond doubt", *Independent Magazine*, August 28, pp. 12–14.

Duffy, Martha (1991) "The war of the noses", *Time*, vol. 138, no. 13 (September 30). Revised June 24, 2001 version available at: http://ti.me/1v4WuDl (accessed September 2014).

Duka, John (1985) "Elizabeth Taylor: Journal of a recovery", *New York Times*, February 4. Available at: http://nyti.ms/1qhxm7u (accessed August 2014).

Dulin, Dann (2003) "Life=Passion", *a&u: America's Aids Magazine*, February. Available at: http://bit.ly/1iz1IWM (accessed June 2015).

Edelson, Sharon (1991) "Elizabeth Taylor: A passion for diamonds", *WWD: Women's Wear Daily*, vol. 161, no. 102, p. 12.

Effron, Lauren (2013) "Elizabeth Taylor confesses 'pure animal pleasure' for Richard Burton in steamy love letter", *ABC News*, November 28. Available at: http://abcn.ws/1x4DZQa (accessed June 2014).

Elizabeth (no other name) (2003) "Quigley's Annual List of Box-Office Champions, 1932–1970", *ReelClassics.com*. Available at: http://bit.ly/1jgPVc8 (accessed April 2014).

Elliott, Andrew, Tobias Greitemeyer, Richard H. Gramzow, Daniela Niesta Kayser, Stephanie Lichtenfeld, Markus A. Maier and Liu Huijun (2010) "Red, rank, and romance in women viewing men", *Journal of Experimental Psychology: General*, vol. 139, No. 3, pp. 399–417.

Elliott, Stuart (1991) "Star vehicle for Taylor: A scent spot", *New York Times*, August 23. Available at: http://nyti.ms/1rkKOMT (accessed September 2014).

Extra staff (2010) "King of pop's secret lover? 'I was Michael Jackson's boyfriend'", *Extra*, April 29. Available at: http://bit.ly/12YQ8wi (accessed October 2014).

Fackler, Maria F. and Nick Salvato (2012) "Fag Hag: A theory of effeminate enthusiasms", *Discourse*, vol. 34, no. 1 (Winter), p. 59–92.

Feeley, Kathleen A. (2004) *Louella Parsons and Hedda Hopper's Hollywood: The Rise of the Celebrity Gossip Industry in Twentieth-century America, 1910–1950*, PhD dissertation, New York: City University of New York.

Ferri, Anthony J. (2010) "Emergence of the entertainment age?" *Social Science and Modern Society*, vol. 47, no. 5, pp. 403–9.

Flynn, Paul (2011) "Elizabeth Taylor: Gay icon", *Guardian*, March 23. Available at: http://bit.ly/VSfrMy (accessed August 2014).

Fontaine, Smokey (2010) "Elizabeth Taylor engaged to a black man", *NewsOne for Black America*, April 9. Available at: http://bit.ly/1xsiTyp (accessed December 2014).

Forrest, Emma (1997) "The last star in the firmament", *Independent*, February 27. Available at: http://ind.pn/Zp1qb6 (accessed October 2014).

Franzero, C. M. (1969) *Life and Times of Cleopatra*, London: Heron Books.

Friedan, Betty (2013; first published 1963) *The Feminine Mystique*, New York: W. W. Norton & Company.

Friedman, Roger (2009) "Jacko not sick, except in head", *Fox News.com*, December 22. Available at: http://fxn.ws/1wANI3d (accessed October 2014).

Frost, Jennifer (2011a) "Hollywood gossip as public sphere: Hedda Hopper, reader-respondents, and the Red Scare, 1947–1965", *Cinema Journal*, vol. 50, no. 2, pp. 84–103.

Frost, Jennifer (2011b) *Hedda Hopper's Hollywood: Celebrity Gossip and American Conservatism*, New York: New York University Press.

Furedi, Frank (2003) "Get off that couch", *Guardian*, October 9. Available at: http://bit.ly/VrYo3r (accessed February 2014).

Gabler, Neal (2009) "Tiger-stalking: In defense of our tabloid culture", *Newsweek*, December 11. Available at: http://bit.ly/1izeB3w (accessed September 2015).

Gainer, Nichelle (2014) *Vintage Black Glamour*, London: Rocket 88.

Galloway, Stephen (2013) "Rock Hudson's wife secretly recorded his gay confession", *Hollywood Reporter*, June 14. Available at: http://bit.ly/1DRvc9U (accessed April 2015).

Gamson, Joshua (1992) "The assembly line of greatness: Celebrity in twentieth-century America", *Critical Studies in Mass Communication*, vol. 9, no. 1, pp. 1–24.

Garavelli, Dani (2011) "Elizabeth Taylor's death has brought down the curtain on the 20th century's greatest love affair", *The Scotsman*, September 11. Available at: http://bit.ly/1geZI4b (accessed: September 2015).

Gardetta, Dave (2002) "The skin you're in", *Los Angeles Magazine*, January, pp. 47–9 and 121–22.

Gates, Anita (1995) "And what's more, Elizabeth Taylor dyes her hair", *New York Times*, May 21. Available from: http://nyti.ms/ZVwjEP (accessed October 2014).

Gerhart, Ann (1993) "Gossip queen tells few of her own secrets", *Philadelphia Inquirer*, September 23. Available at: http://bit.ly/1uQ0oSV (accessed October 2014).

Germain, David and Hillel Italie (2011) "Film legend Elizabeth Taylor dies at 79 in L.A.", *Backstage,* March 23. Available at: http://bit.ly/1n3YFCh (accessed May 2014).

Gies, Lieve (2011) "Stars Behaving Badly: Inequality and transgression in celebrity culture", *Feminist Media Studies,* vol. 11, no.3, pp. 347–61.

Goldman, Russell (2013) "Lance Armstrong admits to doping", *ABC News*, January 17. Available at: http://abcn.ws/1k8XGgp (accessed May 2014).

Gomstyn, Alice and Chris Connelly (2011) "Michael Jackson's Secret World: willing doctors, hospital-grade sedatives", *ABC News*, November 4. Available at: http://abcn.ws/1wknOR8 (accessed October 2014).

Goodman, Ezra (1961) *The Fifty-Year Decline and Fall of Hollywood*, New York: Simon and Schuster.

Graham, Caroline (2011) "She put on a fur coat over her nightdress and fell giggling in the snow", *Daily Mail* April 24. Available at: http://dailym. ai/1oJGYYX (accessed October 2014).

Green, Mary and Stephen M. Silverman (2011) "John Warner: Elizabeth Taylor 'was a fox'", *People*, March 25. Available at: http://bit.ly/1k5fXlN (accessed July 2014).

Greenberg, Zack O'Malley (2010) "The rich afterlife of Michael Jackson", *Forbes*, October 25. Available at: http://onforb.es/1tD5P6h (accessed October 2014).

Gross, Michael (1987) "Elizabeth Taylor's Passion, a perfume", *New York Times*, January 15. Available at: http://nyti.ms/1xDdrck (accessed September 2014).

Gundle, Stephen (2002) "Hollywood glamour and mass consumption in postwar Italy", *Journal of Cold War Studies*, vol. 4, no. 3, pp. 95–118.

Gundle, Stephen (2012) *Death and the Dolce Vita: The Dark Side of Rome in the 1950s*, Edinburgh: Canongate Books.

Gurley Brown, Helen (1962) *Sex and the Single Girl*, New York: Bernard Geis Associates.

Gussow, Mel (2011) "A lustrous pinnacle of Hollywood glamour", *New York Times*, March 23. Available at: http://nyti.ms/1DOEnnL (accessed May 2015).

Gutierrez, Victor (1997) *Michael Jackson Was My Lover*, Palo Alto CA: VMG Publishing.

Guzman, Rafer, Gary Dymski and Michele Ingrassia (2011) "Elizabeth Taylor 1932–2011: Film goddess", *Newsday*, March 24, p. A3.

Hadleigh, Boze (2001) *The Lavender Screen: The Gay and Lesbian Films—Their Stars, Makers, Characters, and Critics,* New York: Citadel.

Haggerty, Ryan (2011) "Elizabeth Taylor in Chicago", *Chicago Tribune*, March 24. Available at: http://trib.in/1laLtZL (accessed May 2015).

Haller, Scot (1985) "The Long Goodbye: Rock Hudson 1925–85", *People*, vol. 23, no. 17. Available at: http://bit.ly/1wM3t84 (accessed August 2014).

Halperin, Ian (2009) *Unmasked: The Final Years of Michael Jackson*, New York: Simon and Schuster.

Hamilton, Denise (1990) "Celebrities vie for sweet smell of success", *Sun Sentinel*, December 16. Available at: http://bit.ly/1qEOSHa (accessed September 2014).

Harris, Daniel (2008) "Celebrity deaths", *Antioch Review*, vol. 66, no. 44, pp. 616–24.

Hefferman, Virginia (2007) "Wow! Ooh! Ugh! Celebrities are just like us", *International Herald Tribune*, July 17, p. 20.

Hersh, Burton (2008) *Bobby and J. Edgar: The Historic Face-Off Between the Kennedys and J. Edgar Hoover That Transformed America*, New York: Basic Books.

Heymann, C. David (1995) *Liz: An intimate biography of Elizabeth Taylor*, London: Mandarin.

Hite, Shere (2004) *The Hite Report: A Nationwide Study of Female Sexuality*, New York: Seven Stories Press.

Hoffmann, Bill (1999) "Liz Taylor: Hudson & Dean had a 'Giant' rift", *New York Post*, June 21. Available at: http://bit.ly/YX2X8l (accessed August 2014).

Hollander, Paul (2010) "Michael Jackson, the celebrity cult, and popular culture", *Culture and Society*, vol. 47, no. 2, pp. 147–52.

Holley, Val (2003) *Mike Connolly and the Manly Art of Hollywood Gossip*, Jefferson NC: McFarland & Co.

Holston, Kim R. (2013) *Movie Roadshows: A History and Filmography of Reserved-Seat Limited Showings, 1911–1973*, Jefferson NC: McFarland & Co.

Hooper, John (2006) "The bitter sweet life", *Guardian*, June 24. Available at: http://bit.ly/1uhlpCY (accessed June 2014).

Hopper, Hedda (1948) "Moppet matures to whistle bait", *Toledo Blade*, August 29, p. 4. Available at: http://bit.ly/1jnbWls (accessed March 2015).

Hopper, Hedda and James Brough (1963a) *The Whole Truth and Nothing But*, Garden City NY: Doubleday.

Hopper, Hedda and James Brough (1963b) "Todd taught Liz everything about sex—good and bad", *Winnipeg Free Press*, March 25, p. 24.

Horn, John, Nicole Sperling and Doug Smith (2012) "Unmasking the Academy: Oscar voters overwhelmingly white, male", *Los Angeles Times*, February 19. Available at: http://lat.ms/PQQUUT (accessed April 2014).

Horton, Donald and R. Richard Wohl (1956) "Mass communication and para-social interaction: observations on intimacy at a distance", *Psychiatry*, vol. 19, no. 1, pp. 215–29.

Howard, Caroline, Kate Pierce, Mehrunnisa Wani and Chris Smith (2014) "100 women who lead the world" *Forbes*, May 28. Available at http://onforb.es/1khSk9u (accessed August 2014).

Hudson, Rock and Sara Davidson (2007) *Rock Hudson: His Story*, New York: Carroll & Graf.

Hughes-Hallet, Lucy (1990) *Cleopatra: Histories, Dreams and Distortions*, London: Bloomsbury.

Israel, Lee (1970) "The Rise and Fall and Rise of Elizabeth Taylor", pp. 340–9 in Gross, Theodore L. (ed.) *Representative Men: Cult Heroes of Our Time*, New York: Free Press.

Jacobowitz, Florence and Richard Lippe (2012) "Elizabeth Taylor: in memoriam 1932–2011", *CineAction*, March 22, p. 44.

Jicha, Tom (1995) "Liz tactics frustrate NBC", *Orlando Sun-Sentinel*, May 11. Available at: http://bit.ly/1sc451M (accessed October 2014).

Kalich, Timothy (1987) "What's in a Smell? The perfume industry is now mainly an American one, and it has a problem or two", *Atlantic*, vol. 260 (October), p. 34–9.

Kaltenbach, Chris (1996) "Gee whiz, it's La Liz on TV", *Baltimore Sun*, February 26. Available at: http://bit.ly/1uLWWVM (accessed September 2014).

Kalter, Suzy (1982) "Dr. Arnold Klein's business is shady but lifesaving—he's out to prevent skin cancer", *People*, May 25. Available at: http://bit.ly/1usSJVw (accessed October 2014).

Kamp, David (1998) "When Liz met Dick", *Vanity Fair*, March. Available at: http://vnty.fr/1xwMZP9 (accessed June 2014).

Kashner, Sam (2011) "Elizabeth Taylor's closing act", *Vanity Fair*, November. Abridged version available at: http://vnty.fr/1KaebpH (accessed September 2015).

Kashner, Sam and Nancy Schoenberger (2010) *Furious Love: Elizabeth Taylor-Richard Burton—The Marriage of the Century*. London: JR Books.

Kaufman, David (2008) "Doris Day's vanishing act", *Vanity Fair*, May. Abridged version available at: http://bit.ly/1EPYw32 (accessed September 2015).

Kehr, Dave (2011) "Elizabeth Taylor 1932–2011" *Entertainment Weekly*, no. 1149, pp. 2–11.

Kelley, Kitty (1981) *Elizabeth Taylor: The Last Star*, London: Coronet.

Kelley, Kitty (1987) *His Way: The Unauthorized Biography of Frank Sinatra*, New York: Mass Market Paperback.

Kennedy, Lisa (2011) "Elizabeth Rosemond Taylor, Feb. 27, 1932–March 23, 2011: A life, her way", *Denver Post*, March 24, p. A.1.

Kilday, Gregg (2012) "Shirley MacLaine's past (Oscar) lives", *Hollywood Reporter*, February 23. Available at: http://bit.ly/1iI5p9r (accessed April 2014).

Kilgallen, Dorothy (1963) "Showgirl refuses to tell on Burton", *Toledo Blade*, June 24, p. 24.

Kilgallen, Dorothy (1964) "Voice of Broadway: Keely Smith starts year with romantic success", *Tanawanda News*, January 15, p. 12.

King, Susan (2013) "'Cleopatra,' A spectacle on-and off-screen", *Los Angeles Times*, May 20. Available at: http://lat.ms/1BQiKWx (accessed March 2015).

Kinsey Institute (n.d) "The Development and Publication of *Sexual Behavior in the Human Male* and *Sexual Behavior in the Human Female*: "The Kinsey Reports" of 1948 and 1953", Available at: http://bit.ly/1oSrkLP (accessed May 2014).

Kinsey, Alfred C., Wardell B. Pomeroy and Clyde E. Martin (1948) *Sexual Behavior in the Human Male*, Philadelphia PA: W. B. Saunders

Kinsey, Alfred C., Wardell B. Pomeroy, Clyde E. Martin and Paul H. Gebhard (1952) *Sexual Behavior in the Human Female*, Philadelphia PA: W. B. Saunders.

Klein, Arnold W., James H. Sternberg and Paul Bernstein (1982) *The Skin Book*, New York: Macmillan.

Klemsrud, Judy (1979) "Liz: superstar takes on Capitol Hill", *Wilmington Morning Star*, February 6, p. 2A. Available at: http://bit.ly/1ARuwym (accessed August 2014).

Korman, Seymour (1958a) "Debbie's lawyer says she'll sue for divorce", *Chicago Tribune*, September 13, part 1, p. 4.

Korman, Seymour (1958b) "Barefoot Liz throws party starring Eddie", *Chicago Tribune*, October 2, part 3, p. 8.

Koski, Lorna (2011) "Elizabeth Taylor: A beautiful pioneer", *WWD: Women's Wear Daily*, vol. 201, no. 61, p. 4.

Lague, Louise (1984) "Richard Burton—lover, drinker, scholar, friend", *People*, vol. 22, no. 8 (August 20), pp. 26–7. Available at: http://bit.ly/1sIC30s (accessed August 2014).

Langer, Cassandra (2013) "Parallel lives—up to a point", *Gay & Lesbian Review*, vol. 1, no. 2 (March/April), pp. 34–5.

Lapham, Lewis H. (1997) "Fatted calf", *Harper's*, vol. 295 (November), pp. 11–14.

Lasch, Christopher (1991) *The True and Only Heaven: Progress and its Critics*, New York: W. W. Norton.

Leafe, David (2013) "The ultimate sexual betrayal—and the guilt that haunted Liz Taylor to the grave", *MailOnline*, April 26. Available at: http://dailym.ai/1gDmLQb (accessed April 2014).

Leaming, Barbara (1989) *If This Was Happiness: A Biography of Rita Hayworth*, New York: Viking.

Lee, Adrian (2011) "Battle of Richard Burton's brides", *Daily Express*, October 11. Available at: http://dexpr.es/1rSn8wx (accessed August 2014).

Lee, Dan P. (2011) "Carpooling: Liz, Jacko, and Marlon: The starriest refugees in history", *New York*, August 27. Available at: http://nym.ag/1ytcwrN (accessed October 2014).

Lee, Richard (1986) "'Heartburn' brings more heartache", *Philadelphia Inquirer*, April 20. Available at: http://bit.ly/1sX6znh (accessed August 2014).

Leerhsen, Charles (1996) "Life after Larry", *People*, vol. 45, no. 9 (March 4), Available at: http://bit.ly/1sKClVl (accessed February 2015).

Lees, Gene (2005) *The Musical Worlds of Lerner and Loewe*, Lincoln NE: University of Nebraska Press.

Leff, Leonard (2008) "Becoming Clifton Webb: A queer star in mid-century Hollywood", *Cinema Journal*, vol. 47, no. 3 (Spring), pp. 3–28.

Leonard, Suzanne (2010) "The 'True Love' of Elizabeth Taylor and Richard Burton," pp. 74–97 in Callahan, Vicki (ed.) *Reclaiming the Archive: Feminism and Film History*, Detroit: Wayne State University Press.

Levy, Emmanuel (1990) "Social attributes of American movie stars", *Media, Culture and Society*, vol. 12, pp. 247–67.

Lewin, Tamar (1982) "Whose life is it anyway? Legally it's hard to tell", *New York Times*, November 21. Available at: http://nyti.ms/1uwCj3b (accessed August 2014).

Libman, Norma (1993) "Traveling with Chen Sam: Liz Taylor's road trips demand double-duty work", *Chicago Tribune*, November 21. Available at: http://trib.in/1S6ZoUf (accessed May 2015).

Life staff (1958) "Tale of Debbie, Eddie and the Widow Todd", *Life*, vol. 45, no. 12 (September 22), pp. 39–40.

Lippert, Barbara (1998) "Rights of Springer", *New York*, April 20. Available at: http://nym.ag/1CvFNEG (accessed October 2014).

Lister, David (2014) "An actor's pain alters how we see them", *i*, February 8, p. 43.

Lofton, Kathryn (2011) "Religion and the American celebrity", *Social Compass*, vol. 58, no. 3, pp. 346–352.

Lord, M.G. (2011) "How she broke the rules", *The Hollywood Reporter*, March 29. Available at: http://bit.ly/1GqtX0x (accessed December 2014).

Lord, M.G. (2012a) *The Accidental Feminist: How Elizabeth Taylor Raised Our Consciousness and We Were Too Distracted by Her Beauty to Notice*, New York: Walker & Company.

Lord, M.G. (2012b) "I am Liz, hear me roar", *W*, February. Available at: http://wmag.co/1yGRAiV (accessed December 2014).

Maddox, Brenda (1977) *Who's Afraid of Elizabeth Taylor? A Myth of Our Time*, London: Granada.

Mahboob, Tahiat (2013) "Elizabeth Taylor's 1976 Trip to Iran, in pictures", *Asia Society*, November 8. Available at: http://bit.ly/1pKimzX (accessed July 2014).

Mangan, Lucy (2012) "TV review: Elizabeth Taylor: The auction of a lifetime; divine women", *Guardian*, April 18. Available at: http://bit.ly/1o3u1cn (accessed July 2014).

Mann, William J. (2009) *How to be a Movie Star: Elizabeth Taylor in Hollywood*, London: Faber & Faber.

Mann, William J. (2011) "Elizabeth Taylor: Movie star, angel of mercy", *The Gay and Lesbian Review Worldwide*, vol. 18, no.4 (July/August) p. 8.

Manning, Harriet J. (2013) *Michael Jackson and the Blackface Mask*, Farnham, UK: Ashgate.

Martin, Douglas (2012) "Judith Crist, a blunt and influential film critic, dies at 90", *New York Times*, August 7. Available at: http://nyti.ms/1lQ8zon (accessed June 2014).

Maslow, Abraham H. (1954) *Motivation and Personality*, New York, NY: Harper.

McCarthy, John P. (1995) "Review: 'Liz: The Elizabeth Taylor Story'", *Variety*, May 24. Available at: http://bit.ly/1sbVs7B (accessed October 2014).

McClellan, Diana (1985) "Pals: Liz had bigger fish to fry", *Weekly World News*, March 26, p. 13. Available at: http://bit.ly/1v0bjt9 (accessed August 2014).

McCracken, Grant David (2005) *Culture and Consumption II: Markets, Meaning, and Brand Management*, Bloomington IN: Indiana University Press.

McDonald, Tamar Jeffers (2006) "Very Little Wrist Movement': Rock Hudson acts out sexual heterodoxy", *Canadian Journal of Communication*, vol. 31, no. 4, pp. 843–58.

McFarland, Stephen (1996) "Forbes hints father was gay", *New York Daily News*, March 1. Available at: http://nydn.us/1rIBBQc (accessed September 2014).

McGraw, Carol (1990a) "Liz Taylor stars in battle over 'Passion' fragrance", *Los Angeles Times*, December 3. Available at: http://lat.ms/1rtyqrX (accessed July 2014).

McGraw, Carol (1990b) "Taylor, ex-boyfriend put the cap on perfume battle", *Los Angeles Times*, December 7. Available at: http://lat.ms/XQv1t4 (accessed September 2014).

McLean, Adrienne L. (1995) "The Cinderella Princess and the Instrument of Evil: Surveying the limits of female transgression in two postwar Hollywood scandals", *Cinema Journal*, vol. 34, no. 3, pp. 36–56.

McLean, Gareth (2012) "Tracey-Ann Oberman on Rock and Doris and Elizabeth", *Radio Times*, October 16. Available at: http://bit.ly/1qCx3bn (accessed August 2014).

McLeland, Susan Elaine (1996) *Fallen Stars: Femininity, Celebrity and Scandal in Post-Studio Hollywood*, PhD dissertation, Austin TX: University of Texas.

McLeland, Susan Elaine (1999) "Elizabeth Taylor: Hollywood's Last Glamour Girl", pp. 227–51 in Radner, Hilary and Luckett, Moya (eds), *Swinging Single: Representing Sexuality in the 1960s*, Minneapolis: University of Minnesota Press.

McNamara, Kim (2011) "The paparazzi industry and new media: the evolving production and consumption of celebrity news and gossip websites", *International Journal of Cultural Studies*, vol. 14, no. 3, pp. 515–30.

Menand, Louis (2010) "Talk stories: Dick Cavett and the battles for late night", *The New Yorker*, November 22. Available at: http://nyr.kr/ZqhrgB (accessed October 2014).

Merton, Robert K. (1938) "Social structure and anomie", *American Sociological Review*, vol. no. 5, pp. 672–82.

Meryman, Richard (1964) "I refuse to cure my public image", *Life*, December 18, pp. 74–85.

Michaud, Chris (2011) "$116 million auction of Liz Taylor jewels breaks record", *Reuters*, US Edition, December 14. Available at: http://reut.rs/1yPYj7l (accessed February 2015).

Monsma, Genevieve (2010) "A Look Back: Beauty chat with Elizabeth Taylor", *More*, undated. Available at: http://bit.ly/1EFMQ10 (accessed February 2015).

Moylan, Brian (2011) "Elizabeth Taylor was worth more money than you imagined", *Gawker*, March 28. Available at: http://bit.ly/1qEEJu0 (accessed September 2014).

Munn, Michael (2008) *Richard Burton: Prince of Players*, New York: Skyhorse Publishing.

Neimark, Jill (1995) "The culture of celebrity", *Psychology Today*, May/June, pp. 54–7; 87–90.

Niven, David (1975) *Bring On the Empty Horses*, New York: Putnam.

Observer-Reporter (Washington, PA) (1983) "Burton admits to alcoholism", *Observer-Reporter*, February 25, p. A3. Available at: http://bit.ly/1pVyn7R (accessed August 2014).

Orbach, Susie (2006; orig. 1978) *Fat Is a Feminist Issue,* London: Arrow Books.

Paglia, Camille (1992) "Elizabeth Taylor: Hollywood's Pagan Queen", pp. 14–18 in Camille Paglia (ed.), *Sex, Art and American Culture*, New York: Vintage Books.

Pearson, Drew (1966) "Burton almost stopped at border by Feighan", *Gadsen Times*, May 1, p. 8. Available at: http://bit.ly/1ixT6yF (accessed June 2014).

Peary, Danny (2014) "Ralph Kiner and Elizabeth Taylor", *The Sag Harbor Express*, February 28. Available at: http://bit.ly/1KG7imM (accessed May 2014).

Pendleton, Austin (1986) "Elizabeth", *Film Comment,* vol. 22, no. 3, pp. 28–31.

People staff (1975a) "Taylor and Burton leave poor Henry Wynberg holding the bags", vol. 4, no. 10, September 8. Available at: http://bit.ly/1mXceFF (accessed July 2014).

People staff (1975b) "Liz un-Burtoned again", *People*, vol. 5, no. 10 (March 15). Available at: http://bit.ly/1BJ6Gmt (accessed March 2013).

People staff (1981) "Old violet eyes is back", *People*, vol. 16, no. 26, December 28. Available at: http://bit.ly/1qr7jw0 (accessed July 2014).

People staff (1985) "To have and to hold", *People*, vol. 23, no. 1, January 7. Available at: http://bit.ly/1moQjEl (accessed August 2014).

Perry, Eleanor (1965) "Who pays the sandpiper calls the tune", *Life*, vol. 59, no. 3, July 16, p. 22.

Petersen, Anne Helen (2010) "Smut goes Corporate: TMZ and the conglomerate, convergent face of celebrity gossip", *Television and New Media*, vol. 11, no. 1, pp. 62–81.

Petersen, Anne Helen (2013) "The Rules of the Game: a century of Hollywood publicity", *Virginia Quarterly Review*, vol. 89, no. 1, pp. 46–59.

Pinker, Steven (1999) *How the Mind Works*, London: Penguin.

Pithers, Ellie (2013) "Elizabeth Taylor: the ultimate rock chick", *Sunday Telegraph*, Fashion section, June 5. Available at: http://bit.ly/1k9ZZ43 (accessed July 2014).

Pomerantz, Dorothy (2012) "Elizabeth Taylor tops 2012 list of the top-earning dead celebrities", *Forbes*, October 24. Available at: http://onforb.es/1v4NxbN (accessed February 2015).

Pomerantz, Dorothy (2014) "Michael Jackson tops Forbes' list of top-earning dead celebrities with $140 million haul", *Forbes*, October 10. Available at: http://onforb.es/1BPftHJ (accessed December 2014).

Porkari, George (aka Lightmonkey) (2013) *Who's the Clown with the Camera? A Very Short History of the Art of the Paparazzi*. Available at: http://www.lightmonkey.net/essays/ (accessed April 2014).

Porter, Darwin and Danforth Prince (2012) *Elizabeth Taylor: There is Nothing Like a Dame*, New York: Blood Moon Productions.

Posner, Gerald (2009) "The Jackson-Liz drug link" *Daily Beast*, June 7. Available at: http://thebea.st/1yY01rc (accessed October 2014).

PR Newswire (2005) "House of Taylor Jewelry, Inc. established through merger with Nurescell Inc." May 23. Available at: http://prn.to/1nQkgU0 (accessed October 2014).

Projansky, Sarah (2014) *Spectacular Girls: Media Fascination and Celebrity Culture*, New York: New York University Press.

Provenzano, Jim (2005) "Dean, James", pp. 89–90 in Claude J. Summers (ed.) *The Queer Encyclopedia of Film and Television*, Berkeley CA: Cleis Press.

Quan, Denis (2009) "Promoter: Michael Jackson 'as healthy as can be'", *CNN.com/entertainment*, May 18. Available at: http://cnn.it/1zdxEW7 (accessed October 2014).

Rawlins, Justin Owen (2013) "Over His Dead Body: Hedda Hopper and the story of James Dean", *Velvet Light Trap*, no. 71, pp. 27–41.

Reed, J.D. (1999) "Elizabeth Taylor", *People*, March 15. Available at: http://bit.ly/VUE63g (accessed February 2015).

Respers, Lisa (2011) "Obsessions: Elizabeth Taylor, queen of cologne", *CNN Online*, March 25. Available at: http://cnn.it/1AxJiYl (accessed September 2014).

Reynolds, Debbie and Bob Thomas (1962) *If I Knew Then*, New York: Bernard Geis Associates.

Riad, Sally (2014) "Leadership in the fluid moral economy of conspicuous consumption: insights from the moralizing talks of Cleopatra and Antony", *Journal of Management History*, vol. 20, no. 1, pp. 5–43.

Rice, Francesa (2013) "Elizabeth Taylor and Richard Burton: The most turbulent love story ever told", *Marie Claire*, July 22. Available at: http://bit.ly/1BM98aI (accessed March 2015).

Richmond, Ray (2005) "What a Dame: Dialogue with Elizabeth Taylor", *Hollywood Reporter*, November 10, pp. 22–3.

Rogers, Martha and Kirk H. Smith (1993) "Public Perceptions of Subliminal Advertising: Why practitioners shouldn't ignore this issue", *Journal of Advertising Research*, vol. 33 (March–April), pp. 10–18.

Romesburg, Don (2000) "April 4, 1995: Hollywood rumors", *Advocate*, no. 826, p. 20.

Rosen, Marjorie (2003) "Elizabeth Taylor: Incomparable, unrepentant, and always intriguing", *Biography Magazine*, October, pp. 68–94.

Ross, Chuck (1996) "Arden whiffs success from Liz's CBS romp", *Advertising Age*, March 4. Available at: http://bit.ly/1DCeolS (accessed September 2014).

Rubenstein, Diane (1997) "'That's the way the Mercedes Benz': Di, Wound Culture and Fatal Fetishism", *Theory and Event*, vol. 1, no.4, pp.1–8. Available at: http://bit.ly/-RubensteinThats (accessed September 2015).

Rubython, Tom (2010) *Shunt: The Story of James Hunt*, Bere Regis, England: Myrtle Press.

Rubython, Tom (2011) *And God Created Burton*, Bere Regis, England: Myrtle Press.

Rudolph, Christopher (2013) "Rock Hudson announced he had AIDS on July 25, 1985" *Huffington Post*, July 25. Available at: http://huff.to/1xWChF6 (accessed April 2015).

Rutten Tim (2010) "Elizabeth Taylor and Richard Burton's fierce, quarrelsome life together", *Los Angeles Times* August 7. Available at: http://bit.ly/1n5wUs1 (accessed December 2014).

Ryan, Harriet (2012) "A-list doctor's star has faded", *Los Angeles Times*, January 1. Available at: http://lat.ms/1gtu82F (accessed September 2015).

Salon staff (2010) "Paglia on Taylor: 'A luscious, opulent, ripe fruit!'" *Salon*, March 24, pp.1–8. Available at: http://bit.ly/1fa708f (accessed April, 2014).

Scheer, Robert (1976) "The Playboy Interview: Jimmy Carter", *Playboy*, vol. 23, no. 11 (November), pp. 63–86.

Scheiner, Georganne (2001) "Look at Me, I'm Sandra Dee: Beyond a white teen icon", *Frontiers: A Journal of Women Studies*, vol. 22, no. 2, pp. 87–106.

Schiller, Lawrence (2012) *Marilyn & Me: A Memoir in Words and Photographs*, Cologne, Germany: Taschen.

Schillinger, Liesl (2012) "Smoldering Subversive: What Elizabeth Taylor did for women's rights", *New York Times*, February 3. Available at: http://nyti.ms/1yZpA94 (accessed December 2014).

Scotsman staff (2011) "Obituary: Dame Elizabeth Taylor, actress", March 23. Available at: http://bit.ly/1o9AUwv (accessed March 2015).

Seal, Mark (2012) "The doctor will sue you now", *Vanity Fair*, March. Available at: http://vnty.fr/1otBiaW (accessed October 2014).

Sedgwick, John (2002) "Product differentiation at the movies: Hollywood, 1946 to 1965", *Journal of Economic History*, vol. 62, no. 3, pp. 676–705.

Sellers, Robert (2011) *Hellraisers: The Life and Inebriated Times of Richard Burton, Richard Harris, Peter O'Toole, and Oliver Reed*, London: St. Martin's Press.

Server, Lee (2002) *Robert Mitchum: "Baby I Don't Care"*, New York: St. Martin's Griffin.

Sessums, Kevin (1997) "Elizabeth Taylor tells the truth", POZ *Magazine*, November. Available at: http://bit.ly/1zCQORg (accessed August 2014).

Sessums, Kevin (2011) "Elizabeth Taylor interview about her AIDS advocacy", *The Daily Beast*, May 23. Available at: http://thebea.st/VN40FW (accessed August 2014).

Sharkey, Jacqueline (1997) "The Diana aftermath", *American Journalism Review*, vol. 19, no. 9, pp. 18–25.

Shin, Gloria (2012a) *White Diamond: Elizabeth Taylor's Adventures in American Empire and the Ecstasy of Postcolonial Whiteness*, PhD thesis, Los Angeles CA: University of Southern California.

Shin, Gloria (2012b) "'If it be love indeed, tell me how much': Elizabeth Taylor, Richard Burton and White Pleasure After Empire", *Reconstruction*, vol. 12, no. 1, paras 1–43 (online only). Available at: http://bit.ly/12srt3j (accessed December 2014).

Shipman, David (1993) "Obituary: Joseph Mankiewicz", *Independent*, February 8. Available at: http://ind.pn/1tYON1D (accessed March 2015).

Siegel, Lee (1993) "Man in Liz Taylor hoax allegedly poses as Mia Farrow's personal shopper", *Associated Press Archive*, January 25. Available at: http://bit.ly/1HunPI3 (accessed May 2015).

Simon, Jeff (2011) "Elizabeth Taylor: Always a star", *Buffalo News*, March 24, A1.

Slade, Brian L. (1996) "Rock Hudson's hollywood", *Harvard Gay & Lesbian Review*, vol. 3, no. 2 (April 30), p. 18.

Slide, Anthony (2010) *Inside the Hollywood Fan Magazine: A History of Star Makers, Fabricators, and Gossip Mongers*, Jackson MS: University Press of Mississippi.

Sloan, Pat (1996) "Liz scent pervades CBS sked", *Advertising Age*, February 12. Available at: http://bit.ly/1mxrZ8t (accessed September 2014).

Small, Collie (1947) "Gossip is her business", *Saturday Evening Post* (Los Angeles), January 11, pp. 14–15, 54–7.

Smith, Emily (n.d) *The James Dean Handbook: Everything you need to know about James Dean*, unknown place of publication: Tebbo. Available at: http://amzn.to/1F5y4l8 (accessed September 2015).

Smith, Liz (1991) "Bride says she's a 'marrying kind of woman'", *Baltimore Sun*, October 7. Available at: http://bit.ly/1vIvhqi (accessed October 2014).

Smith, Susan (2012) *Elizabeth Taylor*, Basingstoke, England: Palgrave Macmillan.

Sneed, Michael, Cheryl Lavin and Kathy O'Malley (1985) "Politics as usual . . . .", *Chicago Tribune*, April 9. Available at: http://trib.in/1q2qVrw (accessed August 2014).

Sobel, Lionel S. (1983) "The Trials and Tribulations of Producing Docu-Dramas: Tales of Elizabeth Taylor, John DeLorean and network program standards", *Entertainment Law Reporter*, vol. 5, no. 3 (August), pp. 1–25.

Sobkowski, Anna (1989) "The sweet smell of success", *Executive Female*, vol. 12, no. 4 (July–August), pp. 41–5.

Spiegel, Claire and Virginia Ellis (1994) "3 doctors cited in Taylor drug case", *Los Angeles Times*, August 11. Available at: http://lat.ms/1N7X67j (accessed April 2015).

Sporkin, Elizabeth (1990) "As fans rally with cards and sympathy, Elizabeth Taylor once again battles for her life", *People*, vol. 33, no. 19. Available at: http://bit.ly/10FjDlY (accessed October 2014).

Spoto, Donald (1995) *A Passion for Life: The Biography of Elizabeth Taylor*, London: HarperCollins.

Sprinkel, Katy (2011) *Elizabeth Taylor: The Life of a Hollywood Legend*, Chicago IL: Triumph Books.

Stars and Stripes (1978) "Foe's wife wonders if Taylor looks mean votes", *Stars and Stripes,* September 8, p. 6.

Stern, Ellen (1994) "Chen Sam I am", *New York*, August 8, pp. 32–3. Available at: http://bit.ly/1KfUIqW (accessed September 2015).

Strang, Fay (2013) "Michael Jackson 'drank six bottles of wine a day in weeks leading to death' claims friend and godfather to his children, Mark Lester", *Daily Mail*, April 29. Available at: http://dailym.ai/1EAtBU4 (accessed November 2014).

Sundaram, Neeraja (2011) "You've Been Hit by a Smooth Liminal: Framing Michael Jackson's ailing celebrity body", *Journal of Communication, Culture and Technology*, vol. 11, no. 2. Available at: http://bit.ly/1q2VtaV (accessed October 2014).

Sweet, Matthew (2005) *Shepperton Babylon*, London: Faber & Faber.

Taraborrelli, J. Randy (2006) *Elizabeth*, New York: Warner Books.

Taraborrelli, J. Randy (2010) *The Secret Life Of Marilyn Monroe,* London: Pan.

Taraborrelli, J. Randy (2011) "A furious kind of love: She married eight times but only Liz Taylor's relationship with Richard Burton truly defined her", *Daily Mail*, March 28. Available at: http://dailym.ai/1rROUfW (accessed July 2014).

Taylor, Elizabeth (1964) *Elizabeth Taylor: An Informal Memoir*, New York: Harper & Row.

Taylor, Elizabeth (1988) *Elizabeth Takes Off,* London: Macmillan.

Taylor, Elizabeth (2002) *My Love Affair with Jewelry,* New York: Simon & Schuster.

The Hollywood Reporter staff (2011) "Elizabeth Taylor fragrances to continue", *Hollywood Reporter*, March 25. Available at: http://bit.ly/1ccPv6R (accessed April 2015).

Thomas, Bob (1949) "Elizabeth Taylor finds her romance is public", *Daytona Beach Morning Journal*, March 31, p. 10. Available at: http://bit.ly/1FmZ2EI (accessed April 2015).

Thomson, David (2005) "Liz's art outshines the bling", *Variety*, November 19, p. A4.

Thomson, David (2011) "Let the story melt away and just gaze: The last film star and expert survivor", *Guardian*, March 25, p. 9.

Thrift, Nigel (2008) "The material practices of glamour", *Journal of Cultural Economy*, vol. 1, no. 1, pp. 9–23.

Tiel, Vicky (2011) "Life with Elizabeth", *Vanity Fair*, August 9. Available at: http://vnty.fr/1ld5uOE (accessed June 2014).

Times of Malta (2011) "Remembering Liz Taylor", March 23. Available at: http://bit.ly/UfzG64 (accessed July 2014).

Toronto Star staff (2011) "Elizabeth Taylor dies at the age of 79", *Toronto Star*, March 23. Available at: http://on.thestar.com/1pZJlMM (accessed July 2014).

Trebay, Guy (2009) "An Appraisal: A sequined glove that mesmerized the world", *New York Times*, June 26. Available at: http://nyti.ms/1NxaToc (accessed April 2015).

Turk, Rose-Marie (1991) "Wedding's over but Liz biz draws 3,000 to see Mrs. Fortensky at mall", *Los Angeles Times,* October 11. Available at: http://lat.ms/ZrD4xl (accessed October 2014).

United Press International/UPI (1987) "Elizabeth Taylor's Passion to be available in limited stores", *Bryan Times* (OH), December 28, p. 8. Available at: http://bit.ly/1DncDZH (accessed September 2014).

United Press International/UPI (1990) "Liz Taylor 'Romance' with 23-year-old a hoax", *Los Angeles Times*, June 11. Available at: http://lat.ms/1cOL7uK (accessed May 2015).

Variety staff (1956) "Review: 'Around the world in 80 days'", *Variety*, October 24. Available at: http://bit.ly/1i6ZlTP (accessed May 2014).

Variety staff (1958) "Review: 'Cat on a Hot Tin Roof'", *Variety*, December 31. Available at: http://bit.ly/1jc5oq7 (accessed April, 2014).

Variety staff (1959) "Review: 'BUtterfield 8'", *Variety*, December 31. Available at: http://bit.ly/1JWD3lO (accessed September 2015).

Variety staff (1980) "Review: 'The Mirror Crack'd'", *Variety*, December 31. Available at: http://bit.ly/1ldhEsk (accessed July 2014).

Verniere, James (2011) "Elizabeth Taylor: An enduring star", *Boston Herald*, March 24. Available at: http://bit.ly/QHnt8F (accessed April 2014).

Vesilind, Emili (2009) "Elizabeth Taylor's perfumes led the way for others", *New York Times*, November 29, Available at: http://lat.ms/16y0m8Y (accessed February 2015).

Vider, Stephen (2012) "Book Reviews: *Hollywood Bohemians: Transgressive Sexuality and the Selling of the Movieland Dream* by Brett L. Abrams", *Journal of the History of Sexuality*, vol. 21, no. 3, pp. 548–50.

Vigo, Julian (2010) "Metaphor of Hybridity: The body of Michael Jackson", *Journal of Pan African Studies*, vol. 3, no. 7, pp. 29–42.

Walters, Rob (2010) *Rogue Males: Richard Burton, Howard Marks and Sir Richard Burton,* Oxford: Satin.

Walther Barnes, Liberty (2014) *Conceiving Masculinity: Male Infertility, Medicine, and Identity*, Philadelphia PA: Temple University Press.

Wanger, Walter and Joe Hyams (2013) *My Life with Cleopatra: The Making of a Hollywood Classic,* New York: Vintage Books.

Weber, Bruce (2009) "Army Archerd, columnist for Variety, dies at 87", *New York Times*, September 9. Available at: http://nyti.ms/YZv3jr (accessed August 2014).

Weiner, Jennifer (1996) "Scents and Sensibilities: Liz Taylor, CBS create a stir—she will be on four tv comedies in one night. So will plugs for her perfume. Call It A

Sitcommercial", *Philadelphia Inquirer*, February 25. Available at: http://bit.ly/ Yi6qOe (accessed September 2014).

Werts, Diane (1995) "'Liz' producer defends merits of miniseries", *Los Angeles Times,* May 20. Available from: http://lat.ms/1D4Bq3H (accessed October 2014).

Whittaker, James (2009) "My drunken evening with Richard Burton", *Daily Express*, August 2. Available at: http://dexpr.es/1kViyin (accessed August 2014).

Wigg, David (2010) "My husband picked up the phone and I said 'I know you're in bed with Liz Taylor': Debbie Reynolds on the pain of losing her husband", *Daily Mail*, April 23. Available at: http://dailym.ai/1pNIvj3 (accessed August 2014).

Williams, Chris (ed.) (2012) *The Richard Burton Diaries,* London: Yale University Press.

Williams, Juliet (2006) "Confessional Culture", pp. 116–17 in William G. Staples (ed.) *Encyclopedia of Privacy, Vol. 1: A-M,* Santa Barbara, CA: Greenwood Publishing.

Wilson, Christopher (2011) "Richard Burton never wrote that 'last love letter'", *Daily Telegraph*, November 9. Available at: http://bit.ly/1ta2pH6 (accessed August 2014).

Wilson, Julie A. (2010) "Star Testing: The emerging politics of celebrity gossip", *Velvet Light Trap*, no. 65, pp. 25–38.

Wilson, Scott (1997) "The Indestructible Beauty of Suffering: Diana and the metaphor of global consumption", *Theory and Event*, vol. 1, no.4. Available at: http://bit.ly/-WilsonIndestructible (accessed September 2015).

Winick, Charles (1961) "Celebrities' Errancy as a Subject for Journalism: A study of *Confidential*", *International Communication Gazette*, vol. 7, no. 4, pp. 329–34.

Wood, Dana (1996) "Liz's pearls of wisdom", *WWD: Women's Wear Daily*, vol. 171, vol. 36 (February 22), p. 3.

Yarbrough, Jeff (2011) "The passion of Elizabeth Taylor", *The Advocate*, March 23. Available at: http://bit.ly/1tRK3dv (accessed August 2014).

Zillow (no other name) (2013) "Howard Hughes' former Lake Tahoe estate for sale", *Forbes*, July 12. Available at: http://onforb.es/1qFy8Bc (accessed May 2014).

Films on Elizabeth Taylor

Burton and Taylor (2013). Directed by Richard Laxton. Written by William Ivory (with extracts by Noel Coward). UK: British Broadcasting Corporation (BBC), BBC America.

Liz & Dick (2012). Directed by Lloyd Kramer. Written by Christopher Monger. USA: Larry A. Thompson Productions, Silver Screen Pictures.

Liz: The Elizabeth Taylor Story (1995). Directed by Kevin Connor. Written by Burr Douglas, C. David Heymann. USA: Lester Persky Productions.

Plays

Rock and Doris and Elizabeth (2012) Produced by Liz Anstee. Written by Tracy-Ann Oberman, UK: CPL production for BBC Radio 4.

The Liz and Dick Show (2013) Produced by Richard Oliver. Written by Dhanil Ali. UK: Cheshire Actor's Studio.

Documentaries

Cleopatra: The Film That Changed Hollywood (2001). Directed by Kevin Burns, Brent Zacky. USA: Prometheus Entertainment, Van Ness Films, Foxstar Productions.

Elizabeth Taylor—England's Other Elizabeth (2001). Directed by Chris Bould, USA: Isis Productions.

Songs quoted in text

"Oh! My pa-pa" (1954) Lyrics by Paul Burkhand, John Turner, Geoffrey Parsons. Published by Shapiro Bernstein & Co.

"The Right Profile" (1979) by Aalon William Butler, Topper Headon, Jerry Goldstein, Mick Jones, Paul Simonon, Joe Strummer. Published by Nineden Ltd., Milwaukee Music Inc., Far-out-music Inc., Universal Music Publishing Group.

INDEX

In this index photographs are indicated in *italics*